WHAT OTHERS ARE SAYING
ABOUT THIS BOOK!

"How could I not enjoy a book that the editor says 'is designed as a springboard for delight in God—the supreme Savior, Sovereign, and Satisfier of the world'? Jason DeRouchie has a sure hand when it comes to guiding a team of scholars. The aroma of his God-centered, Christ-exalting commitments permeate this survey. This is not a book with lengthy and elaborate arguments, but a faithful and attractive rendering of conservative evangelical research into the Bible that Jesus said 'cannot be broken' (John 10:35). I would happily put this in the hand of every church member, praying, as the editor has, that it would 'fuel a greater treasuring of God . . . through Jesus—the divine, crucified, and resurrected Messiah.'"

—John Piper, Founder and Teacher, DesiringGod.org

"Finally! An introduction to the only Bible Jesus had—a survey that tries to makes sense of each book by high-lighting its life-giving message. This volume is invitingly organized and composed, and delightfully illustrated. If this does not inspire the curious and the fearful to read the Old Testament, I don't know what will. We are grateful to Jason DeRouchie and the rest of the contributors for this magnificent resource."

—Daniel I. Block, Gunther H. Knoedler Professor of Old Testament, Wheaton College

"No ordinary survey! This clear, concise, and easy-to-understand text will help church folks and serious students alike grasp the contribution of the Old Testament to the Bible as a single text with a unified plot structure that finds ultimate fulfillment in Jesus Christ. Beautiful pictures and helpful diagrams aid communication in a powerful way. I heartily recommend it!"

—Peter J. Gentry, Professor of Old Testament Interpretation, The Southern Baptist Theological Seminary

"This is one of the most user-friendly surveys of the Old Testament—Jesus' Bible—that I have seen. Written by accomplished scholars under the able direction of Jason DeRouchie, the book is a compelling read from start to finish. DeRouchie's vision for making this an accessible introduction to what for most Christians is an inaccessible part of our Scriptures is admirably accomplished. I highly recommend this book."

—David M. Howard Jr., Professor of Old Testament, Bethel Seminary

"DeRouchie unapologetically explains that this is not a theology of the Hebrew Bible on its own but a Christian Old Testament survey. Now that we have the whole story, how can we not read the first part in light of the whole? This clear and attractive book combines academic rigor with devotional warmth. Each chapter is message-driven; it briefly addresses introductory matters such as authorship and date, but it is not preoccupied with them. The authors have taught Old Testament courses many times, and they know how to connect with students."

—Andy Naselli, Assistant Professor of New Testament and Biblical Theology, Bethlehem College and Seminary

"Jason DeRouchie is a thoughtful man committed to Christ and his church. I'm excited to see this new resource he and his select team of contributors have put together. May the Lord use this book to further the cause of making disciples!"

—Jim Hamilton, Associate Professor of Biblical Theology, The Southern Baptist Theological Seminary

"This is truly a remarkable resource for the student of Scripture, especially those who've struggled to understand the Old Testament and how it relates to the New Testament. Jason DeRouchie has assembled an impressive team of scholars who explain the nature and flow of the Old Testament with an eye toward its fulfillment in the coming of Christ. Unlike your standard (and all too often stodgy) survey of the Old Testament, this volume is written in a vibrant and engaging style and is visually stunning. But best of all, it is distinctively Christ-centered. This will be the book to which I send all future inquisitive students of God's Word. I highly recommend it."

—Sam Storms, Lead Pastor for Preaching and Vision, Bridgeway Church, Oklahoma City, OK

"This book sets new standards for an Old Testament survey. The Christ-centered emphasis is a breath of fresh air. The canonical theology is deep and rich. It is exegetically faithful. The user-friendly features are not just easy to follow; they flat-out arrest your attention at times. In a crowded field of competitors, it is a standout. I commend it highly and plan to turn to it often."

—Jason Meyer, Pastor for Preaching and Vision, Bethlehem Baptist Church, Minneapolis, MN

"*What the Old Testament Authors Really Cared About* is a fantastic, foundational book, well written with insightful detail into the lives and times of the Old Testament authors, yet easy to read and understand. DeRouchie did a wonderful job tying all of the chapters together into a single, well-flowing stream."

—Noah Tremaine, Columbia International University student, Columbia, SC

"Reading this book helped me to see the beauty in the Old Testament, and it gave me a greater appreciation for the faithfulness of God. This book encouraged me to dig deeper into the Old Testament and challenged me to look for connections to the New Testament. I loved how Christ-centered it was, and through it I saw many new foreshadows of Christ in the Old Testament."

—Elise Watters, Bethlehem College student, Minneapolis, MN

"This book was very informative, yet it was also easy to read. The conversational style of the book brought the scholarly aspect of it down to a personal level. *What the Old Testament Authors Really Cared About* definitely contributed to how I will read the Old Testament in the future."

—Rose Prince, Bryan College student, Dayton, TN

"The book did an excellent job introducing and explaining each individual book while simultaneously demonstrating how the whole Old Testament fits together in a compelling way. As a future pastor, this will be a go-to book for teaching my congregation to know and love the Old Testament as part of an effort to be a 'whole-Bible people.'"

—Josh Koehn, Bethlehem Seminary student, Minneapolis, MN

WHAT THE OLD TESTAMENT AUTHORS REALLY CARED ABOUT

A SURVEY of Jesus' Bible

JASON S. DEROUCHIE

EDITOR

Kregel
Academic

For my parents,
Dave and Bonnie DeRouchie
and
Herb and Jane Lenon,
who taught me and my wife
to love God and his Word

CONTENTS

Writings

Appendixes

FIGURES AND MAPS

What the Old Testament Authors Really Cared About

PREFACE

What This Survey Is and Is Not

This manageable survey of Jesus' Bible provides a Christian interpretation of what the Old Testament authors really cared about. That is, it is a Christian examination of the Old Testament's message, as inspired by God through his human agents. This book is *not* ...

- A history of Israelite religion;
- A summary of the events of history;
- A synthesis of the sources behind the text;
- A review of characters in the text;
- A theology of the Hebrew Bible on its own;
- A systematic theology;
- A reflection of the reader.

Rather, following the arrangement of the Jewish canon, this survey attempts to *present the essence of what is revealed in the Old Testament*, with a conscious eye toward the fulfillment found in Jesus as clarified in the New Testament.

The Old Testament makes up the initial three-fourths of our Christian Bible and provides the foundation for a fulfillment and climax manifest in the New Testament, specifically in the person and work of Jesus (Rom. 15:4; 1 Cor. 9:10; 10:6; 2 Tim. 3:16). The New Testament authors cited or echoed the Old Testament at every turn, and they expected their readers to follow along. Not only this, the Old Testament was written in the context of *progressive revelation*, making the Old Testament relate to the New Testament much like an apple seed relates to an apple tree. The latter grows directly out of the former. The first is foundation; the second is fulfillment (or completion), and the two inform one another (Matt. 5:17–18; 11:13–14; Heb. 11:13; 1 Peter 1:10–12).

The Bible portrays the New Testament like an answer key in the back of a math textbook; it provides a check to ensure we are correctly and fully interpreting all the equations, which in this case are found in the Old Testament. With this in mind, the overview of the Old Testament message that follows moves to the New Testament regularly to unpack the long-range trajectories that are evident. Furthermore, the body of the survey includes many Scripture references in order to help you, the reader, assess whether the presentation is an accurate summary of the biblical text.

The Old Testament originally addressed an ancient context that was filled with perspectives, powers, and practices sometimes like but often unlike those of our western world. Not only this, biblical faith sometimes paralleled, at times exploited, and often repudiated the pagan religious ideas and rituals that were part of the ancient Near East. While this survey does not focus intently on Old Testament backgrounds, an introductory chart at the front of every chapter helps acquaint the reader with each book's authorship and audience, time period, geopolitical context, and purpose. Such issues provide the setting for the overview of the book's message that shapes each chapter's body.

This Survey's Arrangement and the "Authorship" of Old Testament Books

Following the lead of Jesus in Luke 24:44, this Christian Old Testament survey follows the three-part structure of the Jewish Hebrew Bible—Law, Prophets, and Writings. The specific arrangement of the biblical books is taken from the oldest known complete Jewish canonical list probably established well before the New Testament (*Baba Bathra* 14b). For more on this issue, see chapter 1.

This survey's title is drawn from the companion New Testament volume—*What the New Testament Authors Really Cared About* (Kregel, 2008)—and was set before the Old Testament project even began. A positive aspect of this title is its stress on authorial intent as the basis for meaning—a conviction held to by all contributors in this volume.

A recognizable challenge, however, is that, while many Old Testament books are explicit regarding who spoke the words recorded (e.g., Moses in Deuteronomy or Isaiah in the book by his name), the final author/compiler of the books themselves is rarely even hinted at. Who was the controlling narrator of the book of Joshua? Although Moses' successor gave us some of the book (Josh. 24:26), his efforts would not have included the account of his death (24:28–32). Or how do we pinpoint a single author for the book of Psalms, which is filled with songs and prayers from the time of Moses through the period of initial restoration (over 1,000 years!) but which some individual(s) collected at a later time?

The anonymity of the final form of Old Testament books, along with the developed compositional history of at least some books (e.g., the Twelve [Minor Prophets], Psalms, Proverbs) and of the canon as a whole, make it difficult to identify an Old Testament book's final "author." Because of these factors, the headings in the message-section of each chapter leave the biblical authors unspecified (e.g., "The Author of Esther Really Cared About…), but the writers of the survey chapters address head-on the question of authorship in each introductory table.

Notes of Thanksgiving

This project has been a joy for me from the beginning, and many individuals have served as stewards of God's grace (1 Peter 4:10) to help this volume come to completion. At the front end, I want to thank the sixteen other contributors for catching the vision for a gospel-saturated Old Testament survey and for working with me to make their contributions sing. Each has a proven ability to communicate the message of the Old Testament effectively to students and laity, and I praise the Lord for these years of collaboration.

Kregel Publishing has provided excellent oversight throughout this project. Kenneth Berding and Matt Williams, editors of *What the New Testament Authors Really Cared About*, were of great help at the early stages, and I express thanks to them for sharing their wisdom and resources. Jim Weaver was the academic acquisitions editor when I began the project, and he consistently modeled godliness and supplied solid guidance and help. Laura Bartlett has been very helpful with marketing and in overseeing the creation of an engaging cover, and Paul Hillman did amazing work in formatting a very difficult book and doing so with grace and charity. I am grateful to the whole Kregel team for serving me and the church so well.

I thank the leadership of Bethlehem College and Seminary for tangibly supporting my calling to spread through writing a passion for the supremacy of God in all things for the joy of all peoples through Jesus Christ. What a blessing it is to serve on a team that so truly seeks to exalt God over all things and that models humility and brotherly love to the glory of Christ.

I am grateful to my wife Teresa DeRouchie and to my friends Stephen Dempster, Keith Eveland, Julie Fredrick, Barry Joslin, Tom Kelby, Bryan and Tamara Krogman, Jason Meyer, Dana Paul, and Preston Sprinkle, all of whom read portions of my own contributions to this book and offered helpful feedback. I also thank Boyd Seevers and Todd Bolen for their help on the book's maps, my colleague Matt Crutchmer for creating Figure 24.3, and my former TA Scott McQuinn for assisting in the editing of the whole and in creating lecture presentation materials.

A number of faculty and students at Bethlehem College and Seminary, Columbia International University, and Bryan College used early drafts of this volume in the classroom, and I am grateful for their engagement and feedback. My treasured brother in Christ, Kenneth Turner, whose sustained encouragement blessed me throughout this project, helped on editing at a number of points and made the book all the better.

One of my seminary students deserves special thanks for his design work in this volume. Joel Dougherty serves as a freelance graphic designer at Disejno LLC, a creative studio launched by him and his wife Beth that specializes in brand strategy, corporate identity development, and logo design (disejno.com). In this book, Joel designed the twelve beautiful maps (building off base-maps supplied in Accordance Bible Atlas) and thirteen of the quality charts or images in the body of the text. He also created the various icons to go along with my K-I-N-G-D-O-M acronym for redemptive history. Many thanks, brother. Your efforts have blessed the church.

A key element in this project's success has been the nearly two-hundred photographs supplied by my dear friend Todd Bolen, who is the creator and overseer of BiblePlaces.com. Since our days together at Jerusalem University College in 1993, his spiritual brotherhood has been a great encouragement to my soul. With this, growing out of his thirteen years of studying and teaching in Israel and its environs, his *Pictorial Library of Bible Lands, Revised Edition* (2012) is an amazing resource for helping Scripture's places, peoples, and events come alive for contemporary readers. He has PowerPoint-ready images for classroom use and high-resolution images for publications. For more information, see BiblePlaces.com.

This book is the first I have written for my family and for the Sunday School class that I have taught for seven years at Bethlehem Baptist Church. Their faces have been before me as I have crafted these pages, and I pray that these people will gain greater awe of God and joy in Jesus as they read this book. I thank especially my wife Teresa, who is such a wonderful gift from the Lord, supporting my ministry endeavors and helping me do them well. My children too love their Daddy so much and have blessed me with words of encouragement and times of play that have allowed this book to come to fruition in a healthy way. They even helped me pick out pictures for this volume, and I am grateful for each of them.

I have dedicated this book to my and my wife's parents, Dave and Bonnie DeRouchie and Herb and Jane Lenon. Their long-standing marital faithfulness and their commitment to train their children in godliness have provided me and my wife a sweet heritage, which we now pass on to our own kids and to the world. I pray the Lord will continue to use both of these couples for the expansion of his kingdom for years to come.

> 3 Great is the Lord, and greatly to be praised,
>> and his greatness is unsearchable.
> 4 One generation shall commend your works to another,
>> and shall declare your mighty acts.
> 5 On the glorious splendor of your majesty,
>> and on your wondrous works, I will meditate.
> 6 They shall speak of the might of your awesome deeds,
>> and I will declare your greatness.
> 7 They shall pour forth the fame of your abundant goodness
>> and shall sing aloud of your righteousness. (Ps. 145:3–7).

For the fame of Yahweh's name, now disclosed in the greatness of the divine, crucified, and resurrected Messiah Jesus!

—Jason S. DeRouchie
Bethlehem College and Seminary

ABBREVIATIONS

AOTC	Apollos Old Testament Commentary
ANET	*Ancient Near Eastern Texts Relating to the Old Testament.* Edited by J. B. Pritchard. 3rd ed. Princeton, NJ: Princeton University Press, 1969
BSac	*Bibliotheca sacra*
BST	Bible Speaks Today
CBC	Cornerstone Biblical Commentary
CC	Concordia Commentary
COS	*The Context of Scripture.* Edited by W. W. Hallo and K. L. Younger. 3 vols. Leiden: Brill, 2003
Int	*Interpretation*
JETS	*Journal of the Evangelical Theological Society*
NAC	New American Commentary
NCBC	New Century Bible Commentary
NICOT	New International Commentary on the Old Testament
NIDOTTE	*New International Dictionary of Old Testament Theology and Exegesis.* Edited by W. A. VanGemeren. 5 vols. Grand Rapids: Zondervan, 1997
NIBCOT	New International Biblical Commentary on the Old Testament
NIVAC	NIV Application Commentary
NSBT	New Studies in Biblical Theology
REC	Reformed Expository Commentary
TOTC	Tyndale Old Testament Commentary
TPC	The Preacher's Commentary
WBC	Word Biblical Commentary

CONTRIBUTORS

Jason S. DeRouchie, PhD, Associate Professor of Old Testament, Bethlehem College and Seminary
Editor, Jesus' Bible: An Overview, The Old Covenant Established: What the Law Is Really About, Leviticus (coauthored with Mooney), Deuteronomy, The Old Covenant Enforced: What the Prophets Are Really About, 1–2 Kings (coauthored with Fowler), The Old Covenant Enjoyed: What the Writings Are Really About, Ruth (coauthored with Miller), Ezra-Nehemiah (coauthored with Aaron)

Daryl Aaron, PhD, Professor of Biblical and Theological Studies, University of Northwestern—St. Paul
Lamentations, Ezra-Nehemiah (coauthored with DeRouchie)

Todd Bolen, PhD, Associate Professor of Biblical Studies, The Master's College
1–2 Chronicles

John C. Crutchfield, PhD, Professor of Bible, Columbia International University
Psalms

Edward M. Curtis, PhD, Professor of Biblical and Theological Studies, Biola University, Talbot School of Theology
Job, Ecclesiastes

Stephen G. Dempster, PhD, Professor of Religious Studies, Crandall University
Genesis, The Twelve

Daniel J. Estes, PhD, Distinguished Professor of Old Testament and Director for the Center of Biblical Integration, Cedarville University
Proverbs, Song of Songs

Donald Fowler, ThD, Professor of Biblical Studies, Liberty University
1–2 Kings (coauthored with DeRouchie)

J. Daniel Hays, PhD, Dean of Pruet School of Christian Studies and Professor of Biblical Studies, Ouachita Baptist University
1–2 Samuel

Chris A. Miller, PhD, Senior Professor of Biblical Studies, Cedarville University
Judges, Ruth (coauthored with DeRouchie)

D. Jeffrey Mooney, PhD, Associate Professor of Old Testament, California Baptist University
Leviticus (coauthored with DeRouchie)

Andrew J. Schmutzer, PhD, Professor of Bible, Moody Bible Institute
Numbers

Boyd Seevers, PhD, Professor of Old Testament Studies, University of Northwestern — St. Paul
Joshua, Daniel

Gary V. Smith, PhD, Adjunct Professor of Old Testament, Bethel Seminary
Isaiah, Esther

Preston M. Sprinkle, PhD, Associate Professor of Biblical Studies, Eternity Bible College
Ezekiel

Kenneth J. Turner, PhD, Professor of Bible, Bryan College
Exodus

Gary E. Yates, PhD, Director of the Master of Theology Program and Associate Professor of Old Testament, Liberty Baptist Theological Seminary
Jeremiah

BOOK OVERVIEW

What the Old Testament Authors Really Cared About is a manageable, message-driven, multi-author, book-by-book, gospel-saturated, theologically rich, thematic survey of the Old Testament written from a conservative, evangelical perspective, targeted toward college and seminary students and local churches, and designed to unpack the lasting message of the initial three-fourths of the Christian Scripture. This survey distinguishes itself from other Old Testament surveys in the following ways.

- Each chapter *synthesizes in three to six themes the lasting message of each book*, focusing on what the biblical authors intended most to communicate within the context of Scripture.

- It is *gospel-saturated and text-based*, portraying the Old Testament as foundation for a fulfillment found in the New Testament and celebrating the hope of Messiah and God's kingdom as it is progressively disclosed in the Old Testament's literary flow.

- It has *a different chapter for each book of Jesus' Bible* (Luke 24:44), following the arrangement of the Jewish canon (Law, Prophets, and Writings) and attempting to show the theological significance of this structure.

- It stresses *the lasting relevance of the Old Testament* through the body of the text and through over 160 sidebars that clarify the Old Testament's relationship to the New Testament or to the twenty-first century.

- *Introductory issues (Who? When? Where? Why?) are condensed* to one-page snapshots of essential information at the beginning of each chapter.

- It is *a collaborative project*, written by seventeen Old Testament scholars from fourteen of the finest conservative, evangelical schools across North America.

- It was written by teachers who have a proven ability to *communicate the message of the Old Testament effectively* to college and seminary students and within the local church, thus making the text very readable for broad audiences.

- *The clarity of the biblical message is enhanced* through nearly two-hundred high-resolution photographs, over eighty charts and tables, and twelve color maps.

- *Its format is simpler and intentionally shorter than many other surveys*, making it a very manageable textbook for a single semester Old Testament survey course or a useful guide for personal or small group devotional reading of Scripture.

[1]Blessed is the man who walks
not in the counsel of the wicked,
nor stands in the way of sinners,
nor sits in the seat of scoffers;
[2]but his delight is in the law of the LORD,
and on his law he meditates day and night.
[3]He is like a tree planted by streams of water
that yields its fruit in its season,
and its leaf does not wither.
In all that he does, he prospers.
Psalm 1:1–3

JESUS' BIBLE: AN OVERVIEW

Who?

God was the ultimate author of Jesus' Bible—what we now call the Old Testament. By his Spirit, the Lord guided dozens of prophets, usually writing in Hebrew, to disclose himself and his will for his people (Deut. 18:18; 2 Tim. 3:16; Heb. 1:1; 2 Peter 1:21). The numerous human authors used a variety of genres to communicate God's words, including genealogies, court annals, prophetic oracles, proverbs, prayers, priestly instructions, and much more. This diversity, however, only adds flavor to the amazing unity of message and purpose evident throughout the whole. Indeed, like its thirty-nine individual books (twenty-four by Jewish numbering), the Old Testament as a whole shows signs of intentional shaping toward a common goal—a quality testifying to the guiding hand of the supreme author.

When?

Through use of sources and under divine guidance, the Old Testament was formed over a more than a thousand-year period (ca. 1450–400 B.C.). As God's Word spoken through human words in history, every book was conditioned by the language, culture, and situations of the time. The material overviews God's perspective on and purposes in world history from creation to the initial stages of Israel's restoration after exile. During this period, five main empires dominated the world scene, each playing a key role in the developing biblical drama: Egypt, Israel, Assyria, Babylon, and Persia. For dates and a sampling of biblical persons and events from these periods, see the chart in the right column.

Where?

The Old Testament arose in the heart of the Fertile Crescent, the birthplace of ancient civilization. This curved region of land stretched from the north in Mesopotamia southward through Canaan to Egypt (see the map "Israel:

The Land Between" in this chapter). In alignment with Israel's mission to serve as an agent of divine blessing to the nations (Gen. 12:3; Exod. 19:5–6; Deut. 4:5–8), Yahweh (the Lord) placed his people geographically in the center of the world (Ezek. 5:5; cf. 38:12). Because kingdom expansion through trade, alliance, or conquest required the northern and southern powers to travel through Israel's Promised Land ("the Land Between"), many of ancient history's major events are highlighted in the Old Testament.

Why?

What we call the Old Testament was written to guide God's people to him and his purposes and to lay a foundation for the kingdom fulfillment found in the New Testament. Through three main divisions (Law, Prophets, Writings), Jesus' Bible overviews the initial stages of God's unfolding plan of redemption and details how the old (Mosaic) covenant was established, enforced, and enjoyed, all in anticipation of God's kingdom consummation realized in Jesus and his church. The message may be summarized as God's kingdom through covenant for his glory, ultimately in Christ.

World Power	Sampling of Biblical Persons and Events
Egypt (ca. 3000–1200)	Abraham (ca. 2100) Moses and exodus (ca. 1446 [1250])
Israel (ca. 1010–930)	David (ca. 1010), temple built (ca. 959) Kingdom divided (ca. 930)
Assyria (ca. 870–626)	Isaiah (ca. 740) Israel (north) exiled (ca. 723)
Babylon (ca. 626–539)	Judah (south) exiled (ca. 605; 597; 586) Temple destroyed (ca. 586)
Persia (ca. 539–323)	Initial restorations (ca. 538, 458, 444) Temple rebuilt (ca. 516)

JESUS' BIBLE: AN OVERVIEW

Jason S. DeRouchie

Carefully Crafted Verses from the Old Testament[1]

"The LORD, the LORD, a God merciful and gracious, slow to anger, and abounding in steadfast love and faithfulness, … forgiving iniquity and transgression and sin, but who will by no means clear the guilty" (Exod. 34:6–7).

"Hear, O Israel: The LORD our God, the LORD is one. You shall love the LORD your God with all your heart and with all your soul and with all your might" (Deut. 6:4–5).

> ### THE DIVINE AUTHOR OF THE OLD TESTAMENT …
>
> - Supplied *authoritative kingdom instruction* for God's people.
>
> - Recorded *the progression and purpose of God's covenants* in redemptive history.
>
> - Distinguished the *Law, Prophets, and Writings*.
>
> - Highlighted *how the old (Mosaic) covenant was established, enforced, and enjoyed*.

"I will make a new covenant with the house of Israel.… I will put my law within them, and I will write it on their hearts. And I will be their God, and they shall be my people" (Jer. 31:31, 33).

---

1. If these five passages do not move you to worship, this book may cause more harm than good. This survey is designed as a springboard for delight in God—the supreme Savior, Sovereign, and Satisfier of the world. Worship is the end for which this book was created. May your study fuel a greater treasuring of God and his ways, for his glory and your good, through Jesus—the divine, crucified, and resurrected Messiah.

But he was pierced for our transgressions; he was crushed for our iniquities; upon him was the chastisement that brought us peace, and with his wounds we are healed (Isa. 53:5).

Let everything that has breath praise the LORD! Praise the LORD! (Ps. 150:6).

The Divine Author of the Old Testament Supplied *Authoritative Kingdom Instruction* for God's People

Jesus never read Romans or Revelation. He never heard sermons on Matthew's Gospel or Peter's epistles. Indeed, the New Testament was not written in Jesus' day, so his only Bible was what we call the *Old Testament*. It was books like Genesis and Deuteronomy, Isaiah and Psalms that shaped Jesus' upbringing and that guided his life and ministry as the Jewish Messiah. It was these Old Testament "Scriptures" that Jesus identified as God's Word (Mark 7:13; 12:36), considered to be authoritative (Matt. 4:3–4, 7, 10; 23:1–3), and called people to know and believe so as to guard against doctrinal error and hell (Mark 12:24; Luke 16:28–31; 24:25; John 5:46–47). Jesus was convinced that what is now the first three-fourths of our Christian Bible "cannot be broken" (John 10:35), would be completely fulfilled (Matt. 5:17–18; Luke 24:44), bore witness about him (Luke 24:27, 46; John 5:39, 46), and called for repentance and forgiveness of sins to be proclaimed in his name to all nations (Luke 24:47). All this Jesus summarized as "the good news of the kingdom of God" (Luke 4:43; cf. Acts 1:3). If we want to know Jesus as best as we can, we must saturate ourselves in the same Scripture he read—namely, the Old Testament!

Jesus had stressed the need for the same "gospel of the kingdom" that he taught to be "proclaimed throughout the whole world as a testimony to all nations" (Matt. 24:14). It was proper, therefore, that the early church continued to preach and teach from Jesus' Bible (the Old Testament), even as the New Testament was being written. For example, Peter observed that the Old Testament prophets predicted the gracious good news of salvation preached to Christians (1 Peter 1:10–12), and he charged believers to pursue holiness *because* the

"If you believed Moses, you would believe me; for he wrote of me. But if you do not believe his writings, how will you believe my words?" (John 5:46–47). *A Torah scroll.*

Old Testament called for it: "as he who called you is holy, you also be holy in all your conduct, *since it is written*, 'You shall be holy, for I am holy'" (1:15–16; cf. Lev. 11:44). Furthermore, Paul taught Christians that the Old Testament "was written for *our* instruction" (Rom. 15:4; cf. 4:22–23; 1 Cor. 10:11).

Like Jesus, Paul believed the Old Testament was all about "the kingdom of God" climaxing in "the Lord Jesus Christ" (Acts 28:23, 31; cf. 20:24–25, 27), and the apostle stressed how this kingdom message pointed both to the Messiah's death and resurrection and to the fruit of global missions that would grow from it (26:23). He was also convinced that the "sacred writings" that were taught to Jewish children are "able to make you wise for salvation through faith in Christ" (2 Tim. 3:15; cf. 1:5; Acts 16:1). It was these "Scriptures" that were "breathed out by God and profitable for teaching, for reproof, for correction, and for training in righteousness, that the man of God may be complete, equipped for every good work" (2 Tim. 3:16–17). And it was this

> Have you considered that you could *correct* a straying Christian brother or sister using the *Old Testament*? This appears to be what Paul teaches in 2 Timothy 3:16. It can be challenging to figure out how to do this rightly, seeing as we are no longer under the old (Mosaic) covenant, but the point still stands—the Old Testament is important for Christians!

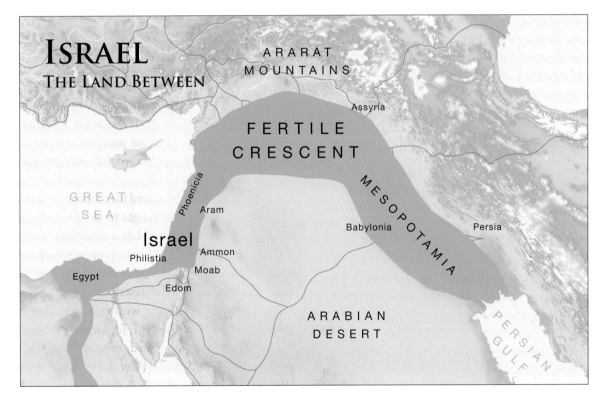

"Word," interpreted in the light of Christ's coming, that Paul called Timothy to preach, so as to fight against the perversion of truth (4:2–4).

The Divine Author of the Old Testament Recorded *the Progression and Purpose of God's Covenants* in Redemptive History

Kingdom Through Covenant Climaxing in Christ

When the Old and New Testaments are read alongside one another, at least seven historical stages are apparent in God's kingdom-building program. The initial five are the foundation for the ultimate fulfillment in the last two. Interwoven into this story of redemption is a progression of five overlapping covenants, which portray the development of God's global purposes with humanity.

Figure 1.1. God's Kingdom-Building Program at a Glance

Old Testament Narrative History	**K**	**KICKOFF AND REBELLION**	1. Creation, fall, and flood (ca. ? B.C.)
	I	**INSTRUMENT OF BLESSING**	2. Patriarchs (ca. 2100–1850 B.C.)
	N	**NATION REDEEMED AND COMMISSIONED**	3. Exodus, Sinai, and wilderness (ca. 1450–1400 B.C.)
	G	**GOVERNMENT IN THE PROMISED LAND**	4. Conquest and kingdoms (united and divided) (ca. 1400–600 B.C.)
	D	**DISPERSION AND RETURN**	5. Exile and initial restoration (ca. 600–400 B.C.)
New Testament Narrative History	**O**	**OVERLAP OF THE AGES**	6. Christ's work and the church age (ca. 4 B.C.–A.D. ?)
	M	**MISSION ACCOMPLISHED**	7. Christ's return and kingdom consummation (ca. A.D. ?–eternity)

Figure 1.2. God's K-I-N-G-D-O-M Story Through Images

Paradise

Blessing to all nations (promise-fulfillment)

Fall, sin, rebellion

Giving of the law

Exile, paradise lost

Penal substitutionary atonement

Waters of judgment

Conquest, kingdom established

Patriarchs

Saving/atoning work of Christ

Much offspring (promise-fulfillment)

Fires of judgment

Land, home, rest (promise-fulfillment)

The interrelationship of the covenants can be portrayed like an hourglass, with the most universal scope occurring at the two ends and the work of Christ at the center. The Adamic/Noahic, Abrahamic, Mosaic, and Davidic covenants are all named in light of the covenant head or mediator through whom God entered into a relationship with his elect. The new covenant is titled in light of its contrast to the "old" Mosaic administration and provides climax to all God's purposes in history (see Jer. 31:31–34; Heb. 8:6–13).

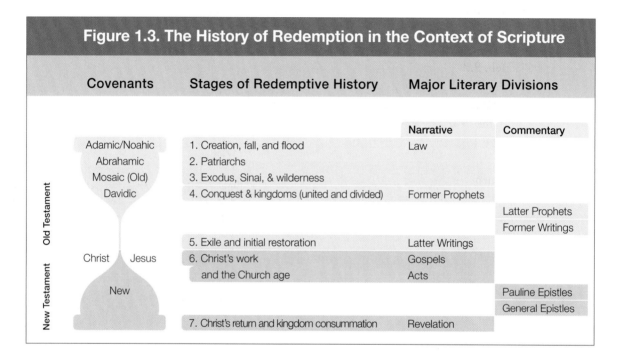

Figure 1.3. The History of Redemption in the Context of Scripture

	Covenants	Stages of Redemptive History	Major Literary Divisions: Narrative	Major Literary Divisions: Commentary
Old Testament	Adamic/Noahic	1. Creation, fall, and flood	Law	
	Abrahamic	2. Patriarchs		
	Mosaic (Old)	3. Exodus, Sinai, & wilderness		
	Davidic	4. Conquest & kingdoms (united and divided)	Former Prophets	
				Latter Prophets
				Former Writings
		5. Exile and initial restoration	Latter Writings	
	Christ Jesus	6. Christ's work	Gospels	
New Testament		and the Church age	Acts	
	New			Pauline Epistles
				General Epistles
		7. Christ's return and kingdom consummation	Revelation	

Significantly, *Jesus' saving work is the fulcrum upon which the entire Bible pivots*. To him all redemptive history points, and from him all fulfillment comes. As Jesus himself said, "Do not think I have come to abolish the Law or the Prophets; I have not come to abolish them but to fulfill them" (Matt. 5:17). The Old Testament is Christo-telic (*telos* is Greek for "goal, end"). Each of the five covenants culminates in the person and work of Messiah Jesus.

- In fulfillment of the *Adamic/Noahic covenant*, Jesus is the Son of Man, last Adam, and image of God (Mark 10:45; 14:62; 1 Cor. 15:45; 2 Cor. 4:4).

- In fulfillment of the *Abrahamic covenant*, Jesus is the offspring of Abraham and agent of universal blessing (Gen. 22:17b–18; Acts 3:25–26; Gal. 3:16).

- In fulfillment of the *Mosaic (old) covenant*, Jesus represents Israel and stands as God's Son, Yahweh's servant, the embodiment of wisdom, the one who fulfilled the law's demands, and the substance of all covenant shadows (Exod. 4:22–23; Isa. 49:3, 5–6; Matt. 3:17; 11:2, 19; 12:42; 13:54; John 2:19–21; Acts 3:25–26; Rom. 5:19; Col. 2:17; Heb. 9:9–12; 10:1).

- In fulfillment of the *Davidic covenant*, Jesus is the King of the Jews and Son of David (Matt. 2:1; 21:9; Luke 1:32–33).

"There shall come forth a shoot from the stump of Jesse, and a branch from his roots shall bear fruit.... Righteousness shall be the belt of his waist, and faithfulness the belt of his loins" (Isa. 11:1, 5). *Almonds on a tree near Aijalon.*

- In fulfillment of the *new covenant* promises, Jesus is the prophet like Moses who was to come and the only true mediator between God and man (Deut. 18:15, 18; Luke 7:16; 22:20; Acts 3:22–26; 7:37; 1 Tim. 2:5; Heb. 8:6; 9:15; 12:24).

The Story of God's Glory in Christ

What accompanies this messianic trajectory is the sustained assertion throughout Scripture that *everything God does is for his glory*. That is, God's ultimate goal at every stage in his kingdom program is the preservation and display of himself as the supreme Savior, Sovereign, and Satisfier of the world, ultimately through his messianic representative. As such, the Bible's grand narrative has rightly been called "The Story of God's Glory."[2] What follows is a brief overview of each stage in God's kingdom-building plan.

> The entire Bible pivots on the person and work of Jesus. To him all redemptive history points, and from him all fulfillment comes.

---

2. See John Piper, "The Goal of God in Redemptive History," in *Desiring God: Meditations of a Christian Hedonist* (rev. and exp.; Sisters, OR: Multnomah, 2003), 308–21. This appendix is not found in the 2011 edition.

"The high mountains are for the wild goats.... O LORD, how manifold are your works! In wisdom have you made them all; the earth is full of your creatures" (Ps. 104:18, 24). *Left: A male Nubian ibex "wild goat" at Machtesh Ramon (photo by Kim Guess); Right: a heard of male Nubian ibex at En Gedi.*

Paradise

Fall, sin, rebellion

Exile, paradise lost

Waters of judgment

KICKOFF AND REBELLION (creation, fall, and flood). As the maker and sustainer of all things visible and invisible, God deserves the highest praise (1 Chron. 29:11; Rom. 11:36; Rev. 4:11). God created humans to image him and commissioned them to display his greatness throughout the world from generation to generation (Gen. 1:26–28). Like a temple paradise, the Garden of Eden was to be a place where Yahweh was exalted over all, and it was to be ever expanding as the first couple would carry God's image to the ends of the earth, thus reflecting, representing, and resembling the divine glory for all to see. However, Adam and Eve failed to honor God rightly, and in Adam, all the rest of humanity sinned, *falling short of God's glory* (Rom. 1:21–23; 3:23; 5:1219). Before subjecting the world to futility in hope (Rom. 8:20–21) and before casting humanity's parents into exile from the garden, the Lord promised to reestablish cosmic order through a male human deliverer, the ministry of whom would display *great glory* through divine grace (Gen. 3:15; John 1:14). Humanity's sustained wickedness after the fall resulted in the flood, but God preserved a remnant whose hope was in the coming redeemer (Gen. 4:25–26; 5:22; 6:8–9), and he confirmed through Noah his covenant with creation (Gen. 6:7–9, 18; 8:21; 9:9–11). At the Tower of Babel, however, such mercy was matched by human self-exaltation over God-exaltation, resulting in more divine judgment (11:1–9, esp. v. 4).

I INSTRUMENT OF BLESSING (patriarchs). It was *to the praise of his glorious grace* that God elected and created a people for himself (Jer. 13:11; Isa. 43:6–7; Eph. 1:4–6). *God's glory* compelled Abraham to leave Mesopotamia (Acts 7:2), so that through Israel the nations of the earth could be restored into relationship with their Creator (Gen. 12:3). Though it would take a miracle, Abraham believed God could do for him what he could not do on his own, and his faith in Yahweh's promise of offspring was counted as righteousness (15:6; cf. 18:14). To exalt his faithfulness and in anticipation of future mercy, Yahweh vowed to fulfill his promise of land to Abraham's offspring (15:17–18) and provided a substitute sacrifice in the place of Isaac (22:12–14). He also reaffirmed that his blessing of the nations would be accomplished through a royal representative, now known to be from Judah, who would destroy evil and reestablish world peace (22:17b–18; 24:60; 49:8–10). For such ultimate good, God sent Joseph to Egypt, preserving the children of Jacob/Israel alive in the midst of famine, while they awaited the Promised Land (45:7–8; 50:20, 24–25).

Patriarchs

Much offspring promised

Land, home, rest promised

Blessing to all nations promised

N NATION REDEEMED AND COMMISSIONED (exodus, Sinai, and wilderness). In fulfillment of his promises, God sustained and multiplied Israel through four hundred years of Egyptian bondage (Exod. 1:7; cf. Gen. 15:13–14). *For the sake of his name and reputation*, God brought the plagues on Egypt, redeemed Israel from slavery through the Red Sea, and preserved his people after their sins in the wilderness (Exod. 9:15–16; 14:4; 32:11–13; Num. 14:13–19; 2 Sam. 7:23; Ezek. 20:9, 14, 21–22; Ps. 106:7–8). *For the display of his holiness*, he gave Israel his law through Moses, called his people to radical love overflowing in obedience, and provided a means of atonement so that they could be near him, his presence alone distinguishing them from the nations (Exod. 19:4–6; 20:3–5; 33:16; Lev. 10:3; Deut. 4:5–8; 6:4–5). He also restated his promise that a deliverer would arise from Jacob who would exercise international influence (Num. 24:17–19). Nevertheless, he did not overcome Israel's hard-heartedness (Deut. 29:4), but he foretold Israel's sustained rebellion and exile (31:16–17, 29) and promised restoration that would exalt God alone as the enabler and gracious sustainer of love for him, of commandment keeping, and of the covenant (30:6, 8).

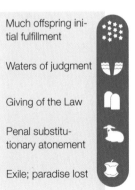

Much offspring initial fulfillment

Waters of judgment

Giving of the Law

Penal substitutionary atonement

Exile; paradise lost

The LORD said to Pharaoh, "By now I could have put out my hand and struck you and your people with pestilence, and you would have been cut off from the earth. But for this purpose I have raised you up, to show you my power, so that my name may be proclaimed in all the earth" (Exod. 9:15–16). *Chefren's Pyramid from Egypt's Old Kingdom (third millennium B.C.). Already built during the days of Abraham, Joseph, and Moses, this is the second largest of the great pyramids in the Giza necropolis on the outskirts of Cairo, Egypt; archaeological excavations are in the foreground.*

Conquest; kingdom established

Typological paradise enjoyed

Land, home, rest— initial fulfillment

Fall, sin, rebellion

GOVERNMENT IN THE PROMISED LAND (conquest and kingdoms). Through the conquest, Yahweh exalted himself before the nations as the only true God, fulfilling his promises to give Israel rest in the land as an echo of the Edenic paradise (Josh. 11:23; 21:43–45; cf. Exod. 15:17). In the Canaanite Rahab's words, "The LORD your God, he is God in the heavens above and on the earth beneath" (Josh. 2:11; cf. 8:24). The majority of the twelve tribes of Israel, however, soon forgot the Lord and progressively became Canaanized (Judg. 2:10–23), which ultimately resulted in their ruin. Refusing to listen to God's gracious appeal via his prophets, the united and divided kingdoms all came to an end, climaxing in the destruction of the temple and exile (2 Kings 17:13–23; ch. 25).

Nevertheless, in the midst of Israel's rise and fall, the Lord graciously renewed his promise of a coming royal redeemer (1 Sam. 2:10), raised up King David as a foreshadow of this deliverer, and declared that through him God's universal kingdom purposes would find fulfillment (2 Sam. 7:12–16; cf. Ps. 2; 72:17). The anticipated savior-king would proclaim Yahweh's end-times reign—the year of his favor and the day of his vengeance (Isa. 52:7; 61:2). He also, while himself guiltless (50:9; 53:9), would, through a substitutionary death, satisfy God's wrath against sin and would, by his righteousness, "make many to be accounted righteous" (53:5, 10–11; cf. John 11:50–52; Rom. 5:19; 2 Cor. 5:21).

In all, one principle governed God's actions during the united and divided kingdoms: "Those who *honor me* I will honor, and those who despise me shall be lightly esteemed" (1 Sam. 2:30). Whether dealing with barren woman or priest, prophet or king, shepherd or warrior, Israelite or foreigner, God acted *for his glory* (Josh. 24:14; 1 Sam. 2:1–10; 6:5–6, 19–20; 12:20–22; 15:22–23; 17:46; 1 Kings 8:43; 18:36–39; 2 Kings 19:19, 34).

D DISPERSION AND RETURN (exile and initial restoration). Yahweh cast Israel from the Promised Land because of their failure to live for him (2 Kings 17:7; 2 Chron. 36:16), but he also promised that, in the latter days, "the God of heaven will set up a kingdom that shall never be destroyed" and that "one like a son of man" would receive "dominion and glory and a kingdom, that all peoples, nations, and languages should serve him" (Dan 2:44; 7:13–14). Isaiah had anticipated *that for his own sake*, the Lord would sustain Israel through exile, return a remnant to the land, and use them as missionaries to represent him rightly in the world (Isa. 48:9, 11): "*For my name's sake* I defer my anger, *for the sake of my praise* I restrain it for you, that I may not cut you off…. *For my own sake, for my own sake*, I do it, for how should *my name* be profaned? *My glory* I will not give to another." Similarly, Ezekiel stated (Ezek. 36:23): "I will vindicate *the holiness of my great name*, which has been profaned among the nations, and which you have profaned among them. And the nations will know that I am the LORD … when *through you I vindicate my holiness before their eyes.*" So it is that Daniel prayed that God would act "for your own sake," redeeming

Exile; paradise lost

Fall, sin, rebellion

his people and forgiving their sin (Dan. 9:15–19). Upon the initial restoration, God called the Jews to rebuild the temple "that I may be glorified" (Hag. 1:8), and he also charged them to *honor and fear him* as the "great King" over all (Mal. 1:6, 14). Sadly, the majority of the restored remained cold to God, and the light of kingdom hope was dimmed in the darkness of sustained slavery (Ezra 9:8–9; Neh. 9:36).

"I have refined you, but not as silver; I have tried you in the furnace of affliction. For my own sake, for my own sake, I do it, for how should my name be profaned? My glory I will not give to another" (Isa. 48:10–11). *A spouted silver jar and a silver bowl from Ur, dated by some to ca. 2600 B.C., almost two-thousand years before Isaiah (from the British Museum).*

Saving/atoning work of Christ

Spiritual conquest; kingdom initiated

Blessing to all nations initial fulfillment

Much offspring initial fulfillment

OVERLAP OF THE AGES (Christ's work and the church age). "But when the fullness of time had come" (Gal. 4:4), God caused the light to dawn in the person of Christ (Matt. 4:16–17; John 8:12). One of the mysterious parts of God's kingdom program was the way Jesus' first coming was as suffering servant, and only in his second coming would he show himself fully as conquering king. In his initial appearing, he proclaimed "the year of the LORD's favor," and only later would he bring "the day of vengeance of our God" (Isa. 61:2; cf. Luke 4:19). "Christ, having been offered once to bear the sins of many, will appear a second time, not to deal with sin but to save those who are eagerly waiting for him" (Heb. 9:28). Today we rest in an overlap of the ages, with Christ having delivered us from "the present evil age" (Gal. 1:4) yet only in a way that lets us taste "the powers of the age to come" (Heb. 6:5). Figure 1.4 attempts to visualize the already-but-not-yet aspects of the kingdom in this overlap of the ages (see esp. Rom. 8:18–24; Eph. 1:3–14; 1 Peter 1:3–13).

With respect to the *already* aspect of the kingdom, for God's reign to be celebrated on earth, his wrath toward the sin of Israel and the world needed to be appeased. So in the fullness of time, after four hundred years of prophetic silence but in direct fulfillment of Old Testament hopes, God the Father sent his eternal Son to earth as the promised, royal deliverer "to give his life as a ransom for many" (Mark 10:45). In the "great exchange" of the ages, God counted every believer's sin to Christ, and Christ's righteousness to every believer:

- "For our sake [the Father] made [Christ] to be sin who knew no sin, so that in him we might become the righteousness of God" (2 Cor. 5:21).

- "And because of [God] you are in Christ Jesus, who became to us wisdom from God, righteousness and sanctification and redemption" (1 Cor. 1:30).

Figure 1.4. Redemptive History and the Overlap of the Ages

First Coming of Christ

Second Coming of Christ

OLD Age, Covenant,* and Creation

Church Age Last Days

NEW Age, Covenant,* and Creation

"Already"

"Not Yet"

Sin and Death

Gospel Proclaimed Through Suffering and Sharing

Righteousness and Life

*At one level, the old and new covenants do not overlap, for Jesus "makes the first one obsolete" and "does away with the first in order to establish the second" (Heb. 8:13; 10:9). At another level, however, because the old (Mosaic) covenant represents the age of death in Adam, the writer of Hebrews can add, "And what is becoming obsolete and growing old is ready to vanish away" (8:13), noting that while "the end of the ages" is already upon us (9:26), the consummation of "the age to come" has not yet been realized (6:5; cf. 2 Cor. 3:11).

- "For as by the one man's disobedience [i.e., Adam] the many were made sinners, so by the one's man's obedience [i.e., Jesus Christ] the many will be made righteous" (Rom. 5:19).

The good news of God's end-times reign is nothing less than *"the glory of God in the face of Jesus Christ"* (2 Cor. 4:6; cf. 1 Tim. 1:11). Jesus lived *for the glory of his Father* (John 7:18; 17:4), and his death and resurrection vindicated *God's righteousness* and exalted *God's glory* (John 12:27–28; 17:1; Rom. 3:25–26). God forgives sins and welcomes believers *for his glory* (Isa. 43:25; Ps. 25:11; Rom. 15:7), and he calls everyone to live *for his glory* always (Matt. 5:16; John 5:44; 1 Cor. 10:31; Phil. 1:11; 1 Peter 4:11), which includes a radical commitment to spreading a passion for God's supremacy throughout the world, both through sharing and suffering (Matt. 5:11–12; 28:18–20).

> It is *right*, *necessary*, and *loving* that God act for his own glory and call us to do the same. It is right because Yahweh alone is preeminent over all things and is therefore worthy of worship (Exod. 34:14; Deut. 32:39). It is necessary because if Yahweh gave his glory to another, declaring something else as being worthy of highest praise, he would stop being God (Isa. 42:8; 48:11). It is loving because Yahweh alone can save (43:10–12) and because in his presence is fullness of joy forever (Ps. 16:11; cf. Matt. 13:44).

Within this context, God promises to honor all who *seek to exalt him* and not themselves (1 Sam. 2:30; Luke 18:14; James 4:6; 1 Peter 5:5), even as they await the "blessed hope, the appearing of the glory of our great God and savior Jesus Christ" (Titus 2:13).

Conquest; kingdom consummated

Fires of judgment

Blessing to all nations

Much offspring consummate fulfillment

Paradise enjoyed

Land, home, rest consummate fulfillment

MISSION ACCOMPLISHED (Christ's return and kingdom consummation). God's mercy, wrath, and power are all directed at making known "the riches of his glory" (Rom. 9:22–23), and only those who "fear God and give him glory" will escape divine wrath when the Son of Man returns *to be glorified* in his saints (Rev. 14:7; 2 Thess. 1:9–10; cf. Matt. 16:27; 24:30; 25:31; John 17:24). Judgment day will come (Rom. 2:5; 2 Peter 3:7), and with it the consummation of the new creation, when the righteous will be perfected (1 Thess. 5:23–24; Heb. 12:23) and *the glory of God* will give light to all (Rev. 21:24). In this day, those ransomed "from every tribe and language and people and nation" will celebrate eternally in the presence of God, declaring, "Salvation belongs to our God who sits on the throne, and to the Lamb!" (Rev. 5:9; 7:10). Here all rest will be realized, pleasures perfected, the curse conquered, and Jesus exalted and treasured forevermore (21:3–4; 22:3–4).

"In that day this song will be sung in the land of Judah: 'We have a strong city; he sets up salvation as walls and bulwarks. Open the gates, that the righteous nation that keeps faith may enter in…. Trust in the LORD forever, for the LORD God is an everlasting rock'" (Isa. 26:1–2, 4). *Jerusalem's Old City walls.*

The Divine Author of the Old Testament Distinguished *the Law, Prophets, and Writings*

The Arrangement of Jesus' Bible

Having overviewed God's kingdom agenda as disclosed in the Bible's narrative history, it is important to consider the shape and significance of the Old Testament's structure. You have probably already noted that the arrangement of books in this survey is different from the order of Old Testament books in most Christian Bibles, which distinguish Law, History, Poetry and Wisdom, and

Prophecy. The reason for the distinction is that the Jewish Bible legitimated and used by Jesus and the apostles appears to have been structured differently.

Specifically, while the Jewish Scriptures contain the same thirty-nine books found in our English Old Testaments, the books themselves are arranged in a different order and grouped in three main divisions: the Law (*tôrâ*), the Prophets (*nĕbîʾîm*), and the Writings (or "the *other* Scriptures," *kĕtûbîm*).[3] It is this three-part canon that Jesus appears to have referred to after his resurrection when he clarified how "everything written about me in the *Law* of Moses and the *Prophets* and the *Psalms* must be fulfilled" (Luke 24:44). In most reckonings, Psalms is the first main book in the Writings (though prefaced by Ruth), and in Jesus' words it appears to provide a title for the whole third division. Because of this three-part structure, the Hebrew Bible is commonly referred to as the TaNaK (or Tanach), an acronym derived from the first Hebrew letters of each of the three major section titles.[4]

> The order of our English Bible is patterned after the Latin Vulgate, which was structured after some arrangements of the Septuagint, the Greek translation of the Old Testament. The sequence of Law, History, Poetry and Wisdom, and Prophecy is likely derived from the Greco-Roman tendency to arrange collections according to chronology and genre. Nevertheless, because the Bible of Jesus and the apostles was arranged according to the Law, Prophets, and Writings (Luke 24:44), doesn't it make sense that we would want to read it in the same order?

This survey follows the most ancient complete listing of the Jewish canonical books, which most likely dates from before the time of the New Testament, perhaps as early as the second century B.C. (*Baba Bathra* 14b) (see Fig. 1.6).[5] Along with the three-part arrangement, the list treats as single

---

3. For examples of the three-fold division outside the Bible, see the prologue to Ben Sira and 4QMMT C.10 in the Dead Sea Scrolls.

4. The biblical evidence also suggests that Jesus' Bible began with Genesis and ended with Chronicles. This fact is clarified in one of Jesus' confrontations with the Pharisees, in which he spoke of the martyrdom of the Old Testament prophets "from the blood of Abel to the blood of Zechariah" (Luke 11:51; cf. Matt. 23:35). This is not a simple "A to Z" statement, for Zechariah's name does not begin with the last letter of any biblical language alphabet. Also, it is not strictly a chronological statement, for while Abel was clearly the first martyr (Gen. 4:4, 8), the Old Testament's last martyr with respect to time was Uriah the son of Shemaiah, who died during the reign of Jehoiakim (609–598 B.C.; see Jer. 26:20–23). Instead, Jesus appears to have been speaking *canonically*, mentioning the first and last martyr in his Bible, for just as Genesis recorded Abel's murder, the end of Chronicles highlighted a certain Zechariah who was killed in the temple court during the reign of Joash (835–796 B.C.; see 2 Chron. 24:20–21).

5. *Baba Bathra* 14b is a baraita, which is an ancient tradition found in the Babylonian Talmud (ca. A.D. 500) that dates from around the time of the Mishnah but was not included in it. Roger Beckwith provides a complete evaluation of the textual data and posits that the arrangement of biblical books in *Baba Bathra* 14b most likely originated from a list drawn up by Judas Maccabaeus around 164 B.C. (see 2 Macc. 2:14–15) (*The Old Testament Canon of the New Testament Church* [Grand Rapids: Eerdmans, 1985], 121–27, 152–53, 198). For a popular-level, succinct summary of Beckwith's conclusions,

books some of those that our English Bibles separate (i.e., 1–2 Samuel, 1–2 Kings, the Twelve Minor Prophets, Ezra-Nehemiah, 1–2 Chronicles).[6] Furthermore, the major prophets are out of chronological order, Ruth is totally separated from its temporal context after Judges, Daniel is not among the Prophets, and Chronicles and Ezra-Nehemiah are placed in reverse chronological order. Is there any logic to this structure?

Figure 1.5. The Structure of the English Old Testament and Jesus' Bible

English OT	Jesus' Bible
Law: Genesis–Deuteronomy	**Law** (*tôrâ*): Genesis–Deuteronomy
History: Joshua–Esther	**Prophets** (*nĕbî'îm*): Joshua–Kings (Former); Jeremiah–Malachi (Latter)
Poetry and Wisdom: Job–Song of Songs	**Writings** (*kĕtûbîm*): Ruth/Psalms–Lamentations (Former); Daniel–Chronicles (Latter)
Prophecy: Isaiah–Malachi	

Anticipations of the Arrangement's Significance

At least two points of significance are readily apparent as one looks at the organization of Jesus' Bible. First, reading the Old Testament through the lens of *God's program of redemption* is both justified and necessary, for the whole Bible is held together by a historical narrative that sketches in chronological order the initial stages of this story.[7] The biblical narrative it-

---

see his "The Canon of Scripture" in *New Dictionary of Biblical Theology* (ed. T. Desmond Alexander et al. [Downers Grove, IL: InterVarsity, 2000]), 27–34.

6. At least in the case of the books of Samuel, Kings, and Chronicles, the reason for the separation appears to be merely pragmatic: the Hebrew Bible used only consonants, and when it was translated into Greek, which included vowels, the books got too long for single scrolls.

7. The only narrative books out of temporal succession are Ruth and Chronicles, which bookend the Writings, the final section of Jesus' Bible. Ruth serves as a preface to the Writings, turning the readers eyes away from the despondency at the end of the Twelve (Minor Prophets) to the hope of complete restoration through the Davidic Messiah. Conversely, Chronicles comes at the end of the Writings and provides an apt conclusion to the Old Testament by summarizing the whole (it begins with Adam and ends with the call to return to Jerusalem from exile) and by heightening anticipation for complete kingdom fulfillment.

self begins in the Law and continues through the Former Prophets and the Latter Writings, into the Gospels, Acts, and Revelation. This (true) story clarifies God's perspective on how the peoples and events of space and time relate to his kingdom purposes, which move from original creation to new creation, from the old (cursed) world in Adam to the new (blessed) world in Christ. As will be made clear, the main character in the redemptive drama is God, who stands supreme over all and who graciously set Israel apart to serve as the channel through which he would overcome the world's plague of sin and replace it with the blessing of salvation.

"The earth lies defiled under its inhabitants; for they have transgressed the laws, violated the statutes, broken the everlasting covenant. Therefore a curse devours the earth, and its inhabitants suffer for their guilt.... Behold, I will create new heavens and a new earth" (Isa. 24:5–6; 65:17). *A cross at Dominus Flevit with Jerusalem and the Dome of the Rock in the background (photo by David Gunderson).*

Figure 1.6. The Arrangement of Jesus' Bible

English Classification/Arrangement		Hebrew Classification/Arrangement			Approx. Dates (all B.C.)
LAW	Genesis	**LAW (tôrā)**	Genesis		The beginning to 1406
	Exodus		Exodus		
	Leviticus		Leviticus		
	Numbers		Numbers		
	Deuteronomy		Deuteronomy		
HISTORY	Joshua	**PROPHETS (nĕbî'îm)** — Former	Joshua		1406–1380
	Judges		Judges		1380–1050
	Ruth		1–2 Samuel		1100–1010 / 1010–970
	1 Samuel		1–2 Kings		970–853 / 853–560
	2 Samuel	Latter	Jeremiah		627–580
	1 Kings		Ezekiel		593–570
	2 Kings		Isaiah		740–700
	1 Chronicles			Hosea	760–730
	2 Chronicles			Joel	600 (?)
	Ezra			Amos	760
	Nehemiah			Obadiah	586 (?)
	Esther			Jonah	770
POETRY/ WISDOM	Job		The Twelve	Micah	737–690
	Psalms			Nahum	650
	Proverbs			Habakkuk	630
	Ecclesiastes			Zephaniah	627
	Song of Solomon			Haggai	520
PROPHETS — Major	Isaiah			Zechariah	520–518
	Jeremiah			Malachi	433
	Lamentations	**WRITINGS (kĕtûbîm)** — Former	Ruth		1200–1150
	Ezekiel		Psalms		
	Daniel		Job		
Minor	Hosea		Proverbs		No specific historical period covered
	Joel		Ecclesiastes		
	Amos		Song of Songs		
	Obadiah		Lamentations		586
	Jonah	Latter	Daniel		605–530
	Micah		Esther		483–474
	Nahum		Ezra–Nehemiah		538–450 / 444–410
	Habakkuk		1–2 Chronicles		1010–970 / 970–538
	Zephanish				
	Haggai				
	Zephaniah				
	Malachi				

Prepared by Jason S. DeRouchie; many of the dates are taken from John H. Walton, *Chronological and Background Charts of the Old Testament* (Grand Rapids: Zondervan, 1994), 12. The Hebrew ordering is from the Jewish baraita *Baba Bathra* 14b.

Second, Jesus' Bible was more than narrative, for it included both the Latter Prophets and the Former Writings (in light brown in Fig. 1.6), two large groupings of mostly poetic books that stand *within* the main storyline and are arranged in descending order of size (Jeremiah to the Twelve and Psalms to Lamentations).[8] As such, we will grasp Scripture's overarching message most clearly only when the history of redemption is read alongside the additional material and placed within the three-part structure. It is through this lens that Jesus and the apostles preached the good news of God's kingdom, manifest in a message of the messiah and missions (Luke 24:44–47; Acts 26:22–23; 28:23).

The Divine Author of the Old Testament Highlighted How the *Old (Mosaic) Covenant Was Established, Enforced, and Enjoyed*

All five of the major covenants play key roles in the unfolding of the seven-stage redemptive drama. However, the most dominant from a literary perspective are the *old* (Mosaic) covenant and the *new* covenant in Christ. Indeed, the early church named the two parts of the Bible after these covenants (Old *Testament* and New *Testament*).[9]

On the whole, the old (Mosaic) covenant represented an age of death. It is true that Jesus' Bible testifies that God always preserved a faithful remnant, and it is only because of this group who preserved and held fast to God's Word—loyal parents, priests, prophets, politicians, and the like—that the first three-fourths of the Bible even exists! Nevertheless, for the majority of Israel, God's call to love him from the heart and to serve as his witnesses in the world was met with stubbornness and lack of faith, which resulted in the breaking of the covenant and the need for a new one (Jer. 31:31–32).

It is Yahweh's special covenant relationship with Israel, instituted at Sinai, that controls the Old Testament's three divisions. The old (Mosaic) covenant is *established* in the Law, *enforced* in the Prophets, and *enjoyed* in the Writings.

---

8. Lamentations is a little longer than the Song of Songs (2011 words vs. 1662 words). Its placement after the Song was likely driven by some of the following desires: (1) to keep together the three books traditionally assigned to Solomon (Proverbs, Ecclesiastes, Song of Songs), (2) to allow the Old Testament's commentary section (the Latter Prophets and Former Writings) to begin and end with books assigned to the prophet Jeremiah, and (3) to provide a transition at the end of the commentary section back into the exilic context departed from at the end of 2 Kings.

9. From the Latin *testamentum*, meaning "will, covenant."

The Law: The Old (Mosaic) Covenant Established

The Law, also called the Pentateuch, is the Bible's first five books. It is devoted to clarifying God's relationship with and purpose for Israel in the context of the world. Genesis provides a "kingdom prologue" that sets the stage for Israel's mission, which is then detailed in Exodus through Deuteronomy. Israel enjoys God's favor for the sake of the nations (Gen. 12:3; Exod. 19:4–6; Deut. 4:5–8), and through Israel God would raise a royal deliverer who would defeat evil and establish universal blessing (Gen. 3:15; 22:17b–18; 49:8, 10; Num. 24:17–19). While Israel's own stubbornness would result in their exile (Deut. 31:16–17, 29), the mercy of Yahweh would triumph in an age of restoration blessing that would benefit Israel and, ultimately, the nations (4:30–31; 30:1–10 with 4:5–8; 32:21).

The Prophets: The Old (Mosaic) Covenant Enforced

The Prophets contain two sections, the first a *narrative history* of Israel's covenant failure and the second a *prophetic commentary* on the people's rebellion that places their sin within the overall scope of God's redemptive plan. Whereas the Former Prophets (Joshua–Kings) focus on *what* happened in Israel's downward spiral from conquest through monarchy to exile, the Latter Prophets (Jeremiah–The Twelve [Minor Prophets]) develop *why* the drama went the way it did. God's covenant enforcers, the prophets, colored Israel's history as an age of darkness, the old (Mosaic) covenant resulting

"This is the one to whom I will look: he who is humble and contrite in spirit and trembles at my word" (Isa. 66:2). *Machtesh Ramon in the Negeb with sunrise.*

in Israel's condemnation (2 Kings 17:14–18; 2 Cor. 3:9). Nevertheless, the narrative and sermons also offer glimmers of light, heightening anticipation for full kingdom fulfillment in a new covenant and setting the stage for the testimony of the Writings.

The Writings: The Old (Mosaic) Covenant Enjoyed

Like the Prophets but in reverse order, the Writings include both commentary and narrative. Unlike the Prophets, however, the Writings are dominated by a positive thrust, giving voice to the faithful remnant who hoped in the consummation of God's kingdom. The commentary of the Former Writings opens with Ruth, which colors all that follows in messianic anticipation. Psalms through Lamentations then clarify *how those hoping in God's kingdom were to live*—that is, how they could maintain satisfaction in God amidst life's pleasures and pains. Following Lamentations, which resituates the reader in the exilic context highlighted at the end of 2 Kings, the narrative resumes in Daniel and continues through Chronicles, detailing God's preservation of a remnant in exile, the people's initial restoration to the land, and the promise of complete kingdom realization. Because the story is unfinished at the end of Chronicles, the reader is pushed into the New Testament for fulfillment, which is ultimately realized in the person of Christ and his church.

The New Testament's Parallel Structure

Intriguingly, the arrangement of the New Testament books in many ways parallels that of the Old. Not only is the narrative-commentary pattern the same (see Fig. 1.7), but also the covenantal structure can be viewed as parallel. The new covenant is *established* in the Gospels, *enforced* in Acts and the Pauline Epistles, and *enjoyed* in the General Epistles and Revelation. The last category may be the most questionable, for the General Epistles and Revelation include covenant enforcement and regularly address tribulation. Can you really call this "joy"? In response, like the Old Testament Writings, which are future-oriented and loaded with trials, joy in the last section of the New Testament is one of persevering hope, experienced through suffering and in light of the glory that is to be revealed at the consummation of the kingdom (Heb. 12:2–3; James 1:2; 1 Peter 1:6–8; 4:13; 1 John 1:4; 2 John 4, 12; 3 John 3–4; Jude 24; Rev. 18:20; 19:6–8).[10]

---

10. David Trobisch argues that the New Testament canon was fixed as early as A.D. 125 and
    originally bore a different arrangement in the commentary section: Matthew, Mark, Luke,

Figure 1.7. The Bible's Covenantal Structure

	Established (Savior)	Enforced (Sovereign)		Enjoyed (Satisfier)	
OLD COVENANT	Law	Former Prophets	Latter Prophets	Former Writings	Latter Writings
NEW COVENANT	Gospels	Acts	Pauline Epistles	General Epistles	Revelation[11]
	Narrative	Narrative	Commentary	Commentary	Narrative

Synthesis and Conclusion

The Bible's Frame, Form, Focus, and Fulcrum

In order to synthesize the Old Testament message, it will be helpful to review what we have already learned regarding what the Bible is about (its *frame*), how it is transmitted (its *form*), why it was given (its *focus*), and around whom it is centered (its *fulcrum*).

- The Frame (Content: What?). The Bible is the revelation of God, who reigns over all, standing as the source, sustainer, and goal of all things (Rom. 11:36). Through creation, fall, redemption, and consummation, this supreme Savior, Sovereign, and Satisfier has been shaping a people for himself in the context of the world. The Bible is about his kingdom building process—God's reign over God's people in God's land for God's glory (Luke 4:43; Acts 1:3; 20:25; 28:23, 31).

John, Acts, James, 1 Peter, 2 Peter, 1 John, 2 John, 3 John, Jude, Romans, 1 Corinthians, 2 Corinthians, Galatians, Ephesians, Philippians, Colossians, 1 Thessalonians, 2 Thessalonians, Hebrews, 1 Timothy, 2 Timothy, Titus, Philemon, Revelation (*Paul's Letter Collection: Tracing the Origins* [Minneapolis: Fortress, 1994]; idem, *The First Edition of the New Testament* [Oxford: Oxford University Press, 2000]; cf. C. E. Hill, "The New Testament Canon: Deconstructio ad Absurdum?" *JETS* 52 [2009]: 101–20; idem, *Who Chose the Gospels? Probing the Great Gospel Conspiracy* [Oxford: Oxford University Press, 2010]). Significantly, regardless of how the New Testament commentary books are ordered, the general pattern "narrative → narrative → commentary → commentary → narrative" remains parallel to the structure of Jesus' Bible.

11. Although Revelation is not strictly "narrative," it does complete the storyline begun in the Old Testament and carried on in the Gospels and Acts. Furthermore, like Chronicles at the end of the Old Testament, which reviews all history from Adam to the initial restoration, Revelation at the end of the New Testament reviews redemptive history from the first coming of Christ unto eternity.

- **The Form (Means: How?).** Throughout redemptive history, God's relationship with his people has been maintained through a series of covenants. The most dominant of these are the old (Mosaic) covenant and the new covenant in Christ, which together provide the thematic structure of the Christian Bible's two parts. Addressing the age of death, the old covenant was *established* in the Law, *enforced* in the Prophets, and *enjoyed* in the Writings. In contrast, the new covenant, which overviews the age of life, was *established* in the Gospels, *enforced* in Acts and the Pauline Epistles, and *enjoyed* in the General Epistles and Revelation.

- **The Focus (Purpose: Why?).** The ultimate goal behind all God's actions is the preservation and display of his glory, and it is to this end that all Scripture points. Because all things are from him, through him, and to him, God's glory is exalted over all things (Rom. 11:36) and should be the goal of our lives (1 Cor. 10:31).

"Let everything that has breath praise the LORD! Praise the LORD!" (Ps. 150:6). *A close-up of a camel in the Judean wilderness.*

- **The Fulcrum (Sphere: Whom?).** Jesus Christ is the one to whom all redemptive history points, and the one from whom all fulfillment comes. The entire Bible is centered on him, who stands as the promised messianic deliverer and who secures reconciliation with God for all who believe in him as the divine, crucified Messiah. A universal call to repentance and whole-life surrender is the natural overflow of Jesus' redemptive, kingdom work.

Figure 1.8. The Bible's Frame, Form, Focus, and Fulcrum

Frame	God's Kingdom
Form	through Covenant (Established, Enforced, and Enjoyed)
Focus	for God's Glory
Fulcrum	in Christ (Savior, Sovereign, and Satisfier)

Stated succinctly, the message of the Christian Scriptures can be synthe-
sized as *God's kingdom through covenant for his glory in
Christn.*[12] Or, put another way, the Bible's call is for
Jew and Gentile alike to magnify God as the supreme
Savior, Sovereign, and Satisfier of the world through
Messiah Jesus. The Old Testament provides the foundation for this message; the New Testament supplies
the fulfillment. Although every synthesis can be found
wanting in light of the depths of God's greatness and mankind's fallen state,
Figure 1.9 is an attempt to capture the entire Bible's message in a single
graphic.

> How would you summarize the Bible's message?
> Here is my attempt: *God's kingdom through cov-
> enant for his glory in Christ.*

A Commencement Challenge

As you read through this Christian interpretation of the Old Testament,
my prayer is that you will encounter God and find yourself changed more
into his likeness. As you revel in the message of his Word, your life should
develop heightened gratitude and hope, greater surrender and commitment,
more intense delight and passion, all toward God in Christ. You should
become more God-exalting and less dependent on things of this world. You
should find yourself less self-absorbed and more ready to pour your life out
in love for others, all in the strength that God supplies.

The prophet Isaiah foretold that, in the age of restoration, the remnant
of Israel and the nations would all "be taught by the LORD" (Isa. 54:13; cf.
Jer. 31:34). John 6:44–45 records Jesus citing this passage and then saying,
"Everyone who has heard and learned from the Father comes to me" (John
6:45). May the Lord now grant you ears to hear, eyes to see, and a heart to
understand, all in a way that helps you move toward Christ in heart and
soul, "from one degree of glory to another" (2 Cor. 3:18).[13]

---

12. I thank my friend and colleague Jason C. Meyer, who first presented to me the simple
     but profound multi-orbed synthesis of the Bible's message as "God's kingdom through
     covenant for his glory (What? How? Why?)."

13. This gift was not granted to most of old covenant Israel (Deut. 29:4; Rom. 11:8), but God
     promised it for all in the new covenant (Deut. 30:6, 8; 2 Cor. 4:6). May it be so for you,
     even as you wait "for our blessed hope, the appearing of the glory of our great God and
     Savior Jesus Christ" (Titus 2:13).

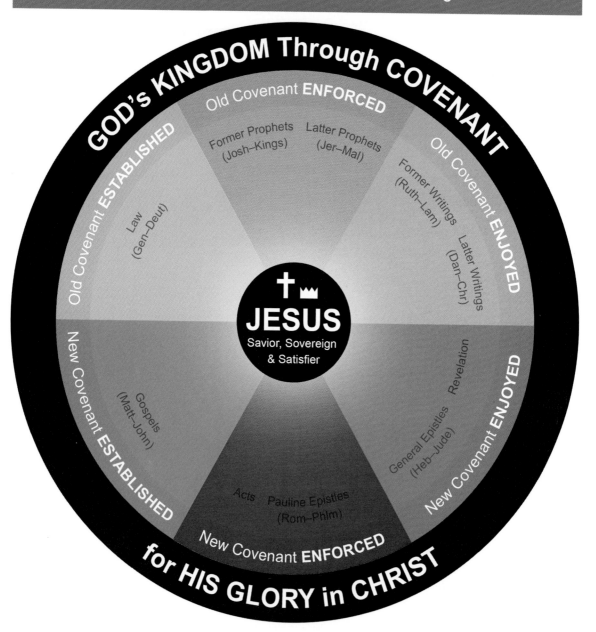

Figure 1.9 The Bible's Structure and Message[14]

GOD's KINGDOM Through COVENANT

Old Covenant ENFORCED

Old Covenant ESTABLISHED

Former Prophets (Josh–Kings)   Latter Prophets (Jer–Mal)

Old Covenant ENJOYED

Former Writings (Ruth–Lam)   Latter Writings (Dan–Chr)

Law (Gen–Deut)

JESUS
Savior, Sovereign & Satisfier

New Covenant ESTABLISHED

Gospels (Matt–John)

Revelation

General Epistles (Heb–Jude)

New Covenant ENJOYED

Acts   Pauline Epistles (Rom–Phlm)

New Covenant ENFORCED

for HIS GLORY in CHRIST

---

14. I thank my friend Miles V. Van Pelt, whose lectures and charts on Old Testament biblical theology at www.biblicaltraining.org initially sparked my vision for this diagram.

KEY WORDS AND CONCEPTS FOR REVIEW

Five world powers	Already but not yet
Fertile Crescent	Law, Prophets, Writings
The Land Between	Program of redemption
For our instruction	Covenant established, enforced, enjoyed
Seven historical figures	Frame, form, focus, and fulcrum
K.I.N.G.D.O.M.	Foundation and fulfillment
Five main covenants	
Story of God's glory	

KEY RESOURCES FOR FURTHER STUDY[15]

Alexander, T. Desmond. *From Eden to the New Jerusalem: An Introduction to Biblical Theology*. Grand Rapids: Kregel, 2009.

Carson, D. A. *The God Who Is There: Finding Your Place in God's Story*. Grand Rapids: Baker, 2010.

Dempster, Stephen G. *Dominion and Dynasty: A Theology of the Hebrew Bible*. NSBT. Downers Grove, IL: InterVarsity, 2003.

Dumbrell, William J. *The Faith of Israel: A Theological Survey of the Old Testament*. 2nd ed. Grand Rapids: Baker, 2002.

Gentry, Peter J., and Stephen J. Wellum. *Kingdom Through Covenant: A Biblical-Theological Understanding of the Covenants*. Wheaton, IL: Crossway, 2012.

Goldsworthy, Graeme. *According to Plan: The Unfolding Revelation of God in the Bible*. Downers Grove, IL: InterVarsity, 2002.

Hafemann, Scott J. *The God of Promise and the Life of Faith: Understanding the Heart of the Bible*. Wheaton, IL: Crossway, 2001.

---

15. As editor of this survey, I have included books in the "Key Resources" lists at the end of each chapter that I believe will be helpful in various ways to the student of the Scriptures. Not all the books listed are unified in their theological perspectives or interpretive approaches, and all claims need to be evaluated carefully up against the Bible, which supplies the highest authority for the Christian.

Hamilton, James M., Jr. *God's Glory in Salvation Through Judgment: A Biblical Theology*. Wheaton, IL: Crossway, 2010.

House, Paul R. *Old Testament Theology*. Downers Grove, IL: InterVarsity, 1998.

Merrill, Eugene H. *Everlasting Dominion: A Theology of the Old Testament*. Nashville: B&H Academic, 2006.

Williamson, Paul R. *Sealed with an Oath: Covenant in God's Unfolding Purpose*. NSBT. Downers Grove, IL: InterVarsity, 2007.

Wright, Christopher J. H. *Knowing Jesus Through the Old Testament*. Downers Grove, IL: InterVarsity, 1992.

THE OLD COVENANT ESTABLISHED: WHAT THE LAW IS REALLY ABOUT

Jason S. DeRouchie

The universal glory of the King of Kings, who reigns through his Messiah: This is the hope to which Genesis through Deuteronomy point. Genesis sets the stage by clarifying both the universal need for divine blessing and the means by which God will restore it—namely, through Abraham and his offspring, called Israel. Exodus, Leviticus, Numbers, and Deuteronomy then detail the institution of the old (Mosaic) covenant, including clarification of Israel's unique role in God's universal kingdom purposes.

Another title for the Law is the Pentateuch, which derives from the Greek *penta* ("five") and *teuchos* ("book, vessel, tool"). While the English word "law" is usually used to render the Hebrew title *tôrâ*, the Bible's first five books contain much more than what is often considered law. Certainly large portions are devoted to guiding justice and deeds of mercy and to directing God's people in how to live rightly in God's world. However, this type of "instruction" is bound up within a narrative plot, which itself *teaches* readers about God and his purposes for and in human history.

Following the worldview-shaping preface in Genesis 1:1–2:3, the Law's narrative backbone details the initial three stages of God's kingdom-building program. The unit places Israel within God's global purposes and provides a theological history from the beginning of time to around 1406 B.C., the year of Moses' death. In the process, it details the fruits and failures of faith in the lives of people like Adam and Eve, Noah and Abraham, Jacob and Joseph, and all the children of Israel. The most dominant human figure is Moses, whose 120-year life is chronicled from birth to death in Exodus through Deuteronomy.

Figure L.1. God's Kingdom-Building Program Narrated in the Law			
	Preface introducing the biblical worldview: God and his purposes for people on this planet		Genesis 1:1–2:3
K	**KICKOFF AND REBELLION**	1. Creation, fall, and flood (ca. ? B.C.)	Genesis 2:4–11:9
I	**INSTRUMENT OF BLESSING**	2. Patriarchs (ca. 2100–1850 B.C.)	Genesis 11:10–50:26
N	**NATION REDEEMED AND COMMISSIONED**	3. Exodus, Sinai, and wilderness (ca. 1450–1400 B.C.)	Exodus–Deuteronomy
G	**GOVERNMENT IN THE PROMISED LAND**	4. Conquest and kingdoms (united and divided) (ca. 1400–600 B.C.)	Joshua–Kings
D	**DISPERSION AND RETURN**	5. Exile and initial restoration (ca. 600–400 B.C.)	Daniel–Chronicles
O	**OVERLAP OF THE AGES**	6. Christ's work and the church age (ca. 4 B.C.–A.D. ?)	Matthew–Acts
M	**MISSION ACCOMPLISHED**	7. Christ's return and kingdom consummation (ca. A.D. ?–eternity)	Revelation

Significantly, Yahweh is unquestionably the main character dominating the Law's entire storyline. In these five books, God creates and judges his world, establishes and renews covenants, and makes and fulfills promises. He rescues and commissions his people, dwells in their midst and forgives their sin, and performs miracles like giving babies to the barren and providing water in deserts. He instructs his own in the path of life, and he displays himself as believable and his promises as desirable.

As is clear from the literary space given to God's work and words through Moses, the Pentateuch was designed to highlight *the establishment of the old covenant*, which provides the literary lens for understanding the Prophets and Writings and anticipates the need for the redeeming work of Messiah Jesus. The nature and purpose of the Mosaic (old) covenant is only understood in light of the Adam/Noahic and Abrahamic covenants that precede, and the covenant itself anticipates both implicitly and explicitly the Davidic and new covenants that follow.

The Law begins by highlighting humanity's unique mission of imaging God, mankind's failure, and the promise of a male descendant of the first woman who would overcome the evil one and reestablish universal peace under God's sovereignty (Gen. 3:15; cf. 22:17b–18; 49:8, 10; Num. 24:17–19). The Law ends by highlighting the unique role Moses played as mediator of the old covenant and by anticipating the foretold "prophet like Moses" (Deut. 34:10; cf. 18:15, 18; Luke 7:16; John 1:21, 25, 45; Acts 3:22–26; 7:37), whose very presence suggests the temporary nature of the Mosaic administration and the long-term need for a new covenant (Gal. 3:23–26; Heb. 8:13; 9:8–15; 12:18–24). Figure L.2 overviews the flow of thought in the Law, and Figure L.3 synthesizes through images the first three stages in God's kingdom-building program, as narrated here.

Figure L.2. The Law at a Glance	
THE LAW: The Old Covenant ESTABLISHED **(Yahweh as Savior)**	
Genesis	Prologue to God's Universal Kingdom: The Need and Provision for Universal Blessing
Exodus	King Yahweh and His Global Purpose through Israel: God's Presence and Israel's Salvation and Mission
Leviticus	Holy Yahweh and the Necessity for Holiness: Pursuing God through His Sanctifying Presence and Promises
Numbers	Faithful Yahweh and His Unfaithful People: Learning to Wait and Follow amidst Seasons of Discipline
Deuteronomy	Israel's Constitution: A Call to Lasting Covenant Relationship and Its Eschatological Realization

Figure L.3. God's K-I-N-G-D-O-M Story Through Images

KEY RESOURCES FOR FURTHER STUDY

Alexander, T. Desmond. *From Paradise to the Promised Land: An Introduction to the Pentateuch*, third ed. Grand Rapids: Baker, 2012.

Schnittjer, Gary Edward. *The Torah Story: An Apprenticeship on the Pentateuch*. Grand Rapids: Zondervan, 2006.

Wenham, Gordon. *Exploring the Old Testament, Volume 1: A Guide to the Pentateuch*. Downers Grove, IL: InterVarsity, 2003.

Genesis

Who?

Genesis is the Bible's first book and is also the initial volume of a small collection called the Law/Torah or Pentateuch. It provides an introduction to information organized around a "biography" of Moses from his birth (Exod. 2) to his death (Deut. 34). Moses is regarded by the biblical record as the principal author of the Pentateuch and by inference the book of Genesis (2 Chron. 25:4; Ezra 6:18; Matt. 19:7; John 5:46; 7:23). He probably had access to ancient records and used them to preface the historical and legal material that now forms the core of the Pentateuch.

Like the rest of the Torah, the language of Genesis (i.e., spelling and grammar) appears to have been updated after Moses to conform to the Hebrew of the rest of the Bible. With this, editing of content also appears to have continued even centuries after the prophet. For example, the presence of Canaanites in Israel at an earlier time seems to have required explanation to later audiences for whom they were a distant memory (e.g., Gen. 12:6; 13:7; cf. 28:19; 36:31). Also, using language that would have been relevant to people in Judah living in exile or after, the text says God brought Abraham up—not from Ur of the Amorites (or the like) but—from Ur of the Chaldeans (15:7; cf. Neh. 9:7), a title attested in other sources no earlier than the eighth century B.C.

When?

Building upon earlier sources, Moses probably wrote the first canonical edition of Genesis amidst the wilderness wanderings during the final forty years of his life (1446–1406 B.C. [though some posit 1250–1210 B.C.]). In doing so, he placed the exodus story within God's global purpose of redemption and showed how the patriarchs ended up in Egypt. Moses or later editors of the book then spelled out more fully the universal and cosmic implications of the exodus salvation by providing the book with a universal history (Gen. 1–11) rooted in ancient traditions.

Where?

Moses would likely have compiled and written the first edition of the book in the wilderness, somewhere between Mount Sinai and the bank of the Jordan River in Moab. Later editorial updating of the book would likely have been performed from within the Promised Land (e.g., Gen. 13:7, 10; 36:1, 8, 19, 43).

Why?

Serving as an introduction to the Law, the Old Testament, and the Christian Bible, Genesis is indispensable for a right understanding of each. As its name suggests, it is a book of beginnings: creation, humanity, history, the fall, redemption, and the nation of Israel. By focusing on God's promise to restore his creation through a human being in the family line reaching from Adam to Abraham to Judah, Genesis provides the main background necessary for grasping the global purpose of Israel and the storyline of the Bible as a whole.

GENESIS

Stephen G. Dempster

Carefully Crafted Verses from Genesis

In the beginning, God created the heavens and the earth (Gen. 1:1).

"I will put enmity between you and the woman, and between your offspring and her offspring; he shall bruise your head, and you shall bruise his heel" (Gen. 3:15).

"Go from your country and your kindred and your father's house to the land that I will show you. And I will make of you a great nation, and I will bless you and make your name great, so that you will be a blessing. I will bless those who bless you, and him who dishonors you I will curse, and in you all the families of the earth shall be blessed" (Gen. 12:1–3).

And [Abram] believed the LORD, and he counted it to him as righteousness (Gen. 15:6).

> ## THE AUTHOR OF GENESIS ...
>
> - Used genealogy to highlight *the divine origin and significance of all creation.*
>
> - Emphasized *the purpose of creation* in relation to its *one, loving, transcendent Creator.*
>
> - Identified *human revolt against God* as the base cause of global wickedness and death.
>
> - Stressed *God's promise to restore creation* through a specific family line and human being.

The Author of Genesis Used Genealogy to Highlight *the Divine Origin and Significance of All Creation*

Genesis has a striking genealogical form. A theological introduction to the book (Gen. 1:1–2:3) is followed by ten "chapters," each beginning with the language of genealogy:

Figure 2.1. Genesis at a Glance

	Introduction: A Creation Proem (Gen. 1:1–2:3)	
1	The Genealogy of Creation (2:4–4:26)	
2	The Genealogy of Adam (5:1–6:8)	Primeval
3	The Genealogy of Noah (6:9–9:29)	History
4	The Genealogy of Noah's Sons (10:1–11:9)	
5	The Genealogy of Shem (11:10–11:26)	
6	The Genealogy of Terah (11:27–25:11)	
7	The Genealogy of Ishmael (25:12–18)	
8	The Genealogy of Isaac (25:19–35:29)	Patriarchal
9	The Genealogy of Esau (36:1–8; 36:9–37:1)	History
10	The Genealogy of Jacob (37:2–50:26)	

At least four purposes are evident in the book's conspicuous organization around the genealogical form. First, the form stressed the importance of *origins*. The book was named appropriately "Genesis" in the Greek translation of the Hebrew Bible. The Greek translators consistently rendered the Hebrew word for "genealogy" with this term, which means "birth" or "beginning." Some of the beginnings that Genesis described were: creation, humanity, family, work, sin, and the first promise of God. Second, by the use of a family tree, the roots of humanity were traced back from the vast variety of races and ethnic groups to one couple, Adam and Eve, who were created in the image of God. This showed the divine imprint placed upon every human being. In the ancient world it was often only royalty that could claim divine origin; Genesis democratized this concept. Every human being had royal dignity! Third, the genealogies showed the importance of descendants—a key motif in Genesis. Fourth, the author was able to trace not only historical roots with this genealogical form but also able to "fast forward" the narrative storyline to reach particular family branches that he wished to spotlight. Thus the initial five genealogies transported the reader through millennia quite rapidly until the sixth genealogy was reached, which focused on Abraham and his family. Then the narrative pace slowed down considerably in order to "showcase" the lives and families of the patriarchs of Israel. In fact the last five genealogies account for approximately eighty percent of the written material in the book of Genesis. This indicated a clear structural division between Genesis 1–11 (primeval history), which generally deals with universal concerns, and Genesis 12–50 (patriarchal history), which specifically describes more national concerns relating to the birth of Israel.

The Author of Genesis Emphasized *the Purpose of Creation* in Relation to Its *One, Loving, Transcendent Creator*

Foundations for the Biblical Worldview

"In the beginning, God created the heavens and the earth." These are the first words of not only Genesis but also the Old Testament and the entire Christian Bible. There are seven Hebrew words in this first sentence, introducing seven days of creation and seven pronouncements of the goodness of creation. The introduction to Genesis (Gen. 1:2–2:3) is a linguistic and theological masterpiece, functioning as a prologue to the book of Genesis in much the same way that John 1:1–18 prefaced John's Gospel. Literarily, this elegant *proem* (poetic prose) provides a panoramic picture of God's magnificent accomplishment in creating the world, while the first "chapter" (Gen. 2:4–4:26) opens the body of the book with a close-up view of God and his creation.

> Psalm 8:5 declares, "You have … crowned him with glory and honor." Based on this explication of being created in God's image, Greek Orthodox weddings include the exchange of crowns rather than rings. In the biblical view, *all weddings are royal,* because all human beings are made in the likeness of the King of the universe. Can you imagine the implications for marriage in any culture if spouses began to treat each other with the royal dignity each deserves (see Song 3:6–11; 6:4–12)?

The proem was designed to shape a proper theological perspective of reality. The world was the product of a deliberate plan and purpose of one transcendent God. Repeatedly, created reality materialized immediately at the command of the divine word: God spoke, and it was so (1:7, 9, 11, 15, 24, 30). The perfection of the final creation is accented by the symmetry of three days of domains (the formless is shaped) balanced by three days of their inhabitants (the void is filled), capped by a seventh day of complete Sovereign rest.

"God said, 'Let there be lights in the expanse of the heavens to separate the day from the night'" (Gen. 1:14). *Sunrise over the Nile River in Minya, Egypt.*

In the ancient world, creation was often seen to be the result of a fight among the gods (*theomachy*); the great whales were demonic sea monsters; and the sun, moon, and stars were important deities. In a single stroke, Genesis 1 demolished these myths. One God created by speaking effortlessly; the whales were created and blessed by him to frolic in the ocean (see Ps. 104:26); the sun and moon were simply "lights," and the stars were barely mentioned. The world was not divine but was rather the divine glory. It was not a dangerous place but a safe and secure place for its inhabitants to thrive and flourish. Seven times was heard the refrain "God saw that it was good" (Gen. 1:4, 10, 12, 18, 21, 25, 31).

Figure 2.2. The Structure of the Creation Week in Genesis 1:1–2:3

DOMAIN (Formless Becomes Shaped)	DOMAIN INHABITANT AND MASTER (Void Becomes Filled)
Day 1 Light	**Day 4** Lights (Sun, Moon, Stars)
Day 2 Sky to Separate "Waters"	**Day 5** Birds, Sea Creatures
Day 3 Dry Land and Vegetation	**Day 6** Land Animals and Humanity
Day 7 Sabbath—Sovereign Rest	

"Valiant Marduk ... trampled upon the frame of Tiamat, with his merciless mace he crushed her skull.... He split her in two, like a fish for drying, half of her he set up and made as a cover, heaven. He stretched out the hide and assigned watchmen, and ordered them not to let her waters escape" (*The Epic of Creation*; cf. Gen. 1:2, 6–8). Elsewhere in the Epic we read: "What [Marduk] thought of in his heart he proposes, 'I shall compact blood, I shall cause bones to be, I shall make stand a human being, let 'Man' be its name. I shall create humankind, They shall bear the gods' burden that those may rest'" (*COS* 1:400; cf. *ANET* 68). *The Babylonian Epic of Creation provides one ancient Near Eastern conception of the world's creation while focusing on the exaltation of Marduk over all gods in return for his fighting on behalf of other deities; this particular tablet written in cuneiform celebrates the elevation of Marduk after his defeat of Tiamat, the goddess of watery chaos (from the British Museum; translation from COS 1:398; cf. ANET 67).*

The creation of humanity in Day 6 represented a climax. The previous creations happened with a simple divine command. Not so with mankind.

There was first a pregnant pause as God addressed himself and for the first time deliberated before creation: "Let us make man in our image, after our likeness" (1:26). This solemn moment showed that humanity emerged from the depths of the divine heart in a way that was not true for the rest of creation.[1] God then clarified mankind's makeup and function: male and female, side by side (1:27), would together "be fruitful and multiply and fill the earth and subdue it, and have dominion" (1:28). In the world of the Bible, only kings claimed to be "images of God," but Genesis states that every human being, as God's representative, bears royal status expressed in having "dominion." While there has been a great deal written about the meaning of the divine image, at the least it indicated a unique relationship between God and humanity. An important implication of this unique divine–human relation was a unique human–creation relationship. Humanity alone of all the creatures of the earth would rule creation, "imaging" God in the world.

> The innate royal status of every human is the real *foundation of Western justice*, since it assumes that every human, by virtue of creation, has certain inherent rights.[2] The significance of this fact is highlighted in S. Tomkins's following account:[3] "In November 1759, a slave ship arrived in the Caribbean ravaged by dysentery. Luckily it ran into the British fleet there, and appealed for help. The only doctor willing to go on board was an evangelical Christian named James Ramsay. His first introduction to the slave trade was a hold full of dying prisoners, covered in blood and excrement. Quitting the navy after a leg injury, he became an Anglican minister in S. Christopher (now St. Kitts) where, as well as his official duties, he enraged the plantation managers by preaching to the slaves and condemning their mistreatment. For fourteen years he faced violent opposition and filled their heads with the notion that they were made in the image of God."

God and His Kingdom Family

The relationship between God and humanity became the focus of attention in Genesis 2, as the transcendent Creator became "up close and personal" with his image. In this text, God was depicted first as a potter crafting the man from the soil (2:7), and then as a master artisan, putting Adam to sleep, extracting one of his ribs, and forming from the man a woman as his partner (2:21–23). Remarkable and unique in the Hebrew Bible is the consistent addition in Genesis 2–3 of the personal name for God, Yahweh (LORD), to the title Elohim (God). It clearly showed that the transcendent Creator of Genesis 1 was the covenantal, personal God of Genesis 2, condescending to "get his hands dirty" in the life of humanity. This was a first condescension in a long series of divine actions that ultimately led to

---

1. G. Von Rad, *Genesis: A Commentary* (Philadelphia: Westminster, 1972), 57.
2. N. Wolterstorff, *Justice: Rights and Wrongs* (Princeton, NJ: Princeton University Press, 2007).
3. S. Tomkins, William *Wilberforce: A Biography* (Grand Rapids: Eerdmans, 2007), 36.

the Word himself becoming flesh and participating in the depths of human life (John 1:14).

The task of humanity was to have a relationship with God and with the rest of creation. The relationship with God was to be marked by dialogue and submission; the relationship with creation, dominion and service. Adam and Eve were thus *servant-rulers*. The first couple's rule of creation was characterized by agriculture and maintenance of the garden, that is, developing it to its full potential. They were to have the free run of creation: to eat and enjoy all the trees in the garden except one—a tree of knowledge of good and evil (Gen. 2:16–17). The forbidden tree represented the sin of moral autonomy, which would erase the boundary between divinity and humanity. By eating fruit forbidden by God, the first couple would determine for themselves good and evil.[4]

> Jesus was the "last Adam" and ultimate human—the truest "image of the invisible God" (1 Cor. 15:45; Col. 1:15, 19). Both the original creation and the new creation came into being through Jesus (John 1:1–3; 1 Cor. 5:17–19; Col. 1:16–19), making him the preeminent Lord over all things (Col. 1:18; Heb. 1:3).

The garden paradise represented the ideal vision of human life: humanity in relationship with God, human beings in relationship with each other and with the rest of creation, coruling it and mastering it. The source of the world's major waterways flowed out from Eden, symbolizing a universal source of life. There was perfect coherence and wholeness. Later, the priest Aaron would bless the people of Israel with this wholeness (Num. 6:24–26). The word used at the climax of the priestly benediction was the Hebrew word *shalom*. When English readers see this word, which is translated "peace," they think of the "absence of tension." Ancient Hebrews would have thought of the presence of health and wholeness. This characterized existence in Eden.

> Many environmentalists trace the roots of the modern ecological crisis to Genesis 1 and the so-called *cultural mandate* for humans to rule the earth. The roots of the environmental crisis, however, can be traced back to Genesis 3, not Genesis 1, where humans serve no higher authority than self!

The Author of Genesis Identified *Human Revolt Against God* as the Base Cause of Global Wickedness and Death

Theologians use the term "the fall" to describe the events of Genesis 3, but this term is an understatement. "Colossal collapse" would be more appropriate. The avalanche of sin and death down the mountain of human

---

4. H. Blocher, *In the Beginning: The Opening Chapters of Genesis* (Downers Grove, IL: InterVarsity, 1984), 131.

history had its origin here. While some may see this account rich with metaphor and caution against reading the text too literally, the writer clearly intended that the first couple were real persons in a real place, tempted to eradicate the divine–human boundary.

"Out of the ground the Lᴏʀᴅ God made to spring up every tree that is pleasant to the sight and good for food" (Gen. 2:9). *Wadi Qilt in the Judean wilderness between Jerusalem and Jericho.*

The snake was the first speaker to discuss the subject of God in the Bible and thus the first theologian.[5] This original "doctor of divinity" called into question God's character with a charge that the divine prohibition extended

---

5. D. Bonhoeffer, *Creation and Fall: A Theological Exposition of Genesis 1–3* (Minneapolis: Fortress, 1997), 111–112.

to all the trees of the Garden (Gen. 3:1)—a lie. A speaking reptile would have shocked an ancient audience. The content of the speech increased the severity of the shock. First, the snake used the term "God" (Elohim) and not "the LORD God," a striking aberration in this section of text. The snake did not know God covenantally—in personal relationship. It only knew about God.

When the first couple sinned (3:6), they did so by choosing the things of the world over the precepts of God (see 1 John 2:16). The result was that couple experienced a distorted vision of life, which revealed their alienation from God and each other (Gen. 3:7–8). For the first time they became aware of each other's nakedness, and it shamed them. The primal original unity was broken. They attempted to hide their nakedness with improvised clothing, and they hid from God among the trees of the garden. Divine presence—once a joy—became a threat.

Judgment and curse resulted. The serpent now slithered along on the ground, a sign of the eventual demise of the sinister power that spoke through the reptile (Rev. 20:2). Wordplays significantly emphasized the judgment upon the couple. The woman (*iššâ*), made from the man (*îš*) as a companion and co-ruler, became a competitor and opponent. She now would give life only through suffering. The man (*ādām*), made from the earth (*ădāmâ*) to rule, now would engage in a relentless struggle with the earth for its goods. The earth would finally win as *Adam* would return to the *Adamah*. Finally, the first couple was banned both from their garden paradise and from the divine presence particularly, symbolized by a tree of life. Adam and Eve were the first in a long line of exiles from Eden (Gen. 3:1–24).

> Every human being is either in Adam or Jesus, dead or alive, part of the old creation or part of the new. This is Paul's point in 1 Corinthians 15:22: "As in Adam all die, so also in Christ shall all be made alive" (cf. Rom. 5:18–19).

The ensuing narrative recounted powerfully the "snowballing" effects of sin and its consequences. The word "curse" occurred five times (3:14, 17; 4:11; 5:29; 9:25). Genesis 4 described the first murder, followed by the ascent of human culture paralleled by the amoral descent into the abyss. The flood was caused by the entire early world *en masse* gripped by violence, aggression, and bloodshed (6:1–6). The post-flood world was no different, as the story

> "We are stardust, we are golden. And we have to get ourselves back to the garden!" So went the theme song of the flower children at Woodstock, New York, in 1969. Through music, drugs, and sex, they sought to re-enter paradise, but Genesis points out that this is possible only by relying on God. In Jesus' words, he alone is the "way" to relationship with the Father (John 14:6), and to those who overcome/conquer, resting in the strength he supplies (15:5; 1 John 4:4), he "will grant to eat of the tree of life, which is in the paradise of God" (Rev. 2:7).

of the tower of Babel represented the concerted attempt by the human community to storm heaven to attempt to erase once again the divine–human boundary—one more symbol of human defiance and autonomy. Humanity and its community, ability, and technology were all marred by sin and death. The pristine creation now became a source of pain and disgust. At the end of the primeval history (chs. 1–11), the ancient reader was forced to confront once more the problematic human condition and wonder about the solution to the fall.

The Lord God "drove out the man, and at the east of the garden of Eden he placed the cherubim" (Gen. 3:24). *Painting in Mar Saba Greek Orthodox monastery east of Bethlehem.*

The Author of Genesis Stressed *God's Promise to Restore Creation* Through a Specific Family Line and Human Being

The First Gospel Promise

From earliest moments following humanity's revolt, God's grace was evident. After Adam and Eve's sin, God sought them out, asking them probing questions (Gen. 3:8–19). The penalty for sin was death, but physical death was postponed. God's grace produced not only a delay in punishment but also a strategy of salvation. Thus the curse on the serpent contained the first sign of hope for the human race and the creation. By cursing the serpent, God limited its power and guaranteed its eventual demise: "I will put enmity between you and the woman, and between your offspring and her offspring; he shall bruise your head, and you shall bruise his heel" (3:15; cf. Luke 10:17–19; Rom. 16:20; Rev. 12:9–11). Early interpreters rightly viewed this text as the "mother of all promises": the *protoevangelion* ("first gospel"). It announced that a conflict between the seed of the woman and the serpent would eventually result in the demise of the latter. The serpent's conqueror would restore the conditions of paradise.

Since this conqueror would be a human descendant, the family tree "form" of the book of Genesis was extraordinarily important! The genealogies moved history toward this divine goal of salvation. The ultimately triumphant seed of the woman was being highlighted, and the genealogical structure facilitated the tracking of the descendants. At the end of a ten-member, pre-flood genealogy, Noah's father named his son in hope that he would bring relief from the curse on the ground (Gen. 5:29). Noah became the saviour of the world as he built a giant ark, which passed through the great deluge of judgment. At the end of a similar post-flood genealogy, Abram was figured as another savior through whom not just

> Speaking of Jesus' victory over evil, John declared, "And the great dragon was thrown down, that ancient serpent, who is called the devil and Satan, the deceiver of the whole world" (Rev. 12:9). While the evil one and his minions are already disarmed (Col. 2:15), we await the fulfillment of God's promise that he "will soon crush Satan under [our] feet" (Rom. 16:20).

> "On the seventh day(?) the ship was completed.... What living creatures I had I loaded upon her. I made go aboard all my family and kin.... Shamash set for me an appointed time.... That appointed time arrived.... I gazed upon the appearance of the storm, The storm was frightful to behold! I went into the ship and battened my door" (The *Epic of Gilgamesh*; cf. Gen. 7). *The Epic of Gilgamesh is perhaps the most famous literary piece from ancient Mesopotamia. Depicted here is a visual of Tablet XI, which contains a (warped) Mesopotamian version of the flood story, here presented in the mouth of the flood-hero himself, Utnapishtim (from the British Museum; photo by Douglas Bookman; translation from COS 1:459; cf. ANET 94).*

one family but all the families of the world would find blessing (11:26; cf. 12:3; 22:17b–18)! Through the patriarchal stories, the seed of the woman would triumph over infertility, captivity, oppression, and famine (12–50). How appropriate, then, that the book of Genesis closed with a lengthy poem that spoke of one from the tribe of Judah would restore nature and rule the nations (49:1–28, see esp. vv. 8–10).

The Means for Universal Restoration

When the chronological span of the primeval history (1–11) is compared with that of the patriarchal history (12–50), the difference is startling. The former covered millennia, while the latter a few centuries! It was as if the clock of *world* history had been waiting for the inauspicious lives of an aged Mesopotamian couple in order to begin the clock of *redemptive* history. Thus with the arrival Abram and Sarai, the unpromising "nobodies" of Mesopotamia, the Genesis narrative made a monumental transition.

Genesis 12:1–3 is the hinge connecting these major units of text and thus it has enormous significance. This is one of the most important texts in the entire Bible, for it outlines a divine plan for the world:

> Now the Lord said to Abram, "Go from your country and your kindred and your father's house to the land that I will show you. And I will make of you a great nation, and I will bless you and make your name great, so that you will be a blessing. I will bless those who bless you, and him who dishonors you I will curse, and in you all the families of the earth shall be blessed."

A number of key promises build to a climax at the end of verse 3, each contrasting ironically with its literary context. First, Abraham must become an exile in order to obtain land. Landlessness was a key motif in the previous chapters (3:24; 4:14–16; 6–9; 11:1–6). Now Abram was told to give up his security and *leave* his homeland to go in search of a land that God would give him. This was no ordinary land but a true Eden-like home.

Second, Abram would become a great "nation." Such a word is unusual in the text, for it referred to a political entity, having a large population, government, and defined territory. Given the age and infertility of Sarai (11:30), this promise was preposterous (cf. 18:13–14)!

Third, Abram was going to become famous with an international reputation—a great "name," with the result that he would be a blessing to other nations. A name! A lasting legacy! International fame was something exceptionally valued in the ancient world and something longed for by the builders of the tower of Babel (11:4). But Abram, a Mesopotamian no-name, was going to become legendary by following God's call.

"Abraham moved his tent and came and settled by the oaks of Mamre, which are in Hebron" (Gen. 13:18). *A Bedouin, tent, and camel near Beersheba (photo by David Bivin).*

Fourth, Abram would emerge victorious in a momentous conflict that would determine the destiny of other peoples: "I will bless those who bless you, and him who dishonors you I will curse." Thus would continue the conflict between the seed of the woman and the serpent.

Fifth, there is the climactic promise—"In you all the families of the earth shall be blessed." Abraham would become the instrument of universal blessing. The world had been under universal curse in Genesis 1–11, but now the solution for that curse had arrived: God would work through Abram. As if to signal the fireworks of God's restoration promises, the word "bless" was repeated five times in this short span of three verses to counteract the five instances of "curse" in the primeval history. Abram represented the way back to paradise!

The Hope of Blessing Affirmed

This program for salvation was developed in embryonic form throughout the rest of Genesis. Abram obeyed God's call and reached Canaan, where he claimed the land for Yahweh by building an altar (12:7). Throughout the rest of his life and that of his descendants in Genesis they wandered through the land building altars or digging wells (12:8–9; 13:4, 18; 22:9; 26:13–25; 28:16–22; 35:6–15; 46:1–2). Ironically, the only land that the patriarchs acquired were grave plots (23:1–20; 50:7–16). However, the last words of Genesis forcefully underscored the concern for land, as both Jacob and Joseph, who were in Egypt, longed for their future burials to occur in Canaan (49:28–33; 50:25; cf. Josh. 24:32). This promise of land became central in the Old Testament, a type or anticipatory picture of the eventual restoration of all creation, which would be the inheritance of all believers (Rom. 4:13).

> Has the rest of the world (Gen. 1–11) been made for Israel (12–50)? Or has Israel been made for the rest of the world? The climactic promise in Genesis 12:3—"In you all the families of the earth shall be blessed"—shows clearly that God set Israel apart for the salvation of the world!

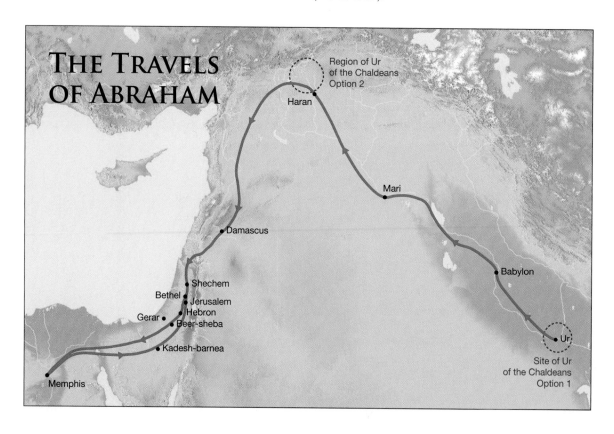

THE TRAVELS OF ABRAHAM

The promise that Abram would become a great nation was partially realized in Genesis. Abram's defeat of major armies in Genesis 14 foreshadowed this role, as did the birth of Isaac and the steady growth of the family from Isaac to Jacob to Jacob's grandchildren. Promises of numerous progeny weaved their way through Genesis, as well as promises of a ruling line of kings (Gen. 13:16; 15:5; 17:6, 16; 28:14; 32:13), from whom a single ruler would come having universal significance (49:8–10; cf. Matt. 1:1; 28:18–20). At the end of Genesis (chs. 37–50), the transition of an Israelite from humiliation to exaltation in Egypt prefigured this rise to greatness for Israel.

The promise of a great name also rippled through the rest of Genesis. Both Abram and Sarai were renamed before the birth of their first child. God changed Abram's name ("my father is exalted") to Abraham ("father of a multitude") to indicate the numerous progeny he would father—a virtual new humanity (Gen. 17:1–7). Likewise, Sarai ("my princess") was renamed Sarah ("princess"), because she

> *Faith* is *trusting God to do for us what we cannot do on our own*. Even though he was old and his wife was barren, Abraham "grew strong in his faith..., fully convinced that God was able to do what he had promised" (Rom. 4:18–21; cf. Gen. 15:6; 18:14). The same held true for Sarah (Heb. 11:11). God is faithful to his Word, so we should trust him as Abraham and Sarah did!

> What could cause Abram to leave pagan comforts (Josh. 24:2) to follow God to a land not his own (Gen. 12:4)? There must have been something so desirable about the promises and so believable about the promise maker (see Acts 7:2) that Abram could not help but trust and obey (Heb. 11:6, 8–10).

"Abraham planted a tamarisk tree in Beersheba and called there on the name of the LORD, the Everlasting God" (Gen. 21:33). *Beersheba from the east.*

would become the mother of a new humanity as well (17:15–16). The name of their child, Isaac ("laughter"), was significant, because it testified to the incredible power of God, of which both Abram and Sarai could not even conceive (cf. 17:17; 18:12). In a dramatic encounter with God that became a defining moment for the entire nation, Isaac's son Jacob ("heel grabber") was renamed Israel ("fighter/striver with God"), thus bestowing on the nation its name. His body bore the wounds of a struggle through which he won blessing from God for his family (32:1–32). Jacob foreshadowed a greater Israel (see Isa. 49:3, 5–6) who in a titanic struggle would emerge victorious but bear deep wounds in winning the blessing for the entire world (52:13–53:12; cf. Acts 3:25–26; Gal. 3:13–14; 2 Cor. 5:21). This latter Israel would be given a name that would be above every name—the name "Lord," and thus he, as Abraham's greater son, would fulfill this incredible promise (Phil. 2:9–10).

"The Jordan Valley was well watered everywhere like the garden of the Lord ... before the Lord destroyed Sodom and Gomorrah" (Gen. 13:10). *The Dead Sea's salty shoreline.*

The stance of other nations and groups to Abraham determined their experience of blessing and curse. This happened throughout Genesis as Lot and his family were saved from the captivity of Mesopotamian kings (ch. 14) and from the wicked city of Sodom (ch. 19). Others were blessed or cursed as they interacted either positively or negatively with Abraham or his descendants (12:9–20; 20:1–8; 21:22–34; 29–31; 34). A particularly poignant scene near the end of the book portrays a weary old Jacob standing before the majestic Pharaoh of Egypt, pronouncing a blessing on him and his house and country (47:7–10). This incongruous picture ironically depicts who had the real source of power.

Finally, the promises climaxed in universal blessing through Abraham. This was more fully developed when the promise was reaffirmed to Abraham after he was willing to sacrifice his only son: "In you all the families of the earth shall be blessed" became "*In your offspring* shall all the nations of the earth be blessed" (22:18; cf. 26:4). By the end of the book of Genesis, Joseph, an Abrahamic descendant, has brought universal blessing after undergoing much suffering. His wisdom literally saved the world during a worldwide famine. And by the end of the Joseph story (49:8–10), there was the promise that *in*

> Paul considered Jesus to be the ultimate *offspring of Abraham* through whom all who believe are blessed (reversing the curse of Adam) and become adopted into God's family (Gal. 3:13–14, 16, 29).

"Joseph went after his brothers and found them at Dothan" (Gen. 37:17). *The view westward from Dothan.*

EXODUS

Who?

Exodus (from Greek *exodus*, "departure") is part of the unified story and literary unit of the Torah, and its authorship is interrelated to the authorship of the whole. Although the Torah is formally anonymous, Jews and Christians have traditionally attributed substantial authorship to Moses, based largely on biblical references outside the Pentateuch to the prophet's "words" or "writings" (Mark 7:10; John 5:47; cf. Josh 8:32) and "the Book/Law of Moses" (e.g., 1 Kings 2:31; 2 Kings 14:6; Ezra 6:18; Luke 24:44; 1 Cor. 9:9; Heb. 10:28). This conclusion is logically consistent with Moses' authoritative position as covenant mediator and specific references within the Pentateuch to his writing activity (e.g., Exod. 17:14; 24:4; 34:27; Deut. 31:9, 24).

The view that Moses was the substantial author of Exodus still allows for later updates of spelling, grammar, or historical-geographical information; minor editorial insertions; and perhaps minor shaping and arranging of material. It is unknown who would have brought Exodus to its final form.

When?

Assuming that Moses is the principal author, Exodus would have been written shortly before his death in the fifthteenth or thirteenth centuries B.C. The discrepancy in the date has to do with harmonizing the biblical and archaeological data for the timing of the exodus. If certain numerical references are taken at face value (esp. 1 Kings 6:1 [480 years from ca. 966 B.C. = 1446 B.C.]; cf. Judg. 11:26; 1 Chron. 6:33–37), then the earlier date is established, placing Moses' death around 1406 B.C. The date of the final form is unknown, but it would have been completed no later than the time of Ezra (ca. 458 B.C.) and likely considerably earlier.

Where?

The exodus story moves from Egypt, through the Red Sea and wilderness, to Mount Sinai. Of these locations, only Egypt is known for certain. There exists around a dozen theories on the exact identity of both the biblical Red Sea and Sinai. Moses would have written the book somewhere in the wilderness between Mount Sinai and the region of Moab, where he died.

Why?

Exodus resumes the narrative begun in Genesis, as the sons of Jacob become "Israel" the nation (Exod. 1:1–7). Both the long stay and the guest-turned-slave status of Israel in Egypt began to fulfill God's word to Abram (Gen. 15:13). The ensuing story of God's judgment of Egypt and deliverance of Israel completed the prediction (Exod. 1–15; cf. Gen. 15:14). The second part of the book focuses on the covenant God established with Israel at Sinai through the mediation of Moses. This covenant, including laws (Exod. 19–24) and the building of the tabernacle (chs. 25–40), became the basis for Israel's mission in the Promised Land.

EXODUS

Kenneth J. Turner

Carefully Crafted Verses from Exodus

Their cry for rescue from slavery came up to God. And God heard their groaning, and God remembered his covenant with Abraham, with Isaac, and with Jacob (Exod. 2:23c–24).

"You yourselves have seen what I did to the Egyptians, and how I bore you on eagles' wings and brought you to myself. Now therefore, if you will indeed obey my voice and keep my covenant, you shall be my treasured possession among all peoples, for all the earth is mine; and you shall be to me a kingdom of priests and a holy nation" (Exod. 19:4–6).

"The LORD, the LORD, a God merciful and gracious, slow to anger, and abounding in steadfast love and faithfulness, keeping steadfast love for thousands, forgiving iniquity and transgression and sin, but who will by no means clear the guilty" (Exod. 34:6–7).

THE AUTHOR OF EXODUS …

- Portrayed the continuing fulfillment of *Yahweh's promises and mission*.

- Stressed *Yahweh's passion to be known* by all in the world.

- Celebrated *Yahweh's power to redeem his people* from slavery.

- Disclosed *Yahweh's gracious provision of his covenant* with Israel.

- Emphasized the significance of *Yahweh's presence* among his people.

- Called *Israel to respond* to Yahweh's disclosure of himself and his will.

The Author of Exodus Portrayed the Continuing Fulfillment of *Yahweh's Promises and Mission*

Exodus offers its own self-contained narrative that progresses from the people of Israel's "filling" Egypt to Yahweh's glory "filling" the tabernacle (Exod. 1:7; 40:34). Topically, the book is dominated by the exodus (chs. 1–15) and the covenant at Sinai, which includes the giving of the law (chs. 20–24) and the construction of the tabernacle (chs. 25–40). These can be restated theologically as several expressions of God's grace: his gracious redemption of Israel (chs. 1–18); his gracious covenant with Israel (chs. 19–24); and his gracious presence in the midst of Israel (chs. 25–40).

Figure 3.1. Exodus at a Glance
God's Gracious Redemption of Israel (Exod. 1–18)
God's Gracious Covenant with Israel (chs. 19–24)
God's Gracious Presence in the Midst of Israel (chs. 25–40)

This story line, however, is not meant to be read in isolation. The opening verses introduce the ensuing drama as a continuation and progression of the story begun in Genesis (Exod. 1:1–7; see Gen. 15:13; 46:27). This fact is emphasized in Exodus 1:7—"But the people of Israel were fruitful and increased greatly; they multiplied and grew exceedingly strong, so that the land was filled with them." This verse draws on the dual themes of creation and covenant by alluding both to the creation mandate (Gen. 1:28; 9:1) and the Abrahamic covenant (cf. 12:2; 15:5; 17:6). In other words, the formation of Israel as an incipient nation (in Exodus) is an outworking of God's purposes in creation and his promises to the patriarchs (in Genesis).

Throughout the book, creational themes appear in (1) the miraculous birth rate of Israelites despite slavery and infanticide (Exod. 1:7, 12); (2) Yahweh's ability to manipulate the created order (human, animal, and inanimate) through the series of signs and plagues in Egypt and through the exodus; (3) Yahweh's explicit claims of ownership of all the earth (8:22; 9:29; 19:4); (4) the natural phenomena attending Yahweh's presence on Mount Sinai (19:16–19); and (5) the creational (Edenic) imagery associated with the tabernacle. By the end of Exodus, the people of Israel (and we as readers) have come to know a fuller manifestation of Yahweh as creator, redeemer, and covenant Lord.

Furthermore, from the perspective of the larger biblical metanarrative, the exodus and the Sinai covenant represent a major progression in God's plan to redeem a fallen world. God's response to and rescue of his people from Egypt is grounded in his "remembering" his covenant promises to the patriarchs (2:24; 6:5; cf. 3:6–4:5). Similarly, following Israel's worship of the golden calf, Moses pleads for divine mercy by appealing to God's promises to multiply Abraham's offspring and give them the land (32:13). Israel, God's "son" (4:22–23), is Abraham's offspring, and God's larger mission to use the elect nation to reach the world shapes the particular way he treats Israel and the particular mission he would give it at Sinai (see esp. 19:4–6). Major lines of continuity, therefore, exist between the Abrahamic covenant and the covenant at Sinai, and recognition of this link helps clarify what God is doing in Exodus.

"A basket made of bulrushes…. She put the child in it and placed it among the reeds by the river bank" (Exod. 2:3). *Papyrus in the Huleh Basin north of Galilee.*

The Author of Exodus Stressed *Yahweh's Passion to be Known* by All in the World

One of the keywords in Exodus is "know." Egyptian leaders' early lack of knowledge was a detriment to Israel (Exod. 1:8; 5:2). But "God knew" (2:25): he knew his people's sufferings, and he knew that the time had come to rescue his people in fulfillment of past covenant promises (2:23–24; 3:7–9). If the battle with Pharaoh was solely to get Israel out of Egypt, then God was incredibly inefficient! Examining the use of "know" and other factors shows that Yahweh's primary concern in the exodus was the revelation and demonstration of his own name and glory.

That All May "Know" Yahweh

The battle with Pharaoh is dominated by "knowing" God through personal experience. The content and results of this experiential knowledge differ between recipients, whether Moses and Israel or Pharaoh and the Egyptians.

God's passion to be known is both right and necessary, for Yahweh alone is God (Exod. 34:14; Deut. 32:39), and to give his glory to another would render something else more worthy and supreme (Isa. 42:8; 48:11). His jealousy for his own renown, however, is also the greatest love he could show the world, for he alone can save (Deut. 4:34–35; Isa. 43:10–12) and in his presence alone is fullness of joy forevermore (Ps. 16:11).

God acts against Egypt so Israel might "know that I am the LORD" (6:7; 10:2). "Yahweh" is God's personal and covenant name (rendered in English Bibles as "the LORD" [small capitals]). While it was used in Genesis (e.g., Gen. 12:8; 15:2, 7), Moses and the present generation of Israel are coming to "know" Yahweh in a much fuller sense, as his presence and fulfillment of past promises are being revealed and actualized in new ways (this is the best way to understand Exod. 6:2–8). At the burning bush, Moses asks about God's name. God responds, "I am who I am" (3:14)—a statement formally related to the proper name Yahweh (i.e., the four consonants *yhwh* are related to the Hebrew verb of existence *hyh*, "to be"). Though it is popular to understand Yahweh/"I AM" to be describing God's incommunicable attributes (e.g., eternality, independence, or unchangeableness), the context points in a couple other directions. First, describing Yahweh as "I AM" may be sort of a non-definition promoting divine freedom; he cannot be manipulated or limited to a short definition (e.g., "I am whoever I say I am"). This fits the broader context because it was common in the ancient world (Egypt included) to think that humans could manipulate the gods by naming or defining them. In contrast, Yahweh is not like any other god and must not be treated as such, especially by his own people. Second, Yahweh as "I AM" may be an affirmation of God's presence with Moses and Israel (e.g., "I am with you, ready to help"). This understanding fits best with the immediate context, in which the assurance of God's presence is a constant theme (e.g., 3:12; 4:12, 15), resulting in the fulfillment of his promises (see 3:15–17). Both options—divine freedom and divine presence—cohere with two later texts in Exodus in which Yahweh

"On all the gods of Egypt I will execute judgments: I am the LORD" (Exod. 12:12; cf. Num. 33:4). *Amon, the Egyptian god of creation and wind (left), and the falcon-headed Horus, the Egyptian god of the king, sky, and vengeance (right) (from the Abydos painted limestone reliefs).*

reflects on his own name (see 33:19 and 34:6–7). Taken together, God chooses to use his divine freedom through the grace and mercy of his presence.

Thus, Moses and Israel come to "know" Yahweh more fully as creator and covenant keeper. Israel's deliverance from Egypt was to be known and remembered as part of a larger, lasting display of Yahweh's power, uniqueness, faithfulness, presence, and promise. Rightly, Israel's first response to its redemption was a song of praise and worship encompassing all these elements (15:1–21).

Conversely, the knowledge of Yahweh brought humiliation, destruction, and death to Egypt. Pharaoh had brazenly asserted: "Who is the LORD, that I should obey his voice and let Israel go? I do not know the LORD.... I will not let Israel go" (5:2). In response, Yahweh was more than happy to answer with a series of signs or plagues, culminating in the destruction of the Egyptian army in the Red Sea. The texts that use "know" with respect to the Egyptians' experience of Yahweh reveal two main concepts. First, Pharaoh and Egypt learned of Yahweh's special relationship with and commitment to his people (7:16; 8:10, 23), fulfilling the promise to Abraham, "him who dishonors you I will curse" (Gen. 12:3). Second, Yahweh is incomparable

Figure 3.2. Yahweh's Mighty Acts Against Egypt

Cycle	Act/Episode	Bible Reference	Explicit Agent of Heart Hardening (ND = non–descriptive)	Fulfillment Formula ("as the LORD said")
1	Nile to blood	Exod. 7:14–25	ND (7:14, 22)	Exod. 7:13, 22
	Frogs	8:1–15	Pharaoh (8:15)	8:15
	Gnats	8:16–19	ND (8:19)	8:19
2	Flies	8:20–32	Pharaoh (8:32)	–
	Death of livestock	9:1–7	ND (9:7)	–
	Boils	9:8–12	Yahweh (9:12)	9:12
3	Hail	9:13–35	Pharaoh (9:34); ND (9:35)	9:35
	Locusts	10:1–20	Yahweh (10:20)	–
	Darkness	10:21–29	Yahweh (10:27)	–
Climax	Death of firstborn	11:1–10; 12:29–32	Yahweh (11:10)	–

to any gods known in Egypt (Exod. 8:10; 9:14–16). Unlike the localized gods of the ancient Near East, Yahweh claims ownership of all the earth (8:22; 9:14, 29), proving it by taking control of all the arenas supposedly under the authority of the Egyptian gods. Truly, Yahweh achieved his goal to gain glory over his divine and human foes (12:12; 14:4, 17–18; 15:11; 18:10–11).

Battle Weapons: Plagues and Pharaoh's Hardened Heart

Exodus 7–12 recounts a series of ten mighty acts of God against Egypt. Literary artistry of the narrative is signaled by the presence of several recurring elements in each episode (e.g., warnings, instructions, Pharaoh's responses, Egyptian magicians), and that the acts increase overall in intensity and scope. The most important observation, though, is the fact that God initiated and sovereignly controlled each act. The so-called "plagues" and the hardening of Pharaoh's heart should be viewed as God's weapons in this battle.

God's powerful deeds against Egypt are commonly called "plagues" (cf. 8:2; 9:3, 14; 11:1). As a series, however, the acts are introduced as "miracles" (4:21) and "signs and wonders" (7:3)—terms used more frequently than "plagues" (8:23; 10:1, 2; 11:9, 10; cf. 7:9). The broader designation "signs" more appropriately highlights the intent of these acts: Yahweh was working for his own glory, which included judgment (connoted by "plagues") but went beyond it. This also helps the Bible reader see the connections between the "signs" of the exodus and the "signs" of Jesus, particularly in the Gospel of John (cf. John 2:11, 18, 23; 3:2; 4:48, 54; 6:2, 14, 26, 30; 7:31; 9:16; 10:41; 11:47; 12:18, 37; 20:30).

> The Gospel of John has close ties with Exodus. It not only focuses on Jesus' visits to Jerusalem during Jewish festivals celebrating the exodus (John 2:13; 5:1; 7:2; 11:55), but also supports claims of Jesus' divinity (1:1, 14; 20:30–31) by developing two sets of parallels between Jesus and Yahweh: Jesus' seven "I AM" statements imply that he is the God who appeared to Moses at the burning bush (6:35; 8:12; 10:7–9, 11; 11:25; 14:6; 15:1), and his seven positive "signs" (miracles) show he is the same God who displayed sovereign control over creation during the battle with Pharaoh (2:2–11; 4:46–54; 5:1–15; 6:1–14, 15–21; 9:1–41; 11:1–45).

Figure 3.2 above indicates that the hardening of Pharaoh's heart is an important subtheme, ending each episode in the drama. Pharaoh's hard heart consistently resulted in his refusal to let Israel leave Egypt. The explicit agent of hardening varies between Pharaoh and Yahweh or is at times not given (e.g., "Pharaoh's heart was hard[ened]"). From one perspective, this is a display of theological balance: Pharaoh's hardening of his own heart emphasized his personal responsibility and guilt; Yahweh's hardening of Pharaoh's heart emphasized divine sovereignty. It would be a mistake,

To Pharaoh, the Lord declared, "For this purpose I have raised you up, to show my power, so that my name may be proclaimed in all the earth" (Exod. 9:16). *Statue of Thutmose III (ca. 1504–1450), likely Pharaoh of the Israelite oppression or, if dated differently, the exodus (from the Luxor Museum).*

however, to consider these two points as "equals," or worse, to think that Yahweh's hardening only "confirms" Pharaoh's initial decisions to harden his own heart. Clearly, Yahweh is in control from the beginning. Before the episodes commence, Yahweh tells Moses that he intends to harden Pharaoh's heart *so that* Israel will not be released immediately (Exod. 4:21; 7:3). These words are confirmed explicitly several times by the recurring phrase, "as the LORD said," even when Yahweh is not the explicit subject of the hardening (see the last column in Figure 3.2). Yahweh wants this battle to drag out in order to reveal his power and glory more fully (9:15–16): "For by now I could have put out my hand and struck you and your people with pestilence, and you would have been cut off from the earth. But for this purpose I have raised you up, to show you my power, so that my name may be proclaimed in all the earth." However we try and settle the philosophical and theological dilemmas of the relationship between God's sovereignty and human responsibility, Yahweh wants to be known and controls how he will be known (see Rom. 9:16–21).

> Through quoting Exodus 9:16, Paul asserted God's prerogative to bestow mercy or hardening on whomever he wills (Rom. 9:17–18). The apostle also stressed that God's sovereign acts of mercy and judgment are intended to bring him glory in the world and that, while we may not fully understand God's ways, we must never scrutinize them (9:19–24; 11:33, 36).

The Author of Exodus Celebrated *Yahweh's Power to Redeem His People* from Slavery

The exodus is to the Old Testament what the cross-resurrection event is to the New Testament. In each case, the great redemptive act (exodus/cross) produces the covenant community of God's people (Israel/church) who are called to serve God and his universal mission. The importance of the exodus is signaled by its constant reference throughout the Old Testament, to motivate covenant fidelity (Exod. 19:4; 20:1), to establish national identity and self-consciousness (e.g., Josh. 2:9–11; Judg. 6:8–13; 1 Sam. 12:6–8; 1 Kings 8:51; Neh. 9:9; 2 Chron. 7:22), to inspire prophetic judgment and hope (e.g., Jer. 7:21–24; 11:1–18; 16:14–21; 34:13; Ezek. 37:24–28; Hos. 11:1), and to produce personal praise and confession (e.g., Pss. 77:14–20; 78:12–55; 80:8; 106:7–14; 114; 136:10–22). In short, the rest of the Old Testament can only be understood in light of the significance of the exodus.

This larger perspective explains why the immediate context of the exodus is surrounded by elements of worship that evoke images of salvation, which in turn serve the biblical meta-narrative. The exodus involves the actual flight from Egypt (Exod. 12:33–42) and the crossing of the Red Sea (ch.

14). These events are preceded by worship instructions (the Passover: 12:1–27, 43–49; 13:1–16) and followed by a worship song (the Song at the Sea: 15:1–21).

"They ruthlessly made the people of Israel work as slaves" (Exod. 1:13). *The Karnak Temple victory inscription of Thutmose III's conquest in Canaan (ca. 1504–1450); his enemies are here shown with arms bound behind their backs.*

Image of Salvation: Substitutionary Sacrifice

The Passover is both a historical event and an annual feast commemorating that event. As an event, it is the reverse of the final plague, the death of the firstborn (Exod. 11:1–10; 12:29–32). The Israelites were to spread lamb or goat's blood on their houses' doorposts and lintels, distinguishing God's faithful people from the Egyptians. When Yahweh would come to destroy all the firstborn in the land, he would "pass over" those houses with the blood, sparing their inhabitants (12:3–13, 21–23). Theologically, this event shows Yahweh's ability to make a distinction between Egypt and Israel (11:7), effectively reversing Egypt's earlier attempts to kill the Israelite children (1:22). As an annual feast, the Passover (with the Feast of Unleavened Bread) would allow for instruction and celebration of Yahweh's protection and provision—the salvation of his people (12:14, 17, 24, 27; 13:8–9, 14–15). Developed more fully in the sacrificial system in

"And when I see the blood, I will pass over you, and no plague will befall you" (Exod. 12:13). *A sacrificial lamb from a Samaritan Passover.*

Leviticus, Passover established the concept of salvation by substitutionary sacrifice, as the death of the lamb yielded redemption (cf. 13:12–15).

> Paul declared, "Christ, our Passover Lamb, has been sacrificed" (1 Cor. 5:7), and John the Baptist proclaimed of Jesus, "Behold, the Lamb of God, who takes away the sin of the world!" (John 1:29). Praise the Lord for the eternal redemption won for us in the Jewish Messiah (cf. 19:14, 31–36; Heb. 9:12–14).

Image of Salvation: Conquest

"Fear not, stand firm, and see the salvation of the LORD" (14:13). The narrative of the crossing of the Red Sea emphasizes Yahweh's desire to display his own glory through Israel's deliverance (14:4, 18). Thus, he hardened the hearts of Pharaoh and the Egyptians, moving them into the final pursuit (12:31–32; 14:4–5, 17). This also set up a moment of decision for Israel: Would the people trust their God or cower in fear? Despite their initial unbelief and grumbling (14:10–12), Yahweh's miraculous intervention and defeat of the Egyptian army inspired proper fear and faith (14:30–31). The ensuing song (15:1–21) puts salvation in right perspective. While noting some benefits for Israel— salvation (v. 2), redemption (vv. 13a, 16), and guidance (vv. 13b, 17)—the song's focus is on the military-like destruction of Egypt by Yahweh, the divine warrior. The active verbs with Yahweh as subject are instructive: "triumphed" (vv. 1, 21); "thrown" horse and rider (vv. 1, 21); "cast" Pharaoh's chariots and host (v. 4); "shatters" the enemy (v. 6); "overthrow" his adversaries (v. 7a); "send out" his fury (v. 7b); "blew" with his wind (v. 10); and "stretched out" his right hand (v. 12). The language and imagery of conquest challenged God's

> Beyond the mere physical redemption from slavery won for Israel in the exodus, God has procured for all believers eternal salvation from sin (Heb. 9:26), death (1 Cor. 15:55–57), and the devil (Heb. 2:14). At the cross, God in Christ "disarmed the rulers and authorities and put them to open shame, by triumphing over them in him" (Col. 2:15; cf. Eph. 1:21).

people to keep a God-centered outlook on their identity and security. Their salvation was a result of God's ultimate quest to gain victory over his enemies.

The Author of Exodus Disclosed *Yahweh's Gracious Provision of His Covenant* with Israel

Israel's arrival at Mount Sinai in Exodus 19 was a critical moment in the nation's history. Israel's stay at Sinai is less than one year, yet its narrative space takes up about a third of the Torah (Exodus 19 through Numbers 10 is 59 of the Law's 187 chapters). Not in the direct route from Egypt to Canaan (the Promised Land), Sinai's location is significant because (1) it was the same place Yahweh engaged Moses at the burning bush (= Horeb, the mountain of God; Exod. 3:1) and (2) Israel's arrival there to worship Yahweh constitutes fulfillment of the divine word (3:12; cf. 5:1; 7:16; 8:28;

10:9, 25–26). At Sinai, Yahweh formalized his relationship with Israel through a covenant, and he revealed to the people how to live in response to his gracious redemption.

The Purpose of the Covenant (Exod. 19)

The covenant at Sinai commenced, not with a code of conduct, but with declarations of Yahweh's gracious election and salvation of Israel (19:4). Unlike a contract, which is driven by a list of rules and conditions, a covenant is about a relationship—a personal commitment between two covenant partners. In response to the gracious redemption (v. 4) and in the light of the amazing mission (v. 6), Israel declared unreserved commitment to Yahweh (v. 8) *before* the legal stipulations were given in chapters 20–23. Obedience to the law would, therefore, be a demonstration of such allegiance, revealing a heart of gratitude for Yahweh's grace. (Note how in the Ten Commandments of Exodus 20 the indicative of redemption [vv. 1–2] and relationship *precedes* all the imperatives of responsibility [20:3–17].)

"Mount Sinai was wrapped in smoke because the Lord had descended on it in fire" (Exod. 19:18). *Jebel Musa, traditional site of Mount Sinai.*

Yahweh's purpose of this covenant amounted to Israel's mission to fulfill the Abrahamic covenant. Living in the context of the entire world, if Israel would be faithful, it would become God's "treasured possession," "a kingdom of priests," and "a holy nation" (19:5–6). The first and third phrases emphasize the special and unique status Israel occupied (cf. Deut. 7:6; 14:2; 26:18–19). Though Yahweh owned all the earth (Exod. 19:5), Israel was of immense value to him; it had been set apart to serve God and display his holiness to the world. The second phrase goes a different direction. As "a kingdom of priests" Israel would serve as mediator between God and the nations (cf. Deut. 4:5–8). The combination of royal and priestly functions recalls God's purpose for humans, who serve as viceroys in God's kingdom (Gen. 1) and priests in God's sanctuary (Gen. 2). Thus, the programmatic statement of Israel's mission in Exodus 19:5–6 shows how Israel can fulfill the (universal) climax of the

> Significantly the new covenant church appropriates and fulfills Israel's mission to be a kingdom of priests and holy nation. Peter clarifies both our responsibility and goal: "You are a chosen race, a royal priesthood, a holy nation, a people for his own possession, that you may proclaim the excellencies of him who called you out of darkness into his marvelous light" (1 Peter 2:9).

Abrahamic covenant: "In you all the families of the earth shall be blessed" (Gen. 12:3).

The Laws of the Covenant (Exod. 20–23)

God came down to the mountain in Exodus 19; his word comes to the people in chapters 20–23. The Ten Commandments (or "Ten Words" in Hebrew) (Exod. 20:1–17; cf. 34:28; Deut. 4:13; 10:4) are distinct from the rest of God's law in that they were spoken directly by God (Exod. 20:1), they were written by his finger (31:18), and their pronouncement yielded its own response from the people (20:18–21). Throughout history, Christians have traditionally counted the "Words" in one of two ways—an issue complicated by the distinctions between the lists in Exodus 20 and Deuteronomy 5. Nevertheless, nearly all interpreters have seen them as the basic covenant

Figure 3.3. The Ten Commandments in Exodus 20:2–17

I am the LORD your God, who brought you out of the land of Egypt, out of the house of slavery.... (v. 2)

C/L/A	O/R	"Word/Commandment"	Interpretation as a "Bill of Rights"
LOVE FOR GOD (Vertical Dimensions)			
1a	1	Have no other gods (v. 3)	Yahweh's Right to Exclusive Allegiance
1b	2	Never make a carved image (vv. 4–6)	Yahweh's Right to the Definition of His Image
2	3	Never take Yahweh's name in vain (v. 7)	Yahweh's Right to Proper Representation
3	4	Remember the Sabbath day (vv. 8–11)	Yahweh's Right to the Israelite's Time and Life
LOVE FOR NEIGHBOR (Horizontal Dimensions)			
4	5	Honor your father and mother (v. 12)	Your Parents' Right to Respect
5	6	Never murder (v. 13)	Your Neighbor's Right to Life
6	7	Never commit adultery (v. 14)	Your Neighbor's Right to Sexual Purity
7	8	Never steal (v. 15)	Your Neighbor's Right to Personal Property
8	9	Never witness falsely against your neighbor (v. 16)	Your Neighbor's Right to Honest Testimony
9	10a	Never covet your neighbor's house (v. 17a)	Your Neighbor's Right to Home Security
10	10b	Never covet your neighbor's household (v. 17b)	Your Neighbor's Right to Household Security

KEY: C/L/A = Catholic, Lutheran, Anglican; O/R = Orthodox, Reformed
Prepared by Kenneth J. Turner and Jason S. DeRouchie. The list of "rights" is adapted from a similar list in Daniel I. Block, " 'You Shall Not Covet Your Neighbor's Wife': A Study of Deuteronomic Domestic Ideology," *JETS* 53/3 (2010): 456.

stipulations, of which the other more detailed laws are social and religious applications. Since the Ten Commandments address the would-be perpetrator of an offense, they might be viewed as a "bill of rights," protecting not our own rights but those of others. The commandments naturally break into two groups: relating to God and relating to one's neighbor.

The detailed legislation that follows the Ten Commandments begins and ends with instructions for worship, which are especially concerned with holiness and loyalty to God alone (Exod. 20:23–26; 23:10–19; see also 22:18–20, 29–31). The rest of the laws can be grouped roughly into two sections. First, the civil laws in 21:1–22:17 involve cases of slavery and freedom (21:1–11), injury and compensation (21:12–36), and property and restitution (22:1–17). Emphasis rests on setting proper limits for justice, such as the law of retaliation ("eye for eye, tooth for tooth"; 21:23–25), which is meant to curb vengeance by having the punishment fit the crime. Also, restricting capital punishment to specific crimes (i.e., murder, kidnapping, assaults against parents, sorcery, bestiality, idolatry) accentuates the areas of life most valued by God—human life, the family structure, and the purity of worship. Second, the laws in 22:21–23:9 focus on caring for those most vulnerable in society (i.e., the sojourner, widow, orphan, and poor). Made up mainly of moral imperatives without prescribed penalties, these laws call for an attitude and standard of behavior that goes beyond the "letter of the law."

"You shall not mistreat any widow or fatherless child. If you do mistreat them, and they cry out to me, I will surely hear their cry, and my wrath will burn, and I will kill you with the sword" (Exod. 22:22–24). *A woman working in a field in the Ephraim hills.*

The Author of Exodus Emphasized the Significance of *Yahweh's Presence* Among His People

Modern readers wonder why the tabernacle occupies thirteen chapters in this book (Exod. 25–31, 35–40). Why was it so important? Every painstaking detail of building instructions (chs. 25–31) and construction (chs. 35–40) points in one direction—the glory of Yahweh that filled the tabernacle was to be taken seriously (40:34)! Patterned after the heavenly archetype, the tabernacle (= "dwelling place") was also God's sanctuary (= "holy place") (25:8–9, 40), and God's presence with his people was a re-actualization of the original creation (29:45–46; cf. 25:8). This structure was heaven on earth, Eden in a fallen world! This connection is highlighted by the 6+1 pattern of the tabernacle instructions. All seven speeches (paralleling the seven days of creation) begin with "the LORD said to Moses" (25:1; 30:11, 17, 22, 34; 31:1, 12). The sixth speech sets apart two humans to oversee the building project (30:1–11), and the seventh calls Israel to keep the Sabbath (31:12–17). A full list of all other potential links would include the various fabrics and curtain designs (25:4; 26:1, 31), the cherubim (25:18–22; cf. Gen 3:24), and the gold lampstand, representing the tree of life (Exod. 25:31–40; cf. Gen 3:22). The tabernacle was the climax of the covenant at Sinai, enabling

Figure 3.4. General Content Distinctions of Old Testament Laws

Rom. 13:8–10. Owe no one anything, except to love each other, for the one who loves another has fulfilled the law. For the commandments … are summed up in this word: "You shall love your neighbor as yourself." Love does no wrong to a neighbor; therefore love is the fulfilling of the law.

Criminal	Laws governing crimes or offenses that put the welfare of the whole community at risk; the offended party is the state or national community, and therefore the punishment is on behalf of the whole community in the name of the highest state authority, which in Israel meant Yahweh. SAMPLE ISSUES: Kidnapping and homicide; false prophecy and witchcraft; adultery and rape.
	Exodus 21:23–25: You shall pay life for life, eye for eye, tooth for tooth, hand for hand, foot for foot, burn for burn, wound for wound, stripe for stripe. *Deuteronomy 17:8–9: "If any case arises … within your towns that is too difficult for you, then you shall arise and go up to the place that the LORD your God will choose. And you shall come to the Levitical priests and to the judge …, and you shall consult them, they shall declare to you the decision."*
Civil	Law governing private disputes between citizens or organizations in which the public authorities are appealed to for judgment or called upon to intervene; the offended party is not the state or national community. SAMPLE ISSUES: Accidental death and assault; theft and destruction of property; limited family issues like premarital unchastity, post-divorce situations, and the mistreatment of slaves.
	Deuteronomy 11:18–20: "You shall therefore lay up these words of mine in your heart and in your soul, and you shall bind them as a sign on your hand, and they shall be as frontlets between your eyes. You shall teach them to your children, talking of them when you are sitting in your house, and when you are walking by the way, and when you lie down, and when you rise. You shall write them on the doorposts of your house and on your gates."
Family	Non-civil, domestic laws governing the Israelite household. SAMPLE ISSUES: Marriage and inheritance; the redemption of land and persons; family discipleship and care of slaves.
	Leviticus 20:25–26: "You shall not make yourselves detestable by beast or by bird or by anything with which the ground crawls, which I have set apart for you to hold unclean. You shall be holy to me, for I the LORD am holy and have separated you from the peoples, that you should be mine."
Ceremonial / Cultic	Laws governing the visible forms and rituals of Israel's religious life. SAMPLE ISSUES: The sacred sacrifice, the sacred calendar, and various sacred symbols like the tabernacle, priesthood, and ritual purity that distinguished Israel from the nations and provided parables of more fundamental truths about God and relating to him.
	Deuteronomy 24:17–18: "You shall not pervert the justice due to the sojourner or to the fatherless, or take a widow's garment in pledge, but you shall remember that you were a slave in Egypt and the LORD your God redeemed you from there; therefore I command you to do this."
Compassion	"Laws" dealing with charity, justice, and mercy toward others. SAMPLE ISSUES: Protection and justice for the weak; impartiality and generosity; respect for persons and property.

Prepared by Jason S. DeRouchie and Kenneth J. Turner. The categories are taken from Christopher J. H. Wright, *Old Testament Ethics for the People of God* (Downers Grove, IL: InterVarsity, 2004), 288–301, which he adapted from Anthony Phillips, *Ancient Israel's Criminal Law: A New Approach to the Decalogue* (New York: Schocken Books, 1970), 2, 13. For an expanded version of this material that includes biblical texts with the sample issues, see Appendix 1, Fig. A.2.

God's original presence with humanity and his presence with Israel on the mountain to remain with the people in the Promised Land (see Exod. 15:17).

Figure 3.5. The Christian and Old Testament Law

Grasping rightly the Christian's relationship to Old Testament law is a very difficult issue, in part because the New Testament contains both positive and negative statements about the law (e.g., Rom. 3:31; Gal. 3:12). Though this topic can be treated only minimally here, a number of basic considerations ought to be kept in mind.

1. The law is given in the context of covenant relationship, not as the basis for it. Israel was called to follow God's ways in response to his redeeming them from Egyptian bondage (Exod. 19:4–5; 20:1–2), and Christians are called to love others in response to the way God first loved us in Christ (1 John 3:16; 4:10–11; cf. Rom. 6:6; 8:3–4).

2. A person without God's Spirit is unable to keep God's law and stands hostile to God in a state of death (Rom. 7:7–8, 13; cf. 1 Cor. 2:14). This is why, within God's plan of redemption, the old covenant law played a unique role in disclosing Israel's hard-heartedness and need for Jesus (Rom. 3:20; 7:7–8; 10:4; Gal. 3:19).

3. It is instructive that the larger purpose of the old covenant—namely, Israel's mission to be a kingdom of priests and a holy nation in order to bless the world—is assumed and fulfilled by God's new covenant people (Exod. 19:6; 1 Peter 2:9; cf. Gen. 12:3; Deut. 4:5–8).

4. While changes are expected with the transition from the old covenant (Israel at Sinai) to the New, care must be taken when considering what exactly is "new" about the new covenant. For example, we know that Jesus' death on the cross put an end to the Old Testament sacrificial system, which was merely a prototype of Jesus' ultimate sacrifice (Heb. 9:23–10:4). Also, the inclusion of the Gentiles into the church makes irrelevant at one level the Old Testament civil legislation or stipulations preserving Jewish distinctiveness (e.g., circumcision, purity regulations) (Eph. 2:15; cf. Acts 15:19–20). Nevertheless, the new covenant still includes law keeping (Heb. 8:8–12; cf. 1 Cor. 9:21; Gal. 6:2; James 1:25; 2:12) but adds to it God's promise to enable the very thing he commands, the essence of which is love (Deut. 30:6; Ezek. 36:27; Rom. 8:13). Even though Christians are not under the old covenant in any way (Rom. 7:6; 2 Cor. 3:5–8), because "all Scripture … is profitable" (2 Tim. 3:16) and was written "for our instruction" (Rom. 15:4; cf. 1 Cor. 9:10; 10:11) and because "love is the fulfilling of the law" (Rom. 13:10; cf. Matt. 7:12; John 13:34; Gal. 5:14), we can, through the lens of Christ, find in the Old Testament law numerous examples of how broad and deep love for God and neighbor is to be operative in this world (cf. 1 Cor. 9:9–11; Eph. 6:1–3; 1 Peter 1:15–16). That is, the Old Testament law provides a paradigm for understanding how to love others, even today (see Gen. 26:5; Rom. 2:13–15, 25–29). Furthermore, through the power of the Spirit of Christ in us, we can fulfill the call to love (Rom. 2:29; 8:4, 9, 13; 13:8–10; Gal. 5:22). While Christians will continue to debate over specific commands (e.g., Sabbath, tithing, tattoos), investigating the actual changes from the old covenant to the new covenant is a helpful place to start.

Prepared by Jason S. DeRouchie and Kenneth J. Turner.

The tabernacle bore a three-tier structure that resembled the nation's experience at Sinai, with its different degrees of "sacred space." At the mountain, three levels of access to Yahweh were marked: (1) Moses alone was given direct access to God's presence at the top of the mountain; (2) the elders were allowed part way up the mountain; and (3) the rest of the people were required to stay at the foot of the mountain (19:10–13, 20–24; 24:1–18). This gradation is matched in the tabernacle: (1) only the high priest could enter the Most Holy Place (once a year), where Yahweh dwelt; (2) the priests alone had access to the Holy Place; and (3) the people worshipped in the courtyard. These details are spelled out more fully in Leviticus, but their introduction in Exodus allows us to see the connection between the revelation at Sinai and the ongoing formal worship of the nation.

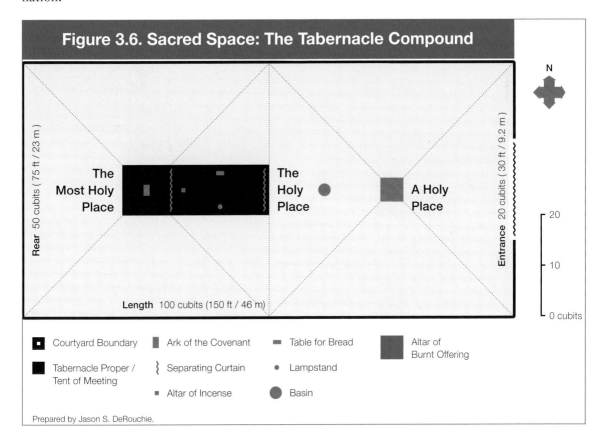

Figure 3.6. Sacred Space: The Tabernacle Compound

Rear 50 cubits (75 ft / 23 m)

Length 100 cubits (150 ft / 46 m)

The Most Holy Place

The Holy Place

A Holy Place

Entrance 20 cubits (30 ft / 9.2 m)

N

20
10
0 cubits

■ Courtyard Boundary   ■ Ark of the Covenant   ▬ Table for Bread   ■ Altar of Burnt Offering
■ Tabernacle Proper / Tent of Meeting   ⸬ Separating Curtain   • Lampstand
■ Altar of Incense   ● Basin

Prepared by Jason S. DeRouchie.

The whole tabernacle compound was 100 cubits x 50 cubits, divided into equal halves. The front half, centering the altar for burnt offerings, represented God as both savior and judge. In contrast, the back half, centering the ark of the covenant (i.e., God's throne), stressed God's kingship over all. While more will be said about sacred space in the next chapter, the following four observations highlight the lasting significance of the tabernacle:[1]

> The Old Testament tabernacle with its pageantry was merely a "copy and shadow" of the ultimate realities found in Christ (Heb. 8:5). Jesus is the superior high priest and sacrifice (9:24–26) and the true temple, wherein humanity can commune with God (Mark 13:1–2; John 2:19). Derivatively, the church is also considered God's temple (1 Cor. 3:16–17; 2 Cor. 6:16), as we await the full and final manifestation of God's presence in the New Jerusalem (Rev. 21–22).

- God's willingness to "tabernacle" among his people emphasized his covenant commitment as provider and protector (Exod. 25:8; 29:45–46; cf. John 1:14).

- God's desire to be present among his people stressed his passion to be known both by Israel (Exod. 29:45–46) and the nations (33:16 with 20:20).

- The tabernacle drew attention to God's holiness and his distinction from humans by regulating and controlling access to the

"The cloud covered the tent of meeting, and the glory of the Lᴏʀᴅ filled the tabernacle" (Exod. 40:34). *Tabernacle model in Timnah Valley just west of the Arabah.*

---

1. Supplied by Jason S. DeRouchie; used by permission.

divine glory by a complex of walls, gates, Levitical guardians, and guidelines.

- Through the centrality of the sin altar and ark of the covenant, respectively, the tabernacle gave hope to sinners that a relationship with Yahweh, the universal King, was possible through the provision of a penal substitute.

The Author of Exodus Called *Israel to Respond* to Yahweh's Disclosure of Himself and His Will

Yahweh's revelation of himself to Israel was also a call for exclusive allegiance evidenced by faith and obedience (Exod. 3:14–18, 31; 14:31; 19:4–6; 20:20; 24:3). Israel demonstrated faith at times (3:31; 14:31), and the book ends on a positive note, as the people's total obedience in constructing the tabernacle is affirmed by Yahweh's taking up residence (40:34). However, a closer look at the people's sporadic response throughout the narrative puts an ominous cloud over their future. The problem facing the Israelites is not Pharaoh's hard heart but their own. In fact, Sinai—the granting of the law and the presence of a holy God—may pose the greatest threat.

A Wayward People

Early signs of trouble are apparent. The Israelites' initial reluctance to trust Moses may be understandable (5:21; 6:12), but their unbelief during the exodus is stunning (14:10–12), especially after all they had witnessed in Egypt. This concern is validated in the desert trip to Sinai, as the people violate the Sabbath (16:27–29) and constantly grumble about their conditions (15:24; 16:2, 7–8; 17:3). The fact that similar sins would take place after they left raised real questions about their covenant commitment (Sabbath violation: Num. 15:32–36; grumbling: Num. 11:1; 14:2, 27, 29, 36; 16:41; 17:5).

The most overt demonstration of brazen infidelity, however, was Israel's worship of the golden calf (Exod. 32). The people had recalled their redemption (19:4), offered and accepted the covenant with Yahweh (19:8), heard his word (20:1–17), seen the cataclysmic effects of his presence among them (20:18), sealed their commitment with blood (24:3–8), and awaited the instructions for the tabernacle so Yahweh could dwell in their midst (chs. 25–31). And how did they respond to such grace and privilege? With impatience

The LORD said to Moses, "They have made for themselves a golden calf and have worshipped it" (Exod. 32:8). *The bull Apis, Egyptian god of fertility, who was possibly a target in the plague on cattle (Exod. 9:1–7; from the Cairo Museum).*

LEVITICUS

Who?

Leviticus is a series of divine speeches with no explicitly cited author. Many scholars have theorized that multiple authors penned the book. However, Moses is by far the central mediating figure in Leviticus, and he is the most likely candidate to have written the material. God frequently speaks to Moses with words of guidance for the people (e.g., Lev. 1:1–2; 4:1–2; 5:14), and Moses is portrayed as God's mouthpiece (8:5, 31; 9:1–2, 6–7, 23; 10:3–6, 12; 24:23). Later biblical figures allude to Leviticus as being from the law (of Moses) (Matt. 22:37–40), and they speak of laws in Leviticus as having come from the prophet's command (Mark 1:44 with Lev. 14:2–32; John 8:5 with Lev. 20:10; cf. Deut. 22:22–24). Thus, there is good reason to assume that Moses wrote the book.

When?

The book's final verse clarifies its contents: "the commandments that the LORD commanded Moses for the people of Israel on Mount Sinai" (Lev. 27:34). As such, Leviticus was likely composed during the forty-year span following this Sinai experience but before Moses' death and Israel's entry into Canaan in ca. 1406 B.C. (though some posit ca. 1210 B.C.).

Where?

The text clearly indicates that the teachings of Leviticus appeared first at Sinai (27:34), and the book as a whole makes up the largest and most central material within the larger Sinai narrative (Exod. 19–Num. 10). If the proposal for authorship and date is correct, the book was likely composed at Mount Sinai or in the wilderness en route to Canaan.

Why?

Although it is often neglected, Leviticus provides a vital canonical witness to God's holiness and to the "good news" announced to the exodus generation (see Heb. 4:2, 6). Anticipating in beautiful ways the work of Messiah Jesus, the book served as a guide to worship and ethics, clarifying how priests and laity were to behave properly before a holy God. It also testifies to God's sustained gracious work announced in the previous books:

1. The opening announcement that "the LORD called to Moses … from the tent of meeting" recalls the end of Exodus when God's presence filled the Tent (Lev. 1:1; cf. Exod. 40:34–38) and reinforces that the holy God had taken initiative to relate with a sinful people (see Exod. 34:9).

2. Affirming Israel's mission to be a "holy people" in the midst of a cursed world (Exod. 19:6), Yahweh called Israel to "be holy, for I am holy" (Lev. 20:26; cf. 11:44–45; 19:2; 20:7; 21:8) and clarified how this would be done—"I am the LORD who sanctifies you" (20:8; cf. 21:8, 15, 23; 22:9, 16, 32).

3. "I … will be your God" (26:12; cf. 11:45; 22:33; 25:38)—Yahweh's covenant commitment made first to Abraham (Gen. 17:8) and then reaffirmed to Israel (Exod. 6:7) would continue.

LEVITICUS

D. Jeffrey Mooney and
Jason S. DeRouchie

Carefully Crafted Verses from Leviticus

"Among those who are near me I will be sanctified, and before all the people I will be glorified" (Lev. 10:3).

"I am the LORD your God.... You shall therefore keep my statutes and my rules; if a person does them, he shall live by them: I am the LORD" (Lev. 18:1–2, 5).

"You shall love your neighbor as yourself: I am the LORD" (Lev. 19:18).

THE AUTHOR OF LEVITICUS ...

- Proclaimed the reality and implications of *God's holiness*.

- Clarified the place of *sacrifice and atonement* in covenant worship.

- Distinguished *the holy and common, the unclean and clean* in covenant worship.

- Called Israel to *display holiness* through the practice of covenant ethics.

"Consecrate yourselves ... and be holy, for I am the LORD your God. Keep my statutes and do them; I am the LORD who sanctifies you.... You shall be holy to me, for I the LORD am holy and have separated you from the peoples, that you should be mine" (Lev. 20:7–8, 26).

The Author of Leviticus Proclaimed the Reality and Implications of *God's Holiness*

In contrast to Genesis and Exodus, which are dominated by a clear story line, Leviticus served principally as a manual for worship and ethics. No group of worshippers in history would have been more convinced of God's love for them than Israel's Sinai generation. Those called to worship in Leviticus had seen love displayed in raw acts of power and redemption, both in deliverance from Egypt's grip (Exod. 7–15) and in forgiveness from sin (Exod. 17; 32–34). Modern worship is often characterized by ethos, talent, polish, and celebration over an assumed love provided by God to his darling worshippers. In sharp contrast, worship in Leviticus is marked by danger, expulsion, personal and corporate ethics, burning flesh, dried blood, sin, impurity, death, and a marked distinction between Israel and their holy redeemer God.

> Within Leviticus, vivid portrayals of God's holiness are interwoven with graphic depictions of salvation through judgment.

Figure 4.1. Leviticus at a Glance

Covenant Worship Chs. 1–16	Guidance for Sacrifices, Consecration of Priests, Clean and Unclean Laws, Day of Atonement
Covenant Ethics Chs. 17–27	Holiness Code, Festivals, Blessings and Curses

Within Leviticus, Moses clearly displayed God alone as supremely holy ("I am holy"—Lev. 11:44–45; 19:2; 20:26; 21:8). While this holiness included Yahweh's unique love for Israel above all other nations (Exod. 19:4–6), it also comprised God's absolute distinction (i.e., transcendence) from every created thing. He must not be taken lightly! On the heels of God's filling the tabernacle (40:34–35), the two sons of Aaron the high priest—Nadab and Abihu—approached God with "unauthorized fire" (Lev. 10:1). We can only theorize what the nature of this act was, but the text is clear that they were violating the heart of priestly responsibilities. The result was definitive: "And fire came out from before the Lord and consumed them, and they died" (10:2; cf. Num. 3:4). Immediately after their death, Moses told Aaron that the younger priests' should have taken God's holiness more seriously (Lev. 10:3).

Unlike the "gods" of Israel's neighbors, Yahweh could not be manipulated, bribed, or controlled by any human action. His purposes were not contingent on the people's libations, prayers, sacrifices, songs, or offerings. He was alive and untamed apart from Israel, and his commitment to them was grounded in grace alone apart from any merit they had. Where he dwelt was holy and implicitly dangerous to any who would treat it as otherwise (10:2; 16:2). Thus, the life of worship had to assume the realistic distinction between the worshipper and the object of worship. Because Yahweh was holy, his people must in turn be holy, relating to God with true repentance (5:5, 17), humility (9:24; 10:3), and dependent surrender (e.g., ch. 19). Only in this way could they enjoy sustained life (i.e., covenant blessings) in relation to God (26:1–13). Carelessly engaging God at the tabernacle or demonstrating the same negligence by unethical living would result in catastrophe—namely, the covenant curses, involving the removal of all divine provision and protection and the loss of their distinct identity and purpose in life (26:14–33).

"In the seventh month, on the first day of the month, you shall observe a day of solemn rest, a memorial proclaimed with blast of trumpets, a holy convocation" (Lev. 23:24). *Jewish man blowing a shofar at the Western Wall, Jerusalem.*

Most people in the world today have "no fear of God before their eyes" (Rom. 3:18). The new covenant call is to "work out your own salvation *with fear and trembling*" (Phil. 2:12), accounting both for the bigness of God and our need for dependence on him (see Jer. 32:39–40).

The Author of Leviticus Clarified the Place of *Sacrifice and Atonement* in Covenant Worship

Unfortunately, the most popular theme in Leviticus is the reason most people fail to read the book. Moses provided a system of regulations concerning sacrifice and atonement that was to help Israel realistically assess, repent from, and gain atonement for their sin, so as to maintain the presence of God in their midst. There are five major offerings that appear in Leviticus. The first, fourth, and fifth dealt with unintentional and intentional sins, whereas the second and third were expressions of gratitude and communion, respectively: (1) the whole burnt offering, (2) the grain offering, (3) the peace offering, (4) the sin (purification) offering, and (5) the guilt (reparation) offering.

Figure 4.2. Major Old Testament Sacrifices and Offerings

1. Burnt	Pre-tabernacle this was the only offering to atone for sin; after the tabernacle it is an optional act of worship that atoned for sins in general, accompanied other offerings, and expressed devotion, commitment, and complete surrender to Yahweh (Lev. 1:1–17; 6:8–13; cf. 8:18–21; 16:24). God alone consumed the burnt offering.
2. Grain	As a recognition of God's goodness and provision, this optional act of worship expressed devotion to God and regularly accompanied other offerings (Lev. 2:1–16; 6:14–23). The priests consumed the grain offering.
3. Peace (Fellowship)	This optional act of worship celebrated the offerer's fellowship with Yahweh and was given in the context of thanksgiving, vows, general praise (i.e., "free will"), or ordination (Lev. 3:1–17; 7:11–36). The offerer consumed the peace offering (except the priestly portions).
4. Sin (Purification)	Mandatory atonement for contamination of God's holy places or objects; the focus was on purification or consecration of individuals or community after specific sins, whether prohibitive ("don't"s) or performative ("do"s), unintentional (negligence or ignorance) or intentional (Lev. 4:1–5:13; 6:24–30; cf. 8:14–17; 16:3–22, 29–34). The priests consumed the sin offering (unless the offering was their own, in which case the whole animal was burned outside the camp).
5. Guilt (Reparation)	Mandatory atonement for desecration of God's holy things or the property of others; the focus was on re-consecration of God's sacred things or people with compensation (restitution of what was violated + 1/5) for specific sins against others, whether prohibitive ("don't") or performative ("do"), unintentional (negligence or ignorance) or intentional (Lev. 5:14–6:7; 7:1–10; cf. Num. 5:6–8). The priests consumed the guilt offering.

Prepared by Jason S. DeRouchie with some material drawn from Richard E. Averbeck, "Offerings and Sacrifices," in *NIDOTTE* 4:1020–21.

The text describes each offering twice. The first descriptions appear in Leviticus 1:1–6:7 and detail the procedures and purposes of the offerings, with special emphasis given to the responsibilities of the laity. The second appear in 6:8–7:10 and clarify the handling, eating, and disposal of the offerings, with special focus given to the work of the priest. The severity of the sacrificial act, namely the destruction of life, conveys the chasm between God's holiness and Israel's natural state. Yet, sacrifice resulted in God's pleasure in and forgiveness or purification of an individual, group, or object.

The Seriousness of Sin and the Need for Sacrifice

Moses presented sin as a concrete act of covenant hostility that had contaminating results. Sin was an Ebola virus-like substance that attached itself to people, animals, the various areas of the tabernacle (Lev. 15:31; 20:3), and the land as a whole (18:25, 27–28; Num. 35:33–34). Through sacrificial worship, Israel effectively dealt with sin of all types, appeasing God's wrath against it. Sacrifice in Leviticus included transfer of sin and impurity *via* the vital act of placing one's hand onto the sacrificial animal (e.g., Lev 1:4; 4:4, 15, 24, 29, 33). By the imposition of hands a declaration was made that "this figure now represents me," whether for a whole life consecrated to Yahweh or, as with the sacrifices related to sin, for a sinful life standing under God's wrath. It further represented the public act of repentance (i.e., casting off sin), which was required of every true worshipper (4:13, 22, 27; 5:2, 3, 4, 5, 17; 6:4, 5; cf. 5:5; 16:21; 26:40; Num. 5:6; 1 John 1:9). Sinners who refused to repent (sinning with a "high hand" in Num. 15:30–31) found no respite in sacrifice (Pss. 24:3–5; 51:16–17; see Heb. 10:26–27). However, those who did publicly lay claim to their sin found forgiveness through the concrete transfer of their sin to the sacrificial animal. The animal's blood in turn became dis-

"If his gift for a burnt offering is from the flock, from the sheep or goats, he shall bring a male without blemish " (Lev. 1:10). *A shepherdess with a lamb in a Negeb riverbed.*

eased with the sin-contamination and in this sense, also functioned as the human's penal substitute.

The Result of Sacrifice: Atonement

God is a holy and just judge who must take sin seriously. For him to remain just, he must punish sin. In Leviticus, atonement is the process by which God purifies and (re-)consecrates his contaminated and desecrated tabernacle and people by pouring out his wrath on the sinner or onto a substitute, thus restoring the relationship and right order. Moses characterized sacrificial blood like a sponge that could soak up (and thus remove) the sins of the true wor-

> Even today, "if we go on sinning deliberately after receiving the knowledge of the truth, there no longer remains a sacrifice for sins, but a fearful expectation of judgment, and a fury of fire that will consume the adversaries" (Heb. 10:26–27). However, when repentance is linked with a true trust in Jesus as our atoning sacrifice, "If we confess our sins, [God] is faithful and just to forgive us our sins and to cleanse us from all unrighteousness" (1 John 1:9).

shipper (Lev. 17:11; cf. Num. 35:33; Heb. 9:22). Through the transfer from sinner to substitute, the sacrificial animal and ultimately its blood would become "diseased" with the worshipper's sins. The priest then deposited the sacrificial blood at various places in the tabernacle compound (depending on whether the sacrifice was for priest or laity) and then burned the sacrificial fat on the altar, thus securing atonement (e.g., Lev. 1:4–5; 4:17–18, 20,

25–26, 30–31, 34–35; 5:9–10). The sin-diseased blood would then remain within the tabernacle compound until the Day of Atonement (ch. 16).

The Day of Atonement was the annual sacred day during which the entire community ritually declared God's holiness and their sinfulness and collectively repented from all sins of the previous year (16:16, 21, 30, 34). To atone for the sins of the priests, the Day of Atonement required a bull for a sin offering and a ram for a burnt offering (16:3); to atone for the sins of the congregation required two male goats for a sin offering and a ram for a burnt offering (16:5). Unlike the daily sacrifices where the priest took diseased animal blood into the holy precincts, on this day the high priest now took uncontaminated (no hand imposition) blood from the bull and one goat into the Holy of Holies and worked his way outward, sprinkling all major worship furniture on the way (16:14–15, 18–19). The

> If our God is a just judge, how could he have freely forgiven Old Testament figures like Rahab the prostitute and David the adulterer and murderer? How was it right for him to accept an animal death to pay for a human offense—especially when "it is impossible for the blood of bulls and goats to take away sins" (Heb. 10:4)? Paul told us that, although "in his divine forbearance he had passed over former sins," God the Father sent his Son as the wrath-bearing, sacrificial substitute in order "to show his righteousness at the present time, *so that he might be just* and the justifier of the one who has faith in Jesus" (Rom. 3:25–26). Because of Christ alone, God is "faithful and *just* to forgive us our sins" (1 John 1:9).

"For the life of the flesh is in the blood, and I have given it for you on the altar to make atonement for your souls" (Lev. 17:11). *The (bronze) altar of burnt offering at the tabernacle model in Timnah Valley just west of the Arabah.*

uncontaminated blood absorbed the sin from every sprinkled place, and by this means the priest purged both sacred space and sacred people (16:27, 30, 33–34) of the sin that had resided there throughout the year. The priest would then transfer all sins of the community onto the remaining live goat (through hand imposition) and send the goat into the wilderness, thus symbolizing the absolute removal of all covenant rebellion and guilt from Israel (16:20–22). In this way, sacrifice produced atonement (16:30, 33–34, etc.) resulting in forgiveness (4:20, 26, 31, 35; 5:10, 13, 16, 18)—purification that reconciled all repentant ones to God and to the community (see e.g., 12:7–8; 14:1–32).

> The sin offerings of the Day of Atonement foreshadowed the wrath-bearing, substitutionary, sufficient work of Messiah Jesus at the cross to remove sin and to secure right relationship between God and his people (Heb. 9:7–14; 13:12; 1 John 2:1–2). Through Jesus' blood, even common people who have no special pedigree or abilities become priests of God with unreserved access into his presence (Heb. 4:14–16; 10:19–22; 1 Peter 2:5, 9; Rev. 5:10).

The Author of Leviticus Distinguished *the Holy and Common, the Unclean and Clean* in Covenant Worship

The Holiness Continuum

One of the challenging features of Leviticus for modern Western readers is its holiness continuum. God directed the priests "to distinguish between the holy and the common, and between the unclean and the clean" (Lev. 10:10). The holy presence of God in the midst of Israel created the need to differentiate this mixture of states and conditions with respect to people, space, and time.

While somewhat difficult to assess, it appears that everything that was not holy was common, and everything common was either clean or unclean. In Leviticus, holiness and uncleanness are completely incompatible, and so every effort is taken to distinguish the two. Holy persons or things could be profaned, thus requiring sanctification to enjoy holiness again. That which was clean could be polluted and rendered unclean. Those things that were unclean could be made clean and further made holy through being sanctified by the priests. While those who were clean could never experience exile from the community, they also were never allowed to approach the Holy Places in the camp.

Whereas cleanness is the normal state or condition of creatures, holiness portrays absolute order and is enjoyed only by grace. Holiness characterizes God himself (Lev. 11:4–45; 19:2; 20:26), and anything that belongs to God is holy:

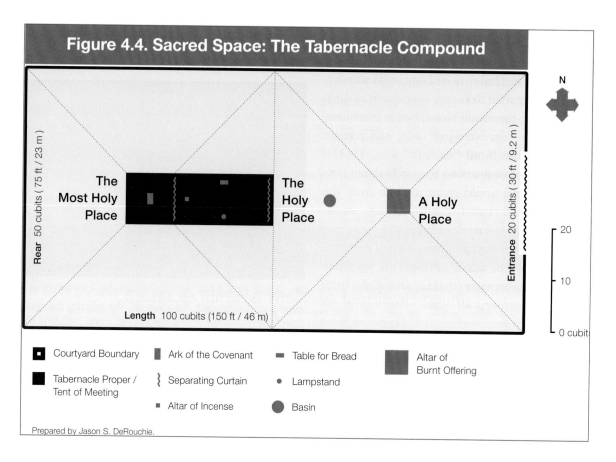

Figure 4.4. Sacred Space: The Tabernacle Compound

Rear 50 cubits (75 ft / 23 m)

The Most Holy Place

The Holy Place

A Holy Place

Entrance 20 cubits (30 ft / 9.2 m)

N

Length 100 cubits (150 ft / 46 m)

20
10
0 cubits

■ Courtyard Boundary ■ Ark of the Covenant ▬ Table for Bread ■ Altar of Burnt Offering

■ Tabernacle Proper / Tent of Meeting ⟩ Separating Curtain • Lampstand

▪ Altar of Incense ● Basin

Prepared by Jason S. DeRouchie.

The increasing level of holiness was represented in the building materials that adorned each sphere. For example, the coverings at the extremities of the compound were made of bland goat-hair cloth, whereas the coverings and curtains of the Holy Places included finely decorated, royal-colored linen. Similarly, the structures developed from plain acacia wood to acacia adorned with bronze and silver to acacia fully covered with gold. The most precious, luxurious materials were reserved for the Most Holy Place, thus drawing a strong contrast between Yahweh and his people. He was holy, and his presence deserved the highest respect. Nevertheless, the King over all also desired a relationship with a people prone to sin—a fact symbolized by the presence of the tabernacle itself. Significantly, to purge each area of the tabernacle compound from sin was to purge the people who worshipped in these areas (Lev. 16:16–19, 30, 33).

Sacred People

Compared with the nations, every Israelite was holy. However, with regard to sacred space and worship, the priests were set apart to God as stewards of holiness, singularly charged to elevate and demonstrate God's holiness to Israel. They were to serve as the authoritative teachers of God's Word (10:10–11; cf. Deut. 31:9–13; 33:10) and as the authoritative agents of righteousness—establishing, maintaining, and restoring the proper creational order of persons and things, land and sanctuary in relation to God. As imagers of God's holiness, the priests wore garments that were patterned off the materials of the tabernacle, with the most precious linens being

> The demand for a physically flawless priest to approach the holy areas (Lev. 21:17–23) is less a negative statement about the disabled and more an eschatological profile concerning the messianic priest who would be the fullness of God's image (Heb. 1:3; 2:17–18; 4:15; cf. 2 Cor. 4:4; Col. 1:15) as well as the one who would approach once and for all to purge the sins of the Israel of God (Heb. 7:27; 9:12, 26–27; 10:10, 12, 14).

closest to their bodies (Exod. 28). Their continual nearness to the Most Holy Place demanded great care, and they were given specific instructions about the movement from unclean to clean and from clean to holy (Lev. 10:10; 21:1–24). The non-Aaronic priests, known generally as Levites, bore the special responsibility of guarding the tabernacle and its sacred objects from mishandling and unwarranted encroachment (Num 3:5–10; 18:1–32; cf. Lev. 10:1–3).

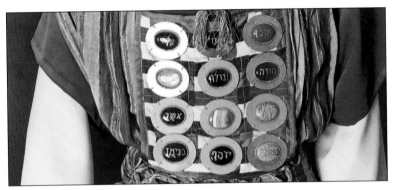

"Aaron shall bear the names of the sons of Israel in the breastpiece of judgment … to bring them to regular remembrance before the LORD" (Exod. 28:29). *The priestly breastpiece found at the tabernacle model in the Timnah Valley just west of the Arabah.*

Sacred Time

The architecture of Israel's worship included a calendar of scheduled high moments of celebration and reflection each year (see esp. Lev. 23). God's greatness as provider and protector was apparent every day, and Israel's cycle of life was filled with reminders of this fact. Some of these feasts or sacred days were somber days of rest, calling for repentance or renewal of covenant commitment (e.g., Trumpets and Day of Atonement).

> God's provision and protection reach their climax in the life and work of Messiah Jesus. Indeed, every feast and sacred day of the Old Testament ultimately pointed to Jesus, who is "the substance" of all matters related to "food and drink, or … festival or a new moon or a Sabbath" (Col. 2:16–17; cf. Rom. 14:5; Gal. 4:10).

Figure 4.5. Israel's Sacred and Civil Calendars with Selected Events

Month: Sacred/Civil		Hebrew Name with Modern Equivalent		Feasts and Sacred Days	Agriculture	Climate
1	7	Abib / Nisan	Mar/April	14: Passover 15–21: Unleavened Bread 21: First Fruits	Barley and flax harvest begins	
2	8	Ziv / Iyyar*	April/May		Barley and general harvest	Spring (Later) Rains
3	9	Sivan	May/June	1: Weeks (Pentecost, Harvest)	Wheat harvest; vine tending	
4	10	Tammuz*	June/July		Vine tending; first grape harvest	
5	11	Ab*	July/Aug	9: Destruction of First Temple	Grape, olive, and fig harvest	Dry Season
6	12	Elul	Aug/Sept		Processing/vintage of grapes, figs, and olives	
7	1	Ethanim / Tishri*	Sept/Oct	1: Trumpets (Rosh Hashanah) 10: Day of Atonement 15–21: Booths (Tabernacles, Ingathering)	Plowing	
8	2	Bul / Marchesvan*	Oct/Nov		Planting barley and wheat	Autumn (Early) Rains
9	3	Kislev	Nov/Dec	25: Dedication (Hanukkah, Festival of Lights)**		
10	4	Tebeth	Dec/Jan		Spring growth	
11	5	Shebat	Jan/Feb		Winter figs	Winter Rains
12	6	Adar	Feb/Mar	13–14: Purim	Pulling flax; almonds bloom; citrus fruit harvest	
		Adar Sheni* ("second Adar")		An additional month added about every three years to enable the lunar and solar calendars to correspond.		

*Names with a single asterisk are not in the Bible. **The feast of Dedication (Hanukkah) was established in the period between the Old and New Testaments to celebrate the rededication of the Jerusalem temple at the time of the Maccabean Revolt in the 164 B.C.; the only biblical reference to is is John 10:22. Prepared by Jason S. DeRouchie; some material adapted from p. 92 in the *NASB Study Bible* edited by Kenneth Barker; copyright © 1999 by Zondervan; other material is adapted from p. 19 in *Chronological and Background Charts of the Old Testament* by John H. Walton; copyright © 1994 John H. Walton. Used by permission of Zondervan. www.zondervan.com

Other days were celebrative, filled, on the one hand, with joy, feasting, and gratitude for God's past deliverance or bounty and, on the other hand, with confident longing for God's future sustaining grace (e.g., Sabbath, Passover and Unleavened Bread, Firstfruits, Weeks, Booths, Purim). The Day of Atonement and the Year of Jubilee marked God's gracious liberating power, both from sin and from debt or servitude, respectively. Every event pointed to the past defining acts of God and the foundation for a worshipping people's future hope.

"His double-month is ingathering. His double-month is sowing. His double-month is late-planting. His month is chopping flax. His month is barley harvest. His month is harvest and measuring (?). His double-month is pruning. His month is summerfruit" (The *Gezer Calendar*). *Likely dated to the time just after King Solomon rebuilt Gezer (1 Kings 9:16), the Gezer Calendar (ca. 925 B.C.) is in Hebrew verse with very early spelling and appears to have been a mnemonic instrument for children (translation from COS 2:222; cf. ANET, 320).*

The Author of Leviticus Called Israel to *Display Holiness* through the Practice of Covenant Ethics

The Need for Holiness

The modern (and postmodern) divorce of worship from ethics does not appear in the book of Leviticus. Rather, the macrostructure of the book evidences that true Godward orientation will result in behavioral transformation. Leviticus 1–16 is a guide to Israel's worship, and Leviticus 17–27 is a guide to their covenant ethics. The two must never be separated. Sadly, few in Israel's history ever learned this fact, as is evident in the way Yahweh's covenant enforcers, the prophets, continually had to use their words to blister all ethic-less "worshippers" (Jer. 6:20; 7:21–23; 14:12; Isa. 1:11–14; 40:16; 66:3; Hos. 6:6; 8:13; Amos 5:21–24; Mic. 6:6–8). Even when the curses of Leviticus 26 came, most of Israel failed to learn from God's disciplining hand (see Lev. 26:18, 21, 23, 27).

Whether priest (21:1–24; 22:1–16) or laity, the holiness God demanded was to be life-encompassing, including all desires and behaviors and all things private and public, civil and ceremonial (11:44–45; 19:2; 20:7–8, 26; 21:6, 15, 23; 22:9). Such a calling portrayed Israel's unique relationship to God and its distinction from its neighbors (18:3–5, 24–30; 20:22–26). God's people were to guard themselves from eating blood and unclean foods

(17:10–16; 20:25), from misappropriating sex (18:6–23; 19:20–21, 29–30; 20:10–21), and from engaging in idolatrous or occult practices (19:31; 20:1–9, 27). They were to keep the Sabbaths (19:3; 26:2) and other sacred days (ch. 23) and be ordered in their sacrificial worship (19:5–8). They were to respect human life (24:17–23); to revere their parents and the elderly (19:3, 32); to be fair in all sales (19:35–36; 25:23–24); and to treat with equity and justice the poor, vulnerable, and sojourner (19:9–10, 13–16, 33–36; 25:25–28, 29–34, 35–55). Ultimately, the call was to "love your neighbor as yourself" (19:18), not abusing others for self-exalting gain but serving others in God-exalting love.

Frequently, Yahweh called Israel to covenant love by reminding them of their redemption from slavery. This call not to forget their past deliverance

"When you reap the harvest of your land, you shall not reap your field right up to its edge, nor shall you gather the gleanings after your harvest. You shall leave them for the poor, and for the sojourner: I am the Lᴏʀᴅ your God" (Lev. 23:22). *Women harvesting on the West Bank of the Nile in Luxor, Egypt.*

functioned in at least three ways. First, remembering the freedom that had been won for them stressed that they were not their own and must, therefore, follow God's ways (11:44–45; 18:3–4; 25:55; cf. 1 Cor. 6:19–20). Second, recalling the pain of persecution they once endured was designed to push them away from being oppressors themselves: "You shall treat the stranger who sojourns with you as the native among you, and you shall love him as yourself, for you were strangers in the land of Egypt: I am the Lord" (Lev. 19:34; cf. 19:36; 25:38, 42; Deut. 10:17–19). Having received love, they were now obligated to give love (see Rom. 1:14; 13:8; 1 Peter 4:10). Third, God recalled his past redeeming grace in order to give his people confidence that he would grant more grace to all who believe: "I am the Lord who sanctifies you, who brought you out of the land of Egypt to be your God: I am the Lord" (Lev. 22:32–33; cf. 26:13, 45). The call to love embodied a "holy sojourner ethic" that avoided the ethical leniency of Egypt from where they were liberated and of Canaan to which they were going. Remembering the pain of their own oppression as sojourners, they now needed to care for the less fortunate and to be mindful of the needs of others. This holy sojourner ethic disallowed the conjoining of adoration for God and cruelty of others. The two cannot coincide, and this remains true even today.

The Means for Holiness

Strikingly, Leviticus includes both the imperative, "You shall be holy to me, for I the Lord am holy" (20:26; cf. 11:44–45; 19:2; 21:8), and the declaration, "I am the Lord who sanctifies you" (22:32; cf. 21:8, 15, 23; 22:9, 16). What was the bridge between Yahweh's statement and Israel's responsibility? The book suggests that God's means of sanctifying his people was through a combination of past and future grace—a feature highlighted in the book's structure, which places the ethical instruction (chs. 17–25) *after* the guidelines for substitutionary sacrifice (chs. 1–7, 16) but *before* the promises of blessing, curse, and restoration blessing (ch. 26).

> The only sin that a person can conquer is sin that has already been cancelled through atonement. To overcome innate rebellion, we need blood-bought power, provided only through the Holy Spirit of Christ in us (Rom. 7:4, 6; 8:13).

With respect to past grace, Leviticus teaches that a person's growth in holy conduct (sanctification) is the *fruit* of one's acceptance with God (justification) (see Rom. 6:7–8, 22; 8:1–4), the latter of which is made possible only by grace alone through faith alone in the unblemished, substitutionary sacrifice alone.[1] This truth is the main point of the only extended narrative within the book (Lev. 8–10). Here atonement is portrayed as the means for enjoying Yahweh's sanctifying presence (9:3–4, 6). Yahweh's fire (= his Spirit) will purify rather than consume only if his wrath toward sin is appeased through the destruction of a sacrificial substitute. By approaching God through the death of this "old man," represented in the slain animal, God's consuming fire sparks a change in the redeemed human heart, resulting in the display of God's holiness in the lives of those restored into relationship with him: "Among those who are near me I will be sanctified" (10:3; cf. 9:5, 7; Eph. 2:13). Stated differently, Yahweh's zeal against sin and for the display of his holiness is magnified through atonement, which in turn ignites a similar, blood-bought zeal against sin and for the display of God's holiness in the life of the newly justified believer. God forgives every person who confesses his sins (Lev. 5:5; 16:21; Num. 5:6), and who trusts Yahweh's willingness to pour his just wrath on a substitute sacrifice (Lev. 17:11; cf. Heb. 9:22). In the process, God manifests his presence to the believer in such a way that results in holy living (Lev. 9:24; 10:3; see Rom. 5:5–6; 7:4, 6; 8:13; Phil. 2:12–13). In contrast, death will come to all who fail to take Yahweh's holiness seriously (Lev. 10:2).

With respect to future grace, the blessings and curses of Leviticus 26 were conditioned on faith-generated obedience, and the covenant promises themselves were designed to motivate this kind of holy living. What was hoped for in the future would affect how people lived in the present (see 2 Peter 1:4). Furthermore, for those able to learn from it, the experience of divine discipline through the curses would itself be a means of grace, softening a hard heart and nurturing persevering dependence (Lev. 26:14, 16, 18, 21, 23–24, 27–28; cf. Heb. 12:10–11).

---

1. The book of Proverbs declares, "He who justifies the wicked … [is] an abomination to the LORD" (Prov. 17:15). Yet Paul declares that God justly "justifies the ungodly," pardoning their sins and counting them righteous and accepted in his sight (Rom. 4:5). This is possible only because of our union with Christ by faith (symbolized in the Old Testament by a sinner's identification with the unblemished, substitutionary sacrifice; Rom. 3:23–24; 5:1; Gal. 2:16; Phil. 3:8–9; Titus 3:5–7). As sinners, we must look outside of ourselves for acceptance with God, for we deserve only judgment. Christ's perfect righteousness and wrath-satisfying death are the only basis for our acceptance with God, and by faith alone (apart from works) our sins are counted to Christ and his righteousness is reckoned to us (Rom. 5:18–19; 2 Cor. 5:21; Phil. 3:9). "But now in Christ Jesus you who once were far off have been brought near by the blood of Christ" (Eph. 2:13). Thanks be to God for his mercy!

At the Feast of Booths, "you shall take on the first day the fruit of splendid trees, branches of palm trees and boughs of leafy trees and willows of the brook, and you shall rejoice before the LORD your God seven days" (Lev. 23:40). *Jewish worshipper at the Western Wall in Jerusalem during the Feast of Booths.*

The Call to Holiness and the New Covenant

In Leviticus 18:5, Yahweh declared, "You shall therefore keep my statutes and my rules; if a person does them, he shall live by them." Israel's history recorded in the Old Testament testifies that the nation as a whole failed in their pursuit of holiness and therefore were unable to enjoy lasting life. As Leviticus 26:27–39 anticipated, Israel's sin resulted in their exile from the Promised Land and the profaning of God's name among the foreign peoples.

Nevertheless, in faithfulness to his covenant promises (Lev. 26:42; cf. Ezek. 16:60), the LORD pledged that, after addressing the problem of Israel's sin (Lev. 26:40–41; cf. Ezek. 36:25), he would display himself as holy *through* a restored remnant in the sight of the nations, resulting in effective witness and new worshippers. In the words of Ezekiel the prophet, "And the nations will know that I am the LORD … when through you I vindicate my holiness before their eyes" (Ezek. 36:23). This is the new covenant hope! "I will put my Spirit within you, and cause you to walk in my statutes and be careful to obey my rules" (36:27).

Today, this side of the cross, God's will remains our "sanctification" (1 Thess. 4:3). And our victory over sin is possible *because* the Spirit of the resurrected, sin-overcoming, death-defeating Christ dwells in us (Rom. 8:7–11). "By the Spirit," we "put to death the deeds of the body," resulting in life (8:13); "the fruit of the Spirit is love…" (Gal. 5:22).

> "As obedient children, do not be conformed to the passions of your former ignorance, but as he who called you is holy, you also be holy in all your conduct, since it is written, 'You shall be holy, for I am holy'" (1 Peter 1:14–16).

Our growth in holiness comes only as an outgrowth of justification and ends in eternal life (Rom. 6:7, 22). Because both justification and eternal life are seen as gifts (3:24; 6:23), "the holiness without which no one will see the Lord" comes to us also as a gift, received through faith (Heb. 12:14). Every fruit of faith is, therefore, a "thanks be to God" kind of obedience (Rom. 6:17). We must work hard in our pursuit of godliness, but we must never do so in a way that replaces grace (1 Cor. 15:10; Phil. 2:12–13; Col. 1:28–29). And all the while we should rest confidently in God's promises, each of which is "Yes" in Jesus (2 Cor. 1:20). "Now may the God of peace himself sanctify you completely…. He who calls you is faithful; he will surely do it" (1 Thess. 5:23–24).

Conclusion

Leviticus provided Israel with guidelines for worshipping and following Yahweh, who is forever holy (Lev. 11:44–45; 19:2; 20:7, 26). Utterly distinct from his world and sovereign over it, Yahweh provided a way for a sinful people to enjoy lasting relationship with him, with sins forgiven, holiness enabled, and life sustained (16:34; 20:8; 22:32; 26:1–13). The detailed discussion of the various sacrifices (chs. 1–7, 16), the expansive overview of how to live for Yahweh (often called the Holiness Code, chs. 17–26), and the inclusion of the sacred calendar (ch. 23) all provided a hopeful prospect for Israel, who anticipated years of life in the Promised Land. Yahweh, nevertheless, warned his people that sustained covenant disloyalty and lack of repentance would ultimately result in their ruin (26:14–39). While they could learn from his disciplining hand (26:18, 21, 23, 27), the story of the rebellion of Israel's religious leaders (10:1–3) and the inclusion of a longer list of curses than blessings both suggest what the rest of Israel's history would show to be true—Israel would turn on Yahweh, spurning his grace and holiness and receiving a just penalty for their sin. Nevertheless, Yahweh promised that even after Israel's rebellion and punishment, he would remember his covenant with Abraham, Isaac, and Jacob, remember his land, remember his covenant with Israel at Sinai, and restore a repentant remnant (26:40–45).

KEY WORDS AND CONCEPTS FOR REVIEW

Holiness	Topography of sacred space
Holy sojourner ethic	Priests
Sacrifices/offerings	Sabbath
Atonement	Feast of Passover and Unleavened Bread
Blood	
Day of Atonement	Feast of Booths
Holy/common	Blessings and curses
Clean/unclean	Means of sanctification

KEY RESOURCES FOR FURTHER STUDY

Gane, Roy. *Leviticus, Numbers*. NIVAC. Grand Rapids: Zondervan, 2004.

Kiuchi, Nobuyoshi. *Leviticus*. AOTC. Downers Grove, IL: InterVarsity, 2007.

Ross, Allen P. *Holiness to the Lord: A Guide to the Exposition of the Book of Leviticus*. Grand Rapids: Baker, 2002.

Wenham, Gordon J. *Leviticus*. NICOT. Grand Rapids: Eerdmans, 1979.

Numbers

Who?

Numbers is essentially the work of Moses, who even kept a record of Israel's traveling itinerary (Num. 33:1–2). This accords with the association of the Pentateuch with Moses throughout the rest of the Bible (e.g., Josh. 23:6, Judg. 3:4; Mal. 4:4; Acts 28:23; Rom. 10:19; 1 Cor. 9:9), along with a number of texts that explicitly assert his writing activity (e.g., Exod. 17:14; 24:4; 34:27; Deut. 31:9, 24) and authorship (Josh. 8:32; John 5:45–47).

The book is filled with what may be called "The Memoirs of Moses," including firsthand accounts of desert life and divine revelation (Num. 2:1; 4:1), lists and censuses (3:15–31; 26:5–51), and details from outside Moses' experience but of current interest to the nation (chs. 22–24). Material was drawn from annalists or scribes (1:16–18; 11; cf. Josh. 1:10) and from books like "The Wars of the LORD" (Num. 21:14–15; cf. 21:17–18, 27–30). Many interpreters question whether the comment about Moses' extreme humility could have come from his own hand (12:3; cf. 1 Tim. 1:15), and other information appears to be post-Mosaic in origin (Num. 32:34–42; cf. Josh. 13:29–31).

When?

The historical period covered in Numbers spans approximately 1445–1406 B.C. (though some posit ca. 1249–1210 B.C.). The first census was taken during the second year after Israel's exodus from Egypt (Num. 1:1), with the second census occurring more than thirty-eight years later (14:20–35; 26:64–65). Moses may have supervised the compilation of the stories in Numbers with minor additional editing occurring at later periods. As an intriguing side note, in 1967 archaeologists unearthed an Aramaic inscription from the eighth century B.C. that cites Balaam the prophet, thus showing that he was known broadly in his day.

Where?

Israel's longest period of wandering was at Kadesh-barnea (13:26; cf. 14:26–22:1). The conquest generation was waiting for Yahweh's command to cross the Jordan and to conquer Canaan (21:1–36:13).

Why?

Numbers narrates the history of Israel's transition from the first to the second generation after the exodus. The book recounts Israel's preparation and journey from Sinai (1:19; cf. 1:1–10:10) through the wilderness of Paran (10:12; cf. 10:11–22:1; Deut. 1:19) and, eventually, to the plains of Moab (Num. 22:2; cf. 22:2–36:13) and into the Transjordan (east of the Jordan River). While the book describes the affairs of the exodus generation, its ultimate aim is instruction, intended for the conquest generation about to enter the Promised Land. It does so by:

1. Compelling Israel to obey Yahweh by describing how covenant breach brought God's discipline on their parents;
2. Inspiring Israel to a proper worship of Yahweh as a response of joy for their deliverance and rest;
3. Encouraging Israel to trust and hope in Yahweh and his promises as they follow God's leading into the Promised Land.

NUMBERS .

Andrew J. Schmutzer

Carefully Crafted Verses from Numbers

"The LORD bless you and keep you; the LORD make his face to shine upon you and be gracious to you; the LORD lift up his countenance upon you and give you peace" (Num. 6:24–26).

"Arise, O LORD, and let your enemies be scattered, and let those who hate you flee before you" (Num. 10:35).

"How long will this people despise me?
And how long will they not believe in me, in spite of all the signs that I have done among them?" (Num. 14:11).

THE AUTHOR OF NUMBERS …
• Developed God's *covenant promises* of offspring and land.
• Explained how Israel responded to *God's gracious presence*.
• Detailed the role of *Moses' mediation* for Israel, as well as other agents.
• Emphasized the *wilderness* as a unique place of *Israel's spiritual maturity*.

The Author of Numbers Developed God's *Covenant Promises* of Offspring and Land

The book of Numbers narrates the *transition* of the Israelites geographically, thematically, and theologically. Geographically, what began at Sinai (Num. 1:1–10:10) soon revolved around Kadesh (10:11–20:13) and culminated in Moab (20:14–36:13). Thematically, the community was formed (1:1–9:14), undertook their journey (9:15–25:18), and prepared for their national settlement (26:1–35:34). Theologically, Israel's redemption underwent the death of the exodus generation (chs. 1–25) before shifting to the generation of conquest (chs. 26–36). Two censuses frame the entire book; the first became a memorial to a fearful generation (ch. 1), and the last, a pledge of hope to their children (ch. 26). Each phase of encampment included law-giving, future promises, rebellion, and divine discipline. Clearly, God's promises to Abraham did not have a simple fulfillment.

> Numbers illustrates that *each generation* has a fresh opportunity to follow God. With the flow of Leviticus and Numbers in mind, Peter called his audience to holiness (1 Peter 1:15–16) and then reminded them, "You were ransomed from the futile ways inherited from your forefathers … with the precious blood of Christ" (1:18–19). The sins of parents do not have to be replayed in our lives.

"In the second year, in the second month, on the twentieth day of the month, … the people of Israel set out by stages from the wilderness of Sinai" (Num. 10:11–12). *Camels resting in the Sinai desert near Ein Hudra.*

Israel's future hope was grounded in the past promises of God. God's covenant with Abraham focused principally on promises of *blessing* (Gen. 12:3; cf. 22:18) and *nationhood* (12:2), the latter of which included God's commitment (1) to multiply offspring (13:16; 15:5; 17:2, 6; 22:17) and (2) to give land (13:15, 17; 15:18; 17:8). All of these elements are critical in

Numbers. Apparent throughout the book is a tension between the promises themselves and their delayed fulfillment.

Figure 5.1. Numbers at a Glance	
Time Frame	First Census—More than One Year after the Exodus (Num. 1:1)
Geography	From Sinai (1:1–10:10)—Community Formed and Tabernacle Constructed
	Through the Wilderness (10:11–22:1)—Internal Focus and Threats
	To the Plains of Moab (22:2–36:13)—External Focus and Threats
Time Frame	Second Census—More than Thirty-Eight Years Later (26:64–65)

From the outset, Canaan was the assumed goal, and the final chapters following the second census (Num. 27–36) gave hope that the objective would indeed be reached. The body of the book, however, raised serious

"The people journeyed to Hazeroth…. [Due to her leprosy,] Miriam was shut outside the camp seven days, and the people did not set out on the march till Miriam was brought in again" (Num. 11:35; 12:15). *The Sinai desert near Hazeroth.*

warnings to future generations about the need to remain true in one's God-orientation. Numbers 1–10 focus on Israel's preparation and departure from Sinai to claim the Promised Land (10:29; cf. 14:16; 32:11; Gen. 12:7). The census of Numbers 1 was designed to calculate the people's numerical strength, for war was on the horizon (Num. 10:35). However, in Numbers 11–25, the realization of both offspring and land is seriously diminished. Because of repeated rebellion, divine judgment ensued that affected the prospect of people and land (14:8, 22–24, 30–31; 20:12). In contrast to viewing the land as God's sure, gracious gift, the ten scouts gave "a bad report of the land" (13:32), leaving only Caleb and Joshua believing and calling the land "exceedingly good" (14:7).

For good reason, Yahweh viewed the community's unwillingness to enter the land as a "despising" of him and a failure of faith (14:11). Shockingly, the majority of Israel not only begged to return to Egypt (14:1–4)—a reversal of God's redeeming intervention—but they even called Egypt "the land flowing with milk and honey" (16:13; cf. Exod. 3:8)! Ironically, it was the money-grubbing prophet, Balaam, who rightly acknowledged the superiority of Yahweh and the ultimate end of Israel's journey (Num. 23:22–24; 24:8, 17–19). An outsider saw what was actually happening, whereas

Figure 5.2. The Balaam Account and the Abrahamic Promises

Cycle 1		Num. 22:2–35
Introduction: Balaam is "Called," a Donkey Responds		22:2–6
Balaam's First Meeting with God		22:7–14
Balaam's Second Meeting with God		22:15–20
Balaam's Third Meeting with God		22:21–35
Angel and Donkey: Round 1		vv. 22–23
Angel and Donkey: Round 2		vv. 24–25
Angel and Donkey: Round 3		vv. 26–35
Cycle 2		Num. 22:36–24:25
Introduction: Balaam's Oracles		22:36–40
Balaam's First Blessing of Israel	(= "offspring," see Gen. 13:16)	22:41–23:12
Balaam's Second Blessing of Israel	(= "protection," see Gen. 17:8)	23:13–26
Balaam's Third Blessing of Israel	(= "land," see Gen. 12:3; 17:6)	23:27–24:25
First Element of Blessing	("those who bless ... curse")	vv. 3–9
Second Element of Blessing	("a ruler ... out of Jacob")	vv. 15–19
Third Element of Blessing	("Ah, who can live?")	vv. 20–24

God's "treasured possession" were blind to the reality of God's plan (see Exod. 19:5–6; Deut. 7:6). Within Numbers, hope burns most brightly in the oracles of Balaam (Num. 22:2–24:5).

Balaam's oracles expanded on the promises to Abraham (Gen. 12:1–3), giving hope in their fulfillment by stressing that God is "not [a] man" who would "change his mind" (Num. 23:19). Despite these announcements, Balaam was portrayed as a greedy pagan who was complicit with the Israelites' sin of sleeping with the Moabite women (31:16; cf. Deut. 23:4–5).

In Chapters 26–36, the conquest generation found hope. This part of Numbers does not record any Israelite death. Instead, the text records that land divisions were made and boundaries were set for territories not yet conquered (Num. 26:53–56; 33:51–56; 34:1–15). It also records the various offerings that were to be made annually at set times in the sacred calendar (chs. 28–29). In spite of national infidelity, future possession was assumed (15:2), and inheritance problems were addressed in anticipation (27:1–11; 36:1–12). Battles were won around the perimeter of the Promised Land (31:1–32:42), serving as a "down payment" on the fuller promises yet to be realized. Nevertheless, stress was also made that the land could be forfeited by failing to take God seriously (33:55–56; 35:33–34; cf. Lev. 26; Deut. 28, 29, 32).

> The Bible consistently portrays Balaam as a false teacher, greedy for profit (Josh. 13:22; 2 Peter 2:15; Jude 11). His life provides a warning against coveting and immorality (Rev. 2:14) and reminds us of our need to seek God's glory above all else (1 Cor. 10:31)!

> The goal of Israel's election was not land but relationship. The Promised Land was the *context* of Israel's fellowship with God and would provide a spiritual barometer (Gen. 17:1; Ps. 78:56–64). Ultimately, the "rest" and "inheritance" Israel sought can be found only in Messiah Jesus (Deut. 12:9; Matt. 11:29; Eph. 2:11–22; Heb. 4:3, 5).

The Author of Numbers Explained How Israel Responded to *God's Gracious Presence*

God's Presence for Israel

Numbers reveals God's *delivering, sustaining,* and *loving* presence for Israel. His presence was first demonstrated *in* Egypt, where he "courted" the national heart of Israel, who soon proclaimed: "Who is like you, O Lord, among the gods?" (Exod. 15:11). God's gracious presence not only

"Moses sent [men to spy out the land of Canaan] from the wilderness of Paran, according to the command of the Lord" (Num. 13:3). *Nahal Paran from the south.*

Figure 5.3. Old Testament Feasts and Sacred Days

	Time Frame with Modern Equivalent		Nature and Purpose	Scripture References
Sabbath	Weekly: 7th day	Saturday	A day of rest for people and animals in order to recall God's sovereignty over creation and the freedom won for all at the exodus and to trust his future provision	Exod. 20:8–11; 31:12–17; Lev. 23:3; Num. 28:9–10; Deut. 5:12–17; Matt. 12:1–14; 28:1; Luke 4:16; John 5:9, 17; Acts 13:42; Col. 2:16; Heb. 4:1–11
Passover and Unleavened Bread	Spring: 14th/15th–21st of first month (Abib)	Mar/April (Easter)	A special memorial day with a meal of roasted sacrificial lamb, bitter herbs, and unleavened bread followed by a week of assemblies, offerings, and meals with unleavened bread, all designed to recall God's great and hasty deliverance of Israel from Egypt	Exod. 12:1–20; 13:3–10; 23:15; 34:18; Lev. 23:4–8; Num. 9:1–14; 28:16–25; Deut. 16:1–8; Matt. 26:17; Mark 14:1, 12–26; John 2:13; 11:55; Acts 12:3; 1 Cor. 5:6–8; Heb. 11:28
Firstfruits	Spring: 21st of first month (Abib)	Mar/April (Easter)	The presentation of the initial barley harvest with burnt and grain offerings to celebrate Yahweh's provision of crops	Lev. 23:9–14; Rom. 8:23; 1 Cor. 15:20–23
Weeks (Pentecost, Harvest)	Spring: 1st of third month (Sivan)	May/June (Pentecost)	The presentation of the initial wheat harvest with various offerings as a dedicatory festival of gratitude for Yahweh's bountiful provision of harvest	Exod. 23:16; 34:22; Lev. 23:15–21; Num. 28:26–31; Deut. 16:9–12; Acts 2:1–4; 20:16; 1 Cor. 16:8
Trumpets (Later: Rosh Hashanah, the Jewish New Year)	Fall: 1st of seventh month (Ethanim / Tishri)	Sept/Oct	A solemn, restful day of spiritual preparation and resolution	Lev. 23:23–25; Num. 29:7–11
Day of Atonement (Yom Kippur)	Fall: 10th of seventh month (Ethanim / Tishri)	Sept/Oct	A solemn, restful day of fasting and sacrifices of atonement to cleanse priests and people, tabernacle and land from the sin and defilement of the year	Lev. 16; 23:26–32; Num. 29:7–11; Rom. 3:24–26; Heb. 9:7–14; 10:3, 19–22; 13:11
Booths (Tabernacles, Ingathering)	Fall: 15th–21st of seventh month (Ethanim / Tishri)	Sept/Oct	A week of harvest celebration, living in booths, and offering sacrifices to memorialize Yahweh's providential care through the wilderness and to express gratitude for harvest	Exod. 23:16; 34:22; Lev. 23:33–36, 39–43; Num. 29:12–38; Deut. 16:13–15; Zech. 14:16–19; John 7:2, 37
Sabbath Year	7th year	Same	A year of rest for the land to secure future productivity and to trust Yahweh for his provision	Exod. 23:10–11; Lev. 25:1–7
Year of Jubilee	50th year	Same	A year of cancelling debts, freeing servants, and returning estates to help the poor and to stabilize society by fighting oppression	Lev. 25:8–55; 27:17–24; Num. 36:4
Purim	Spring: 14th–15th of twelfth month (Adar)	Feb/Mar	Two days of feasting and giving presents to commemorate God's deliverance of the Jewish nation in the days of Esther	Esth. 9:18–32

Prepared by Jason S. DeRouchie; some material adapted from pp. 164–65 in the *NASB Study Bible* edited by Kenneth Barker; copyright © 1999 by Zondervan. Used by permission of Zondervan. www.zondervan.com

established a privileged relationship with Israel but also enhanced God's reputation among the nations (Num. 14:13–17, 21, cf. Exod. 9:16; cf. 8:10[6]; 9:14; 11:7). Numbers 6:24–26 expresses God's deep affection for Israel, for he called the priests to bless them in this way: "The Lᴏʀᴅ bless you and keep you … make his face to shine upon you … be gracious to you … lift up his countenance upon you and give you peace" (cf. Gen. 12:1–3; 27:1–40; Deut. 7:14–16; 28:1–14). The result would be that God's "name" would rest upon Israel (Num. 6:27). This was God's desire, and here peace, security, and prosperity merge.

Yet Israel quickly forgot their sustaining and present God. Yahweh's powerful arm, which had delivered Israel from Egypt, soon reappeared in God's pained questions: "Is the Lᴏʀᴅ's hand short-ened?" (Num. 11:23; cf. Exod. 15:16) and "How long will they not believe in me, in spite of all the signs that I have done among them?" (Num. 14:11). Nevertheless, God declared that "all the earth shall be filled with the glory of the Lᴏʀᴅ" (14:21). Furthermore, his presence would be with Israel in the land, if they would only serve God alone (35:34). However, gaining the Promised Land without God's presence would miss the whole point, for Israel's redemp-tion was for *relationship*, not mere land claim (see Ps. 44:3; cf. 4:6; 31:16).

> One of God's greatest gifts to his people is his presence, for it alone can give the greatest satisfaction for the longest amount of time: "You make known to me the path of life; in your presence there is fullness of joy; at your right hand are pleasures forevermore" (Ps. 16:11). What a gift that the one with universal authority (Matt. 28:18) is with his own, even to the end (28:20).

God's Fatherhood of Israel

Israel was a child prone to rebellion, and God's parenting was both merciful and just (Num. 11:11–14; 14:11; 25:10). In reflection, Moses later stated: "I said to you, '… the Lᴏʀᴅ your God carried you, as a man carries his son, all the way that you went until you came to this place.' Yet in spite of this word you did not believe the Lᴏʀᴅ your God" (Deut. 1:29, 31–32). Similarly, he noted, "Know then in your heart that, as a man disciplines his son, the Lᴏʀᴅ your God disci-plines you" (8:5).

In Numbers, Moses' sustained recollection of Israel's rebellions provided a paradigm for the na-tion's subsequent history: (1) resentment of God's rule and his leaders' authority, (2) chronic attraction to idolatry, (3) fearfulness and divisions, and (4) di-vine judgment and national disaster. While God

> Hebrews uses Israel's wilderness failures to chal-lenge the church to persevere, even when times get hard (esp. Heb. 3:7–4:13). In suffering, we are called to recognize that God our Father is disciplining us "for our good, that we may share his holiness," and that such fatherly care will yield "the peaceful fruit of righteousness to those who have been trained by it" (12:10–11).

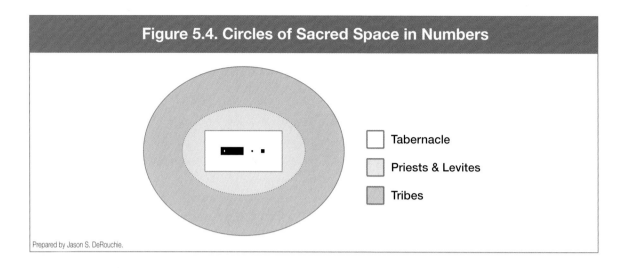

Figure 5.4. Circles of Sacred Space in Numbers

Prepared by Jason S. DeRouchie.

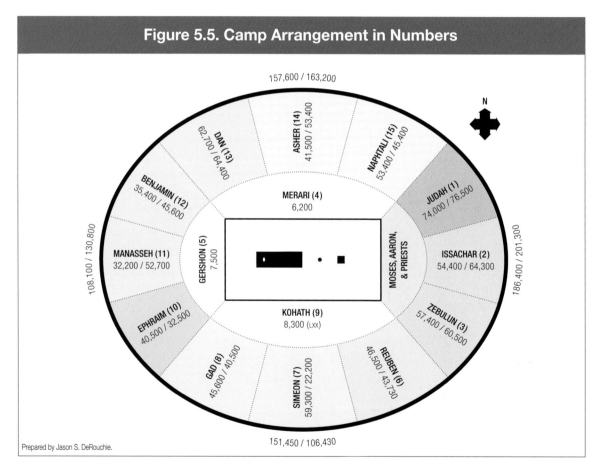

Figure 5.5. Camp Arrangement in Numbers

Prepared by Jason S. DeRouchie.

would still graciously dwell with his fickle people, precautions for his potent presence had to be built into Israel's worship. God's abiding presence will not be mocked!

God's Presence in and before Israel

One striking component of Numbers is that it uses the very structure of Israel's camp to stress the need for the centrality of Yahweh in all of life. As early as the census of Numbers 1, the twelve tribes are distinguished from the Levites (cf. Exod. 32:25–29). The Levites would camp on the inner circle between the tabernacle and the tribes to guard the tabernacle "so that there may be no wrath on the congregation of the people of Israel" (Num. 1:53). Violators could be executed (1:51; 5:10, 38; 16:13; 18:7), and Israel's past infidelity toward God, notably in the golden calf incident, showed that the people's future relationship with God could be jeopardized through covenant failure (Exod. 32:9–10; Num. 14:12; cf. Deut. 1:19–40; Ps. 95:10–11). God's holy presence must be taken seriously, and the camp design helped focus on this fact!

> The strategic placement of the tribe of Judah and family of Aaron at the entrance to the tabernacle appears to anticipate the mediatory role of the ultimate King and High Priest, Jesus Messiah (1 Tim. 2:5; Heb. 9:15; 12:24).

The text details the exact location of each tribe and the placement and function of the levitical and priestly families, all in relation to the tabernacle

"The people of Israel … came into the wilderness of Zin…. And the Lᴏʀᴅ said to Moses and Aaron, 'Because you did not believe in me, to uphold me as holy in the eyes of the people of Israel, therefore you shall not bring this assembly into the land that I have given them'" (Num. 20:1, 12). *Nahal Zin, the southernmost border of the Promised Land (Num. 34:3), east of Kadesh-barnea, from which the spies were first sent out (13:21); the left view is from the northwest toward Edom.*

(Num. 2–4). God established three concentric circles of *sacred space*, with his presence at the middle, bringing his blessing through an outward trajectory, first to the priests and levites and then to the tribes. This layout calibrated the intense relational presence of God that was accessible to everyone, but in varying degrees.

> With Israel's wilderness failures in mind, the writer of Hebrews called the church to guard against "an evil, unbelieving heart, leading you to fall away from the living God" (Heb. 3:12; cf. Ps. 95:7–11). He also said that, like us, they too heard "good news," but because they did not unite their hearing with persevering faith, leading to obedience, they did not enter God's rest (Heb. 4:1–2, 6; cf. Num. 14:11).

The three-tiered ordering is again highlighted through the dedication of the external camp, the priesthood, and the tabernacle, respectively (chs. 5–8), and then through the glory cloud appearing over the tabernacle in the midst of the camp (ch. 9). We are then told that God not only would dwell with Israel but that he would also go before it as guide and warrior (14:10; 16:19). Seated upon his portable throne, the ark of the covenant (10:35–36; cf. Isa 37:16), Israel's King would secure its victory, so long as Israel followed its God (Num. 14:39–45; 21:1–3; 31:1–12; cf. Exod. 15:3; Isa. 63:1–6; Rev. 11:17–18). Wherever and whenever the pillar of cloud and fire moved, the community must follow (Num. 9:15–23; cf. Exod. 13:21–22).

Israel enjoyed the presence of Yahweh, and the structure of the camp provided a "sacred compass" for the people. So long as they maintained the compass settings, aligning with his sacred ordering, they would walk rightly in God's way.

The Author of Numbers Detailed the Role of *Moses' Mediation* for Israel, as Well as Other Agents

Moses' Mediation Faces Opposition

Throughout Numbers, God's leaders play a central role in representing him before the congregation. Figures like Aaron (Num. 18, esp. v. 1) and Eleazar (20:22–29; cf. 25:10–13) as priests and Joshua as Moses' successor (27:18–23) were set apart, but chief among the leaders was Moses himself, who uniquely mediated the revelation of God to Israel (1:1; 12:2,

"Whenever the cloud lifted from over the tent, after that the people of Israel set out, and in the place where the cloud settled down, there the people of Israel camped" (Num. 9:17). *Tabernacle model in Timnah Valley just west of the Arabah (photo by Becky Weolongo Booto).*

6–8; 27:16–17; 36:13). Strikingly, when Moses' role of mediation began in Exodus, so did opposition to his leadership and those associated with him (e.g., Exod. 5:20–21; 14:11–12; 16:8; 17:2). Earlier negative reactions of the community only intensified in Numbers.

For example, the gifting of the seventy elders (Num. 11:24–30) incited Miriam and Aaron against Moses, and they asked, "Has the LORD indeed spoken only through Moses?" (12:2; cf. Exod. 15:20–21). Later, hostility emerged from Korah, Dathan, and Abiram against Moses and Aaron: "All in the congregation are holy.... Why then do you exalt yourselves above the assembly of the LORD?" (Num. 16:3). This moved Yahweh to kill 250 people in judgment (16:35), which in turn led to a full-scale rebellion against Moses (16:42–43) and to a destructive plague from Yahweh. Aaron quickly offered incense to Yahweh, placating his wrath, but 14,700 people died (16:47–49)! In a later event, which Jesus alluded to when speaking to Nicodemus (John 3:14–15), Israel "spoke against God and against Moses," insisting to return to Egypt and loathing the food and drink God was providing (Num. 21:5). As a result, God sent fiery serpents whose bites killed many in the community (21:6). Upon the people's plea for relief, God instructed Moses to place a bronze serpent on a pole and specified that any bitten person who looked upon it would live (21:8–9). A final example opposition occurred when Israel entered into a sexual "free-for-all" with Moabite women and began worshiping the Baal of Peor. Phinehas, grandson of the priest Aaron, acted decisively, and God withdrew his fierce anger—described as another "plague" (25:8; cf. 11:33; 14:37; 33:4). Plagues were a sure sign of the people's covenant violation, as anticipated in Leviticus 26:22 (cf. Deut. 32:24b), and by them God brought sudden and fatal injury. How long would Israel resist the direction of God through his ordained leaders?

> In an echo of the destroying Edenic serpent, God brought serpents against Israel as curse for their rebellion (Num. 21:6; cf. Gen. 3). Looking in faith toward an elevated representation of this curse was the means God gave for the stricken to live (Num. 21:8–9). In anticipation of his own elevated death on the cross, Jesus declared: "And as Moses lifted up the serpent in the wilderness, so must the Son of Man be lifted up, that whoever believes in him may have eternal life" (John 3:14–15). Jesus, who knew no sin, took on himself the curse for our sin, and only in putting our faith in him as our substitute can we know life (Gal. 3:13; 2 Cor. 5:21; cf. Heb. 4:16).

Moses' Intimacy with God and Rebellion Like the Rest

In Numbers, God often talks very personally with Moses (Num. 15, 17–19). Indeed, some mediation for Israel required Moses to intimately intercede *with* God by "face-to-face" dialogue (7:89; cf. Exod. 33:11; Deut. 34:10). Through the fiery "glory" of God, Moses would hear "the voice speaking to him from above the mercy seat that was on the ark of the testimony" (Num. 7:89b; cf. 11:25; 12:5, 8; 14:10; 16:19, 42; 20:6). Frequently Moses blasted God with deep and penetrating questions, the answers of which could change Israel's entire future (11:10–15, 21–22; 14:13–20; 16:22). From the routine complaints of the people, a pattern of *intercessive-dialogue* emerges: (1) the people's complaint, (2) God's anger and threat, (3) Moses' intercession, (4) and a commemorative name tagged on the location of the event (e.g., Num. 11:1–3; cf. Gen. 18:23–32).

Figure 5.6. Some of Moses' Responses to God in Numbers

- "Why have you dealt ill with your servant?" (Num. 11:11)

- "Where am I to get meat to give to all this people?" (11:13)

- "Shall all the fish of the sea be gathered together for them, and be enough for them?" (11:22)

- "Now if you kill this people as one man, then the nations who have heard your fame will say, 'It is because the LORD was not able to bring this people into the land that he swore to give to them'" (14:15–16a)

- "'Please pardon the iniquity of this people, according to the greatness of your steadfast love....' Then the LORD said, 'I have pardoned, according to your word.'" (14:19–20)

- "O God, the God of the spirits of all flesh, shall one man sin, and will you be angry with all the congregation?" (16:22)

According to Paul, the "old ministry" of the Israelite covenant through Moses had its moment of glory in the luminescent face of the prophet (2 Cor. 3:7–11; cf. Exod. 34:29–35). Even more glorious, however, is the "new ministry" of the Spirit, which not only casts out fear of judgment but also creates lasting, glorious changes in the lives of believers (2 Cor. 3:11, 18; Phil. 3:21; cf. John 1:1–14; Heb. 8:8–13).

Even though Moses had unparalleled access to God matched with impeccable integrity and moral poise (Num. 12:3; cf. Deut. 34:7, 10–12), God held Moses (and Aaron) to a higher standard (see James 3:1). And like the Israel he led, Moses too dishonored God, failing in his faith and failing to reach the Promised Land (Num. 20:10–12). The gracious gift of law was not enough to alter the rebellious hearts of the people, and death was the only result (cf. Rom. 7:12–13).

The Author of Numbers Emphasized the *Wilderness* as a Unique Place of *Israel's Spiritual Maturity*

Though the exodus generation had anticipated a quick entrance into the Promised Land, the people's own lack of faith created a long wilderness experience. The nation that struggled to trust needed first to shed its "slave identity"—but Egypt had a harder time leaving Israel!

In Numbers, Yahweh's response to the sin of his people and leaders is not the same gracious "pass" we found in the book of Exodus. Rather, the community deteriorated, and God now judges swiftly. For example, like Exodus, Numbers records Yahweh sending manna and quail, but now "while the meat was yet between their teeth, ... the LORD struck down the people with a very great plague" (Num. 11:33; cf. 11:4–15, 31–35; Exod. 16). Similarly, as in Exodus 17, God used Moses to bring water from a rock, but in Numbers the manner of Moses' action is portrayed as sinful: "You did not believe in me, to uphold me as holy." As such, Moses and Aaron were condemned to die *outside* the Promised Land (Num. 20:12; cf. 20:24, 28; 27:12–14). Twice, God threatened to wipe out Israel, but in Numbers Moses dissuaded the Lord by *quoting back to him* the famed statements of Yahweh's loyal love, originally spoken by God himself (14:12, 17–19; cf. Exod. 32:10; 34:6–7).

"From Mount Hor they set out by the way to the Red Sea, to go around the land of Edom" (Num. 21:4). *The region of Ezion-geber in the Eilat (Elath) Mountains and by the Red Sea's Gulf of Aqaba (see Deut. 2:8; photo by Matt Floreen).*

Sharp terms of complaining and judgment bracket the dark middle of Numbers (Num. 11:1–3; 25:1–18). This section contains seven "rebellions," symmetrically ordered:

A *General Testing* (11:1–3)
   B *Monotonous Food* (11:4–34)
      C *Leadership* (ch. 12)
         X Enemies (chs. 13–14)
      C' *Leadership* (chs. 16–17)
   B' *Lack of Water* (20:1–13)
A' *General Testing* (21:4–9)

As is clear from the above structure, chapters 13–14 mark the fatal changeover between the exodus and conquest generations. Against the pleas of Moses and Aaron (14:5–10), the people grumbled (14:1–4), and God lamented to Moses (14:11; cf. Ps. 15:1–2). God's heart revealed the pain and anger of a wounded lover (Num. 14:26). After talking further with Moses (14:13–33), God was persuaded to forgive Israel (14:20), but he also set consequences in motion. Ironically, the children would enjoy what their parents rejected (14:31–32), but they would also "suffer for your unfaithfulness" (14:33). God announced his judgment (14:21–25), explaining how *retribution* (i.e., "eye for eye") works: "What you have

> After drawing on ten different episodes from Numbers 11–25, Paul emphatically stated, "Now these things happened to them as an example, but they were written down for our instruction, on whom the end of the ages has come" (1 Cor. 10:11). What a powerful historical lesson and ongoing warning.

"They set out and camped on the other side of the Arnon, which is in the wilderness that extends from the border of the Amorites" (Num. 21:13). *Nahal Arnon aerial from the west overlooking the Dead Sea and a close-up from within the canyon.*

said in my hearing I will do to you" (14:28). The people's plea for a wilderness-death would be granted (14:2; cf. vv. 32–33).

The community's forty years in the wilderness were stained by conflict with God (Num. 32:13; Deut. 8:2–3, 16; Ps. 78:17–21; Neh. 9:16–18). As Moses would declare on the plains of Moab, "From the day you came out of the land of Egypt until you came to this place, you have been rebellious against the LORD" (Deut. 9:7; cf. 2 Kings 21:15). The antithesis of safety and supply, the wilderness was essentially negative—a place of hunger, chaos, and death. Surrounded by the cursed reality that results from sin, Israel was to learn about the necessity of persevering faith in Yahweh. The wilderness provided a buffer between liberation and land, and God used it as a crucible for developing Israel's trust in its liberating King.

> Matthew's Gospel capitalizes on this wilderness motif and forty days/years as the unique environment where the Divine Son's call was also be tested in food, protection, and worship (Matt. 4:1–11). Whereas Israel was a "son" who tested God (Exod. 4:22), Jesus proved to be an obedient "Son" who trusted in the care of his Father and refused to test him (Matt. 4:7; cf. Deut. 6:16; 8:5; Hos. 11:1). God tests us for development, not destruction, "that we may we share in his holiness" (Heb. 12:10; cf. James 1:13–14).

Figure 5.7. Israel's Ten Testings of God

Numbers 14:21–23. "But truly, as I live, and as all the earth shall be filled with the glory of the LORD, none of the men who have seen my glory and my signs that I did in Egypt and in the wilderness, and yet have put me to the test these ten times and have not obeyed my voice, shall see the land that I swore to give to their fathers."

1.	When Israel expressed fear at the Sea, as Pharaoh approached (Exod. 14:11–12)	6.	At Rephidim, when the people were thirsty and quarreled with Moses and tested God (Exod. 17:1–2)
2.	Three days into the wilderness at Mara, when Israel complained that the spring was bitter and they were thirsty (Exod. 15:24)	7.	At Sinai, when Israel worshipped the golden calf (Exod. 32:1–6)
3.	Two-and-a-half months after the exodus in the wilderness of Sin, when Israel complained that they were hungry (Exod. 16:2–3)	8.	At Taberah, when Israel complained about their misfortunes and God's fire consumed some of the camp (Num. 11:1)
4.	In Israel's failure to eat all daily manna (Exod. 16:20)	9.	At Taberah, when some complained that they were sick of manna and hungry for other food (Num. 11:4)
5.	In Israel's failure to gather enough manna to sustain them through the Sabbath (Exod. 16:27)	10.	At Kadesh, when the ten spies expressed lack of faith in God (Num. 14:1–4)

Prepared by Jason S. DeRouchie; adapted from *ʿArakin* 15a, *Babylonian Talmud*.

Deuteronomy

Who?

Deuteronomy largely consists of Moses' final sermons, which he spoke (Deut. 1:3, 5; 4:44; 5:1; 29:1) and transcribed (31:9, 22, 24; 32:45) for the Israelites who would live in the Promised Land (1:3, 35, 39). Later biblical figures affirmed the book's Mosaic authorship (Josh. 8:32; John 5:46–47), nature, and authority (e.g., Josh. 1:7–8; 1 Kings 2:3; 2 Kings 23:25; Mark 10:3–5; Acts 3:22–23; Rom. 10:19). Furthermore, Joshua—Moses' successor (Josh. 1:7–8; 8:32; cf. Deut. 3:38; 34:9)—and King David (1 Kings 2:3; cf. Deut. 17:18) had written copies of something called "the Book of the Law (*tôrâ*)" or "the Law of Moses," the former of which is the title Moses gave to his Deuteronomic material (Deut. 29:21; 30:10; 31:26).

All this stated, someone other than Moses, living in the Promised Land, finalized the book's form. This person introduced the whole (1:1–4), clarified geo-historical data (2:10–11, 20–23; 3:9, 11, 13b–14; 10:6–7), and seamed together Moses' messages (e.g., 1:5; 4:41–43, 44–5:1a; 29:1). He then commented on the prophet's death and succession (34:1–9), concluding, "there has not arisen a prophet since in Israel like Moses" (34:10–12; cf. 18:18).

When?

Moses delivered and wrote his final messages around 1406 B.C. (though some posit ca. 1250 B.C.) at the end of Israel's forty years in the wilderness—just before his death and Israel's conquest of the Promised Land west of the Jordan River (1:1–4; 4:1–5; 31:1–3, 9, 14, 24). The final form would have appeared during Israel's tenure in the land, probably in the early years following the conquest (before 1000 B.C.), though others suggest a time just prior to the exile (before 586 B.C.) or during the period of initial restoration (after 538 B.C.).

Where?

Moses gave his final words east of the Jordan River near Beth Peor in what was formerly the territory of Moab (1:1, 5; 3:29; 4:46; 29:1; cf. Num. 21:26); from here, the Promised Land to the west was considered "beyond the Jordan" (Deut. 3:20, 25; 11:30; cf. Num. 32:19). In contrast, the final editor of Deuteronomy was within the Promised Land, viewing Moses and Israel's placement in Moab as "beyond the Jordan" (Deut. 1:1, 5; 3:8; 4:41, 46–47, 49).

Why?

The collection of Moses' messages in Deuteronomy provided Israel with a constitution for governing their lives in relation to God and his world within the Promised Land. It also provides the new covenant community clarity on the nature of covenant love and various ways love can be manifest (30:6, 8). As "the Book of the *tôrâ*," it served as God's manual of "instruction,"

1. Reminding Israel of Yahweh's greatness by stressing his uniqueness and his past and future grace toward them, including ultimate restoration after exile;
2. Providing a lasting witness against Israel's sin (31:26–29; cf. 28:58–63; 29:19–21);
3. Clarifying for Israel how to enjoy lasting covenant relationship (6:4–9; 17:18–20; 30:9–10; 31:10–13; 32:44–47).

DEUTERONOMY

Jason S. DeRouchie

Carefully Crafted Verses from Deuteronomy

"Hear, O Israel: The LORD our God, the LORD is one. You shall love the LORD your God with all your heart and with all your soul and with all your might" (Deut. 6:4–5).

"Take to heart all the words by which I am warning you today, that you may command them to your children, that they may be careful to do all the words of this law. For it is no empty word for you, but your very life, and by this word you shall live long in the land that you are going over the Jordan to possess" (Deut. 32:46–47).

THE AUTHOR OF DEUTERONOMY ...

- Provided a *constitution* for guiding Israel's relationship with God.

- Stressed the importance of taking *God and his Word* seriously.

- Emphasized the *centrality of love* in one's relationship with God.

- Detailed the *perils* of sin, the *pleasures* of surrender, and the *promise* of grace.

- Defined the goal of love as *God-exalting influence* on the nations.

- Affirmed the *supremacy of Yahweh God* over all.

"There is none like God, O Jeshurun, who rides through the heavens to your help, through the skies in his majesty.... Happy are you, O Israel! Who is like you, a people saved by the LORD, the shield of your help, and the sword of your triumph!" (Deut. 33:26, 29).

The Author of Deuteronomy Provided a *Constitution* for Guiding Israel's Relationship with God

Perhaps no other book colors the tapestry of biblical thought like Deuteronomy. Standing climactically as the final installment in the Pentateuch and concluding the account of Moses' life, it clarified for the post-wilderness generation the significance of all that precedes, and it provided them with a constitution for guiding their covenant relationship with Yahweh in the Promised Land. It also supplied the Bible's later writers with a lens through which to interpret Israel's covenant history and clarified what humanity's response to Yahweh should be in this sometimes challenging world.

Why did Deuteronomy have such influence? A key reason is that the book served as a document of covenant *renewal* for all who would live in the Promised Land (thus the title *Deutero-nomos*, "second law"). As part of the fulfillment of his covenantal promises to the patriarchs (Deut. 1:8; 7:8; cf. Gen. 15:18; 17:7) and in alignment with what he started with the exodus generation at Sinai (Horeb) (Deut. 5:2–3; 29:1), Yahweh in Deuteronomy reaffirmed and developed his special covenant relationship with Israel just prior to their entry into Canaan (29:1, 12–15). For all who would dwell in the land, therefore, Deuteronomy's exposition of the earlier covenant materials would be a guide, governing life in relationship with Yahweh until the

> Like the New Testament's twin towers, John and Romans, Deuteronomy provides answers to all the major worldview questions: *Who or what governs reality? Who are we? Where are we? What is valuable in this world? What has gone wrong in this world? What is the solution?* As you read, try to answer these questions as Moses would have.

"These are the words of the covenant that the LORD commanded Moses to make with the people of Israel in the land of Moab, besides the covenant that he made with them at Horeb" (Deut. 29:1). *Camels in the plains of Moab, opposite Jericho (see Num. 36:13).*

promises given to Abraham were fulfilled (see Gal. 3:23–29). To heed the instruction would result in sustained life and blessing; to ignore would result in curse and ultimately death (Deut. 11:26–28; 30:15–18).

Deuteronomy presents itself as a collection of Moses' three "farewell sermons" (1:5–4:43; 4:44–29:1; 29:2–30:20), a song of warning (32:1–43), and the prophet's death-bed blessing (33:2–29), all wrapped into the grand narrative of God's kingdom-building work begun in Genesis. Moses termed his own material "the Book of the *tôrâ*" (29:21; 30:10; 31:26)—God's manual of "instruction" governing life in the Promised Land. In it Moses clarified the nature

> Jesus and the apostles frequently preached from Deuteronomy, citing it or alluding to it more than one-hundred times in the New Testament! Do we take Deuteronomy as seriously as they did?

of lasting covenant relationship and pleaded as a pastor on behalf of a loving covenant "father" who was calling for the sustained love of his "sons" (6:5; 14:1; 32:5–6; cf. Exod. 4:22). Israel must listen to Moses' teaching so they can "learn to fear the LORD your God, and be careful to do all the words of this law" (Deut. 31:12). Later, the prophet stressed (32:47): "It is no empty word for you, but your very life, and by this word you shall live long in the land that you are going over the Jordan to possess." He also emphasized that in the age of restoration following the curse (i.e., the new covenant), when God does a love-enabling work in the hearts of his people (30:6), the teachings of Deuteronomy would still be important (30:8): "And you shall again obey the voice of the LORD and keep all his commandments that I command you today" (cf. Jer. 12:16; 31:33; Isa. 2:2–3; 42:1–3; Mic. 4:1–3).

Figure 6.1. Deuteronomy at a Glance

Literary Structure	Ancient Near Eastern Treaty Echo
Superscription (1:1–4)	Title/Preamble (1:1–4)
Moses' 1st Sermon: God's Past Grace and Israel's Covenant Future (1:5–4:43)	Historical Prologue (1:5–4:43)
Moses' 2nd Sermon: The Nature of Lasting Covenant Relationship (4:44–29:1)	Stipulations (4:44–26:19)
Moses' 3rd Sermon: A Paradigm for a New Covenant after Exile (29:2–30:20)	Document Clause (27:1–8; 31:9, 24–26)
Moses' Arrangements for the Future, Including His Warning Song (31:1–32:47)	Public Recitation (27:9–26; 31:10–13)
Moses' Final Blessing and Death (32:48–34:8)	Blessings and Curses (27:12–26; 28:1–68)
Postscription (34:9–12)	

The Author of Deuteronomy Stressed the Importance of Taking *God and His Word* Seriously

Throughout his messages, Moses emphasized that Israel would enjoy life in the Promised Land only in a context of surrender to, dependence on, and trust in Yahweh and his revelation. The people must keep God and his Word central, for "man does not live by bread alone, but man lives by every word that comes from the mouth of the LORD" (Deut. 8:3; cf. Matt. 4:4).

Moses believed life could be enjoyed only when one closely follows God, for turning away would be to choose death over life (Deut. 30:15–20). The prophet stressed both that "[the LORD] is your life" (30:20) and his words are "your very life" (32:47), thus showing the amazing grace of God in disclosing his will to us. (Law does not have to be burden!) God is the initiator, graciously giving directions; having experienced grace, we respond

"You shall read this law before all Israel in their hearing. Assemble the people, men, women, and little ones, and the sojourner within your towns, that they may hear and learn to fear the LORD your God, and be careful to do all the words of this law" (Deut. 31:11–12). *Jewish men and boys with a Torah scroll at the Western Wall, Jerusalem.*

by following his lead and thus sustain our experience of life that can only be found in relationship to him. "I will never forget your precepts, for by them you have given me life" (Ps. 119:93). In such a context, Moses charged Israel to hear and follow "the statutes and rules ... that you may live" (Deut. 4:1) and then emphasized that, in contrast to the tragic deaths of all who had followed Baal of Peor, "you who held fast to the LORD your God are all alive today" (4:4; cf. 6:24).

A willingness to follow implies surrender to the leader (reverence/fear) as well as dependence on and trust in the leader's readiness to guide one to the promised destination (faith). Within the biblical framework, obeying God (following) is rightly understood only as an outgrowth of a proper disposition toward Yahweh's awe-inspiring nature (fear) and promises (faith).

The Bible emphasizes that *fearing* the Lord is the generator for holy living (Exod. 20:20; Prov. 1:7; Jer. 32:39–40; Phil. 2:12). It also stresses that a lack of such fear results in judgment (Matt. 10:28; Rom. 3:18). In line with this canonical perspective, Deuteronomy teaches that true obedience grows out of a heart that reveres Yahweh's supremacy. This is clear from the book's stress that fearing God must precede and give rise to following his ways. As seen most clearly in Deuteronomy 6:1–3; 17:19–20, and 31:11–13, the full pattern is as follows (see also Deut. 4:10; 5:23–29; 6:1–2, 24; 10:12–13; cf. John 5:24–25; 6:44–45):[1]

The Reading or Teaching of God's Word → Hearing God's Word → Learning to Fear God → Obeying God = Life

Significantly, this progression emphasizes that the fear of God that produces dependent and productive living results only from God's gracious disclosure of himself and his will in a way that captures the hearts of his people.

Faith in the God of promise is a natural outgrowth of fearing Yahweh, for a true encounter with the living God proves both his believability and the desirability of lasting relationship with him

> The old covenant saw obedience as the fruit of a heart-encounter with God. But Deuteronomy also made clear that Israel was spiritually deaf (never receiving the gift of "hearing") and would therefore never follow God (Deut. 29:4; 31:16, 20, 27, 29) until the day he would change their heart (4:30–31; 30:6, 8, 11–14). In echo of both Moses and Isaiah, Jesus said (John 6:44–45): "No one can come to me unless the Father who sent me draws him.... Everyone who has heard and learned from the Father comes to me."

---

1. Daniel I. Block, "The Grace of Torah: The Mosaic Prescription for Life (Deut. 4:1–8; 6:20–25)," *BSac* 162 no.1 (2005), 15.

(Heb. 11:1, 6). Throughout the Bible, faith is future-oriented in that God's people trust him to accomplish for them what they cannot do on their own (Gen. 15:6; Rom. 4:18–22; Heb. 11:1, 6). A heart of God-dependence rather than self-reliance is the root; obedience is the fruit (Deut. 29:18–19; cf. 1 John 3:7). Just as there is no true faith without obedience (1 Cor. 13:2; James 2:17, 26), so also there is no true obedience without faith (Rom. 14:23; Heb. 11:6).

Deuteronomy's commitment to what Paul termed the "obedience of faith" (Rom. 1:5; 16:26; cf. 6:17–18) is clearly evident in the way Moses addressed Israel's initial failure to enter the Promised Land. After affirming that Israel rebelled against God's Word (Deut. 1:26), the prophet asserted that Israel's ultimate failure was in not "believing" God (1:32–36; 9:23; cf. Num. 14:11; 20:12; 2 Kings 17:14). The generation that first sought to enter the land lacked faith overflowing in obedience, and this lack of persevering surrender ultimately resulted in their ruin. In the words of the writer to the Hebrews, Moses preached "*good news*" to the wilderness generation, but "the message they heard did not benefit them, because they were not united by faith with those who listened" (Heb. 4:2; cf. Rom. 9:32; Jude 5). The writer then added, "Those who formerly received the good news failed to enter because of disobedience" (Heb. 4:6).

Believers today should still revere God's Word! Two Gospel writers stress this fact by narrating Jesus' use of Deuteronomy 8:3 in his own battle with the devil: "Man shall not live by bread alone, but by every word that comes from the mouth of God" (Matt. 4:4; cf. Luke 4:4).

"Following the leader" is more than a kids' game; it should be the pattern of our lives in relationship to God. In both the old and new covenants, real obedience to the Lord flows out of a heart that is awed by his greatness, takes seriously his Word, is surrendered to his ways, trusts in his promises, and looks to him for help.

The Author of Deuteronomy Emphasized the *Centrality of Love* in One's Relationship with God

What should such God-centered, faith-filled, Bible-saturated living look like? Some may immediately respond, "Keeping the Ten Commandments!" This is a reasonable assertion, in view of the foundational place of the Ten Words both in the Law (Exod. 20:2–17; Deut. 5:6–21) and in the rest of Scripture (e.g., Hos. 4:2; Jer.

7:8–11; Matt. 19:18; Rom. 13:9). Strikingly, however, in Deuteronomy and elsewhere, the Ten Words are seen as illustrations of a more fundamental call—namely, to love God and neighbor. As Jesus stressed, these two commands uphold "all the Law and the Prophets" (Matt. 22:37–40; cf. Mark 12:29–31). Similarly, Paul wrote that all other commandments are "summed up in this word: 'You shall love your neighbor as yourself'" (Rom. 13:9; cf. Gal. 5:14; James 2:8).

A Call to Covenant Love

Deuteronomy suggests that "loving God" is the supreme command, the first step in a godward life (Deut. 6:4–5): "Hear, O Israel: The LORD our God, the LORD is one. You shall love the LORD your God with all your heart and with all your soul and with all your might." Love for God is the spring from which love of neighbor flows (10:12, 19; cf. Lev. 19:18). Loving God and neighbor summarizes *what* God's people were to do; the Ten Words (the "testimonies") and all the additional "statutes and rules" clarify *how* God's people were to do it (see Deut. 4:45; 12:1; 26:16). Love toward God and neighbor is the essence of covenant relationship.

The Context and Scope of Covenant Love

Intriguingly, in order to clarify for Israel in an understandable way the contours of relating to God, the Lord appears to have adopted and adapted international treaty language for his own purposes. In a world where suzerain "fathers" (i.e., big kings) committed to "love" their vassal "sons" (i.e., small kings) and where vassal "sons" were called to "love" their suzerain "fathers" and their fellow vassal "brothers," Yahweh approached Israel as the covenant Lord who sought to make a people his treasure. In accordance with the "love" he had for the patriarchs (4:37; 10:15), he set his affections on Israel, electing them (7:6; 14:2), redeeming them (7:8), becoming their covenant "king" (33:3, 5), and protecting them through the wilderness (23:5). As such, he was Israel's "father" (32:6) and they were his adopted "sons" (14:1) in order that they might become God's "inheritance" (4:20; 9:26, 29; 32:9), "treasured possession," and "holy people" (7:6; 26:18–19; cf. Exod. 19:5). In response to such grace, Israel was called to "love" Yahweh (Deut. 6:5), the effect of which included loving their "brother" (10:19; cf. 14:27–29; 15:11; Lev. 19:18)—a title representative of everyone (male and female) in the covenant community (Deut. 15:12), unless specified otherwise (13:6). Like the faith that produces it, love for God and one's neighbor is a human *response* to God's covenant initiating and sustaining grace.

The immediate context of Deuteronomy 6 suggests that "love" for Yahweh was to be a life-encompassing, community-embracing, exclusive commitment to the Sovereign One. This definition is first suggested by the call of Deuteronomy 6:5 to love Yahweh with all one's *heart, soul* (being), and *might* (substance).[2] Most likely, rather than detailing three distinct parts of a person, these elements characterize three expanding, yet overlapping, human spheres of life, all of which are to proclaim God's supremacy. "Heart" relates to all that is internal—one's desires, emotions, attitudes, perceptions, *and* thoughts. "Soul" refers to one's entire being—all that is part of the "heart" plus everything outward: one's body, words, actions, reactions (e.g., Gen. 2:7; Lev. 26:11). Finally, "might" is not only physical strength but also all that one has available for honoring God, which would include one's spouse, children, house, land, animals, wardrobe, tools, and toys. All that we are and have should ring out, "My God is Yahweh!"

This interpretation of the call to holistic covenant surrender to Yahweh is further supported in the verses that follow. Not only are the hearers to have Moses' call to covenant love etched on their hearts (Deut. 6:6; cf. Jer. 31:33), but also they are to impress the words upon their children at all times and in all settings, spreading a passion for

"You shall bind [these words] as a sign on your hand, and they shall be as frontlets between your eyes" (Deut. 6:8). *Jewish men with phylacteries at the Western Wall, Jerusalem.*

The old covenant called for *internal* surrender and loyalty to God (Deut 4:39; 6:5–6; 8:5; 10:12–13, 16; 11:18; 26:16; 32:46), but for only a small remnant of Israel did the call reach the heart and produce a godward life (e.g., Pss. 37:31; 40:8; 119:10–11; Isa. 51:7). In contrast, *every member* of the new covenant is empowered by God to love him and others rightly—not perfectly yet, but truly (Deut. 30:6, 8; Jer. 31:33–34; Ezek. 36:26–27; cf. Rom. 8:4–9, 13; 13:8–10).

---

2. S. Dean McBride Jr., "The Yoke of the Kingdom: An Exposition of Deuteronomy 6:4–5," *Int* 27 (1973): 304; Daniel I. Block, "How Many Is God: An Investigation into the Meaning of Deuteronomy 6:4–5," *JETS* 47 no. 2 (2004): 202–4.

God's supremacy on to the next generation (Deut. 6:7; cf. 6:20–25; 11:19). Furthermore, an allegiance to God above all else is to govern both the nature of one's actions ("as a sign on your hand") and the object and manner of one's focus ("as frontlets between eyes") (6:8; cf. 21:7; Exod. 3:9, 16). Finally, all that takes place in the home ("on the doorposts of your house") and community ("in your [city] gates"), in private and in a crowd, is to proclaim that God is truly the king (Deut. 6:9). Covenant love for Yahweh is indeed a life-encompassing, community-embracing, exclusive commitment that calls for every closet of our lives to be filled with radical God-centeredness.

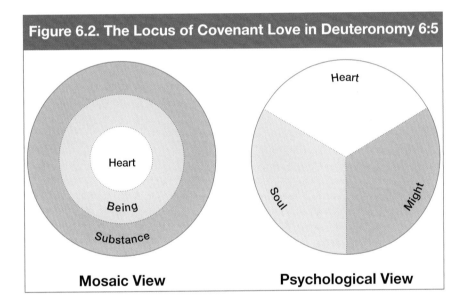

Figure 6.2. The Locus of Covenant Love in Deuteronomy 6:5

Heart
Being
Substance

Mosaic View

Heart
Soul
Might

Psychological View

The Nature of Covenant Love

Immediately after calling God's people to covenant love, Moses characterized this God-centered existence in two ways, both of which are echoed and developed throughout the rest of the book. To love God is (1) to *remember* Yahweh amidst the pleasures of life (6:10–25) and (2) to *remove* all obstacles that could hinder a God-centered existence (7:1–26). These fruits of the supreme command are then developed in chapters 12–26, wherein Moses described "the statutes and rules" Israel must heed (12:1; 26:16) and called them to follow "righteousness and righteousness alone" (*contra* ESV) in every area of life (16:20). The Sovereign One is passionate about *right order* in his world, and only when he is taken seriously is true *righteousness*

"The LORD gave me the two tablets of stone written with the finger of God" (Deut. 9:10). *A remnant of Hammurabi's Law Code (1790 B.C.) from Nippur during the Old Babylonian Kingdom (from the Istanbul Archaeological Museum).*

manifest (cf. 6:25; 24:13; cf. Rom. 2:13; 1 John 3:7–10). Although some have unhelpfully titled chapters 12–26 the "Deuteronomic Law Code," all of the instruction is pastoral. This is a sermon, giving hands and feet to the supreme command.

As noted earlier, love for God and neighbor summarized *what to do*, and the detailed "statutes and rules" (12:1; 26:16) in chapters 12–26 clarified for Israel *how to do it* during their tenure in the land. For them, love would include three spheres: righteousness in community worship (12:1–16:17), righteousness in community oversight (16:18–18:22), and righteousness in daily community life (19:1–26:15). As one skims over this material, what becomes clear is that Yahweh's guidance addressed all aspects of human existence, whether criminal offenses, civil cases, family relationships, societal norms, or community worship (see Fig. 3.4). Most instructions were themselves concrete expressions of love for others, whereas some were symbolic, filled with pageantry that pointed to heart realities that Israel itself was to recognize. How gracious of God to spell out for his people the right way to live (see 4:5–8)! The psalmist recognized the significance of this gift (Ps. 19:9–10): "The rules of the LORD are true, and righteous altogether. More to be desired are they than gold, even much fine gold; sweeter also than honey and drippings of the honeycomb."

> Because *all* scriptural commands are about loving our neighbor (Rom. 13:8–10; Gal. 5:14), Paul could use Deuteronomy's wisdom to challenge believers in their life of love, even though Christians are not under the old covenant (Deut. 25:4 in 1 Cor. 9:7–10; cf. 2 Tim. 3:16; Eph. 6:1–3; 1 Peter 1:15–16). Moses and the later prophets anticipated this exact type of internalized application of Deuteronomy's laws in the new covenant age (Deut. 30:6, 8; Jer. 12:16; 31:33; Ezek. 36:27)!

The Author of Deuteronomy Detailed the *Perils* of Sin, the *Pleasures* of Surrender, and the *Promise* of Grace

Throughout the book, the main challenge to a God-centered, fulfilled existence is the deceitfulness of sin manifest in two overlapping contexts: prosperity and paganism. As Israel entered the Promised Land, they needed to recognize how quickly riches or success can lead to self-reliance and to forgetting God as the ultimate provider (Deut. 6:10–12; 8:10–18; 9:4; 29:19; 32:15). They also needed to be aware how easily the wrong crowd or an immoral setting can pull people away from God (7:3, 4, 16, 25; 11:16; 17:17). All members of the community, therefore, needed to be intentional to sustain their surrender and God-ward focus. God takes sin seriously, and his people should too!

Motivation: Perils, Pleasures, and Future Grace

In Deuteronomy, Moses motivated Israel to battle sin and to love God by reaffirming the blessings and curses of Leviticus 26. Yahweh pledged to continue to *protect* his people and to *provide* for them, given they continue to live as his people—remaining loyal to him from the heart (28:1–14; 30:3–10). However, he also warned against trading joy for pain and rest for discipline through faithless, self-exalting rebellion (11:16–17; 28:15–68; 29:19–21).

Promises motivate people by creating either desire or dread. In the words of Peter, "He has granted to us his precious and very great promises, so that through them you may become partakers of the divine nature, having escaped from the corruption that is in the world because of sinful desires" (2 Peter 1:4; cf. Rom. 4:18–21). In both the old and new covenants, believers come to look more like God and to battle the deceitful allurements of the evil one by focusing on that which is more desirable—God's promises! We will make different choices in the present if we truly believe that the outcome of one decision over another will produce more satisfying results. By believing God's Word, hope is created, and what we hope for tomorrow changes who we are today.

The covenant promises of blessing, curse, and restoration blessing in Deuteronomy 27–32 (and Lev. 26) address both spiritual and physical wellbeing, but the focus is on the latter (e.g., national security and influence, personal health and fertility, productivity, etc.). If Israel, with humble, God-honoring hearts, would not "go after other gods" (Deut. 28:14) but would carefully "do *all* his commandments" (28:1), God would remain with them (Lev. 26:11–12), and they would always enjoy bountiful food, successful pregnancies, victory in battle, and more (esp. 28:1–14; cf. Lev. 26:3–13).

> For Christians, *physical* health, wealth, and safety are a future hope (Isa. 65:17–25; 1 Cor. 9:25; Rev. 21:4) and not something that should be expected today. For although the obedience of Jesus has won us every *spiritual* blessing (Eph. 1:3; 2 Cor. 6:16), the old age still continues, and with it suffering, which identifies the believer with Christ (e.g., Luke 9:23; Rom. 8:17) and is necessary for sanctification (Rom. 5:3–5; 1 Tim. 3:12; James 1:2–4; 1 Peter 1:6–8).

Strikingly, Deuteronomy is clear both in its explicit statements and in its inclusion of longer lists of curses than blessings that, while Israel would enjoy sporadic communal blessings (e.g., Israel's victory over Jericho and Ai in Josh. 5:13–8:29), the general pattern for them would be sin and the experience of curses (esp. Deut. 31:16–17, 26–29 with 27:15–26; 28:15–68; cf. 4:25–28). Their rebellion, like Adam's before them, would bring about the just judgment of God, climaxing ultimately in the curse-bearing work of Messiah Jesus (Gal. 3:13–14).

"You shall tear down their altars and dash in pieces their pillars and burn their Asherim with fire. You shall chop down the carved images of their gods and destroy their name out of that place" (Deut. 12:3). *Remnants of Canaanite worship in Gezer, these standing stones or "pillars" were never destroyed because the Israelites "did not drive out the Canaanites who lived in Gezer" (Josh. 16:10) (photo by Daniel Frese).*

Nevertheless, as anticipated by Moses (Deut. 30:3–10; 32:34–43; 33:26–29; cf. 4:29–31) and clarified by the later prophets, the Eden-like, utopian picture of joy portrayed in the blessings and restoration blessings will come to full expression in the new heavens and new earth (Isa. 51:3; 65:17; Ezek. 36:35; Rev. 21:1–4; 22:1–5). In that day, God's wrath and curse will be no more (Deut. 30:7; 32:43; Rev. 22:3), and believers, who now enjoy every spiritual blessing (Eph. 1:3; 2 Cor. 6:16), will then receive their full inheritance (Eph. 1:14; 1 Peter 1:4).

Foundation: Perils, Pleasures, and Past Grace

The reward in sight, Moses was also intentional to clarify the foundational reasons why Israel must continue to take seriously

God, his Word, and his promises. Specifically, Deuteronomy spends much time reminding Israel of their past experience of divine power, judgment, and grace (Deut. 32:18) in order to nurture confidence in God's promise of future grace and judgment (11:26–28; 30:15–18). Moses asserted that Yahweh's past grace to Israel through both revelation and forgiveness was the basis for their future-oriented faith and the obedience that was to flow from it.

For the Israelites to persevere with God in the present, they needed to look back, remembering their unworthiness to receive God's affection (7:7; 9:6–8, 22–24) and the seriousness with which he had taken their past sins (1:35). They also needed to remember Yahweh's vowed commitment to the patriarchs and to their offspring (1:8; 9:5; cf. Gen. 12:1–3; 15:18; 17:7; 22:16–18), the freedom Yahweh alone gave them from slavery (Deut. 5:15; 6:22–23), the gracious provision that Yahweh alone supplied them through the wilderness (2:7; 8:3–4; 29:5–6), and the fact that they alone among all the nations of the world were set apart to be Yahweh's people (7:6; 14:2; 26:18; cf. Exod 19:5–6). Israel's redeemer, therefore, deserved their allegiance, and out of obligation, gratitude, and anticipation, they needed to live for him alone.

Israel's Problem: Hard-Heartedness

Yet Israel was "rebellious" (Deut 1:26, 43; 9:7, 23–24; 21:18, 20; 31:27), "unbelieving" (1:32; 9:23; 28:66), and "stubborn" (9:6, 13; 10:16; 31:27), and in God's eternal purposes climaxing in Jesus, he did not change their hard hearts: "To this day the LORD has not given you a heart to understand or eyes to see or ears to hear" (29:4; cf. Rom. 11:8, 10)! As such, the people's doom was sure, and Moses himself declared that Israel would enter the Promised Land and break the covenant by rebelling against Yahweh (Deut. 30:1; 31:16, 20, 27, 29). In turn, Yahweh, who is always just and upright in his actions (32:4), would bring upon Israel the curses, climaxing in their exile from the Promised Land (4:25–28; 29:18–28; 31:16–21; cf.

Paul recognized that most of old covenant Israel did not follow God but "were hardened, as it is written, 'God gave them a spirit of stupor, eyes that would not see and ears that would not hear, down to this very day'" (Rom. 11:7; cf. Deut. 29:4). But ethnic Israel's rejection opened the door for salvation to reach the Gentiles (Rom. 15:10; cf. Deut. 32:43). And this, in accordance with Deuteronomy 32:21, is designed to make the elect of Israel jealous and ultimately turn to God (Rom. 10:19; 11:11–12, 25–26).

Dan. 9:11). Like Adam and Eve before them, they would be separated from God's life-giving presence, all because of the hardness of their hearts (see Rom. 8:7–9; 1 Cor. 2:14; Eph. 4:18).

through whom believing Jews and Gentiles alike are brought back to God, experiencing the blessing of life forevermore (Acts 3:25–26; Gal. 3:8, 13–14, 16, 29; Eph. 2:11–18).

Any relationship between Yahweh and a sinful humanity demands reconciliation through an atoning sacrifice, for which the sacrifices of Leviticus provided only a shadow (Heb. 8:5; 10:1). Because of this fact, Messiah Jesus' redeeming and purifying work on the cross supplies the only ultimate ground for anyone's right-standing with God—past, present, and future (8:6; 10:10, 14, 18; Rom. 3:24–26; 5:19; 2 Cor. 5:21). Christ's atoning work is also the foundational grace upon which all Christian living is based, and it alone secures the promise of all future grace (Rom. 15:8; 2 Cor. 1:20; Gal. 3:29). As Paul proclaims, because God gave us his Son, we can be sure he will also meet all our needs (Rom. 8:31–32), and because we have experienced such mercy, we should live lives surrendered to him (12:1). In fulfillment of Deuteronomic anticipation (Deut. 30:6; cf. Jer. 31:33; Ezek. 36:26–27), such love-filled living is a result of a divinely generated new birth (John 3:5–8; 6:63) or heart surgery (Rom. 2:15, 29)—a fruit of Christ's Spirit in us (8:4, 9–11; Gal. 5:6, 22), which ultimately will result in Christ-honoring witness (Acts 1:8), lasting life (Rom. 6:22; 8:13; Gal. 5:25; cf. John 6:63), and the exaltation of God's name in the world (Ezek. 36:22–23, 27; Heb. 13:20–21; 1 Peter 4:11).

Lasting Covenant Relationship: Grace from Start to Finish

Before God's people ever exert future-oriented faith that creates hope resulting in love of others, God graciously initiates the relationship and graciously makes amazing promises that stimulate a different kind of living. Deuteronomy testifies that God's choice of Israel and his initial working on their behalf had everything to do with the promises he had made to the patriarchs and with his unmerited love for his people and had nothing to do with any greatness *of* Israel (Deut. 7:7–8) or any greatness *in* Israel (9:5–6)—they were stubborn (9:6, 13; 31:27)! Furthermore, the surrendered, dependent following (i.e., the obedience of faith) that God demanded would ultimately only be experienced because of this same divine grace, for God was not only the gracious promise maker but the one who would make the promises desirable to a divinely reshaped heart. In the end, therefore, the perpetuation of covenant relationship would ultimately be grounded in, motivated by, and dependent on the experience and hope of divine grace and only secondarily and responsively on the obedience of faith. Faith, hope, and love are merely human responses to God's covenant-initiating and sustaining grace—praise the Lord!

"The Rock, his work is perfect, for all his ways are justice. A God of faithfulness and without iniquity, just and upright is he" (Deut. 32:4). *Dead Sea cliffs aerial opposite Moab, north of Engedi.*

The Author of Deuteronomy Defined the Goal of Love as *God-Exalting Influence* on the Nations

Deuteronomy portrays the goal of Israel's love as God-exalting witness in the world. Yahweh, the only God (4:35, 39; 6:4), holy (26:15; 32:51), sovereign over all things (10:14), the creator of mankind (4:32) and Israel (32:6), and the overseer of nations (32:8), must always act for his own exaltation, for to make anything else more important than himself would render him not God. Because Yahweh is God, he must be jealous for his people's affections (4:24; 5:9; 29:20; 32:16, 21) and must act to maintain right order (righteousness) in the world (4:8; 16:20; 32:4), wherein he is recognized as supreme. In separating Israel for himself, he created them with mission. Their fearing and obeying God would bear the missional purpose of seeing the worship of Yahweh reestablished on a global scale.

In Genesis, God's sovereign rest—kingdom peace—was aggravated through humanity's rebellion and its resulting curse (Gen. 3:14, 17; 4:11; 5:29; 9:25). The gracious creator of all, however, set in motion the solution to the problem, initially through the first statement of gospel in Genesis 3:15 and then by focusing through Abraham and his offspring this promise of the defeat of evil and reversal of the curse (12:2–3; 22:17b–18). In Exodus, God restressed Israel's mission of imaging his supremacy and of standing as a mediator between God and the rest of humanity (Exod. 19:5–6).

Deuteronomy expressed this same goal of God-exaltation by blending a call to covenant love with the unique treasure of God's presence and the necessity of worldwide influence for the glory of God.

The most explicit text is Deuteronomy 4:5–8, where, after calling Israel to heed Yahweh's commands (Deut. 4:5–6a), Moses clarified the reason why obedience (i.e., love in action) was imperative—namely, a godly witness in the world (4:6b–8)! If Israel would live wisely, their lifestyle would attract the attention of the nations (4:6b), who would stand amazed at God's nearness to Israel (4:7) and at the uprightness of his revelation (4:8). Israel's heeding of God's commands would result in the display of God's greatness in the sight of the world (cf. Matt. 5:16).

> Drawing on imagery found in Deuteronomy, Peter emphasized that the church's identity and mission are the realization of what Old Testament Israel was to be and do: "You are a chosen race, a royal priesthood, a holy nation, a people for his own possession, that you may proclaim the excellencies of him who called you out of darkness into his marvelous light" (1 Peter 2:9).

The rest of Deuteronomy affirms Israel's mission mindset. The people's God-centered living would result in international renown (Deut. 26:19; 28:1), with the world standing in awe of Yahweh's people in light of his favor toward them (28:9–10). The global jealousy directed at Israel, however, would in time be turned on its head. For "in the latter days" (31:29; *contra* ESV), after Israel had disobeyed God's Word, receiving both destruction and shame at the hands of the nations (28:25, 37) and profaning God's name through bad witness (29:24; cf. Ezek. 36:20), Yahweh would act on behalf of his "servants" (i.e., those that had [re-]surrendered to God's supremacy, Deut. 32:36). In light of the jealousy that Israel's disloyalty caused God, Yahweh would cause them to be jealous toward the nations (32:21;

cf. Rom. 10:19–11:26), would avenge his enemies (Deut. 32:35, 41, 43; cf. Rom. 12:19; Heb. 10:30), would atone for the polluting effects of sin (Deut. 32:43), and would have compassion on his servants (32:36). From the perspective of at least some Old Testament manuscripts and Paul, this last move would result in worldwide joy, a feature that suggests the inclusion of the nations (Gentiles) in the people of God (32:43, KJV, NASB, NIV, HCSB; cf. Rom. 15:10).

The Author of Deuteronomy Affirmed the *Supremacy of Yahweh God* over All

The governing truth at the core of Israel's worldview was Yahweh's supremacy over all things: he alone is God (Deut. 4:35; 6:4; 33:26). Missions exists because a global recognition of this fact needs to be rekindled.

Yahweh alone is God—a rock (32:4, 15, 18, 30–31), a great (5:24, 7:21, 10:17; 11:2; 32:3) and consuming presence (4:24; 9:3; 33:2) that stands unique in his perfections. With respect to his character (32:3–4), Yahweh is perfectly merciful (4:31; 13:17; 30:3), loving (5:10; 7:8, 13; 10:15, 18;

"The LORD is God in heaven above and on the earth below; there is no other" (Deut. 4:39). *Sunrise over Moab from across the Dead Sea in Engedi.*

23:5), loyal (5:10; 7:9, 12), faithful (7:9; 32:4), holy (26:15; 32:51), eternal (33:27), impartial (10:17–18), and just (32:4). He is fully distinct from his creation (7:21; 10:17) yet fully present and active in it (4:7; 6:15; 7:21; cf. 1:45; 31:17). With respect to his power (3:24; 32:39), he is the creator of humanity (4:32), the overseer of nations (32:8), the universal judge (9:4; 18:12; 32:41, 43), and the sole controller of all things in heaven and on earth (4:39; 10:14; cf. Heb. 1:3). "See now that I, even I, am he, and there is no god beside me; I kill and I make alive; I wound and I heal; and there is none that can deliver out of my hand" (Deut. 32:39).

Yahweh alone is Israel's "father" (32:6)—their redeemer (4:20; 4:34; etc.), covenant maker (29:1), warrior (1:30; 3:22), protector (33:26–29), guide (1:33; 8:2; 32:12), instructor (1:3; 4:2; 6:1–2), prayer answerer (4:7; 9:19; 10:10), provider (2:7; 8:16–18), disciplinarian (8:3, 5; 11:2), tester (13:3), judge (1:17; 5:9; 7:10), restorer (4:40–31; 30:1–10; 32:34), and savior (4:31; 33:29). Because he is God, he is jealous for his people's love (4:24; 5:9; 32:16, 21) and deserves their life-encompassing, community-embracing, exclusive commitment (6:4–5). Because he is God and is by nature both good and just (32:4), he must hate and punish sin (7:4; 8:19–20; 9:8, 19, 20, 22; 29:20; 31:17). He must detest all influences that subvert his rule and all satisfactions that do not ultimately result in humility, gratitude, and praise (7:25–26; 12:31; 32:16). God's people must tenaciously battle against all forms of idolatry (5:7; 6:14), for the preeminent one from whom, through whom, and to whom all things exist demands respect (Rom. 11:36; Col. 1:16).

> Moses would have agreed with Paul that God is the source, sustainer, and goal of all things (Rom. 11:36)!

Yet this respect is a natural response for those who have truly experienced the covenant initiating and sustaining grace of this amazing God. Consider his grace, believe his promises, walk in love, and find your heart satisfied in him. Moses declared such "good news" for those who would respond in faith, hope, and love! "There is none like God, O Jeshurun, who rides through the heavens to your help, through the skies in his majesty.... Happy are you, O Israel! Who is like you, a people saved by the LORD, the shield of your help, and the sword of your triumph! Your enemies shall come fawning to you, and you shall tread upon their backs" (Deut. 33:26, 29).

"Then Moses went up from the plains of Moab to Mount Nebo.... Moses the servant of the Lord died there" (Deut. 34:1, 5). *Mount Nebo summit from the northeast.*

Summary

Deuteronomy is all about pursuing a lasting covenant relationship with God. Moses treated the book as a *charter* (or constitution) for guiding life in relation to Yahweh. And within its pages he detailed the relationship's *context* (taking God and his Word seriously), *essence* (the centrality of love), *foundation* and *means of perpetuation* (grace), *purpose* (God-exalting influence), and *Lord* (Yahweh God).

KEY WORDS AND CONCEPTS FOR REVIEW

Constitution	Righteousness
The Book of the *tôrâ*	Contexts of sin
Fear	God's promises: blessings and curses
Faith	Heart circumcision
Obedience of faith	Grace
Covenant love	Israel's mission
Supreme command	Governing truth in Israel's worldview
Heart, soul, might	

KEY RESOURCES FOR FURTHER STUDY

Block, Daniel I. *Deuteronomy*. NIVAC. Grand Rapids: Zondervan, 2012.

Craige, Peter C. *The Book of Deuteronomy*. NICOT. Grand Rapids: Eerdmans, 1976.

McConville, J. Gordon *Deuteronomy*. AOTC. Downers Grove, IL: InterVarsity, 2002.

Wright, Christopher J. H. *Deuteronomy*. NIBCOT. Peabody, MA: Hendrickson, 1996.

THE OLD COVENANT ENFORCED: WHAT THE PROPHETS ARE REALLY ABOUT

Jason S. DeRouchie

Since the early stages of Genesis, readers have anticipated Israel's control of the Promised Land (Gen. 15:16; 17:8). Within this earthly realm Israelite kings would rule, and from it the promised royal deliverer would rise, overcoming evil and reestablishing global peace with God (17:6; 49:8, 10; Num. 24:17–19; Deut. 17:14–20). The Law concluded with Israel on the brink of entry, receiving a charge to go into the land on mission. They were to display the greatness of Yahweh by following his Word given through Moses and by overcoming all obstacles to radical God-centeredness (Deut. 4:5–8; 7:2). Yet the Lord had also declared that, following the prophet's death, "this people will rise and whore after the foreign gods among them in the land that they are entering, and they will forsake me and break my covenant that I have made with them" (31:16; cf. 2 Kings 17:13–15). Their covenant rebellion would result in their ruin, climaxing in their exile from the land!

The middle portion of Jesus' Bible details this sinful journey to destruction, giving direct stress to God's *enforcement of the Mosaic (old) covenant*. The Former Prophets provide a *narrative history* that clarifies God's perspective on *what* happened to Israel from their conquest of the Promised Land to their exile from it. The Latter Prophets then offer *prophetic commentary* that develops *why* Israel's story went the way it did.[1] Both units cast dark shadows over Israel's covenant history, portraying most of the nation as faithless and wayward. However, they also draw attention to

---

1. "Former" and "Latter" here refer not to time but to placement in the Old Testament. As one reads through the Bible, the "former" grouping comes first, the "latter" grouping second.

God's faithfulness and mercy, stressing a coming new covenant and affirming the consummation of the kingdom through a Judean royal redeemer, shown now to be in the line of David.

Joshua, Judges, Samuel, and Kings together describe the fourth stage in God's kingdom-building program. They survey the time of conquest and the downward spiritual spiral in the days of the judges through the

Figure P.1. God's Kingdom-Building Program Narrated in the Former Prophets			
	Preface introducing the biblical worldview: God and his purposes for people on this planet		Genesis 1:1–2:3
K	**KICKOFF AND REBELLION**	1. Creation, fall, and flood (ca. ? B.C.)	Genesis 2:4–11:9
I	**INSTRUMENT OF BLESSING**	2. Patriarchs (ca. 2100–1850 B.C.)	Genesis 11:10–50:26
N	**NATION REDEEMED AND COMMISSIONED**	3. Exodus, Sinai, and wilderness (ca. 1450–1400 B.C.)	Exodus–Deuteronomy
G	**GOVERNMENT IN THE PROMISED LAND**	4. Conquest and kingdoms (united and divided) (ca. 1400–600 B.C.)	Joshua–Kings
D	**DISPERSION AND RETURN**	5. Exile and initial restoration (ca. 600–400 B.C.)	Daniel–Chronicles
O	**OVERLAP OF THE AGES**	6. Christ's work and the church age (ca. 4 B.C.–A.D. ?)	Matthew–Acts
M	**MISSION ACCOMPLISHED**	7. Christ's return and kingdom consummation (ca. A.D. ?–eternity)	Revelation

united and divided kingdoms into the exile—a period of more than eight-hundred years (ca. 1406–586 B.C.).[2] These four books are often called the "Deuteronomistic History" because they evaluate all characters and events in light of Deuteronomy's covenant principles (Josh. 1:8; Judg. 3:4; 2 Kings 18:12; 21:8). Monarchs were judged in accordance with the rule of the king in Deuteronomy 17:14–20 (1 Sam. 10:25; 1 Kings 2:3; 2 Kings 23:25), and the blessings and curses detailed in Deuteronomy 27–28 guided the Lord's response to his people's covenant disloyalty (Judg. 2:15; 2 Kings 22:13). The new covenant vision of restoration in Deuteronomy 30 also stands behind the Davidic covenant hope laid out in 2 Samuel 7. In light of this close tie with the covenant, this section of narrative is justly called the *Former Prophets*.

With the conclusion of 1–2 Kings, Israel's narrative history pauses to allow for commentary, the first part of which comes in the *Latter Prophets*. According to the Jewish reckoning, this section is made up of four books: the three major (large) prophetic volumes of Jeremiah, Ezekiel, and Isaiah and the single collection of twelve minor (short) prophetic works called the Twelve (Hosea–Malachi). All four books are anthologies, substantially made up of prophetic sermons delivered mostly during the period of history addressed in 2 Kings.[3]

While the story of the Former Prophets includes many of Yahweh's prophets as characters, the Latter Prophets capture in full some of these prophets' extended messages. In these books, Yahweh's heavenly ambassadors speak God's words, enforcing his covenant with Israel and declaring judgment against the nations. The prophets charged Israel with Mosaic (old) covenant violation (indictment) (Jer. 9:13–14; Ezek. 22:26; Isa. 5:24), called them back to covenant faithfulness (instruction) (Amos 5:14–15; Mal. 4:4), warned them of the covenant curses (Jer. 44:23; Mal. 2:2), and promised the covenant restoration blessings for those who would learn from the divine discipline (Jer. 31:31–34; Isa. 19:24–25). In a world of sin, the prophets were gifts of God's grace, urging all who would listen to return to the only true Savior, Sovereign, and Satisfier.

Following the Law's concluding emphasis on Moses' unique and temporary prophetic role as covenant mediator (Deut. 34:9–12), the Prophets open and close with explicit stress on the central place of God's law given through

---

2. 586 B.C. is the year of Babylon's destruction of Jerusalem. Although 2 Kings 25 overviews this event, the chapter ends by recording how the exiled Judean King Jehoiachin was removed from prison and given a seat of honor in Babylon, an event that occurred around 561 B.C.
3. The clear exceptions are the books of Haggai, Zechariah, and Malachi, which contain explicit messages from the period of initial restoration after exile.

Moses. In Joshua 1:7–8, Yahweh called Moses' successor Joshua to be "careful to do according to all the law that Moses my servant commanded" and to "meditate on it day and night." Then in Malachi 4:4, Yahweh called his people to "remember the law of my servant Moses" (Mal. 4:4). Until the "prophet like Moses" would arise and establish a new covenant (Deut. 34:10; cf. 18:15, 18; Luke 7:16; John 1:21, 25, 45; Acts 3:22–26; 7:37), Israel's foundation for understanding God and his purposes would be Moses' words in the Pentateuch. The old (Mosaic) covenant, therefore, is the lens through which to read the Prophets.[4] Figure P.2 overviews the flow of thought in the Prophets, and Figure P.3. synthesizes through images the single stage in God's kingdom-building program narrated here.

Figure P.2. The Prophets at a Glance	
THE PROPHETS: The Old Covenant ENFORCED **(Yahweh as Sovereign)**	
FORMER (Narrative)	
Joshua	Yahweh's Covenant Faithfulness and the Call for Israel's Covenant Faithfulness
Judges	Israel's Covenant Faithlessness and the Need for God's Kingship
1–2 Samuel	The Importance of Honoring Yahweh and the Davidic Kingdom Hope
1–2 Kings	Covenant Failure, Kingdom Destruction, and the Hope of Kingdom Restoration
LATTER (Commentary)	
Jeremiah	Israel's Lack of Covenant Loyalty and the Eschatological Promise of Covenant Loyalty
Ezekiel	Israel's Loss of God's Presence and the Eschatological Promise of His Spirit
Isaiah	Israel's Rejection of God's Kingship and the Eschatological Promise of His Universal Kingdom
The Twelve	Israel's Spiritual Unfaithfulness and the Eschatological Promise of Divine Faithfulness

---

4. Only in Joshua 1:2, 7 and Malachi 4:4 is the mediator of the old covenant ever called "Moses *my* servant." This link along with the similar call to heed the law suggests that the book of Malachi was intentionally placed as the conclusion of the Prophets. Further support for this conclusion is found in the fact that, just as the end of the Law anticipated the coming of the "prophet like Moses" (and with him the new covenant) (Deut. 34:10), Malachi 4:5–6 predicted the coming of a new "Elijah the prophet," who would help restore the community of God. Of all Old Testament prophets after Moses, Elijah is portrayed in Kings as the chief covenant enforcer, whose ministry pointed to and substantiated the ministry of the original Moses. Malachi's ending, therefore, suggests that a "prophet like Elijah" would accompany, support, and legitimate the ministry of the "prophet like Moses"—a fact played out in the lives of John the Baptist and Jesus (see Matt. 11:11–14; 17:19–13). In conclusion, it is noteworthy that the links between the end of the Law and the end of the Prophets on the one hand and the beginning and ending of the Prophets on the other imply that Malachi himself may have arranged the Latter Prophets and the Twelve within it, thus securing that his final appeal be seen as an echo of the opening scene of Joshua and in parallel with the end of Deuteronomy.

Figure P.3. God's K-I-N-G-D-O-M Story Through Images

KEY RESOURCES FOR FURTHER STUDY

Former Prophets

Hamilton, Victor P. *Handbook on the Historical Books*. Grand Rapids: Baker, 2001.

Howard, David M., Jr. *An Introduction to the Old Testament Historical Books*. Chicago: Moody, 1993.

Satterthwaite, Philip E., and J. Gordon McConville. *Exploring the Old Testament*, vol. 2: *A Guide to the Historical Books*. Downers Grove, IL: InterVarsity, 2005.

Latter Prophets

J. Daniel Hays, *The Message of the Prophets: A Survey of the Prophetic and Apocalyptic Books of the Old Testament*. Grand Rapids: Zondervan, 2010.

McConville, J. Gordon. *Exploring the Old Testament*, vol. 4: *A Guide to the Prophets*. Downers Grove, IL: InterVarsity, 2003.

Smith, Gary V. *The Prophets as Preachers: An Introduction to the Hebrew Prophets*. Nashville: B&H, 1998.

VanGemeren, Willem. *Interpreting the Prophetic Word: An Introduction to the Prophetic Literature of the Old Testament*. Grand Rapids: Zondervan, 1990.

"Thus says the Lord: 'The people who survived the sword found grace in the wilderness; when Israel sought for rest, the Lord appeared to him from far away. I have loved you with an everlasting love; therefore I have continued my faithfulness to you'" (Jer. 31:2–3). *An aerial from the east of the mountains south of Wadi Farah in the hill country east of Shiloh and northwest of Jericho that Joshua allotted to the tribes of Ephraim and Manasseh.*

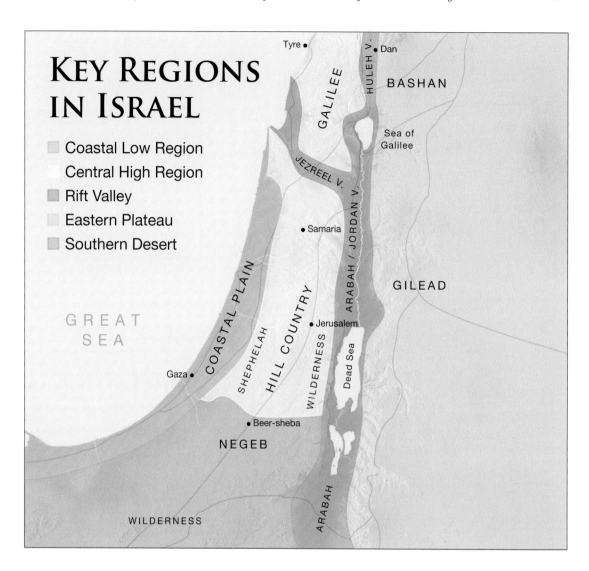

KEY REGIONS IN ISRAEL

- Coastal Low Region
- Central High Region
- Rift Valley
- Eastern Plateau
- Southern Desert

Tyre

Dan

HULEH V.

GALILEE

BASHAN

Sea of Galilee

JEZREEL V.

Samaria

COASTAL PLAIN

SHEPHELAH

HILL COUNTRY

WILDERNESS

ARABAH / JORDAN V.

GILEAD

GREAT SEA

Gaza

Jerusalem

Dead Sea

Beer-sheba

NEGEB

ARABAH

WILDERNESS

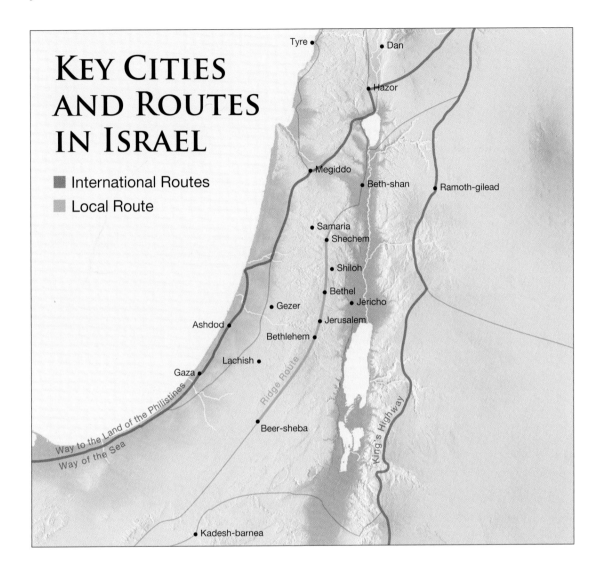

KEY CITIES AND ROUTES IN ISRAEL

■ International Routes
■ Local Route

Tyre • ● Dan

● Hazor

● Megiddo
  ● Beth-shan   ● Ramoth-gilead

● Samaria
  ● Shechem

● Shiloh

● Bethel
  ● Jericho
● Jerusalem

● Gezer

Ashdod ●
  Bethlehem ●

Lachish ●

Gaza ●

Way to the Land of the Philistines
Way of the Sea

Ridge Route

King's Highway

Beer-sheba ●

● Kadesh-barnea

JOSHUA

Who?

Statements about Joshua's writing (Josh. 8:32; 24:26) and of his instructing others to write (18:8) show that Joshua had at least some part in compiling the book that bears his name. Using "we" and "us" (2:17–20, etc.) further supports authorship by an eyewitness. However, the frequent use of "to this day" (4:9; 7:26, etc.) indicates that an undetermined amount of time passed from the events until the completion of the text. The account of Joshua's death (24:28–32) clearly points to a later author, as does the reference to the later Book of Jashar (10:13), dated no earlier than David (see 2 Sam. 1:18). Other statements seem to suggest a time of writing during the early monarchy—the presence of Canaanites in Gezer (Josh. 16:10) seems to predate Solomon (1 Kings 9:16), whereas the dwelling of Judahites in Jebus (Josh. 15:63) suggests a time after David's conquest (2 Sam. 5:6–16). Perhaps Joshua began the book, and someone in the time of David or Solomon finished it. The author(s) apparently wrote for the Israelites after the conquest and/or during the early monarchy.

When?

The Israelites' conquest of Canaan began forty years after the exodus. First Kings 6:1 seems to date the exodus at 1446 B.C., with the conquest beginning about 1406 (cf. Judg. 11:26). By contrast, some believe certain archaeological evidence (e.g., the destruction of certain cities and the sudden appearance of hundreds of new villages) fits better with a date of conquest approximately 150 years later. More information is needed to reconcile these perspectives.

Where?

The conquest of Canaan carried the combatants through most of the land. They began east of the Jordan River opposite the city of Jericho in east-central Canaan. Israel's army crossed the river to Jericho and then ascended into the central highlands for the battles at Ai and Gibeon. The army then swept south through the southern hills and lowlands, and finally they moved to northern Canaan for a decisive victory over a coalition there.

Why?

The author(s) wrote to give an interpretive account of the conquest, as well as to demonstrate God's character and actions and his people's needed response. God is faithful to his Word, and his people must be faithful to it as well! The book details how the faithful, sovereign, and holy God gave to Israel their promised homeland. It also stresses that the Israelites' subsequent fortunes in the land depended on their unity and their covenantal loyalty to God. Today believers are not promised land like the Israelites of Joshua's time, but we are promised other benefits because of our relationship to God, and we must demonstrate obedience and faith to him as well.

Boyd Seevers

Carefully Crafted Verses from Joshua

There has been no day like it before or since, when the LORD heeded the voice of a man, for the LORD fought for Israel (Josh. 10:14).

Thus the LORD gave to Israel all that he swore to give to their fathers.... Not one of all their enemies had withstood them, for the LORD had given all their enemies into their hands. Not one word of all the good promises that the LORD had made to the house of Israel had failed; all came to pass (Josh. 21:43–45).

"Choose this day whom you will serve.... But as for me and my house, we will serve the LORD" (Josh. 24:15).

THE AUTHOR OF JOSHUA ...

- Clarified *God's perspective on Israel's conquest* of Canaan.

- Emphasized *the character of Israel's God* in light of the conquest.

- Stressed *the need to know and heed God's expectations* for his people.

- Defined *Israel's relationship to the Promised Land*.

The Author of Joshua Clarified *God's Perspective on Israel's Conquest* of Canaan

Covering Israel's conquest and division of Canaan, the book of Joshua portrays God's perspective on these central events that ultimately gave birth to the kingdom of Israel. Picking up directly after the death of Moses (Josh. 1:1; cf. Deut. 34:5), the account seamlessly continues the national

give Israel the land (Deut. 1:8; 6:10), and the book of Joshua stresses God's fulfillment of his word. God remained trustworthy, and the conquest proved this fact—"Not one word of all the good promises that the LORD had made to the house of Israel had failed; all came to pass" (Josh. 21:45; cf. 1:3–6). The end of the book stresses God's faithfulness by recording that Joseph's bones were buried in the Promised Land in direct fulfillment of the hope-filled dying request of the patriarch some four-hundred years before (24:32; cf. Gen. 50:25)! God always accomplishes what he says he will do!

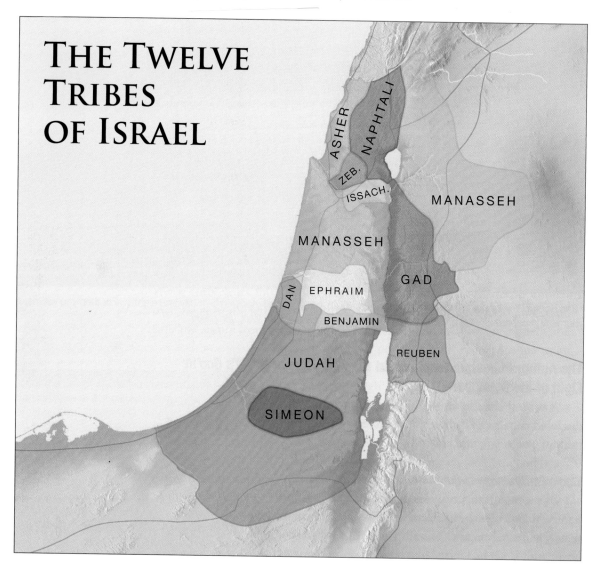

THE TWELVE TRIBES OF ISRAEL

God's Sovereignty over Nature and Nations

The Israelites' faithful God was able to give Israel the land of Canaan because he owns the whole earth (Exod. 19:5; Ps. 24:1) and exercises control over the world and its processes. Israel entered Canaan only after God blocked the Jordan River at flood stage (Josh. 3:15–17). Israel defeated the enemy coalition at Gibeon because God sent hail and then halted the sun (10:11–14). They continued their victories, in part, because God drove out their enemies with hornets (24:12). Israel's sovereign God controlled both nature and nations, and he alone determined who would dwell in Canaan. As anticipated more than a generation earlier (see Exod. 15:15–16), testimonies of Yahweh's victories over Egypt and the eastern kings had made their way to Canaan, and all the peoples feared Israel's God (Josh. 2:9–11; 5:1; 6:1; 9:24). The giants who had caused Israel to tremble forty years earlier (Num. 13:31–33; cf. Deut. 1:28; 9:2) were easily defeated (Josh. 11:21–23). God hardened the hearts of the local inhabitants so they would resist and face defeat, surrendering their land to his people (10:12; 11:20; 24:11). Even the Canaanite Rahab understood a fact of which we must continually remind ourselves: "the Lord your God … is God in heaven above and on the earth beneath" (2:11; cf. Heb. 11:31).

The Lord said to Joshua, "On the seventh day you shall march around the city [of Jericho] seven times…. Then all the people shall shout with a great shout, and the wall of the city will fall down flat" (Josh. 6:4–5). *Left: a close-up of Jericho; Right: an aerial from the east of Jericho and cliffs in the direction of Ai.*

God's Holiness and Its Demands

This sovereign God was also holy, as demonstrated by his expectations for people. To the Canaanites, God demonstrated his holiness in judgment. Their sin had apparently reached full measure (see Gen. 15:16; Deut. 9:5), and through Israel he took their lives and land as a consequence. God's expectations and accountability related to the Israelites as well: "Only be strong and very courageous, being careful to do according to all the law that Moses my servant commanded you ... that you may have good success wherever you go" (Josh. 1:7). Even standing in God's holy presence demanded a humble response (5:15). When the Israelites did not meet God's standard (7:1), he punished them with defeat and death, both individually and corporately (7:11–26). When they did meet his standard, he gave them victory after victory.

God the Warrior on Behalf of His Faithful People

God was Israel's warrior, and so long as his promise "I will be with you" remained true, so too would the promise "No man shall be able to stand before you all the days of your life" (1:5). Just as God had done against Egypt at the Red Sea (Exod. 15) and against Sihon and Og in the Transjordan (Num. 21:23–26, 33–35), so also Yahweh led Israel into Canaan ready to give victory to his people if they would be faithful to him.

> The same faithful, sovereign, holy God who helped Israel in Joshua's day is no less willing and able to meet his people's needs today, whatever they may be.

Fortunately, Achan's theft and deception at Jericho was not the norm for the Israelites during the initial conquest. We are told that "Israel served the Lord all the days of Joshua, and all the days of the elders who outlived Joshua and had known all the work that Lord did for Israel" (Josh. 24:31). And because they usually met God's standard of dependence, Israel benefited from his help (1:7–9).

God fought as a warrior to give Israel victory over a superior foe. Only such divine aid could explain the victory at Jericho, given the divinely directed but highly unusual strategy (ch. 6). God again gave specific instructions that led to the victory at Ai (8:1–2, 18–19). Only God's supernatural help enabled Israel to defeat a coalition of armies at Gibeon (10:11–14). His continued aid also helped in the successful campaign in southern Canaan (10:29–43). Israel succeeded because "the Lord fought for Israel" (10:14; cf. Acts 7:45)!

The Author of Joshua Stressed *the Need to Know and Heed God's Expectations for His People*

The author of Joshua wrote about the conquest of Canaan not only to record the past but also to teach his audience what they needed to do in the future to build on their earlier successes. Clearly the author wanted Israel to act as a united whole, and above all, to obey God's commands.

"Joshua spoke to the LORD ..., 'Sun, stand still at Gibeon, and moon, in the Valley of Aijalon.' And the sun stood still, and the moon stopped, until the nation took vengeance on their enemies" (Josh. 10:12–13). *An aerial of Gibeon (top) and Nebi Samwil (bottom) from the south.*

Israel's Need for Unity

The accounts in Joshua show that Israel succeeded when they acted in unison but failed when they were divided. After the conquest, two and a half tribes would live east of the Jordan, but they still remained a part of the whole nation. Joshua made sure they helped the other tribes with the conquest (Josh. 1:12–15), and afterward the nation narrowly avoided civil war when the two groups appeared to have different loyalties (22:9–34). During the conquest they lost one battle waged by only part of the army (7:3–5) but later won when the "whole army" took part (8:1, 3). Unity was essential for Israel.

Israel's Need for Obedience

Israel needed unity to win, but most of all, their success depended on their obedience to God (1:7–8). In one sense, God's promise to give the Israelites the land was unconditional (Deut. 1:8; 6:10). But in another sense, their ability to enter, maintain control, and enjoy it to the fullest depended on their obedience (Deut. 4:1). When Israel failed to obey God's instruction or to ask his direction, they lost a battle and a city (Josh. 7:1; 9:14–15). Most of the book, however, records Israel's successes, for during this time they generally did heed God's commands, regardless of how difficult or strange the orders appeared. They obeyed instructions to cross a swollen river even though they lacked the means to carry it out (ch. 3). The men obediently circumcised themselves at Gilgal, which exposed them to danger in enemy territory (5:2–9; see Gen. 34:24–29). They followed God's strategy at Jericho even though parading themselves before the enemy defied good military tactics, and their strategy for penetrating the city's walls included only trumpets and voices. Then they destroyed the entire city with its goods regardless of how badly they may have wanted or needed the spoils (Josh. 6:24; cf. Heb. 11:30). The Israelites obediently killed the enemy (Josh. 10:40) and destroyed their military resources (11:6, 9) as commanded by God. God-exalting, humble obedience by the people and

> Regardless of when or where you live or what you are trying to accomplish for God, the sovereign Lord calls his people to only one lifestyle: trust and obey, regardless of how challenging or odd his commands may appear.

"Joshua … captured Hazor and struck its king with the sword, for Hazor formerly was the head of all those kingdoms [in northern Canaan].… And he burned Hazor with fire" (Josh. 11:10–11). *Left: in the foreground, a four-room house at Hazor from the period of the judges and Israelite kingdoms; Right: a reconstruction of an Israelite four-room house at Eretz Israel Museum.*

their leader ensured success (11:15–16): "Joshua … left nothing undone of all that the LORD had commanded…. So Joshua took all that land."

The Author of Joshua Defined *Israel's Relationship to the Promised Land*

The Promised Land is a central motif in the book of Joshua. The author not only explained how God delivered the land of Canaan to the Israelites but also showed what they must do to take full advantage of this blessing. First, the author went into great detail clarifying which regions and cities belonged to each tribe (Josh. 13–21), both to stress God's great faithfulness to his word (21:43–45) and perhaps to alleviate the potential for future misunderstandings. He then emphasized how Israel could finish conquering their inheritance and afterward hold onto it. Simply put, Israel needed to obey God and stay faithful to the covenant he had made with them at Mount Sinai. Joshua warned (23:6–8): "Be very strong to keep and to do all that is written in the Book of the Law of Moses … that you may not mix with these nations remaining among you … or bow down to [their gods], but you shall cling to the LORD your God just as you have done to this day." Joshua likewise warned that if Israel violated the covenant, "the anger of the LORD will be kindled against you, and you shall perish quickly from off the good land that he has given you" (23:16).

"And the west boundary [of Judah] was the Great Sea with its coastline" (Josh. 15:12). *View northward along the Mediterranean Sea coastline on the beach of Ashkelon, one of three Philistine coastal cities designated to Judah (Josh. 13:3; Judg. 1:18).*

Figure 7.2. Old Testament Yahweh Wars of Judgment

Deut. 7:9–10. Know therefore that the LORD your God is God, the faithful God who keeps covenant and steadfast love with those who love him and keep his commandments, to a thousand generations, and repays to their face those who hate him, by destroying them. He will not be slack with one who hates him. He will repay him to his face.

General

1. Yahweh does the fighting and alone gives victory—thus Yahweh's wars are often called "holy" wars (Exod. 14:14; Deut. 1:30; 20:4; Josh. 23:3; Neh. 4:20; cf. Deut. 1:42; Josh. 1:9; chs. 7–8; Prov. 127:1b).

2. War is a religious undertaking, thus requiring various forms of self-denial and sacrifice (Exod. 19:15; Deut. 23:9–14; Josh. 5:1–15; 1 Sam. 13:1–15; 21:4–5; cf. 2 Sam. 11:1–13; 1 Cor. 7:5).

3. All precious metals won in battle belong to Yahweh; pagan shrines are destroyed (Num. 18:14; Deut. 7:5, 25–26; Josh. 6:19, 24).

4. Violators become the enemy (Num. 33:55–56; Deut. 8:19–20; cf. 7:4; 13:12–18; Josh. 7:11–12, 19–26).

	Judgment Wars of Annihilation	Judgment Wars of Defense and Subjugation
Nature	5. Yahweh's aggressive wars of retributive judgment against sustained wickedness and rebellion—nothing to do with racism, nationalism, or prejudice; enemies of war are Yahweh's enemies, having worshipped other gods and having shown progressive and persistent hostility against Yahweh and his people (Deut. 7:9–10; 9:5–6).	5. Yahweh's responsive wars of retributive judgment against aggressive hostility toward God and his people; enemies of war are Yahweh's enemies, having stood against Yahweh by refusing terms of peace and/or by assertively bringing war against Israel (Deut. 20:1, 10–15).
Purpose	6. (a) To root out wickedness by punishing sin (Deut. 7:9–10; 9:5–6; 1 Sam. 15:3, 18; cf. Gen. 15:16; Rom. 6:23); (b) to cleanse the land from defilement (Lev. 18:24–30; Isa. 24:4–6); (c) to protect God's people from apostasy and ultimate destruction (Exod. 23:33; Num. 33:35–36; Deut. 7:3–4, 25; 8:19–20; 20:16–18); (d) to display the greatness of God and his people (Exod. 15:11–18;	6. (a) To halt aggressive hostility against Yahweh and his people and (b) to display the seriousness of refusing Yahweh's terms of peace (Deut. 20:12–13).

Limits	7. Yahweh alone initiates judgment wars of annihilation and specifies the opponents; where God uses human agency, as in the conquest of the Promised Land, war is only at his direction through a recognized prophet (Gen. 15:16; Exod. 23:23–33; Num. 13:1–2; 33:50–56; Deut. 2:19, 24, 37; 7:1–5, 16–26; 20:1–18; 24:17–19; Josh. 1:1–5; 9:14–15; 1 Sam. 23:1–5; cf. Isa. 53:10; Acts 2:23; 4:27–28).	7. The borders of Israel's Promised Land, within which all the tribal allotments fell (Gen. 17:8; Num. 34:1–12; Deut. 34:1–4; Josh. 13–21), and the borders of Israel's promised kingdom (Gen. 15:18–21; Exod. 23:31; Deut. 1:7; 11:24; Josh. 1:4; cf. 1 Kgs. 4:21–24) were not coterminous. Assuming all enemies within the Promised Land were destroyed (see judgment wars of annihilation), judgment wars of defense began when an enemy outside Israel's tribal borders aggressively encroached into the Promised Land; judgment wars of subjugation began when a nation outside the Promised Land but within the political sphere of sovereignty promised to Israel refused to surrender to Yahweh's terms of peace and thus become Israel's vassal (Deut. 20:11).
Army	8. All able-bodied men over twenty participate (Num. 26:2; cf. 32:6, 16–17, 26–27; Josh. 1:14).	8. While participation in judgment wars of defense and subjugation appears to have been a "public duty," new home owners, new business owners, and newly married men were excused from war (Deut. 20:5–8; 24:5; cf. Judg. 7:2–3; 1 Sam. 8:11–12).
End	9. Battle concluded when the entire enemy population is annihilated, including men, women, and children (Deut. 7:2, 16; 20:16; 25:19; cf. Deut. 2:34; 3:6; Josh. 6:21; 8:2, 26; 10:40; 11:14; 1 Sam. 15:3).	9. Battle concluded when enemy aggression ceases and all armed enemy warriors are destroyed (Deut. 20:13).
Spoils	10. Once 3 and 9 are met, God's people may enjoy all other spoils of war (Deut. 2:34–35; 3:6–7; Josh. 8:2, 27; 11:14).	10. Once 3 and 9 are met, all other spoils of war, including women, children, and animals, may be incorporated into Israel's community (Deut. 20:14).
Examples	Flood (Gen. 6:5–7, 11–13); incineration of Sodom and Gomorrah (Gen. 18:20–21; 19:24–25; Jude 7); conquest of Canaan (Gen. 15:16; Deut. 7:25–26; 9:5–6; 20:16–18); destruction of the Amalekites (Exod. 17:14; Deut. 25:17–19; 1 Sam. 15:3, 18).	Plagues and destruction of Egypt after Pharaoh's refusal to let Israel go (Exod. 7–15); Deborah and Barak's defeat of Sisera (Judg. 4–5); Israel's battles against the Philistines, including David's defeat of Goliath (1 Sam. 4, 13:1–6, 14, 17, etc.); David's numerous victories over the border countries, resulting in "rest from all his surrounding enemies" (2 Sam. 7:1; 8:1–14; cf. 1 Kings. 4:21–24); God's overpowering of Sennacherib in the days of Hezekiah (2 Kings. 19:32–37); perhaps the deaths of Ananias and Sapphira (Acts 5:1–11) and Herod Agrippa I (12:23).

Cross of Christ (Isa. 53:4–9; Rom. 3:25; 4:24–25; 2 Cor. 5:21; 1 Peter 2:22–25; 1 John 4:10); Final judgment day of Yahweh (Joel 2:11; Amos 5:18–20; 1 Thess. 5:2–3; 2 Thess. 1:5–10).

Prepared by Jason S. DeRouchie.

For modern believers, our relationship with God has similarities and differences compared with that of the Israelites in Joshua's day, including how we relate to the Promised Land. Like the ancient Israelites, we are also called into fellowship with God, but under a different covenant.

> Simple obedience flowing from faith is still the key to properly relate to God in the new covenant. "This is the love of God, that we keep his commandments.... And this is the victory that has overcome the world—our faith" (1 John 5:3–4).

Under the Mosaic covenant, God committed to give Israel the land, and they enjoyed and controlled it according to their obedience. In our day, the new covenant neither promises us a share in that land nor is restricted to ethnic Israelites. Our covenant includes Gentiles (Isa. 56:3–7; 66:18–23), who also share in God's blessings by entering his non-physical, spiritual kingdom (Col. 1:13–14) through adoption as God's children (Rom. 8:14–25). Though we are also promised the earth in some fashion (Matt. 5:5; Rom. 4:13; cf. Ps. 37:3–11), our ultimate inheritance is kept in heaven (1 Peter 1:3–5) and will climax with eternal fellowship with the triune God in the new heavens and new earth (Rev. 21:1–7). For now, obedient believers can enjoy God's rest (Heb. 4:1–11) as well as loving fellowship in a new community of believers (John 13:34–35), and ultimately we will enjoy dwelling with God face to face in the new Jerusalem (Rev. 21–22).

"Not one word of all the good promises that the Lord had made to the house of Israel had failed; all came to pass" (Josh. 21:45). *Men on donkeys on the Ascent of Adummim between Jericho and Jerusalem on the border of Judah and Benjamin (Josh. 15:7; 18:17).*

Conclusion

The book of Joshua ends by saying, "Israel served the Lord all the days of Joshua, and all the day of the elders who outlived Joshua and had known all the work that the Lord did for Israel" (Josh. 24:31). The conclusion is silent, however, as to whether Israel would continue following God. As we turn the page into the book of Judges, this question looms as a dark cloud bringing a storm. Joshua's own charge clarifies the book's final call (24:15): "Choose this day whom you will serve…. But as for me and my house, we will serve the Lord."

KEY WORDS AND CONCEPTS FOR REVIEW

To this day	Holy
Conquest	Warrior
Canaan	Wars of judgment
Faithful	Unity
Covenant	Obedience
Sovereign	Promised Land

KEY RESOURCES FOR FURTHER STUDY

Davis, Dale Ralph. *Joshua*. Fearn, Scotland: Christian Focus, 2005.
Hess, Richard S. *Joshua*. TOTC. Downers Grove, IL: InterVarsity, 2008.
Howard, David M., Jr. *Joshua*. NAC. Nashville: B&H, 1998.
Hubbard, Robert L., Jr. *Joshua*. NIVAC. Grand Rapids: Zondervan, 2009.

JUDGES

Who?

The book of Judges is an anonymous composition with no references to its authorship. There are, however, both early (Judg. 1:21, 29) and late elements (21:25)—facts that suggest a later editor used some early source material in the book's final composition.

In contrast to what the English word implies, the "judges" of this book did not normally hold court or make legal decisions. Processes and people (elders or family heads) were in place to handle civil questions, and priests taught and ruled in religious matters. The judges in this period were deliverers raised up by Yahweh to lead Israel militarily and to govern them.

When?

The events of the book happened from the death of Joshua until the rise of Samuel. There is no scholarly consensus on when the book was written. Some internal evidence appears to point to an early date before David (1:21, 29), whereas some editorial comments no doubt come from the period of the divided monarchy (18:30). As such, a definitive date of origin is lacking.

Where?

Because the book is focused upon the settlement of the land, the events of the book occurred within the borders of Israel's Promised Land, except for the occasion when a judge would press the battle against a neighboring people group (3:30; 8:10; 11:32–33; 16:23).

Why?

The book of Judges provided Israel with a theological interpretation of their history from the death of Joshua to the time of Samuel. The author of Judges:

1. Recorded how sin compromised Israel's national identity and mission;
2. Traced how Israel's covenant disloyalty forfeited blessings and brought curses;
3. Described the moral failure of the judges and the need for a virtuous king;
4. Highlighted the covenant faithfulness of Yahweh in providing for Israel's need.

JUDGES

Chris A. Miller

Carefully Crafted Verses from Judges

And all that generation also were gathered to their fathers. And there arose another generation after them who did not know the LORD or the work that he had done for Israel. And the people of Israel did what was evil in the sight of the LORD and served the Baals (Judg. 2:10–11).

So the people of Israel lived among the Canaanites, the Hittites, the Amorites, the Perizzites, the Hivites, and the Jebusites. And their daughters they took to themselves for wives, and their own daughters they gave to their sons, and they served their gods (Judg. 3:5–6).

In those days there was no king in Israel. Everyone did what was right in his own eyes (Judg. 21:25).

> ## THE AUTHOR OF JUDGES ...
>
> - Recorded how *sin compromised Israel's national identity and mission.*
>
> - Traced how Israel's *covenant disloyalty forfeited blessings and brought curses.*
>
> - Described *the moral failure of the judges and the need for a virtuous king.*
>
> - Highlighted *the covenant faithfulness of Yahweh* in providing for Israel's need.

The Author of Judges Recorded How *Sin Compromised Israel's National Identity and Mission*

Just before Joshua died, he warned the people three times to get rid of their foreign gods in order to properly serve Yahweh (Josh. 24:14–24). Three times the people responded that they would indeed serve Yahweh, but, conspicuously, they never agreed to give up their idolatry. Their silence in the matter was deafening, and the story of Judges displayed Joshua's insight into the tendencies of his people. Instead of destroying the pagan culture of Canaan, they absorbed it and became just like the nations around them, losing their unique identity as the people of God.

"Manasseh did not drive out the inhabitants of Beth-shean and its villages…, for the Canaanites persisted in dwelling in that land" (Judg. 1:27). *Excavations at Beth-shean of a Canaanite temple from the time of the Israelite conquest.*

The book of Judges opens with the settlement of the land appearing to go well, as Judah took the lead and began to dispossess the land's inhabitants (Judg. 1:3–18). However, the tone quickly turns ominous, for Judah failed to fully conquer the Philistines, and the other tribes failed to dislodge the Canaanites within their territories (1:19–36). With a brilliant rhetorical device, the author contrasted the Israelite excuse for this failure ("because they had chariots of iron," 1:19) with the Lord's judgment on their disobedience (2:1–5). Ultimately, the problem was Israel's lack of faith and not the power of their opposition.

This initial failure led to even more failure and a definable downward cycle into pagan behaviors. The cycle can be described as (1) Israel turned to the idolatry of the Canaanites, (2) Yahweh disciplined them by giving them into the hands of their enemies, (3) the people cried out to Yahweh, and (4) Yahweh faithfully raised up judges to deliver them (2:11–16). This cycle occurs at least six times in the book (3:7, 12; 4:1; 6:1; 10:6; 13:1), but, sadly, it was more than just a two-dimensional reality. At the end of each cycle, the people "turned back and were *more corrupt* than their fathers" (2:19), so that a downward spiral more accurately describes the tragic course of the nation and the book.

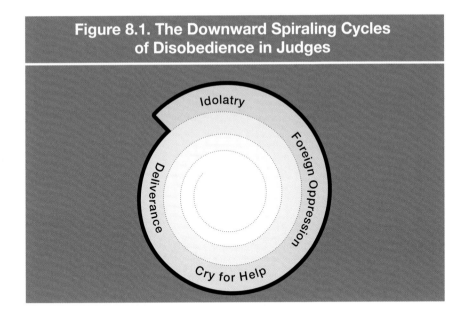

Figure 8.1. The Downward Spiraling Cycles of Disobedience in Judges

Idolatry

Foreign Oppression

Cry for Help

Deliverance

This downward trajectory became clear through the lenses of their *idolatry* and their *morality*. First, the people began to *worship the gods* of the Canaanites. The author stated this initially in a general way (3:6) and then offered concrete examples in the rest of the book. For example, in a particularly ironic scene during Jepthah's rule, Yahweh counseled Israel sarcastically, "Go and cry out to the gods whom you have chosen; let them save you in the time of your distress" (10:14). Perhaps the most revealing statement comes from the mouth of Micah, who, when his idols were stolen, cried out: "You take the gods that I made ... and go away, and what have I left?" (18:24). The attentive reader wants to shout, "You have the God of Abraham, Isaac, and Jacob!" However, we also know that Micah was so spiritually deaf that he could not hear.

> When the people of God consciously or unconsciously adopt the values of their unredeemed neighbors, their witness loses all credibility and power.

Figure 8.2. Judges at a Glance

Introductory Failure (1:1–3:6)	The Judges (3:7–16:31)						Concluding Failure (17:1–21:25)
	Othniel	Ehud	Deborah	Gideon	Jepthah	Samson	
	3:7–11	3:12–20	4:1–5:31	6:1–10:5	10:6–12:15	13:1–16:31	

"I said, '... you shall break down their altars.' But you have not obeyed my voice" (Judg. 2:1). *A pagan sacrificial altar in Megiddo from the period following the flood and just before Abraham.*

Figure 8.3. The Attractions of Idolatry

1. **Guaranteed** (Physical and visible)	**Do you ever pray and feel that God is not there?** An idol was a visible, tangible, physical representation that was considered to transmit the presence of a deity.
2. **Selfish and Works-Oriented** (Materialism; legalism)	**Are you ever prone toward self-righteousness or tempted with materialism?** Through "feeding" offerings to an idol/god, people believed they obligated the god to multiply their crops, fertility, cattle, etc.; therefore, "worship" was driven by the pursuit of earthly profit or pleasure, and blessing was considered a wage earned (Hos. 2:12; 9:1; Mic. 1:7; Rom. 4:4; Eph. 5:5; Col. 3:5).
3. **Easy** (Ethical relativity; no covenant obligations)	**Do you ever find it easier to please men rather than God or to love yourself over others?** Idolatry called for frequent and generous outward sacrifices with no covenantal, heart-generated, ethical obligations to the gods or neighbors.
4. **Convenient** (Anywhere; anytime)	**Do you ever find that following God gets in the way of your own agenda?** While the expectation for frequent and generous offerings were expected, such "worship" of idols could be performed whenever and wherever one so chose—"on every hill and under every green tree" (1 Kings 14:23; 2 Kings 17:10; cf. Deut. 12:2).
5. **Normal** (Everybody's doing it)	**Are you ever prone to follow the crowd, even when you know the majority is wrong?** Idolatry was the way of life in the ancient world and stood in direct contrast to Israel's minority view that there was a single God over all, who redeemed a people for relationship (Deut. 4:32–40). Three features characterized most ancient idolatry: 1. polytheism (believing in or worship of more than one god) (2 Kings 17:16); 2. syncretism (the [inconsistent] amalgamation of different religions/worldviews) (2 Kings 17:33); 3. pantheism (the belief that God and the universe are somehow one or that nature is a manifestation of the divine) (Jer. 8:2).
6. **Logical** (Specialization system)	**When you are sick, would you rather see a specialist or a general practitioner?** Ancient people believed in three categories of gods: personal, family, and national. Yahweh was Israel's national god, but many paid homage to other deities in family or personal worship. National gods were considered to govern specific geographical regions (see 1 Kings 20:23, 28; 2 Kings 5:15, 17; Jon. 1:3). And all "gods" were considered specialists in some aspect of world or nature, controlling life, death, light, evil, water, etc. (e.g., Baal of Canaan, the young weather god; Ashtoreth his consort, the mother goddess of love and fertility; Chemosh of Moab, the god of war; and Dagon of Philistia, the god of grain [Judg. 2:11, 13; 11:24; 16:23]). Such specialization made it logical for people to seek "expert" help rather than go to Yahweh, who had to manage all things.
7. **Sensuous** (If it feels good, do it)	**Do you ever turn away from God toward worldly pleasures?** Focused on what is earthly, idolatry was gratifying to the physical senses and fleshly desires. It could include bowing down and kissing idols (1 Kings 19:18); an array of visual images and smells (Ezek. 8:10–12); cutting of the body, loud cries, and weeping (1 Kings 18:28; Ezek. 8:14); heavy feasting, drinking, and drunkenness (Amos 2:8; Acts 15:20–21; 21:25; 1 Cor. 8:4–13); and "sacred sex." The latter included temple prostitution, wherein it was believed that engaging in symbolic intercourse on the temple compound would stimulate the gods to produce fertility on earth (1 Kings 14:24; 2 Kings 23:7; Jer. 5:7; Ezek. 23; Amos 2:7–8; Mic. 1:7; Job 36:14).

Prepared by Jason S. DeRouchie with some material adapted from Douglas K. Stuart, *Exodus* (NAC; Nashville: B&H Academic, 2006), 450–54.

Figure 8.4. The Six Judge Cycles

		Judge	Tribe of Origin	Enemy Opposition	Scripture
I	1.	Othniel	Judah	Mesopotamia	Judg. 3:7–11
	2.	Ehud	Benjamin	Moab	3:12–30
		Parenthesis 1: Governorship of Shamgar			3:31
	3.	Deborah and Barak	Ephraim	Canaan	4:1–5:31
II	4.	Gideon	Manasseh	Midian	6:1–9:57
		Parenthesis 2: Governorship of Tola and Jair			10:1–5
	5.	Jephthah	Gilead	Ammon	10:6–12:7
		Parenthesis 3: Governorship of Ibzan, Elon, and Abdon			12:8–15
	6.	Samson	Dan	Philistia	13:1–16:31

Prepared by Chris A. Miller and Jason S. DeRouchie.

"They went after other gods, from among the gods of the peoples who were around them, and bowed down to them. And they provoked the LORD to anger" (Judg. 2:12). *A bronze figurine of the Canaanite god, El, from the time of the Judges; found in Megiddo, one of the northern Canaanite cities that the tribe of Manasseh failed to conquer (Judg. 1:27) (from the Oriental Institute, USA).*

As the Israelites worshiped Canaanite gods, they also adopted their *morality*. When Jephthah made his vow involving the possibility of human sacrifice (11:30–31), he was giving in to pagan notions of appeasing the gods. Samson married outside the covenant community and was ultimately overcome by his immoral relationship with another Philistine woman (16:1–31). In the final saga of the book, the men of Benjamin defended members of their tribe who were so morally debased that the author of Judges painted their debauchery in colors borrowed from the palette of Sodom and Gomorrah (Gen. 19:1–11; Judg. 19:11–30).

By intermarrying with the Canaanites and worshiping their gods, Israel became just like those whom they were commanded to dispossess. Thus they lost their national identity and failed in their mission to live as the people of Yahweh in the land.

The Author of Judges Traced How Israel's *Covenant Disloyalty Forfeited Blessings and Brought Curses*

Deuteronomy clearly taught that obedience to the covenant drew one closer to Yahweh and resulted in fullness of life (Deut. 28:1–15), while disobedience moved one in the opposite direction (28:16–68). One might also say that covenant loyalty allowed Israel to fully enjoy what it meant to be made in God's image, and disloyalty to the covenant effectively dehumanized Israelite society. Being designed in God's image meant mankind was blessed with the ability to think, to feel, to love, to rule over the earth, and to participate in the blessing of re-creation (Gen. 1:26–28).

Each of these descriptions served as a measure of just how much Israel forfeited by their waywardness.

The ability to *think* correctly began to erode with the hesitance of Barak (Judg. 4:8–9), the idolatry of Gideon (8:27), and the foolish vow of Jephthah (11:30–31). This erosion picked up steam with Samson's poor choices in women (chs. 14–16). Depravity then found a climax in the last stories of the book involving the men of Benjamin, who foolishly defended the immorality and brutality of the Gibeonites (20:13), and the contrived choices of the rest of the nation to provide wives for the six-hundred remaining Benjamites (21:8–23). By the end of the book, Israelite society has spun totally out of control, and the conscientious reader wonders whether anyone in all of Israel was capable of a truly rational decision.

Although God made humans *relational* beings, there are no satisfying relationships noted in the book after the story of Achsah (1:12–15). Instead, we find only a father who sacrificed his own daughter (11:39), illicit relationships with pagan prostitutes (16:1–4), and brutal, superficial marriages (14:16–17; 19:4–30; 21:12–23).

Instead of *ruling* over people with tender care, the powerful exploited the weak (18:14; 19:14–31), and, rather than enjoying the blessing of *passing on life*, the people in Judges became quite good at taking it. Abuse and death begin to seem normal by the end of the book. By disobedience to the covenant, Israel turned it back on life and came face to face with the dehumanizing effects of sin and death.

> Jesus said, "The thief comes only to steal and kill and destroy. I came that they may have life and have it abundantly" (John 10:10). Turning to God always brings life; moving away from him brings death.

The author of Judges also communicated this idea powerfully through his portrayal of dysfunctional male-female relationships and of the fate of women, the treatment of whom served as a barometer of the nation's relationship with God. Women particularly suffered the effects of sin when the nation turned from the covenant. The first woman mentioned in the book, Achsah, the daughter of Caleb and wife of Othniel (1:12–15), was a singular example of a blessed woman and thus served as a foil for all who came after her. She was blessed by her father (rather than being killed by him!), inspired a man to great acts of obedience to God (rather than seducing him into sin), and married within the covenant community (rather than taking a Canaanite spouse)! But in Judges 4, the subtle, downward progression began with Jael. Unlike later women in the book, she was not harmed but was forced into the unlikely role of military hero, simply because Barak refused to accept his mission without the aid of a woman (4:9). Later, Jephthah's daughter became an innocent victim of her father's foolish decisions (11:39), and Samson's wife was burned to death as a consequence of his actions (15:6). The woman who was brutalized (ch. 19) was never even given a name. By this subtle literary device, she was denied any identity and personhood; she was dismembered and all too easily forgotten. All the women of Benjamin were destroyed in a civil war (20:48), and those found from other tribes to replace them were either intentionally orphaned by brutal destruction of their immediate families (21:11–23) or kidnapped by desperate Benjamite bachelors. If true and undefiled religion is to care for widows and orphans in their distress (James 1:27), there is none to be found in the book of Judges. When sin infected the culture, it corrupted the God-ordained relationships between men and women with women suffering from abusive male dominance.

"Barak went down from Mount Tabor with 10,000 men following him. And the Lord routed Sisera and all his chariots and all his army before Barak by the edge of the sword" (Judg. 4:14–15). *A view eastward of Mount Tabor from the Nazareth ridge.*

The Author of Judges Described *the Moral Failure of the Judges and the Need for a Virtuous King*

In the first three chapters, the author recounted the stories of Caleb and his future son-in-law, Othniel. Both men accomplished great victories in settling the land through their fearless leadership and unhesitating faith in Yahweh (Judg. 1:10–13), and, even though the record of Othniel's judgeship was short (3:7–11), it was still remarkable because of what it did *not* include. There was no hint of idolatry or exploitation of others or even hesitation to fulfill his mission. He delivered the nation by following after Yahweh—something that can be said of only one other judge, the left-handed loner named Ehud. Beyond these three at the beginning of the book, however, each successive judge showed progressively flawed character and lack of moral leadership, punctuated by the final two stories.

Barak could not be coaxed to lead the army alone and only agreed to do so when accompanied by a woman (4:9). Gideon was even more tentative and cautious than Barak, forcing God through a series of confirming hoops before he would act (6:15–22, 36–40; 7:10–15). Although he officially refused to replace Yahweh as king, he foolishly began to act like one anyway when he assumed a harem (8:30) and made personal idols (8:27). These seeds took root and grew in one of his sons, Abimelech, who proclaimed himself king and allowed Baal worship (9:1–57). Standing as the counter image of the godly Caleb, Jephthah doomed his daughter to infertility by taking her life. Samson's flirtatious ways with immoral women cast him in the role of the fool of Proverbs, doomed to destruction and motivated only by lust and personal vengeance. In his final act of deliverance, he cried out to God for help in avenging the Philistines, but his motive was hollow: "for my two eyes" (16:28). To be fair to Samson (and the other judges), it is true that he at least cries out to God, which is an indication of his faith in Yahweh (see Heb. 11:32). However, his motives and choices always reveal a conflicted set of loyalties. By contrast, when David called upon God for help against the same enemy, it was the honor of Yahweh that motivated him (1 Sam. 17:26—"Who is this uncircumcised Philistine, that he should defy the armies of the living God?").

The final two stories of the book (Judg. 17–18, 19–21) provide the perfect punch line for the plot developed in the first sixteen chapters. These episodes focus on the lack of moral leadership, which was clarified by the author's reminder, "In those days there was no king in Israel" (17:6; 18:1; 19:1; 21:25). In the context of the book, the author was not simply lamenting the lack of a monarchy, but especially the lack of virtuous, godly leadership.

Samson's parents said to him, "Is there not a woman … among all our people, that you must go to take a wife from the uncircumcised Philistines?" (Judg. 14:2–3). *A view south into the Sorek Valley, the region of Timnah, from which Samson chose his pagan bride.*

The first story involved a man named Micah who stole money from his mother and confessed his theft only out of the fear of being cursed (17:1–5). His mother then rewarded her son by converting the stolen money into an idol. Micah then made more idols and a shrine and installed one of his sons as priest. His every value and choice was made in violation of the covenant, and all of this error happened in just the first five, concentrated verses of Judges 17! The reader questions, "How could any of this have ever happened among God's people?" The next verse immediately responds (17:6): "In those days there was no king in Israel. Everyone did what was right in his own eyes." The story worsened as the emptiness of Micah's idolatry was exposed by Dan, an entire tribe of Israel, which was as corporately selfish and morally bankrupt as Micah himself (17:14–26).

> If the book of Judges illustrates what happens when there is no virtuous king in the midst of Israel, what will our lives look like when Jesus is not Lord of all?

The last episode (chs. 19–21) shockingly captures the state of the nation in terms of immorality and inhumanity. The sting of the tragic story is that it all happened because of the poor choices of those in charge. In reality this could have been prevented if someone with moral strength had stood up and said, "Stop, we're now going to follow the Lord." Thus, the final editorial comment of the book is that everyone did as they saw fit because there was no *virtuous* leader in Israel (21:25). This conclusion leaves the reader haunted by the needless failure and wondering whether a person even exists with the requisite virtue to rescue the nation. The answer comes, of course, in the book of Samuel, where God provides not just a king (Saul), but a covenant-keeping king (David), whose godly leadership rescued the nation from the spiritual and societal chaos of the judges. And even David, for all his virtue, was also a flawed leader who only served as a signpost to his descendant, Jesus, who by his ultimate virtue and self-sacrificial leadership redeemed not only Israel but also all nations of the earth (Gen. 12:3).

The Author of Judges Highlighted *the Covenant Faithfulness of Yahweh* in Providing for Israel's Need

Although the book of Judges focuses on the unfaithfulness of the nation, this dark theme indirectly illuminates the faithfulness of Yahweh. He gave them the land and the ability to fully conquer it. He gave them his covenant promises, and they returned the favor by quickly forgetting him (Judg. 2:11). However, in the midst of the people's rebellion, Yahweh never forgot what he had sworn.

Even when the idolatrous nation cried out to God for help, one wonders whether the people were really sorry for their sin or just the painful consequences of it. Only once in the book did the author explicitly mention a confession of sin and repentance from idols (10:16), and the deeper decline into sin afterwards leads the reader to believe that their repentance was at

"Then Jerubbaal (that is, Gideon) and all the people who were with him rose early and encamped beside the spring of Harod. And the camp of Midian was north of them, by the hill of Moreh, in the valley" (Judg. 7:1). *Left: a look northward from Mount Gilboa toward the Harod Valley and Hill of Moreh; **Right**: the spring of Harod, at which Gideon chose his three-hundred men, each of whom lapped "the water with his tongue, as a dog laps" (Judg. 7:5) (both photos by David Bivin).*

best short-lived and probably superficial. Israel broke nearly every part of the deuteronomic covenant, and God could have righteously expelled them from the land. But in his patient mercy and covenant love, he persisted. In the next episode of Israel's history, God would use Samuel and David to save the people from the death-giving cycles from which they could not save themselves.

Summary

In the scope of literary genre, Judges is a tragedy. The ending of the book of Joshua had raised the question as to whether Israel would remain faithful to the Lord after the death of Moses' successor. The answer in Judges is clear. After Joshua and the elders of his day died, "there arose another generation after them who did not know the LORD or the work that he had done for Israel" (Judg. 2:10). In just a single generation, the whole nation forgot their redeemer (2:12) and "did what was evil in the sight of the LORD" (2:11; 3:7, 12; 4:1; 6:1; 10:6). Whereas at Sinai "the LORD became king" of all Israel's tribes (Deut. 33:5), now it could be said, "In those days there was no king in Israel. Everyone did what was right in his own eyes" (Judg. 17:6; 21:25; cf. 18:1; 19:1). In accordance with God's promise in Deuteronomy, "the hand of the LORD was against them for harm" due to their covenant rebellion (2:15; cf. Deut. 31:29). Nevertheless, Israel's Scriptures still testified to the promise of a royal deliverer who would overcome the curse (Gen. 3:15; 22:17b–18; 49:8–10; Num. 24:17–19), and as the first episode of 1–2 Samuel records, in the dark days of the Judges, there were still some individuals hoping in this figure (1 Sam. 1:9–10).

KEY WORDS AND CONCEPTS FOR REVIEW

Judges	Canaanite
National identity	Attractions of idolatry
Covenant loyalty and disloyalty	Moral leadership
Mission	Idolatry
Downward spiral of disobedience	Baals

KEY RESOURCES FOR FURTHER STUDY

Block, Daniel I. *Judges, Ruth*. NAC. Nashville: B&H, 1999.

Davis, Dale Ralph. *Judges*. Fearn, Scotland: Christian Focus, 2007.

Wilcock, Michael. *The Message of Judges*. BST. Downers Grove, IL: Inter-Varsity, 1993.

Younger, K. Lawson. *Judges*. NIVAC. Grand Rapids: Zondervan, 2002.

1–2 SAMUEL

Who?

The Bible does not tell us who wrote 1–2 Samuel. Although the man Samuel is a key player in the early chapters, he dies in 1 Samuel 25:1, about halfway through the story. The text never implies that he was the author of the book named after him. Since 1–2 Samuel is located within the Prophets portion of the Hebrew canon, perhaps David's court prophets Nathan or Gad (1 Chron. 29:29) wrote a major portion of it. But this is mere speculation. Because 1–2 Samuel has numerous literary connections with 1–2 Kings, many scholars feel that the final form of 1–2 Samuel took shape in the sixth century B.C. near the final events of 1–2 Kings. However, again, we are not at all certain of this. First and Second Samuel were originally written in Hebrew as one unified book. Later in history, when it was translated from Hebrew into Greek, the Greek translation took up more space and would no longer fit on one scroll. Thus in the Greek Septuagint, the translators split the book of Samuel into two parts, placing what is now 1 Samuel on one scroll and placing 2 Samuel on another scroll. Hebrew Bibles did not split the book into two until the fifteenth century A.D.

When?

The historical setting for the opening of 1 Samuel is around 1100 B.C., and the final events at the end of 2 Samuel occurred in 971 B.C. We do not know for certain when 1–2 Samuel was written. Some scholars feel that it was penned shortly after the death of David, but others place the final composition in the sixth century B.C.

Where?

If 1–2 Samuel was composed by David's court prophets, then it was probably written in Jerusalem. The events of the story take place primarily in Israel, Philistia, and Ammon.

Why?

Although the book of Joshua indicates that Israel started out fairly well in their attempt to live in the Promised Land in accordance with God's Torah (Law), by the end of the book of Judges Israel had abandoned any serious attempt to obey God. Who would rescue Israel from the mess they had created? The answer was David, and 1–2 Samuel presents the rise and reign of David, the "bigger than life" hero, who restored true worship of Yahweh and, in essence, completed the conquest that Israel began back in the book of Joshua. Full of promise and potential, David looked very much like a "messiah" or deliverer. However, for all of his virtue, he was still only a mere man, and 1–2 Samuel also describes his sinful actions and the terrible consequences, leaving readers still looking for the great deliverer to come.

1–2 SAMUEL

J. Daniel Hays

Carefully Crafted Verses from 1–2 Samuel

"Those who honor me I will honor, and those who despise me shall be lightly esteemed" (1 Sam. 2:30).

But the people ... said, "No! But there shall be a king over us, that we also may be like all the nations, and that our king may judge us and go out before us and fight our battles" (1 Sam. 8:19–20).

"The LORD sees not as man sees: man looks on the outward appearance, but the LORD looks on the heart" (1 Sam. 16:7).

THE AUTHOR OF 1–2 SAMUEL ...

- Explained the *transition in Israel's leadership* from judges to monarchy.

- Demonstrated the need to take seriously *Yahweh's holy, powerful, and dangerous presence.*

- Displayed *God's ideal for kingship* by contrasting Saul's failures with David's successes.

- Underscored the crucial role of *God's covenant with David* in redemptive history.

- Portrayed *David's sin and its consequences* to show the need for one greater than David.

"I will raise up your offspring after you, who shall come from your body, and I will establish his kingdom. He shall build a house for my name, and I will establish the throne of his kingdom forever" (2 Sam. 7:12–13).

The Author of 1–2 Samuel Explained the *Transition in Israel's Leadership* from Judges to Monarchy

Chronologically, 1–2 Samuel follows immediately upon the heels of the terrible situation in the book of Judges. The Israelites had not completed the conquest as Yahweh commanded, and because of Israel's continued sin and disobedience, foreigners regularly overran and oppressed them. Indeed the Philistines (a new group of immigrants like the Israelites) threatened to displace them! The tribe of Dan had even abandoned the Promised Land of their inheritance, embraced idolatry, and moved north. The priesthood was corrupted and true worship of Yahweh was lost. The sad truth was that the Israelites had become as sinful and corrupt as the wicked Canaanites, whom they were supposed to displace. The end of Judges portrayed Israel in a theologically and politically disastrous situation. The question emerging from the text as we turn from Judges to 1–2 Samuel is "Who will save them from their mess?" David is a central part of God's answer in 1–2 Samuel.

Figure 9.1. Samuel at a Glance

From Corrupt Priest to Corrupt King: The Transition from Judges to Monarchy (1 Sam. 1–15)
Who Will Be King? The Contrast between Saul and David (1 Sam. 16–31)
The Rise of David and the Restoration of Israel (2 Sam. 1–10)
David's Fall: The Bathsheba Affair (2 Sam. 11–12)
The Consequences of Sin: The Unraveling of David's Kingdom (2 Sam. 13–20)
The Good and the Bad: A Summary of David and His Kingdom (2 Sam. 21–24)

The book opens with the tabernacle at Shiloh. We are told the old high priest Eli was lazy and inept, and his two wicked and corrupt sons were serving as the functioning priests (1 Sam. 2:12–25). The Philistines were dominating Israel (4:1–11), and there was no effective leadership in the country. Not only this, but also "the word of the LORD was rare in those days; there was no frequent vision" (3:1).

> Using the same language as 1 Samuel 3:1, Proverbs 29:18 declares that chaos reigns where God's Word does not: "Where there is no prophetic vision the people cast off restraint, but blessed is he who keeps the law."

As 1–2 Samuel progresses, the nation dramatically transitions from being led by judges to being ruled by kings. Samuel, the central character of the early chapters (1 Sam. 1–8), was himself a transitional figure. He was a prophet (3:20), the last judge (7:15–17), and the one who inaugurated the monarchy (8:22; 10:1, 24–25; 16:13). Samuel also began the recovery of the true worship of Yahweh (7:3–14; 12:1–25). Saul, the first king, would flounder and fail (chs. 9–31), but his successor David exploded onto the scene as the one who would deliver the nation from the disaster seen in the book of Judges. David built a strong monarchy, completing the conquest Joshua started, capturing Jerusalem, moving the tabernacle to Jerusalem and making it his capital, and reestablishing a true God-ward orientation in the land (1 Sam. 16–2 Sam. 10). The contrast is startling. Note also that neither Samuel nor David was from the priestly tribe of Levi, and thus neither of them was technically qualified to be priests. Yet both Samuel and David carried out many priestly functions, and they both played crucial roles in restoring a God-honoring environment in Israel. David demonstrated that under the monarchy the king would play a critical role in maintaining proper worship of Yahweh. Thus one of the central themes presented in 1–2 Samuel is the transition in leadership from ineffective judges (and corrupt priests) to the effective monarchy of David, in which the king also led (like a priest) in worshipping God rightly.

> Like Melchizedek of old (Gen. 14:18; cf. Ps. 110), 1–2 Samuel anticipates that the ultimate, anointed deliverer of Israel and the world would embody both the offices of king (1 Sam. 2:10) and priest (2:35–36), a fact the writer of Hebrews linked to Messiah Jesus (Heb. 7).

"Now [Hannah's husband Elkanah] used to go up year by year from his city to worship and to sacrifice to the LORD of hosts at Shiloh, where the two sons of Eli, Hophni and Phinehas, were priests of the LORD" (1 Sam. 1:3). *Viewed from the west, Shiloh was the earliest resting place of the tabernacle and central sanctuary in the Promised Land (Josh. 18:1; Judg. 21:19).*

The Author of 1–2 Samuel Demonstrated the Need to Take Seriously *Yahweh's Holy, Powerful, and Dangerous Presence*

Part of Yahweh's covenant promise to the Israelites was that he would personally dwell in their midst (Exod. 25:8; 29:45–46; 40:34–38). This presence of Yahweh was one of the greatest blessings of the covenant relationship. Although the glory of Yahweh filled the entire tabernacle (40:34–38), Yahweh's presence was focused on the ark of the covenant, the throne of God. The ark was a fairly small rectangular box (approx. 4 ft. x 2½ ft. x 2½ ft.) covered with gold inside and out. On top of the ark was a gold lid (the mercy seat) with gold cherubim on either side. Here resided God's sacred presence (see 25:22).

Yahweh's dwelling with Israel brought tremendous power for blessing, but due to his holiness, Yahweh's presence was also dangerous to all who failed to take him seriously. Through three episodes about the ark of the covenant, the author of 1–2 Samuel emphasized the extreme importance of recognizing the holiness, power, and danger that came with the God's presence (1 Sam. 4:1–7:17; 2 Sam. 6:1–23; 15:24–29).

> In the New Testament, God's presence is embodied in Jesus ("God with us," Matt. 1:23; cf. John 1:14; 2:19), lived out through the church (Acts 2), and enjoyed in the restored paradise of God (Rev. 21:3; 22:3–4; cf. Ezek. 48:35).

In the first episode, Israel foolishly and dramatically lost the ark. The corrupt priests Hophni and Phinehas took the ark into a battle against the Philistines, thinking that they could manipulate God's power to ensure victory over the enemy. After all, was it not the ark that provided victory for Israel in the days of Joshua (Josh. 3:1–17; 6:12–21)? Yet magical fetishes do nothing to Yahweh, who will not be controlled by anyone! The Philistines defeated Israel, killed Hophni and Phinehas, and captured the ark (1 Sam. 4:1–11).

This is where the story gets interesting. How could Israel lose the presence of Yahweh, a critical component in the covenant? What would happen to their relationship with God? Also, in the ancient world people in general thought that if one nation defeated another nation it indicated that the gods of the victorious nation were more powerful than the gods of the defeated nation. Was this true? Had Dagon, god of the Philistines, defeated Yahweh, god of Israel?

The Philistines took the ark back to Ashdod, one of their major cities, and placed it as a captured prize in their temple before their primary god Dagon. Yahweh then began to demonstrate that it was he who would emerge the victor, not Dagon or the Philistines! On the next day, the Philistines found the statue of Dagon lying face down before the ark, "bowing down" in obeisance to Yahweh. They propped him back up, but on the following day, they again found Dagon prostrate before Yahweh. However, this time his head and hands were removed, an action often taken against defeated kings. Yahweh was demonstrating to the Philistines that he had defeated Dagon, and not vice versa (5:1–5). As a sign of this reality, Yahweh then attacked the Philistines, sending what appears to be a plague of tumors among them and terrifying them in city after city (5:6–12). Eventually the Philistines gave in, paying gold tribute to Yahweh to try to appease him. They placed the ark and the gold in an ox-drawn cart, and then watched as the "unmanned" wagon returned Yahweh's throne to Israel.

Strikingly, this entire true saga reads much like a military campaign. Yahweh first defeated Dagon, the god of the Philistines. Then Yahweh, by himself, moved along through Philistine territory capturing city after city. The defeated Philistines in turn paid him gold tribute, and he then returned victoriously by himself to his land. Sinful Israel had been defeated by the Philistines, but the all-powerful presence of Yahweh had not!

> God is always the primary mover in this world; we are not! The repeated use of "the hand of the LORD" in the ark narrative reminds us that God needs nothing from us and is fully capable of bringing about his will by himself without use of other means (1 Sam. 5:6, 7, 11; 6:3, 5, 9; cf. Acts 17:25).

The second story about the ark appears in 2 Samuel 6:1–23. Israel's situation is now much different. David the new king had captured Jerusalem and desired to move the ark of the covenant to his new capital (2 Sam. 5:6–12). But there were complications, for Yahweh had given strict and explicit instructions through Moses about how the ark should be handled and moved (Exod. 25:13–15; Num. 4:15; 7:9; cf. Josh. 3:1–5). Yahweh had clearly stated that the ark was to be carried only by Levites using poles. David, however, ignored this rule, and placed the ark in a cart, just as the Philistines had done. He then accompanied the ark with an army, making it a military procession rather than a religious-like festival (with priests). Along the way, the oxen, which were pulling the wagon, stumbled, and a man named Uzzah touched the ark in order to steady it. Yahweh immediately struck him dead. (Recall from the earlier story in 1 Samuel 4–6 that Yahweh was quite able to stay on the Philistine cart without any human help or guidance.) Thus Yahweh stressed

> Even David could not trifle with Yahweh's powerful and holy presence. May we, therefore, guard our actions, knowing that "[our] body is a temple of the Holy Spirit" (1 Cor. 6:19–20).

the power and danger of his holy presence. Not even David, king of Israel and servant of Yahweh, could take liberty with the manner of handling the ark, the focal point of God's presence. Upset at first, David learned his lesson and completed the journey with proper worship and respect for God's throne. Interestingly, 1 Chronicles 15:15 adds that David now had the Levites carry the ark with poles, just as Moses had instructed.

The final mention of the ark of the covenant in 1–2 Samuel comes in a brief episode from a low point in David's life (2 Sam. 15:24–29). David's son Absalom and much of the nation with him had turned against the king, putting David's life in danger (15:1–13). As the king fled Jerusalem, his faithful priest Zadok brought out the ark, using Levites with poles to move it correctly this time. Yet David sent Zadok and the ark back into Jerusalem. Probably realizing that his relationship with Yahweh had been damaged by his adulterous affair with Bathsheba and the murder of Uriah (chs. 11–12), David questioned whether he could truly enjoy the favor of Yahweh's presence. He was thus reluctant to bring the ark of God with him as he fled

"He struck some of the men of Beth-shemesh, because they looked upon the ark of the LORD…. Then the men of Beth-shemesh said, 'Who is able to stand before the LORD, this holy God?'" (1 Sam. 6:19–20). *The ark of the covenant at the tabernacle model in the Timnah Valley just west of the Arabah.*

Jerusalem (15:25–26). Indeed, like Adam and Eve before him who were crippled by the devastating consequences of sin, David went into exile, separated from the sacred space and presence. Eventually David was reestablished as king and made it back to Jerusalem, but the book is silent about his reunion with Yahweh, and political troubles continued to plague Israel's former hero (chs. 19–21; cf. 1 Kings 2:2–4).

The Author of 1–2 Samuel Displayed *God's Ideal for Kingship* by Contrasting Saul's Failures with David's Successes

The account in 1–2 Samuel of the transition from judge to king must be read theologically, for God has a sermon to proclaim through this true retelling. One of the most central messages is found in the sustained contrast between the first king, Saul, and the second king, David. In the middle portion of the book, Saul is portrayed as a terrible royal figure, while David is a terrific one (1 Sam. 8–2 Sam. 10). By distinguishing these two individuals, Yahweh reveals his ideal for kingship, as first set forth in Deuteronomy 17:14–20.

> In the Bible, human characters are most important when they point the reader to God. The New Testament makes much of David because in his successes, after his failures, and in his memorial, he directs us back to God's power, mercy, and promises.

In 1 Samuel 8 the people of Israel confronted Samuel and demanded that he appoint a king "to judge us like all the nations" and to "go out before us and fight our battles" (vv. 5, 20). Their motives were clearly wrong, and Yahweh viewed their request as a rejection of his rule over them. Nonetheless, Yahweh instructed Samuel to give them a king (8:22), and in chapters 9–10 this king is identified as Saul. He became a king who reflected the people's desires and motives—large in stature (9:2; 10:23) but weak in character and faith, and he soon proved to be a failure (e.g., 13:13–14; 15:22–29; 17:11). Yahweh then raised up David, not a big man physically (16:12), but one whose heart was for God (Yahweh's kind of king) (16:7; cf. Deut. 17:14–20). David would be incredibly successful, at least initially.

The contrast between David and Saul is stark. Saul is introduced as looking somewhat like a buffoon; he was searching aimlessly for his father's lost donkeys (1 Sam. 9:1–20). This is not a portrayal of the future king that would inspire confidence! Even after Samuel anointed him to rule, Saul timidly shirked the responsibility of his position and tried to hide among the animals and baggage (10:20–24). But Saul had several assets. Not only was Samuel his advisor, but also he was a foot taller than anyone else in Israel (9:2; 10:23), a feature that would be quite helpful for a warrior-king who would lead his people in battle. Even more importantly, he received Yahweh's Spirit to empower him (10:6–10), followed by an initial God-empowered victory over the Ammonites (11:1–15).

Samuel next anointed David, who from the beginning was quite different than Saul. First, while not big in size, he was big in heart. Yahweh had declared that Saul's kingdom would be given "to a neighbor of yours, who is better than you" (1 Sam. 15:28). This "goodness" is then clarified during Samuel's search among Jesse's sons for the new king, for God avowed, "Man looks on the outward appearance, but the LORD looks on the heart" (16:7). While Saul was introduced as searching for lost donkeys, David is intro-

THE KINGDOM OF SAUL

Damascus

Tyre

Megiddo

Shechem

ISRAEL

Gezer

Jericho

Ashdod

Jerusalem

Gath

Gaza

Beer-sheba

duced as tending his father's sheep, anticipating his ultimate vocation as shepherd-king of Israel (16:11; cf. 2 Sam. 5:2; Ps. 23:1).

The contrast between David and Saul was portrayed most graphically through the encounter with the Philistine warrior Goliath (1 Sam. 17). Goliath was a heavily armed and well-trained Philistine, whose height towered above most Israelite men, whose own average height at this time was just over five feet. Some Hebrew manuscripts describe Goliath's height at six cubits and a span (about 9 ft. 9 in.), while more older manuscripts—most notably the Dead Sea Scrolls—place

> Leaders were often called shepherds, to stress their call to provide and protect. Thus God told David, "You shall be shepherd of my people" (2 Sam. 5:2), and he promised Israel that in the new covenant age he would provide "shepherds after my own heart, who will feed you with knowledge and understanding" (Jer. 3:15). Jesus identified himself as the good shepherd (John 10:1–18; cf. Jer. 23:1–8; Ezek. 34:1–31), and elders are called "pastors (lit., shepherds)" (Eph. 4:11), charged to watch over "all the flock" and "to care for (lit., shepherd) the church of God" (Acts 20:28; cf. 1 Peter 5:2).

it at four cubits and a span (about 6 ft. 9 in.). Even at 6 feet 9 inches, Goliath was more than a foot taller than most of his enemy—that is, all but Saul, of whom we are told was himself a foot taller than anyone else in Israel (9:2). Israel had wanted a king who could fight their battles, and they had one (8:20). Not only this, Saul was one of the few in Israel who had armor to

"The Philistines stood on the mountain on the one side, and Israel stood on the mountain on the other side, with a valley between them. And there came out from the camp of the Philistines a champion named Goliath" (1 Sam. 17:3–4). *From the northeast, Azekah and the Valley of Elah (1 Sam. 17:1–2), where David defeated Goliath.*

match Goliath's (13:19–22; 17:38), so he was the obvious choice to challenge the Philistine warrior. It was Saul's responsibility to deal with Goliath. Yet as Israel's king cowered in fear, it was David, a mere shepherd boy, who valiantly ran out to defeat Goliath. In David's own words (17:45–47):

> "You come to me with a sword and with a spear and with a javelin, but I come to you in the name of the LORD of hosts, the God of the armies of Israel, whom you have defied. This day the LORD will deliver you into my hand, and I will strike you down and cut off your head. And I will give the dead bodies of the host of the Philistines this day to the birds of the air and to the wild beasts of the earth, *that all the earth may know that there is a God in Israel,* and that all this assembly may know that the LORD saves not with sword and spear. For the battle is the LORD's, and he will give you into our hand."

Even at this point in time, David acted like God's ideal king, in contrast to Saul, who acted cowardly. The rest of 1 Samuel continues to reflect the contrast between Saul, the rebellious and rejected king, and David, Yahweh's royal choice. Saul tried repeatedly to kill David (18:12–29; 19:1–24; 23:7–29), while David twice spared Saul's life (24:1–22; 26:1–25). Saul massacred an entire town of Israelites, including a number of priests (22:6–19), while David protected and provided for the one survivor (22:20–23). Still unable to subdue the Philistines, Saul eventually died in battle against them (ch. 31).

> "Those who honor me I will honor, and those who despise me shall be lightly esteemed" (1 Sam. 2:30). In 1–2 Samuel, this principle remained true for barren woman, priest, king, warrior, and shepherd boy, and it still holds true today. "Everyone who exalts himself will be humbled, but the one who humbles himself will be exalted" (Luke 18:14; cf. 1 Peter 5:5).

As David rose to power and united the country, the contrast between him and Saul continued. David defeated the Philistines (2 Sam. 5:17–25) and restored true worship of Yahweh (ch. 6). Yahweh in turn blessed him with a special covenant (ch. 7) and gave him victories over numerous neighboring nations (chs. 8–10).

Yahweh clearly wanted a king who placed his faith in him rather than in human abilities or military forces, a king characterized by humility as well as bravery, and a king who would place true worship of Yahweh at the center of his life. In Hannah's word from the beginning of the book (1 Sam. 2:9–10): "[The LORD] will guard the feet of his faithful ones, but the wicked shall be cut off in darkness, for not by might shall a man prevail. The adversaries of the LORD shall be broken to pieces; against them he will thunder in heaven. The LORD will judge the ends of the earth; he will give strength to his king and exalt the horn of his anointed."

"The men of Israel fled before the Philistines and fell slain on Mount Gilboa.... Saul took his own sword and fell upon it" (1 Sam. 31:1, 4). *Cows grazing above the Jezreel Valley on Mount Gilboa, where Saul and his three sons died (1 Sam. 31:8).*

The Author of 1–2 Samuel Underscored the Crucial Role of *God's Covenant with David* in Redemptive History

One of the most important chapters in this two-volume book is 2 Samuel 7. David was firmly established as king and had moved the ark of the covenant to Jerusalem, involving the entire nation in a joyful celebration of Yahweh's presence. Boldly and rightly he had stated that humility was the only proper disposition before Yahweh's presence (2 Sam. 6:21–22). Now, in 2 Samuel 7, the king declared to his prophet Nathan that he intended to build a proper temple for Yahweh (7:2). However, using a wordplay, Yahweh responded that David would not build God a "house" but that he, Yahweh, would build David a "house" (7:5–16). The Hebrew word for "house" is often used figuratively to mean "palace," "temple," or "dynasty." In 7:1–7, David proposed to build Yahweh a "temple/house," whereas in 7:8–17 Yahweh promised to establish an eternal Davidic "dynasty/house" with a kingdom that would last forever (7:16).

Yahweh's promise to David in 2 Samuel 7:5–16 was the longest recorded speech by God since the time of Moses, underscoring the significance of this event in the biblical story. This is a critical moment in the theological history of the entire Bible, and this promise would have huge ramifications for the rest of biblical history (and all of human history as well). As 1–2 Kings sadly chronicles, Israel and Judah would rebel against Yahweh and chase after idols. The prophets would warn of coming terrible judgment (the Assyrian and Babylonian invasions), based on the warning curses of Deuteronomy 28:15–68 (among others). Yet the prophets would also look to the future and talk about a glorious time of

"The king and his men went to Jerusalem against the Jebusites.... David took the stronghold of Zion, that is, the city of David" (2 Sam. 5:6–7). *Excavations of Israelite walls from the time of Israel's united and divided kingdoms along the eastern slope of the City of David in Jerusalem looking south over the Kidron Valley.*

restoration when Yahweh would send a special One to rule righteously over Israel and the nations. The prophets regularly based their hope for this coming messianic deliverer on the promise (covenant) that Yahweh made with David back in 2 Samuel 7 (Jer. 23:5; 30:9; 33:14–26; Ezek. 34:23–24; 37:24; Isa. 9:7; 55:3; Hos. 3:5; Amos 9:11). This promise was

> The New Testament consistently declares Jesus to be the fulfillment of God's promise to David for a righteous King who would rule forever (Matt. 1:1; 9:27; 12:23; Mark 10:48; 12:35–37; Luke 18:38–39; 20:41–44; Rev. 5:5; 22:16).

also enshrined in Israel's worship, celebrated especially in Psalms 89 and 132.

The Author of 1–2 Samuel Portrayed *David's Sin and Its Consequences* to Show the Need for One Greater Than David

In 2 Samuel 11, David, the clear human hero of 1–2 Samuel, committed adultery with Bathsheba and then schemed to have her husband killed. The attentive reader should be stunned by this turn of events. How could this happen? And why does the author tell us of such tragedies? (Note the account is not found in 1–2 Chronicles.)

In the overall narrative theology of 1–2 Samuel, the significance of this event cannot be overstressed, for David's sin with Bathsheba functions as a critical pivot in the story of his life and in the redemptive history of the Old Testament. While earlier rumblings are heard (e.g., 1 Sam. 13:14; 15:28), the official account of David began in 1 Samuel 16 and continues to 1 Kings 2, where the text records his death. Prior to his affair with Bathsheba, just about everything in David's life was positive. From 1 Samuel 16 through 2 Samuel 10, David was the successful hero—brave, valiant, humble, and trusting in Yahweh. He whipped the bad guys with class and flair, and everybody loved him. "Saul has struck down his thousands, and David his ten thousands," sang the Israelite women (1 Sam. 18:7). He was God's hero in the ideal of Deuteronomy 17:14–20. Theologically, within the biblical story, David was the answer to Israel's mess depicted at the end of the book of Judges, when "there was no king in Israel" and "everyone did what was right in his own eyes" (Judg. 21:25). David completed the conquest that stalled after Joshua died, and he expanded the borders of Israel (2 Sam. 8–10), coming very close to reaching the size of the Promised Land Yahweh promised to Abram in Genesis 15:18–19. David established Jerusalem as the capital and placed the ark of Yahweh there, thus restoring the central sanctuary and true

> Recalling the special place God's instruction was to have for the king (Deut. 17:18–20), David exhorted Solomon to be a man of the Word (1 Kings 2:2–3). This foundational principle for successful leadership hasn't changed!

worship of God to Israel. His was the kingship upon which all future kingships in Israel would be measured (e.g., 1 Kings 9:4–5; 14:8; 15:3–5).

Yet right as David reached his peak, he stumbled and fell. While hanging out at home, having skipped out on leading his troops to war (2 Sam. 11:1–2), he looked down from his rooftop at a beautiful (and married!) woman bathing in her yard below (11:2–3). He took her, committed adultery with her, and she became pregnant (11:4–5). After failing to implicate her husband Uriah in the pregnancy (because he was off at war), David had Uriah intentionally killed in battle (murdered, if one is honest) (11:5–27). The gripped reader watches in horror as our hero crumbles. Yahweh also watches … with anger (11:27).

Nathan the prophet confronted David (ch. 12). David quickly repented, and Yahweh remarkably forgave him (12:13). Oh, what amazing grace won for us in the ultimate Son of David (Rom. 3:23–26)! But forgiveness from Yahweh does not mean the removal of all negative consequences. After this affair, everything in David's life changed, and his story took a decidedly negative turn. His life, his kingdom, and his "house" (i.e., family) unraveled. Absalom his insolent son rebelled against him, and most of Israel sided with Absalom against their former hero (2 Sam. 15:13), resulting in David's need to flee Jerusalem (15:14–31). Note the ironic contrasts. Earlier David killed Goliath with his sling, became the most popular man in Israel, captured Jerusalem, and brought the ark of the covenant to be with him in Jerusalem. Now David had to flee Jerusalem in humiliation as most of Israel (and even his own son) turned against him. He parted company with Yahweh's presence (i.e., the ark of the covenant) (15:25–29), and then, in the midst of his retreat, an angry Israelite pelted him with rocks (16:5–14), an ironic contrast to his earlier glorious victory over Goliath. Although later his rebellious son Absalom was killed and David was restored to Jerusalem (chs. 18–19), things were never the same, and the old glorious days of David were gone with the wind. Another rebellion broke out (ch. 20, foreshadowing the future civil war and split between David's tribe Judah and the rest of Israel (19:42–43; 20:2; cf. 1 Kings 11:30–33; 12:19–20). Israel's old nemesis the Philistines (whom David had defeated and vanquished earlier) rose up again, and in 2 Samuel 21:15–22 David is once again fighting the Philistines and their huge warriors. This time, however, the had-been champion is weak and has to be rescued by others. The

> Psalm 51 records David's cry of repentance to Yahweh after his affair with Bathsheba. "Have mercy on me, O God…. According to your abundant mercy, blot out my transgressions…. Against you, you only, have I sinned…. Create in me a clean heart, O God…. Take not your Holy Spirit from me. Restore to me the joy of your salvation" (Ps. 51:1, 4, 10–12).

David portrayed after Bathsheba is a far cry from the David prior to that disastrous affair.

Thus we can see that David's adultery (2 Sam. 11) is a pivotal, life-changing event in the story of David. The point that the author of 1–2 Samuel seems to be making is that David, for all of his wonderful virtues and enviable character, was still a weak and frail human, with feet of clay. He was not the ultimate Messiah promised to Eve (Gen. 3:15), Abraham (22:17b–18), and Judah (49:10) and anticipated by Balaam (Num. 24:17–19) and Hannah (1 Sam. 2:10). While in many ways aligning with the Deuteronomic ideal (Deut. 17:14–20) and thus giving hope in God's purposes, his match was not perfect. While almost restoring Israel, David's own sinfulness proved to be his undoing, and most of his accomplishments unraveled. We as readers, therefore, are called to shift our gaze forward in anticipation, sustaining our faith in Yahweh's promise that he would raise up a righteous "son of David"—one who would not crumble before temptation and whose kingdom would last forever…. Jesus is this son, the great, conquering "descendant of David" (Rev. 22:16; cf. 5:5)! The Lord God has given him the "throne of his father David, and he will reign forever, and of his kingdom there be no end" (Luke 1:32–33). "Hosanna to the Son of David! Blessed is he who comes in the name of the Lord!" (Matt. 21:9; cf. 1:1; 12:23).

> The affair with Bathsheba and the consequential crumbling of David remind us that David is not the Messiah. We are not to put our trust in those who are merely human, but rather we are to trust in Jesus, the God-man and true Messiah who emerges victorious where David failed (see Ps. 146).

Summary

The book of Samuel narrates the transition in Israel's leadership from judges to monarchy and demonstrates the need to take seriously Yahweh's holy, powerful, and dangerous presence. God honors those who honor him (whether barren woman, shepherd boy, or king), but he thwarts the purposes of all who stand against him, whether priest, king, or warrior (1 Sam. 2:9, 30; 2 Sam. 22:28). In contrast to Saul's failures, David's successes display God's ideal for kingship, yet David's sin and its consequences stress the need for one greater than David. As such, 1–2 Samuel closes with hope still kindled for a greater David of whom it could accurately be proclaimed, "I will establish the throne of his kingdom forever" (2 Sam. 7:13).

"You save a humble people, but your eyes are on the haughty to bring them down" (2 Sam. 22:28). *A view north eastward from the City of David to the Mount of Olives, which David ascended as he fled Jerusalem after Absalom's conspiracy (2 Sam. 15:30).*

KEY WORDS AND CONCEPTS FOR REVIEW

Judges	Philistines
Monarchy	Davidic covenant
Ark of the covenant	House/temple/dynasty
Presence of Yahweh	Deuteronomic ideal for kingship
The ark narratives	Bathsheba
Jerusalem	Psalm 51
Saul vs. David	Son of David

KEY RESOURCES FOR FURTHER STUDY

Arnold, Bill T. *1 and 2 Samuel*. NIVAC. Grand Rapids: Zondervan, 2003.

Bergen, Robert D. *1, 2 Samuel*. NAC. Nashville: B&H, 1996.

Davis, Dale Ralph. *1 Samuel* and *2 Samuel*. Fearn, Scotland: Christian Focus, 2001, 2007.

Tsumura, David. *The First Book of Samuel*. NICOT. Grand Rapids: Eerdmans, 2007.

1–2 KINGS

Who?

Little evidence exists for the authorship of 1–2 Kings, though the Jewish Talmud attributed the book to Jeremiah. However, while the accounts of the release of Jehoiachin from the Babylonian prison that end each book are almost identical (2 Kings 25:27–30; Jer. 52:31–34), this event from around 561 B.C. likely happened at least a decade after Jeremiah's death in Egypt.

Because 1–2 Kings overviews more than four-hundred years of royal history in two different kingdoms, no single eye witness put the material together. As such, it is probably best to think of "composition and completion" or "source data and final editing." The book itself states that the one(s) who finished the book relied on official court records (1 Kings 11:41; 14:19, 29; etc.). Along with these "annals," other sources must have been drawn from for the Elijah and Elisha narratives and the expanded sections devoted to select kings (e.g., chs. 3–11; 16–22). Finally, the fact that the record of Sennacherib's siege of Jerusalem in 2 Kings 18:13–20:19 is recounted almost identically in Isaiah 36:1–39:8 implies a shared source.

This book began as a single volume in the Hebrew but expanded into two parts in the Greek. While sources were used, the final author(s) took liberty in selection and in providing a theological-covenantal perspective on the establishment and destruction of the divided kingdom.

When?

First and Second Kings is a document whose publication suggests both a process and an event. The book could not have been completed earlier than its last chapter (2 Kings 25 and residency in Babylon around 561 B.C.). The likelihood is that most of the book was composed before the time of Josiah (ca. 640–609 B.C.) but did not achieve its present form until the Judeans were fully settled in Babylonia. Furthermore, a comparison of the Hebrew of 1–2 Kings with the Greek translation suggests there were a number of editions before the final form we have today.

Where?

Because the text makes frequent reference to royal annals, at least the source-data for most of the events recorded in 1–2 Kings were written down before the exile began. It seems likely, however, that the volume was finalized somewhere in Babylon. Additionally, the professional nature of the writing suggests that scribes were utilized in the composition—a fact that implies an urban origin where such scribes would have been centralized.

Why?

While the reasons for writing these books are not specifically stated, a number of fairly obvious reasons are available.

1. To provide a "national history" that covered the monarchical period.
2. To explain to the exilic and post-exilic communities the catastrophic loss of land, temple, and heritage.
3. To allow the prophets to clarify the consequences of covenant failure.
4. To show that hope still existed for God's people, because by Jerusalem's fall the promised royal deliverer in the line of Judah had yet to arise.

CHAPTER 10

1–2 KINGS

Donald Fowler and
Jason S. DeRouchie

Carefully Crafted Verses from 1–2 Kings

"Will God indeed dwell on the earth? Behold, heaven and the highest heaven cannot contain you; how much less this house that I have built!" (1 Kings 8:27).

"How long will you go limping between two different opinions? If the LORD is God, follow him; but if Baal, then follow him" (1 Kings 18:21).

THE AUTHOR OF 1–2 KINGS …

- Stressed the *role of kingship* in the nation's disobedience, division, and destruction.

- Showed the *importance of Yahweh's prophets* in Israel's history.

- Measured *kingdom success* in the light of past covenants.

- Gave *hope for kingdom restoration* beyond exile.

They despised his statutes and his covenant … They went after false idols and became false … and sold themselves to do evil in the sight of the LORD, provoking him to anger. Therefore the LORD was very angry with Israel and removed them out of his sight (2 Kings 17:15, 17–18).

Before [Josiah] there was no king like him, who turned to the LORD with all his heart and with all his soul and with all his might, according to all the Law of Moses, nor did any like him arise after him (2 Kings 23:25).

The Author of 1–2 Kings Stressed the *Role of Kingship* in the Nation's Disobedience, Division, and Destruction

The book of 1–2 Kings overviews the rise and fall, division and destruction of what began as the united nation of Israel. As suggested in the book's title, this history deals primarily with the office of kingship—specifically the positive or, more commonly, negative influence Israel's leaders had on the kingdom's destiny. The book opens with King David "old and advanced in years" (1 Kings 1:1) and in need of a successor, who ultimately was identified as his son Solomon through Bathsheba (1:28–30). Gifted with wisdom, riches, and honor from God, Solomon established Israel in his day as chief among all kingdoms of the ancient world, and all other nations paid him tribute (3:13–14; 4:20–21). In his early years, he built Yahweh a temple in Jerusalem, passionately seeking "that all the peoples of the earth may know that the LORD is God; there is no other" (8:60). As he aged, however, his heart became corrupt, turning away from the Source of his strength to go after the various gods of his many foreign wives (11:1–8). The result was tragic and set the entire nation on a course of destruction: "Since … you have not kept my covenant and my statutes that I have commanded you, I will surely tear the kingdom from you and will give it to your servant…. I will not tear away all the kingdom, but I will give one tribe to your son, for the sake of David my servant and for the sake of Jerusalem that I have chosen" (11:11, 13). So it was that one ruler's failure led to the division of the kingdom in 930 B.C.

> In his better years, Solomon wrote, "Pride goes before destruction, and a haughty spirit before a fall" (Prov. 16:18). He would have done well to heed his own advice.

Figure 10.1. The Makeup of the Southern and Northern Kingdoms

	Southern Kingdom—Judah	Northern Kingdom—Israel
Size	1(2) tribes	10 tribes
Dynasties and Kings	1 dynasty (of David)/20 kings (only two fully loyal: Hezekiah and Josiah)	10 dynasties/20 kings* (all wicked, esp. Jeroboam I and Ahab)
Capitals	Jerusalem	Samaria
Worship Centers	Jerusalem	Bethel and Dan
Economic Status	Struggling	Wealthy
Destruction	586 B.C. by Babylon	723 B.C. by Assyria

* The total number of northern kings lowers to nineteen and the dynasties to nine if Tibni from 1 Kings 16:21–22 is not included. Prepared by Jason S. DeRouchie.

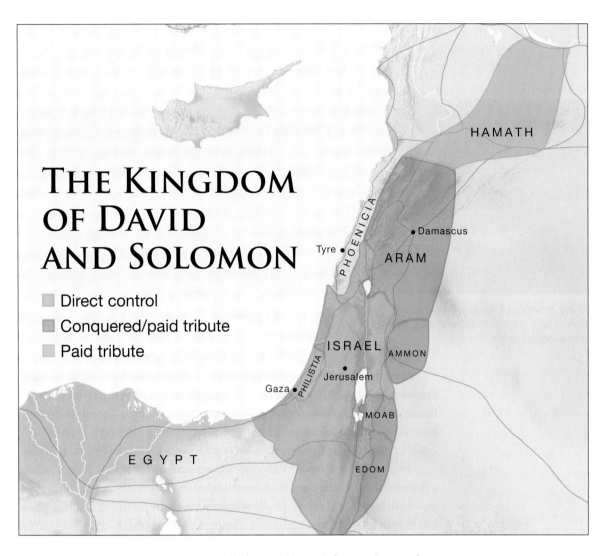

THE KINGDOM OF DAVID AND SOLOMON

- Direct control
- Conquered/paid tribute
- Paid tribute

The northern tribes were now called "Israel," and the southern tribes, "Judah." The northern coalition initially followed Jeroboam I, the wicked idolater who altered the sacred calendar, built temples throughout the territory, and established special sanctuaries of worship at Bethel and Dan, in direct violation to God's Word (1 Kings 12:25–33; cf. Deut. 12:2–32). Significantly, the history of the northern kingdom was scathed by ten successive dynasties, military strife, and deep covenant rebellion against the Lord. After Jeroboam I, *each* of the nineteen other northern kings "did what was evil in the sight of the LORD and walked in the way of Jeroboam and in his sin which he made Israel to sin" (1 Kings 15:34; cf. 2 Kings 17:22). As a

Figure 10.3. The Kings of the Divided Kingdom

Kings of Judah (Southern Kingdom)			Kings of Israel (Northern Kingdom)			
1.	Rehoboam	930–913 B.C.	1.	Jeroboam I	930–909 B.C.	I
2.	Abijah	913–910				
3.	Asa	910–869	2.	Nadab	909–908	
			3.	Baasha	908–886	II
			4.	Elah	886–885	
			5.	Zimri	885	III
			6.	(Tibni)	885–880	IV
			7.	Omri	885–874	V
4.	Jehoshaphat	872–848*	8.	Ahab	874–853	
5.	Jehoram I	853–841*	9.	Ahaziah	853–852	
6.	Ahaziah I	841	10.	J(eh)oram II	852–841	
7.	Athaliah[†]	841–835	11.	Jehu	841–814	VI
8.	J(eh)oash I	835–796	12.	Jehoahaz	814–798	
9.	Amaziah	796–767	13.	J(eh)oash II	798–782	
10.	Azariah II	792–740*	14.	Jeroboam II	793–753*	
	(Uzziah)		15.	Zechariah	753	
			16.	Shallum	752	VII
11.	Jotham	750–732*	17.	Menahem	752–742	VIII
			18.	Pekahiah	742–740	
12.	Ahaz	735–715*	19.	Pekah	752–732*	IX
13.	Hezekiah	729–686*	20.	Hoshea	732–723	X
14.	Manasseh	696–642*	**Exile of Israel by Assyria, 723 B.C.**			

* Date includes a coregency or overlapping reign.
† Originally the wife of Jehoram I, Athaliah became sole ruler of Judah after the death of her son Ahaziah I.

15.	Amon	642–640
16.	Josiah	640–609
17.	Jehoahaz	609
18.	Jehoiakim	609–598
19.	Jehoiachin	598–597
20.	Zedekiah	597–586

Exile of Judah by Babylon, 586 B.C.

Prepared by Jason S. DeRouchie. Most dates are from Edwin R. Thiele, *The Mysterious Numbers of the Hebrew Kings* (rev. ed.; Grand Rapids: Kregel, 1994), 10; the only change is the start date of Hezekiah's reign (729, not 715), based on the clear reading of the Hebrew Masoretic text and the arguments of Leslie McFall, "Did Thiele Overlook Hezekiah's Coregency?" *BSac* 146 (1989): 393–404.

When asked to get a second opinion, Ahab stated, "There is yet one man by whom we may inquire of the LORD, Micaiah the son of Imlah, but I hate him, for he never prophesies good concerning me, but evil" (1 Kings 22:8). Significantly, it was the words of Micaiah that came true, and it meant Ahab's demise (22:17, 19–23).

In 1–2 Kings, what Yahweh's prophets proclaimed consistently occurred, whether it was the division of the empire (1 Kings 11:30–39), the punishment of idolatry (13:2), the ending of dynasties (14:10–11), the covenant curse of drought (17:1), the death of individuals (21:23), victory or defeat in battle (20:13–14, 28; 22:17, 19–23), the healing of diseases (2 Kings 5:10), or the provision of food (7:1). The accuracy of the prophetic predictions was supposed to validate that they were from God and thus motivate the people to return to Yahweh (see Deut. 18:21–22). Sadly, few in Israel listened to the prophetic voice.

The Performing of Miracles

The book of 1–2 Kings never records any monarch performing miracles, but it testifies to many prophets doing extraordinary ones, most significantly Elijah and Elisha. Some of the accounts include more mundane events, like multiplying oil in a jar (1 Kings 17:8–16; 2 Kings 4:1–7), finding a lost ax head (2 Kings 6:5), or protecting fellow prophets from eating a poisoned meal (13:14–19). Other times, however, the miracles are more grandiose, as when Elijah raised a widow's son from the dead (1 Kings 17:17–24), when Elisha did the same for a Shunamite woman (2 Kings 4:18–37), or when Elisha's decaying bones revived a dead man who had been thrown into the same grave (13:20–21).

Along with always fulfilling the prophetic word, Yahweh confirmed the truthfulness of his prophets by enabling them to per-form feats contrary to the laws of nature. Prophetic miracles helped prove that Yahweh was indeed over all and knew all. This fact is evident in the words of the widow after Elijah raised her son from death: "Now I know that you are a man of God, and that the word of the LORD in your mouth is truth" (1 Kings 17:24). Similarly, in the prophetic confrontation on Mount Carmel, after Elijah prayed and Yahweh brought fire out of heaven, consuming "the burnt offering and the wood and the stones and the dust" and licking "up the water that was in the trench," the onlookers turned from Baal and de-clared, "The LORD, he is God; the LORD, he is God" (18:38–39). The mir-acle substantiated the message and the messenger, just as Elijah prayed it would: "Let it be known this day that you are God in Israel, and that I am your servant, and that I have done all these things at your word" (18:36).

> Jesus compared Nazareth's hostility at his own prophetic role to the northern kingdom's sinful unre-sponsiveness during the prophetic ministries of Elijah and Elisha (Luke 4:24–27).

The Confrontation of Israel and Judah's Kings

As Yahweh's mouthpieces, prophets were called to urge people, "Turn from your evil ways and keep my commandments and my statutes, in accordance with all the Law that I commanded your fathers" (2 Kings 17:13). Sadly, though consistently warned by the prophets, the people "would not listen, but were stubborn, as their fathers had been, who *did not believe* in the LORD their God" (17:14).

"Ahab sent to all the people of Israel and gathered the prophets together at Mount Carmel. And Elijah came near to all the people and said, '… If the LORD is God, follow him; but if Baal, then follow him'" (1 Kings 18:20–21). **Left:** *Mount Carmel's western heights overlooking the Mediterranean Sea—the region where Elijah defeated the prophets of Baal;* **Right:** *a statue at Muhraqa of Elijah's triumph.*

While non-Yahweh prophets abounded in the ancient world, there appears no exact parallel to the way Yahweh's prophets confronted kings in order to preserve and maintain a people's relationship with their god. In the earliest stage of Israelite kingship, the prophet Samuel confronted Saul for various violations of God's instructions (e.g., 1 Sam. 13:11–14; 15:13–35), and then the prophet Nathan addressed David with the dreaded, "You are the man!" (2 Sam. 12:7), following the king's sin with Bathsheba. In 1–2 Kings, this ministry of rebuke and judgment continued, creating the following prophetic pattern:

> *Yahweh's king or people rebelled → Yahweh raised up a prophet → the prophet announced Yahweh's judgment → the prophet's words came true*

Significantly, in 1–2 Kings it is usually the most covenantally wicked kings who received the most extended discussion. After Solomon, the two receiving greatest focus are Jeroboam I and Ahab.

The first prophetic confrontation in 1–2 Kings occurred when the prophet Ahijah dramatically announced to Jeroboam I that mighty Solomon's kingdom would be divided and part of it given to him (1 Kings 11:29–39). It was also Ahijah who later predicted that Jeroboam and his family would be destroyed due to their iniquity (14:7–11), and just as the prophet declared, so it happened (15:29). Similarly, God had sent an unnamed prophet to Jeroboam I, who predicted nearly two hundred years in advance that a king named Josiah, one of the two wholly righteous kings of Judah, would burn the bones of Jeroboam's apostate priests of Bethel (13:1–3). When Jeroboam tried to arrest the nameless prophet, the king's hand "dried up, so that he could not draw it back to himself" (13:4). Ultimately, 2 Kings 23:15–16 records that the prophet's words came true.

After King Solomon, the monarch receiving most space in the text is Ahab. He was gifted with success through the ministry of a nameless prophet, who twice revealed to him how God would give him victory over the invading Syrian (i.e., Aramean) army (1 Kings 20). However, because after his victory he released the Syrian king on whom Yahweh had declared a war of judgment (a crime similar to Saul's failure to kill Agag, the Amalekite, in 1 Sam. 15), the same prophet announced that Ahab would die, life for life (1 Kings 20:35–43). Later, the prophet Micaiah prophesied similarly (22:17), and then the narrator wrote of the battle: "A certain man drew his bow at random and struck the king of Israel between the scale armor and the breastplate" (22:34). Thus the northern kingdom's greatest warrior died, less the victim of a "random" arrow than of the prophetic word that God used to guide the arrow to its divinely ordained destination.

> The powerful story of Ahab's demise gives us confidence that God can be trusted to deal with wicked leaders … in his time and in his way. The kingdoms of mighty overseers like Hitler and Stalin are long gone, while God's kingdom continues to grow and prosper. "Vengeance is mine, I will repay" (Rom. 12:19).

The Confrontation of Other Nations' Kings

Central in the worldview of the author of 1–2 Kings is the conviction that Israel's God is Lord over all the kings of all nations. Yahweh raised up Hadad of Edom and Rezon of Damascus to serve as "adversaries" to the disobedient Solomon (1 Kings 11:14, 23). Through a prophet's words, Yahweh also guided Ahab to defeat the arrogant Ben-Hadad of Damascus (20:13–14, 28). Most dramatically, however, Yahweh's wrath was poured out on Sennacherib, the "great king" of Assyria, thus showing how God responds to royal arrogance that rejects his kingship over all. Through his messengers, Sennacherib declared, "Who among all the gods of the lands have delivered their lands out of my hand, that the LORD should deliver Jerusalem out of my hand?" (2 Kings 18:35). In response, King Hezekiah of Judah pled for Yahweh to save and to show himself supreme (19:19). Through his prophet Isaiah, Yahweh then declared (19:22, 28): "Whom have you mocked and reviled? … Against the Holy One of Israel! … Because you have raged against me …, I will turn you back on the way by which you came." During the night, the Angel of Yahweh destroyed 185,000 in the camp of Assyria, and Sennacherib fled home, only to die there by the sword of his own sons (19:35–37).

This most dramatic divine act portrays Yahweh's response to royal arrogance that rejects his supreme kingship. In the New Testament, Herod Agrippa I's failure to glorify God brought a similar fate (Acts 12:21–23). Death is the only result for those who persist in dishonoring God (Rom. 3:23; 6:23).

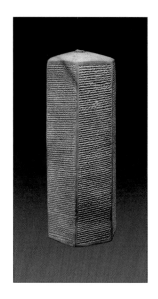

"As for Hezekiah, the Judean, I besieged forty-six of his fortified walled cities and surrounding smaller towns, which were without number…. I conquered (them)…. He himself, I locked up within Jerusalem, his royal city, like a bird in a cage." (*The Prism of Sennacherib* [from the Oriental Institute, USA; translation from *COS* 2:303; cf. *ANET*, 288]). *What Sennacherib failed to record was the devastating loss Yahweh struck upon him after he defied Yahweh, who is "God alone" (2 Kings 19:19).*

The Author of 1–2 Kings Measured *Kingdom Success* in the Light of Past Covenants

The Evaluation of the Kings of Israel and Judah

This book uses a formulaic, annalistic pattern for recording and evaluating all the kings in the northern and southern kingdoms. It approaches the kingdoms chronologically and in parallel, using the following recurrent pattern:

1. Notice of when the king came to reign (in Israel or Judah) in relation to another king
2. Statement about how long the king reigned and in what capital
3. The name of the king's mother (for Judean kings only)
4. The king's religious policy:
   - *Israel*: Did he practice the "sins of Jeroboam son of Nebat," maximizing idolatry and rebellion and minimizing God's presence in Jerusalem (e.g., 1 Kings 16:25–26)?
   - *Judah:* Was he faithful to Yahweh "like David," and did he remove "the high places," thus calling attention to God's presence in Jerusalem (e.g., 1 Kings 15:1–6)?
5. A source for further information about the king
6. Information about the king's death, burial, and succession

As is clear from the "religious policy" statements above, one of the author's main goals in the book was to evaluate each monarch as "good" or "evil," depending on his *covenant commitment to Yahweh*. Interestingly, this ethical evaluation of each king is one of the Bible's most distinctive historical qualities. In the ancient world, kings guarded carefully what was written of them, resulting in historical records being turned into royal propaganda. In contrast, the writer of 1–2 Kings produced a history whose primary purpose was to proclaim not the greatness of earthly kings but the greatness of Yahweh over all. That is, 1–2 Kings is distinctly theological, addressing how each king responded, whether rightly or wrongly, to Yahweh and his purposes.

> Yahweh is the main subject and/or object of every biblical narrative. That is, Bible stories are primarily about God, not humans. Our first interpretive question should always be, "What does this story tell me about God?"

The Covenantal History of 1–2 Kings

First and Second Kings provides a *covenantal evaluation* of the kings of Israel and Judah. In order to do so, the book spends much time building connections with previous covenants.

Echoes of the Abrahamic and Davidic Covenants

For example, 1–2 Kings opens by showing how Israel had become a massive nation (*progeny/heirs*) (1 Kings 4:20; cf. Gen. 22:17a), living in their *land* (1 Kings 4:21; cf. Gen. 15:18), ruled by *kings* (1 Kings 1:1; 4:1; etc.; cf. Gen. 17:6, 16), and *blessing* their neighbors (1 Kings 4:34; 10:1–13; Gen. 12:3). These are all echoes of the Abrahamic covenant.

Similarly, the narrator recorded that the dynastic promises Yahweh gave to David were renewed with Solomon, giving explicit stress that Israel's kings must "pay close attention to their way, to walk before me in faithfulness with all their heart and with all their soul" (1 Kings 2:4; cf. 8:25–26; 9:4–5; 2 Sam. 7:5–16). Furthermore, Yahweh's preservation of the Davidic line after Solomon's failure was said to be "for the sake of David" (1 Kings 11:13, 32; 2 Kings 8:19; 19:34), and the kings of Judah are consistently judged on whether they followed God "like David" (2 Kings 14:3; cf. 1 Kings 11:4, 6, 33, 38; 14:8; 15:3, 11; 2 Kings 16:2; 18:3; 22:2). Finally, as will be highlighted more fully at the end of this chapter, the book ends by drawing attention to God's preservation of the Davidic line, thus grounding Israel's future hope in the kingdom promises made to David (2 Kings 25:27–30; cf. 1 Kings 11:39).

Echoes of the Mosaic (Old) Covenant

These points noted, it is the Mosaic (old) covenant that appears to provide the primary lens for understanding the portrait of destruction of the united and divided kingdoms in 1–2 Kings. This connection is set forth first in the early chapters where David charges Solomon to reign *under Yahweh's leadership*: "Keep the charge of the LORD your God, walking in his ways and keeping his statutes, his commandments, his rules, and his testimonies, as it is written in the Law of Moses, that you may prosper in all that you do and wherever you turn" (1 Kings 2:3). These words echo the chief responsibility of every king as laid out in Deuteronomy 17—namely that he be a *man of the book*, not replacing Yahweh but representing Yahweh before the people and showing the people what it means to have God as the Lord of your life (Deut. 17:18–19): "And when he sits on the throne of his kingdom, he shall write for himself in a book a copy of this law…. And he shall read in it all the days of his life, that he may learn to fear the LORD his God by keeping all the words of this law and these statutes." *By including this allusion, the author of 1–2 Kings invites the reader to interpret the monarchic history in the light of Deuteronomy and the other covenant materials.*

This same invitation is developed in Solomon's prayer of temple dedication, which is filled with allusions to the Mosaic covenant (1 Kings 8), and in the account of Josiah's finding the lost Book of the Law/Covenant and, in response, leading the nation in covenant renewal and reform (2 Kings 22–23). With the *Shema* in mind (Deut. 6:4–5), the narrator closed the account of Josiah by noting, "Before him there was no king like him, who turned to the LORD with all his heart and with all his soul and with all his might, according to all the Law of Moses" (2 Kings 23:25; cf. 18:5–6).

One final way the books emphasizes a connection with the Mosaic covenant is through its allusions to the breaking of the "forbidden four"—those prohibitions found in Deuteronomy 17:14–17 that stressed that the king must not

- Be a *foreigner*;
- Acquire large numbers of horses (*militarism*);
- Take many wives (*marriage alliances*, the common way to form international bonds);
- Accumulate large amounts of gold and silver (*materialism*).

"Pharaoh king of Egypt had gone up and captured Gezer and burned it with fire, and had killed the Canaanites who lived in the city, and he had given it as dowry to his daughter, Solomon's wife; so Solomon rebuilt Gezer" (1 Kings 9:16–17). *A chambered Solomonic gate at Gezer (photo by Daniel Frese).*

Although the first warning was never violated, 1–2 Kings discloses how often the rulers of the united and divided kingdoms sought power, influence, and wealth, only to their own demise. For example, while the book does not record any battles Solomon fought, it does tell us that he had fourteen-hundred chariots along with twelve-thousand horsemen (1 Kings 10:26). We also learn that it was Solomon's numerous diplomatic marriages that led him away from Yahweh (11:1–8) and that the king abused his God-given wealth (3:13) by forcing the Israelites into work gangs to erect his expansive building projects (9:15–23; cf. 1 Sam. 8:16–17), which included religious structures for his wives' gods (1 Kings 11:7–8).

The Monolith Inscription of Shalmaneser III describes a great battle fought at Qarqar (in modern day Syria) in 853 B.C. between Assyria and an anti-Assyrian coalition. We are told the latter included Ahab of Israel, who contributed ten-thousand infantry and two-thousand chariots, the largest number in the alliance and one equal to that of Assyria itself! Though Ahab's kingdom was apparently great of strength, the Bible stresses that Yahweh alone gave the king victory *and* defeat (1 Kings 20:13; 22:16–17, 19–23)!

The same tale reoccurs with the northern king Ahab, who is known from extra-biblical texts to have been a preeminent militarist but whose successes *and* failures the Bible strikingly and appropriately attributes to Yahweh (20:13; 22:16–17, 19–23). Ahab's diplomatic marriage with the Phoenician princess Jezebel brought about his ruin, for Jezebel, arguably the most notorious woman in the Hebrew Bible, led this northern king to turn from Yahweh (16:31), incited the murder of nearly all Yahweh prophets (18:4), persecuted Elijah to the point of despair (19:14), and had innocent people murdered out of greed (21:1–16). As for wealth, whereas Solomon had an ivory throne (10:22), Ahab had an ivory palace (22:39), but he remained discontent, even murdering Naboth in order to acquire his vineyard (21:1–16).

Power, influence, and wealth continue to be temptations today, and the record in 1–2 Kings should give due warning to all readers.

Ironically, right after Solomon's death, his kingdom was divided (1 Kings 12:16–20), and only five years later, King Shishak of Egypt invaded Judah and claimed the bulk of Solomon's treasures (14:25–28). Similarly, all that remains of Omride ivory are scattered artifacts from Samaria.

> Royal power, influence, and luxury, so impressive and noteworthy, are as fleeting as those who possess them (Pss. 37:14–15; 49:16–17; 146:3–4; 1 Tim. 6:7).

The Covenant Failure of the Kings of Israel and Judah

As has been shown, the concept of covenant permeates 1–2 Kings, and it is only in this context that the national demise and destruction can be understood. Solomon's failure was seen as a breach of "covenant" (1 Kings 11:11), as was the people's rebellion at the time of Ahab (19:10). The exile itself is said to have been caused because Israel "transgressed [the LORD's] *covenant*, even all that Moses the servant of the LORD commanded" (2

"The king of Assyria carried the Israelites away to Assyria…, because they did not obey the voice of the LORD their God but transgressed his covenant, even all that Moses the servant of the LORD commanded" (2 Kings 18:11–12). *Assyrian King Sennacherib's Lachish Siege Reliefs (from the British Museum):* **Left:** *Assyrian sling throwers and archers attack Lachish, one of Judah's southwestern border stations;* **Center:** *an Assyrian siege-engine protected by archers pushes up an incline while some Israelite defenders fight from a tower and others carry their goods from the town;* **Right:** *King Sennacherib seated on this throne receives booty taken from Lachish while the Israelite exiles kneel before him in homage; an inscription before the king reads, "Sennacherib, king of the world, king of Assyria, sat upon a nîmedu-throne and passed in review the booty (taken) from Lachish (La-ki-su)" (ANET, 288).*

Kings 18:12). What massive reversal occurred from the beginning of Solomon's reign to the destruction of the twin kingdoms! By the end of the book, most kings have been rebellious, the people's numbers have been greatly reduced, most of those living have been exiled from their land, and the blessings have been removed. There is a covenantal crisis at stake with respect to the earlier promises. However, there is no question as to which of the parties was guilty of covenant violation. It was the north and south's sustained failure to follow Yahweh, initiated mostly by their leaders, that brought about their expulsion from the land.

The Author of 1–2 Kings Gave *Hope for Kingdom Restoration* Beyond Exile

By the end of the book, the tragedy of the nation's *tôrâ* violation seems complete with the loss of land, leadership, temple, and freedom. Upon the mention of Judah's exile (2 Kings 25:21), the book concludes with two contrastive episodes that together capture the overall message of the book. The first highlights the negative influence of the royal family (i.e., David's descendants) on the people's experience of exile (25:22–26); the second stresses Yahweh's unrelenting faithfulness to keep his kingdom promises made to David (25:27–30).

We are told that, after the destruction of Jerusalem when King Nebuchadnezzar of Babylon appointed Gedaliah to be governor of all Judeans left in the land, a group of radicals, led by a member of the "royal family," assassinated the governor and his party. As a result, all those remaining in the land fled to Egypt, out of fear of the Babylonians (25:22–26). Back to Egypt! This is alarming, for Egypt was the place of past slavery—the place from which God had rescued his people. Not only this, Yahweh had declared through Moses, "You shall never return that way again" (Deut. 17:16), and Jeremiah had warned, "If you set your faces to enter Egypt and go to live there, then the sword that you fear shall overtake you there in the land of Egypt, and the famine of which you are afraid shall follow close after you to Egypt, and there you shall die" (Jer. 42:15–16; cf. Deut. 28:68). Nevertheless, David's own family was leading the way back to the grave. This was the story of Israel's destruction.

> The darkness of Israel's exilic situation in Egypt and elsewhere, especially in the north, sets the stage for portraying the age of restoration as a new exodus, this time not from physical oppression alone but from the spiritual bondage that brought it about (Jer. 16:14–16; Ezek. 20:34–38; Isa. 11:11, 16; 12:1–5)!

However, God's kingdom story was not over! Indeed, out of the depths, God would act to fulfill his past promises, originally given to Moses (Deut. 30:1–10) and reaffirmed to David (2 Sam. 7:12–16). The final episode of 1–2

"[King Nebuchadnezzar] burned the house of the LORD and the king's house and all the houses of Jerusalem" (2 Kings 25:9). *The coming of night over Jerusalem.*

Kings highlights again that not all of David's relatives are dead. Indeed, in his thirty-seventh year of exile, King Jehoiachin, Judah's last Davidic monarch, was released from the Babylonian prison and given a place of honor above all other "kings who were with him in Babylon," an honor that included daily dining with the great king and a regular allowance, all the remaining days of his life (2 Kings 25:27–30). Earlier Yahweh had declared that, although he would "afflict the offspring of David," he would not do so forever (1 Kings 11:39)! God's promises never fail, and the very presence of Jehoiachin meant that hope remained for the day when the greater "Son of David" would rise to power!

Conclusion

Filled with numerous names, places, and events over a four-hundred-year period, 1–2 Kings provides Yahweh's perspective on the rise and fall of the kingdoms of Israel and Judah and temporarily brings to an end the narrative history begun in Genesis and the story of Israel's covenant rebellion detailed in the Former Prophets. The book's portrait of Yahweh captures the heart of its message: Israel's God is transcendent yet relational, gracious yet just, always faithful to his Word, both to curse and to bless, and ever committed to preserve the throne of David.

Did the narrator close the book with a hint to a sequel? Certainly the final form of the canon suggests such. Grounded in Yahweh's promise through Moses of future restoration after curse (Deut. 30:1–10), Solomon had pled for God to forgive and restore the repentant remnant after exile (1 Kings 8:46–53). Furthermore, the prophets anticipated this restoration to include a new covenant (Jer. 31:27–37), a new Jerusalem (31:38–40), a new temple, and a restored priesthood (Ezek. 40–48), all of which are applied in various ways by the New Testament authors (e.g., Luke 22:20; Rev. 3:12; 11:19; 20:6; 21:2, 22). The point here is that Yahweh promised that the history of Israel—a redeemed, faithful Israel—would continue into the future.

You will recall that after an extended commentary section in the Latter Prophets and Former Writings, the Old Testament in its Hebrew ordering ends with a series of books that detail the history of the remnant during the period of initial restoration (Daniel through 1–2 Chronicles). In these Latter Writings, however, the history is revitalized, filled with life and longing for the consummate kingdom of God. Clearly, Yahweh was not through with his chosen people at the end of 1–2 Kings, and the rest of the Bible details the continued covenantal story.

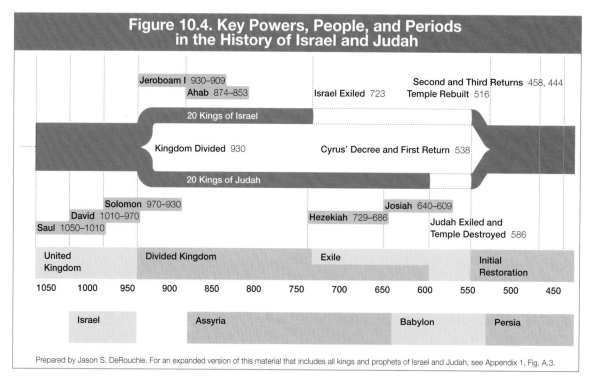

Figure 10.4. Key Powers, People, and Periods in the History of Israel and Judah

Prepared by Jason S. DeRouchie. For an expanded version of this material that includes all kings and prophets of Israel and Judah, see Appendix 1, Fig. A.3.

KEY WORDS AND CONCEPTS FOR REVIEW

Solomon	Elijah and Elisha
Divided kingdom makeup	Religious policies
723 B.C.	Book of the Law/Covenant
586 B.C.	Chief responsibility of a king
Jeroboam I and Ahab	Forbidden four
Hezekiah and Josiah	Hope of restoration
Prophet	Message of 1–2 Kings
Prophetic functions	

KEY RESOURCES FOR FURTHER STUDY

Davis, Dale Ralph. *1 Kings* and *2 Kings*. Fearn, Scotland: Christian Focus, 2005, 2007.

House, Paul R. *1, 2 Kings*. NAC. Nashville: B&H, 1995.

Konkel, August H. *1 & 2 Kings*. NIVAC. Grand Rapids: Zondervan, 2009.

Provan, Ian W. *1 and 2 Kings*. NIBCOT. Peabody, MA: Hendrickson, 1995.

JEREMIAH

Who?

The book of Jeremiah is a collection of Jeremiah's messages and a narrative record of key events from his ministry in Judah's final days as a nation. Jeremiah was a priest who also served as one of Yahweh's prophets during the reigns of Judah's last five kings until Jerusalem fell to the Babylonians in 586 B.C. Jeremiah remained in the land of Judah until a faction of Jews took away him and his scribe Baruch as hostages to Egypt around 580 B.C.

Jeremiah and Baruch appear to have been largely responsible for the contents of the book (Jer. 36:4–21; 43:1–7; 45:1–5). After working with Jeremiah to compose an early scroll of the prophet's messages, Baruch likely continued to collect messages and narratives of Jeremiah throughout his ministry. A final editor perhaps added the appendix concerning the fall of Jerusalem in Jeremiah 52.

There are significant differences between the Hebrew (MT) and Greek (LXX) versions of Jeremiah. The LXX is significantly shorter (by 2,700 words), has a different arrangement, and may reflect an earlier version of the book. The Hebrew version was likely completed shortly after the prophet's death.

When?

Jeremiah began his prophetic ministry in 627 B.C. and recorded, with Baruch's assistance, the first scroll of his prophetic messages in 605 B.C. When King Jehoiakim destroyed this scroll, Jeremiah and Baruch composed an expanded version. Jeremiah died ca. 580–570 B.C., and the last event mentioned in the appendix of chapter 52 (the release of Jehoiachin from prison) occurred in ca. 561 B.C.

Where?

Jeremiah ministered in Judah before and after the fall of Jerusalem until he was taken away to Egypt near the end of his life.

Why?

Yahweh called Jeremiah as a prophet to Judah and to the nations at large and gave him a twofold commission "to tear down" and "to build up" (1:10; 24:6; 31:4, 28; 42:10; 45:4). The book reflects Jeremiah's dual message of judgment and salvation:

1. Explaining why Yahweh brought the judgment of exile upon his people—i.e., Judah had flagrantly violated Yahweh's commands and had been like an unfaithful wife toward Yahweh in chasing after other gods;

2. Demonstrating Judah's unbelief through narrative accounts of how various individuals and groups had rejected Jeremiah's message and persecuted him as Yahweh's messenger;

3. Offering hope for Israel's future by promising that Yahweh would restore his people from exile, forgive their sins, and establish a new covenant that would reverse the failures of the past.

JEREMIAH

Gary E. Yates

Carefully Crafted Verses from Jeremiah

"My people have committed two evils: they have forsaken me, the fountain of living waters, and hewed out cisterns for themselves, broken cisterns that can hold no water" (Jer. 2:13).

Thus says the LORD: "Let not the wise man boast in his wisdom, let not the mighty man boast in his might, let not the rich man boast in his riches, but let him who boasts boast in this, that he understands and knows me" (Jer. 9:23–24).

"I will raise up for David a righteous Branch, and he shall reign as king and deal wisely and shall execute justice and righteousness in the land" (Jer. 23:5).

THE AUTHOR OF JEREMIAH ...

- Presented *Yahweh's case against Judah* for its covenant infidelity.

- Documented *Judah's refusal to repent and to heed* Jeremiah's message.

- Voiced *the prophet's anguish* over his calling and ministry.

- Portrayed *Babylon as God's instrument and object of judgment.*

- Emphasized *the global extent of Yahweh's judgment and salvation.*

- Promised *restoration and a new covenant* between Yahweh and his people.

"I will make a new covenant with the house of Israel and the house of Judah.... I will put my law within them, and I will write it on their hearts. And I will be their God, and they shall be my people" (Jer. 31:31, 33).

Figure 11.1. Chronology of the Classical Prophets

World Power	Prophetic Period	Israel	Judah	Foreign Nation Focus
Assyria (870–626 B.C.)	8th–early 7th century	Jonah (ca. 770)		Assyria (Nineveh)
		Amos (ca. 760)		
		Hosea (ca. 760–730)	Isaiah (ca. 740–700)	
			Micah (ca. 737–690)	
			Nahum (ca. 650)	Assyria (Nineveh)
Babylon (626–539 B.C.)	Late 7th–early 6th century		Habakkuk (ca. 630)	
			Zephaniah (ca. 627)	
			Jeremiah (ca. 627–580)	
			Joel (ca. 600?)	
			Obadiah (ca. 586?)	Edom
			Ezekiel (ca. 593–570)	
			[in Babylon]	
Persia (539–323 B.C.)	Late 6th–5th century		Haggai (ca. 520)	
			Zechariah (ca. 520–518)	
			Malachi (ca. 433)	

Prepared by Jason S. DeRouchie; Most of the dates for the prophets are taken from John H. Walton, *Chronological and Background Charts of the Old Testament* (Grand Rapids: Zondervan, 1994), 52.

The Author of Jeremiah Presented *Yahweh's Case Against Judah* for Its Covenant Infidelity

During the final years of the southern kingdom, Jeremiah served as one of Yahweh's prosecuting attorneys. The prophet made the case that the people of Judah—like their sister Israel to the north—had violated their covenant with God, and he warned that Yahweh was about to judge them with military defeat and exile (Jer. 11:1–5). In the Promised Land, life and blessing in relation to Yahweh were conditioned upon obedience to Yahweh's commands; to turn from him was to move away from life toward death. Death was what Israel to the north had chosen, and now Judah was doing the same—running from God like an unfaithful wife, prostituting herself after many lovers (2:20; 3:2, 20–21; 5:7). Specifically, the primary sin of Israel and Judah was the worship of false gods (5:19). Unlike the pagan peoples around them who would have never betrayed their national gods, Judah had traded their relationship with the true God for "gods" that held no true power (2:10–11). The people had abandoned the source of real life for "broken cisterns" that could never provide what would truly satisfy (2:12–13). Judah's idolatry included the repulsive practice of offering their children as human sacrifices (7:31–32; 19:2, 6; 32:35). And at the end of Jeremiah's ministry, the Jews in Egypt even believed the fall of Jerusalem was due to their neglect of the Queen of Heaven (44:15–19). The reality was that no matter how much Judah multiplied its gods, these idols would never be of help in its time of trouble (10:1–5; 11:12–13).

"As you have forsaken me and served foreign gods in your land, so you shall serve foreigners in a land that is not yours" (Jer. 5:19). *Left: dating at least to Israel's divided kingdoms, the temple at Arad in the Negeb includes both Holy of Holies (upper left) and sacrificial altar (bottom right); Right: a close-up of the Holy of Holies with standing stones used in pagan worship.*

Judah's idolatry also had ethical consequences and led to disregard of the demands Yahweh placed upon his people. Those in Judah became like the gods they worshipped, having eyes but not seeing and ears but not hearing (5:21; cf. 2:5; Ps. 115:8). They believed that ritual and sacrifice could take the place of obedience to Yahweh's commands (Jer. 7:9, 21–26, 31; 26:4–5). The result was that fraud, violence, dishonesty, and a lack of concern for the poor and needy permeated Judah's society at large (5:26–

> Jeremiah taught that Israel's covenant with Yahweh included both responsibilities and blessings and that ritual and sacrifice could never take the place of heartfelt obedience (Jer. 5:26–29; 7:4–11; 11:2–5)

29; 6:7, 28; 7:5–6; 9:6, 16). While under the pressure of Babylonian siege, Zedekiah and the people of Jerusalem made a covenant to release their Hebrew servants in accord with the provision of the Mosaic law that they were not to permanently enslave their own countrymen (34:8–22; cf. Exod. 21:1–11; Lev. 25:39–46; Deut. 15:12–18). However, they reneged on their promise when the Babylonian army temporarily withdrew. As a result, the people of Judah would know what it was like to lose their own freedom when the Babylonians took them away as captives.

Figure 11.2. Jeremiah at a Glance

Prologue (Jer. 1)
Oracles of Judgment against Jerusalem and Judah (chs. 2–25)
Narratives: Judah's Unbelief and the Warnings of Exiles (chs. 26–29)
Oracles of Israel's Salvation and Promise of a New Covenant (chs. 30–33)
Narratives: The Fall of Jerusalem and the Punishment of Judah (chs. 34–45)
Oracles of Judgment Against Foreign Nations (chs. 46–51)
Epilogue (chs. 52)

Corrupt leadership was largely responsible for Judah's spiritual condition. Following the righteous reign of Josiah, the last four kings of Judah were ungodly and disobedient. Yahweh had promised that David's sons would rule "forever" over Israel, but he had conditioned the blessing of each individual king upon obedience to the Mosaic law (2 Sam. 7:13–16; 1 Kings 2:4). Jeremiah exhorted the kings to be like their father Josiah in practicing justice (Jer. 22:2–5, 15–16), but they did not listen. Jehoiakim was a prime example of this lack of concern for justice, as he oppressed the people in order to expand and remodel his palace (22:13–17). Jeremiah warned that covenant unfaithfulness would bring an end to the Davidic kingdom (22:2–5; cf. 13:19; 17:24–27) and that judgment would fall on each of Judah's last four rulers.

- Jehoahaz would die in Egyptian exile (22:10–12).

- Jehoiakim would die and not be given a proper burial (22:18–19).

- Jehoiachin would not return from Babylonian exile, and none of his sons would sit on the throne (22:24–27).

- Zedekiah would be taken away as a captive to Babylon (21:7; 34:3–5).

The future hope for the Davidic dynasty lay in the promise that Yahweh would raise up an ideal David, the Messiah. He would be "a righteous Branch" (23:5), unlike Zedekiah ("the LORD is my righteousness") who had failed to live up to his name.

Figure 11.3. The House of David: Yahweh's "Signet Ring"

The House of David rejected: "Though Coniah [Jehoiachin] . . . were the signet ring on my right hand, yet I would tear you off" (Jer. 22:24).

The House of David restored: "I will take you, O Zerubbabel . . . and make you like a signet ring, for I have chosen you" (Hag. 2:23).

Judah's spiritual leaders were no better than their civil leaders and often spearheaded the opposition to Jeremiah. Jeremiah characterized both prophets and priests as "godless" (23:11) and greedy for gain (6:13). The speech of Jeremiah's prophetic opponents was "falsehood"—the delusions of their own minds, for they had not stood in the council of Yahweh to receive his word (23:16–27; 24:10; 28:15; 29:21–23). They proclaimed "peace, peace," while forgetting that Judah's flagrant sins demanded punishment (6:14; 8:11; 26:6–9). The Babylonian invasion would dash these hopes (8:15; 14:19), showing how false their belief was that Yahweh would protect his covenant people no matter what (7:4; 8:19).

Figure 11.4. Categories of Prophetic Oracles

Indictment	Statement of the offense (specification of covenant stipulations violated)
Judgment/Warning	Declaration of the punishment to be carried out (warning or promise of covenant curses)
Instruction	Clarification of the expected response (call to heed covenant stipulations)
Salvation/Aftermath	Affirmation of future hope or deliverance (promise of covenant restoration blessings)

Prepared by Jason S. DeRouchie; adapted from p. 54 in *Chronological and Background Charts of the Old Testament* by John H. Walton; copyright © 1994 by John H. Walton. Used by permission of Zondervan. www.zondervan.com.

"Can the Ethiopian change his skin or the leopard his spots? Then also you can do good who are accustomed to do evil. I will scatter you like chaff driven by the wind from the desert ... because you have forgotten me and trusted in lies" (Jer. 13:23–25). *A leopard at Yotvata Hai-Bar Nature Reserve.*

The Author of Jeremiah Documented *Judah's Refusal to Repent and to Heed* Jeremiah's Message

The message of Jeremiah offered Judah a final opportunity to repent and avoid the catastrophic judgment of the Babylonian exile. However, the book of Jeremiah documents the national rejection of the prophet's message. As was characteristic of all of Israel's history, the people stubbornly refused to turn from their sinful ways (Jer. 5:3; 7:13, 25–26; 19:15; 35:15). As such, the people and leaders of Judah brought the judgment of exile upon themselves (26:5; 29:19; 32:33; 34:14–17; 36:31; 37:14; 40:3; 42:13, 21; 43:7; 44:16, 23).

When the prophet called the people to return to the "ancient paths" of God's law, "They said, 'We will not walk in it'" (6:16). When he sounded the trumpet warning of impending disaster, they responded, "We will not pay attention" (6:17). Because they blatantly refused to heed the prophet's warnings (18:12; 44:16), there was nothing left but for Yahweh to bring the covenant curses. Jesus would later experience the same rejection and unbelief from his generation when he came announcing the gospel of God's kingdom (Matt. 23:29–39).

> Jesus declared in Matthew 5:11–12: "Blessed are you when others revile you and persecute you and utter all kinds of evil against you falsely on my account. Rejoice and be glad, for your reward is great in heaven, *for so they persecuted the prophets who were before you.*"

Rejection of the Prophetic Word in Jeremiah 1–25

Jeremiah 1–25 particularly highlights Judah's missed opportunity to avoid divine judgment. The book opens with repeated calls for Judah to "return" to Yahweh by renouncing their sinful ways (Jer. 3:12–14, 22; 4:1–4, 12–14; 6:8). Yahweh's calls for repentance were extremely gracious in that Judah had been like an unfaithful wife toward him (2:20; 3:2, 20). Deuteronomy 24:1–4 stipulated that if a husband and wife divorced, the husband was not allowed to remarry this woman ever again (lit., "may not take her again as his wife"—24:4) if she married another man. In light of the fact that Israel and Judah had turned to many lovers, Jeremiah asked if it was even possible for them to "return" to Yahweh as their husband (3:1–3). The precedent of the Mosaic law would suggest not, but Yahweh invited his unfaithful partner to return to him anyway. Figuratively speaking, Yahweh loved his people so much that he was willing to break his own law in order to take them back.

In his "Temple Sermon" in chapter 7 (ca. 609 B.C.), Jeremiah made a passionate call for the people of Judah to reform their ways so that they might avoid judgment (7:3–7; cf. 26:2–6). When the nation rejected the offer to repent and be spared, Yahweh commanded the prophet not to pray for the people (7:16; 11:14; 15:1). Intercession for the people was pointless because the sentence of judgment had become irrevocable. Jeremiah's Temple Sermon was thus a decisive moment and turning point in Judah's history (see also 26:1–19). Jesus borrowed Jeremiah's image of the temple as a "den of robbers" when driving out the money changers and condemning the false worship of his own day (Matt. 21:13; cf. Jer. 7:11).

After the Temple Sermon, the calls for Judah to "return" diminish and then disappear. Calls to repent appear only three times in chapters 11–20 (Jer. 13:15–17; 17:19–27; 18:25) and do not appear at all

> The writer of Hebrews asserted, "It is a fearful thing to fall into the hands of the living God" (Heb. 10:31). Judah experienced this dreadful reality because of their sustained rejection of Yahweh's Word. May we learn from their failure and seek the Lord.

in chapters 21–25. Yahweh's patient endurance with his rebellious people had finally reached its breaking point.

Figure 11.5. Jeremiah's Two Visits to the Potter (chs. 18–19)

Jeremiah's first visit: Jeremiah observes the potter reshaping ruined clay (Judah still has the opportunity to repent; Jer. 18)

People's response: **"We will follow our own plans, and will every one act according to the stubbornness of his evil heart"** (18:12).

Jeremiah's second visit: Jeremiah purchases and smashes a clay jar (Judah's judgment has become unavoidable; ch. 19)

"And the vessel he was making of clay was spoiled in the potter's hand, and he reworked it into another vessel…. Then the word of the LORD came to me: 'O house of Israel, can I not do with you as this potter has done?'" (Jer. 18:4–6). *A potter at Eretz Israel Museum, Tel Aviv (photo by Kim Guess).*

What the Old Testament Authors Really Cared About

Disdain for the Prophetic Word in Jeremiah 26–45

Jeremiah 26–45 consists largely of narrative accounts of various episodes from Jeremiah's life and ministry. The books of Jeremiah and Jonah are unique among the prophetic books in their focus upon the prophet's life. However, the goal of these narratives in Jeremiah is not to provide a biography of Jeremiah's life, but rather to convey the theological message that *the judgment of exile came because of rejection of the prophetic word*. Various individuals, from the kings of Judah down to the common people, reflected the pervasiveness of Judah's unbelief through their responses to Jeremiah's preaching (37:1–2).

This section of the book documents the intensity of the opposition to Jeremiah's preaching. Jeremiah encountered hostile opposition from various political and religious leaders in Judah and endured severe physical abuse and persecution:

- People and leaders called for Jeremiah's death after his Temple Sermon (26:7–11)

- Hananiah opposed Jeremiah's message and promised that the Babylonian exile would be short (ch. 28)

- Shemaiah the priest wrote from Babylon calling for Jeremiah's censure and arrest (29:24–28)

- Jehoiakim destroyed Jeremiah's scroll and sought to punish the hidden prophet (36:19–26)

- Jeremiah was imprisoned at various places and times during the reign of Zedekiah (32:2; 33:1; 37:13–15; 38:13, 28; cf. 20:1–6)

- Jeremiah was thrown into a cistern and left to die (38:1–13)

- Jeremiah was kidnapped and taken away to Egypt (43:4–7)

Judah's unbelief was so deeply ingrained that even the destruction of Jerusalem in 586 B.C. did not turn the people from the error of their ways. In Jeremiah 40–44, the condition of the Jews who remained in the land of Palestine following the fall of Jerusalem was exactly the opposite of what was envisioned for the future restoration of Israel in Jeremiah 30–33. Unlike the righteous leadership of the future Messiah (30:9; 33:14–26), Ishmael, a member of the royal family, murdered Gedaliah and brutally killed a number of other Jews and Babylonian soldiers in an apparent attempt to restore the Davidic throne (41:1–10). Instead of having a new heart to obey (31:31–34), Johanan and his followers went down to Egypt in direct disobedience to the word of Jeremiah (43:1–7). Rather than the transformation and blessing of the new covenant, the Jews in Egypt then rebelled to the point of severing their covenant ties with Yahweh. They brazenly declared that they would not obey the prophet and that they would continue in their pagan practices (44:16–19). In response to their vows to do evil, Yahweh swore that he would destroy the Jewish remnant in Egypt and that only a tiny minority of them would ever return to their homeland (44:20–30).

"A wolf from the desert shall devastate them … because their transgressions are many, their apostasies are great" (Jer. 5:6). *A gray wolf at Yotvata Hai-Bar Nature Reserve.*

The book of Jeremiah provides a reminder that *response to the word of God is a matter of life and death*. In contrast to the national unbelief that led to death and exile (35:17), there are limited examples of positive response to Jeremiah's preaching. Yahweh promised to preserve the life of Baruch, Jeremiah's faithful scribe, in the midst of national calamity (45:1–5). Yahweh gave the same assurance to Ebed-Melech, the royal official, who convinced Zedekiah to rescue Jeremiah from the cistern, where officials opposed to the prophet's message had left him to die (39:15–18; cf. 38:7–13). The irony is that this foreigner from Cush had greater respect for the prophet's authority than Jeremiah's fellow Jews. Jeremiah also commended the clan of the Rechabites as a model of faithfulness and promised that this small family would survive the Babylonian exile (35:1–19). The Rechabites had remained faithful to the vow of their forefather Jonadab to never drink wine or engage in viticultural activities. If the

> Jeremiah anticipated turmoil of bitter loss to precede the great, new covenant restoration: mothers would become childless at the hands of Babylon (Jer. 31:15). Matthew considered this devastation to anticipate the tumult of death in Bethlehem that sparked Joseph, Mary, and Jesus' "exile" into Egypt (Matt. 2:13–18)—all before the Messiah's return to announce God's coming kingdom (4:17) and to inaugurate the new covenant (26:28).

Rechabites had remained faithful in following the wishes of their ancestor, then the people of Judah should have taken Yahweh's commandments even more seriously. The limited examples of obedience and faithfulness point to the sad reality that only a tiny portion of Judah's population responded positively to Jeremiah's preaching. The majority of the people would know only Yahweh's wrath.

The Author of Jeremiah Voiced *the Prophet's Anguish* over His Calling and Ministry

Jeremiah is known as the "weeping prophet" for good reason. His deeply personal anguish over the extreme opposition and difficulties he encountered is evident in a series of prayerful laments that are known as Jeremiah's "confessions" (Jer. 11:18–23; 12:1–6; 15:10–21; 17:14–18; 18:18–23; 20:7–18). These prayers reflect intense emotion as Jeremiah spoke concerning himself, his enemies, and God.

Like Job, Jeremiah cursed his birth and wished that he had never been born (15:10; 20:14–18). The prophet questioned why the wicked prospered (12:1–2) while suffering and opposition had been his reward for faithfulness to his calling (15:16–17; 17:16: 18:20). Jeremiah called for Yahweh to execute justice on his enemies (11:20; 15:15; 17:18; 20:12), and for judgment to even fall on their children and descendants (18:18–23). Jeremiah directed strongly accusatory language toward Yahweh himself. By causing Jeremiah to experience unending pain as his spokesman, Yahweh had been like "a deceitful brook" with no water (15:18). Jeremiah felt "deceived" and "overpowered" because he was compelled to speak the divine word even when he knew the "terror" that opposition to the message would bring into his life (20:7–10).

The Christian reader struggles with whether Jeremiah's confessions represent an appropriate response to God or with how they might serve as a model of prayer for today. However, these types of laments appear on the lips of righteous individuals throughout the Old Testament and are especially prominent in the Psalms. Jesus himself prayed the lament psalms as he faced the difficulties of living out the Father's will (see Matt. 27:46 with Ps. 22; Heb. 5:7).

> The "confessions" of Jeremiah remind us that we can pray to God with absolute honesty about our emotions and experiences.

Jeremiah's prayers for the destruction of his enemies were in accord with the standards of God's covenantal justice. He prayed for them to be carried off to slaughter (Jer. 12:3) because they had led him as a lamb to the slaughter (11:19). The prophet's prayers for judgment to fall on his enemies' families must be understood from the perspective of Old Testament curse language and the fact that Yahweh had promised to visit the sins of the wicked on their offspring who continue to hate him (Exod. 20:5; 34:7). Jeremiah's enemies were the enemies of Yahweh and rebellious members of the covenant community, fully deserving of the curses that Yahweh had threatened to bring upon his disobedient people.

"The LORD once called you 'a green olive tree, beautiful with good fruit.' But with the roar of a great tempest he will set fire to it, and its branches will be consumed" (Jer. 11:16). *Green olives.*

Yahweh did not ignore Jeremiah's laments or condemn the prophet for praying inappropriately. Yahweh reassured Jeremiah that he would be with him and would protect him from every danger that came his way (Jer. 15:20–21). At the same time, Yahweh gently challenged the prophet to remain faithful to his calling in spite of the difficulties and opposition (12:5; 15:19). Even in his despair, Jeremiah expressed his confidence that Yahweh was faithful and would ultimately deliver him from his enemies (20:11, 13).

Jeremiah's "confessions" also spoke to his role as mediator between Yahweh and his people. At one level, Jeremiah's anguish reflected the deep pain that Yahweh felt in abandoning his people and giving them over to judgment (9:1–3; 10:19–20; 14:17–18). At another level, Jeremiah's prayers for vindication also provided a model for how the exiles could pray as they repented of their sinful past and petitioned for Yahweh to deliver them from bondage and execute justice against their enemies (10:23–25; 14:19–22). From the perspective of the Old Testament canon, Jeremiah's laments prepare the reader for the prayers of the exiles that are found in Lamentations.

The Author of Jeremiah Portrayed *Babylon as God's Instrument and Object of Judgment*

Babylon, Agent of Divine Wrath

Jeremiah wanted the leadership of Judah to understand the Babylonian crisis from a theological perspective, rather than merely a political or military one. Judah's real problem was its broken relationship with Yahweh;

Babylon was only the human instrument of divine judgment. In the early stages of his ministry, Jeremiah warned that a powerful army would attack Judah "from the north" if Judah did not turn from its sinful ways (Jer. 1:13–14; 4:5–9; 5:14–17; 6:1–8, 22–24). Their attack would cause the land of Judah to become "without form and void," as if creation itself had been undone (4:23; cf. Gen. 1:2). The anonymity of this approaching army made the prophet's threats even more ominous. Jehoiakim's disregard of Jeremiah's warnings of coming judgment (Jer. 7:12–15; 26:3–6; 36:20–26) led to the Babylonian capture of Jerusalem in 597 B.C. (25:1–11). When the Babylonians arrived, Jehoiachin had been king for only three months and was taken away with a second wave of exiles. The Babylonians then placed Zedekiah on the throne as a puppet ruler.

"Year 7: in Kislev the king of Babylonia called out his army and marched to Hattu. He set his camp against the city of Judah (*Ya-a-ḫu-du*) and on 2nd Adar he took the city and captured the king. He appointed a king of his choosing there, took heavy tribute and returned to Babylon" (*The Babylonian Chronicle*). One of a series of clay cuneiform tablets known as *The Babylonian Chronicle. This piece details the capture of Jerusalem in 597/598 B.C. and the exile of King Jehoiachin, who spent most of his life in a Babylonian prison (see 2 Kings 25:27–30) (from the British Museum; translation from COS 468; cf. ANET 564).*

Jeremiah counseled Zedekiah that submission to Babylon was the only way that Judah could avoid total destruction (21:8–10; 38:1–3, 17–23). The king was not to think that Yahweh would miraculously deliver Jerusalem from the enemy (21:2–5) or that a military alliance with Egypt could provide a solution to the crisis (37:7–10). King Nebuchadnezzar of Babylon had replaced the Davidic king as Yahweh's "servant" (25:9; 27:6) and Yahweh had granted him dominion over the nations. Resistance to Babylon was futile (ch. 27; 38:2–3). Yahweh had given Jerusalem into Nebuchadnezzar's hand and would fight as the leader of the Babylonian army when they besieged the city (21:3–7; 34:2–3, 20–22). Jeremiah's message represented a reversal of earlier holy war traditions where Yahweh had fought for Israel against their enemies. Now Judah had become the enemy, and she would be judged accordingly (see Deut. 8:19–20).

It is little wonder that Judah's leaders viewed Jeremiah as a traitor who was weakening the war effort and that they took extreme measures to silence his message of "surrender or be destroyed" (Jer. 38:2–4). When Zedekiah ultimately decided in favor of rebellion against Babylon, Jeremiah's

Figure 11.6. Jeremiah's Message: "Submit to Babylon"

Before Jerusalem's Fall	After Jerusalem's Fall
To the exiles in Babylon: "Seek the welfare of the city where I have sent you into exile" (Jer. 29:7).	*To the Jews remaining in the land of Judah*: "Serve the king of Babylon, and it shall be well with you" (40:9).
To King Zedekiah: Surrender to Babylon and live (21:8–10).	*To Johanan after Gedaliah's assassination*: "Do not fear the king of Babylon, of whom you are afraid" (42:11).

prophecies of destruction were fulfilled. After a two-year siege, the city of Jerusalem was captured in 586 B.C., the city and temple were burned, and Zedekiah was deported along with many others from the land of Judah (39:1–10; ch. 52).

Jeremiah remained in the land of Palestine after the fall of Jerusalem and continued to preach that submission to Babylon was the key to Judah's survival. The Jews living in the land ignored this advice in two specific ways and brought further disaster upon themselves. First, Ishmael led a group of insurgents to assassinate Gedaliah, the Babylonian-appointed governor of Judah (41:1–2). Ishmael and his men also slaughtered a garrison of Babylonian soldiers and brutally murdered a group of Jewish pilgrims before escaping to Ammon (41:4–10). Second, a military officer named Johanan led a contingent of Jews to flee to Egypt to avoid Babylonian reprisals for the attack on Gedaliah after Jeremiah had advised them to remain in the land and to not fear the king of Babylon (42:9–11; 43:1–7). Johanan and his followers took Jeremiah and Baruch with them as they fled to Egypt. The assassination of Gedaliah led to a fourth deportation to

"Behold, I am watching over them for disaster and not for good. All the men of Judah who are in the land of Egypt shall be consumed by the sword and by famine, until there is an end of them" (Jer. 44:27). *Elephantine Island from the East Bank of the Nile. During the Persian occupation of Egypt (beginning ca. 343 B.C.), there is evidence of a Jewish presence at Elephantine, including a temple where worship of Yahweh was mixed with worship of Khnum, the Egyptian god of creation and water.*

Babylon in 582 B.C. Jeremiah's final recorded message is a warning that Babylon would extend its dominion to Egypt and inflict judgment on the Jews who thought they could hide from Yahweh and the Babylonian army (ch. 44).

Babylon, Recipient of Divine Wrath

Significantly, Jeremiah also taught that Babylon's dominion over Judah and the nations was temporary. Judah's exile would last for seventy years (25:11–12; 29:10), and Yahweh would then turn his wrath against the Babylonians and punish them for their own sins (25:13–14). After causing other nations to drink the cup of God's wrath, Babylon itself would fall down drunk and never rise again (25:15–29).

The oracles against the nations in Jeremiah 46–51 conclude with an extended oracle against Babylon in chapters 50–51. Babylon, the "hammer" and "war club" (50:23) used by God to judge other nations, would now be broken and shattered (51:21–25). Judah and Babylon would experience a reversal of fortunes. Babylon, the enemy from the north that had attacked Zion, would now itself be attacked by an enemy "from the north" (50:3, 9).

> Yahweh is indeed over all things and uses even wicked nations to accomplish his purposes, while still holding them responsible for their sinful actions (Jer. 25:9–14; 50:23; 51:21–25).

Babylon would receive exactly what it had done to Judah. Yahweh would fight with the armies attacking Babylon in order to deliver and vindicate Israel (50:33–35; 51:5–6). Babylon would be destroyed and reduced to ruins like Sodom and Gomorrah (50:39–40; 51:36–37, 58, 62). The conquest of Babylon by Cyrus and the Persians in 539 B.C. brought the historical fulfillment of Jeremiah's prophecies against Babylon.

The Author of Jeremiah Emphasized *the Global Extent of Yahweh's Judgment and Salvation*

As the God who is sovereign over all, Yahweh's judgment would fall on all nations, including superpowers like Egypt and Babylon (Jer. 25:12–13, 19; chs. 46; 50–51), as well as the smaller states surrounding Israel (chs. 47–49; cf. 25:20–25). Yahweh himself would wage war against the nations (46:10; 47:4, 6–7; 49:8–10, 35–38), judging them for their prideful arrogance (46:8; 48:7, 14, 29–30; 49:4, 16), mistreatment of Israel (48:27; 49:1–2; 50:11), and worship of idols (48:7, 35). The false gods of these peoples would share in their humiliation (46:25; 48:7; 49:3; 50:2). The oracles against the nations in Jeremiah 46–51 refer to the judgment of historical peoples before, during, and after Judah's fall to Babylon. However, their placement at the end of the book of Jeremiah gives them a future-focus, and the way in which Yahweh has judged his enemies in the past is representative of how he will judge all peoples in the future. The name "Babylon" appears with reference to the final enemy that God will destroy in the end times in Revelation 17–18, reflecting that this final world power will be like historical Babylon in its rebellion against God and its hatred of God's people.

Judgment is not God's only word for the nations in the book of Jeremiah. Remarkably, God promises to "restore the fortunes" of the Ammonites (48:47), Moabites (49:6), and Elamites (49:36), the same expression used to refer to the restoration of Israel in chapters 30–33. Jeremiah promised that Yahweh would "plant" Israel's wicked neighbors after uprooting them, just as he would do for Israel, if these nations would renounce their idols and turn to him (12:14–17). The larger tragedy of Israel's disobedience to Yahweh was that they had failed to be the instrument of God's blessing to the nations as envisioned by the Abrahamic covenant (4:1–3; cf. Gen 12:3).

> God's plan has always been to include the nations/Gentiles in the blessings of Israel's future salvation (Gen. 12:3; Jer. 3:17; 4:2; 12:14–17; 30:8–9; 48:47; 49:6, 36).

The Author of Jeremiah Promised *Restoration and a New Covenant Between Yahweh and His People*

The book of Jeremiah presents an overturning of the story of Israel's salvation found in the rest of the Old Testament. In Exodus through Joshua, Yahweh brought the people out of Egypt and gave them the land of Canaan as their promised possession. In Jeremiah, Judah leaves their homeland to go into exile, and Jeremiah is taken away to Egypt. The final message of Jeremiah is a proclamation of judgment against the sinful Jews living in Egypt (Jer. 44). Exile and return to Egypt were the climactic covenant curses that Moses had warned of prior to entry into the Promised Land (Deut. 28:64–68).

Although it appeared that the events surrounding the exile had brought the relationship between Yahweh and Israel to an end, Jeremiah promised that Yahweh would bring his people home from exile, forgive their sins, and establish a new covenant in place of the old one that had been irrevocably broken. This message of renewal and restoration is strategically positioned in the "Book of Consolation" (Jer. 30–33) found at the center of Jeremiah. In it Yahweh promised to "restore the fortunes" of his people (30:1, 18; 32:44; 33:11, 26).

In Jeremiah's lifetime, Israel had experienced an overturning of the exodus, but the future restoration would be a new exodus even greater than the first (16:14–15; 23:7–8). Yahweh would bring his people home from various places of captivity (30:3, 10–11; 31:8; 32:37). There would be a reversal of fortunes in that as Israel returned home, the nations that had oppressed it would be sent away into exile (30:16). God's people would once again "serve" the Lord rather than their foreign oppressors (30:8–9). Yahweh's deliverance would turn the sorrow and mourning of the past into dancing and celebration (31:4, 12–17). The people would rebuild their broken cities (30:18; 31:38–40) and once again enjoy the agricultural bounty of the Promised Land (31:5, 14). The Davidic dynasty would be restored, and the future Messiah would rule with justice (23:5–6; 30:9;

"Like these good figs, so I will regard as good the exiles from Judah.... I will set my eyes on them for good, and I will bring them back to this land.... Like the bad figs that are so bad they cannot be eaten, so I will treat Zedekiah the king of Judah, his officials, the remnant of Jerusalem who remain in this land, and those who dwell in the land of Egypt. I will make them a horror to all the kingdoms of the earth" (Jer. 24:5–6, 8–9). *Baskets of bad and good figs.*

31:21; 33:14–26). The historical breach between Israel and Judah would be healed and they would become one people (3:18; 33:7).

Yahweh also promised that he would make a new covenant with the house of Israel and Judah that would surpass the covenant he made with Israel at Mount Sinai (31:31–34). There would be forgiveness for sins and erasure of the failures of the past (31:34; 33:8). More importantly, there would be divine enablement for his re-unified people to permanently obey God's commandments (31:33). Writing the law on the heart and mind meant that Yahweh would provide a spiritual transformation that would give Israel the internal desire and disposition to obey God's commands. Ezekiel's prophecies clarified that this transformation would come about through the giving of the Holy Spirit (Ezek. 36:26–27). Israel would finally have the power to turn from its sinful ways (Jer. 31:18–19).

The problem with the old covenant was not the Mosaic law itself, which stood as a gracious gift from a redeeming, present God to guide Israel's life and witness (Deut. 4:5–8; 6:20–25; cf. Rom. 2:19–20; 7:12). Yahweh had set his love on Israel and called it to love and serve him from the heart (Deut. 6:5; 10:12, 15–16; Jer. 4:4), but Israel's heart never changed (Jer. 17:1; cf. Deut. 29:4).

> Yahweh's new covenant with Israel promised forgiveness for past sins and enablement for future obedience. The New Testament teaches that Christians today enjoy the blessings of the new covenant through the work of Messiah Jesus (Luke 22:20; Heb. 8:8–13; 9:16–18) and that Jesus came to bring the deliverance of Israel from its enemies promised by Jeremiah and the prophets (Luke 1:68–74).

Indeed, the problem with the old covenant was the sustained stubbornness and rebelliousness of the people (Jer. 4:4; 5:23; 16:12; 17:1) and the fact that the covenant's nationalistic nature meant that the covenant community was made up of a small remnant who truly knew Yahweh and a large majority that did not. The new covenant would resolve this problem by providing spiritual transformation for *all* who belonged to the covenant: "They shall all know me, from the least of them to the greatest … for I will forgive their iniquity" (31:34; cf. Deut. 30:6). Ultimately, it is the work of Messiah Jesus that makes this possible, "to the Jew first and also to the Greek" (Rom. 1:16). The restored remnant of Israel and the nations, with hearts now surrendered to Yahweh and the royal descendent of David (Jer. 23:5; 30:9), would never again have to experience judgment and exile for disobedience to Yahweh's commands, and they would forever enjoy the fullness of blessing in the Promised Land (32:39–41): "I will give them one heart and one way, that they may fear me forever, for their own good and the good of their children after them. I will make with them an everlasting covenant, that I will not turn away from doing good to them. And I will put the fear of me in their hearts, that they may not turn from me. I will rejoice in doing them good, and I will plant them in this land in faithfulness, with all my heart and all my soul."

"I will rejoice in doing them good, and I will plant them in this land in faithfulness, with all my heart and all my soul" (Jer. 32:41). *A man plowing near Mizpah (photo by Nathan Foreman).*

Summary

Jeremiah was appointed "a prophet to the nations," and his ministry was "to pluck up and to break down, to destroy and to overthrow, to build and to plant" (Jer. 1:5, 10). While the prophet wept over Judah's covenant infidelity, most of his hearers refused to turn back to God, choosing instead to identify themselves with the pagan nations that awaited divine wrath. Babylon was Yahweh's agent of ruin against Judah, destroying Jerusalem and the temple and proving God's faithfulness to his promise to bring curse on all who failed to fear him and who sought satisfaction and life in what could not supply (2:13, 19). Judah's dark night was not the final word,

EZEKIEL

Who?

Ezekiel was a Jerusalem priest, who was exiled to Babylon in 597 (Ezek. 1:1–3). His name means "may God strengthen/harden," which probably reveals the faith of his parents who gave him the name, though it is ironic that God would indeed "harden his face/forehead" (3:8–9) to prepare him for the difficult ministry that lay ahead.

The first verse of the book appears to place Ezekiel at thirty years old when Yahweh called him to be a prophet (1:1). Nearly all we know about Ezekiel's personal life is that he was married, but Yahweh took his wife's life midway through his ministry (24:15–24). We can also assume that his very unique—even bizarre—prophetic service took a toll on his psychological disposition. Ezekiel was frequently awestruck by fantastic visions of the divine glory and of strange creatures (chs. 1, 3, 10). To clarify the point of his message, he was also commanded to perform physically challenging "sign acts" or dramas (4:4–5:4; 12:1–6). He witnessed extraordinary visions of mass slaughters (chs. 9, 38–39), of otherworldly rivers (47:1–12) and structures (chs. 40–43), and of untold images of the underworld (32:17–32). Amazingly, the book gives no proof that anyone ever listened to his voice. Ezekiel, no doubt, was a weathered man, able to stand only by the strength of his God.

When?

Ezekiel was taken away in exile to Babylon in 597 B.C. and was called to his prophetic ministry in 593 B.C. (1:1–3).

The last recorded prophecy in the book comes in 571 B.C. (29:17). Thus his prophetic ministry spanned approximately twenty-three years.

Where?

Ezekiel's entire prophetic ministry occured while he is in exile in Babylon. Ezekiel was called to ministry while he was by the Chebar canal in Tel-Abib, Babylon (1:3; 3:15). However, a large part of his ministry grew out of his house in Babylon where he was bound (3:25).

Why?

Yahweh called Ezekiel to preach messages of judgment and salvation to the Jewish exiles in Babylon. Most of these messages made no call for repentance but announced an impending doom. This is why Ezekiel was prohibited from "rebuking" the Israelites (3:26). Instead, the prophet announced the forthcoming judgment of Yahweh that would fall upon Jerusalem (i.e., 586 B.C.). The fulfillment not only would validate him as a prophet (2:5, 7; 33:33) but would help all "know that I am the Lord"—a clause that occurs more than seventy times in the book! Significantly, despite the rebellion of Israel and the judgment that it evoked, Yahweh promised also to transform and restore a remnant of Israel to a right relationship with him. In the end, as the prophet foresaw, Yahweh would be there (48:35), dwelling in the midst of his people (37:26–27).

EZEKIEL

Preston M. Sprinkle

Carefully Crafted Verses from Ezekiel

"Son of man, I send you to the people of Israel, to nations of rebels, who have rebelled against me. They and their fathers have transgressed against me to this very day" (Ezek. 2:3).

"And I will give you a new heart, and a new spirit I will put within you. And I will remove the heart of stone from your flesh and give you a heart of flesh. And I will put my Spirit within you, and cause you to walk in my statutes and be careful to obey my rules" (Ezek. 36:26–27).

"My dwelling place shall be with them, and I will be their God, and they shall be my people. Then the nations will know that I am the LORD who sanctifies Israel, when my sanctuary is in their midst forevermore" (Ezek. 37:27–28).

THE AUTHOR OF EZEKIEL …
• Emphasized *God's sovereignty* over creation and especially over Israel.
• Accentuated the temple as mediating *God's glorious presence* on earth.
• Believed that *God abhors sin and will judge* it accordingly.
• Affirmed that *salvation* is possible only by *God's relentless, unmerited grace.*

The Author of Ezekiel Emphasized *God's Sovereignty* over Creation and Especially over Israel

The entire Bible testifies to Yahweh's sovereign rule over creation. The book of Ezekiel begins and ends with this affirmation.

The Glory of God from Beginning to End

The opening vision in Ezekiel 1 underscores Yahweh's universal sovereignty, as the prophet was awestruck by a magnificent vision of God's glorious presence, incarnated, as it were, in the likeness of one "with a human appearance" and seated on a throne (Ezek. 1:22–28). Thrones, of course, are where kings sit, and this throne rested above an "expanse" (1:22) and over four extraordinary creatures, each having four faces: that of a lion, a bull, an eagle, and a man. The "expanse" is likely an echo of the expanse (or sky) above the earth in Genesis 1:6 and thus points to Yahweh's supremacy over the world. The faces seem to represent human and non-human creatures, with "four" signifying totality (e.g., "four corners" of the earth = the entire world). While bizarre, the chapter's

"[The living creatures] had a human likeness, but each had four faces, and each of them had four wings.... As for the likeness of their faces, each had a human face...the face of a lion...the face of an ox...[and] the face of an eagle" (Ezek. 1:5–6, 10). ***Left:*** *the colossal winged lion with human head, a guardian spirit of Assyrian King Ashurnasirapal II (ca. 860 B.C.) found at Nippur, south of Nineveh;* ***Center and Right:*** *two guardian spirits with wings, the body of a man, and faces of man and eagle—also from Ashurnasirapal II's collection at Nimrud (all three images from the British Museum; center and right photos by Mark Borisuk). Whereas these winged creatures were "gods" in ancient Mesopotamia, Ezekiel portrays them merely as ministers to the true "Almighty" One, seated on the throne, whose own appearance was indescribable.*

point is clear—Israel's God is Lord over all creation, including every creature and every location—not only of the land of Israel but also of Babylon!

At the end of the book, we find another vision depicting Yahweh's sovereignty, only this one spans nine chapters (chs. 40–48). Earlier, Yahweh's presence had departed from the temple, ultimately resulting in its destruction (8:3–4; 9:3; 10:4, 15–19; 11:22–24). Now, Ezekiel saw God's glory returning to the throne of God's temple (43:1–9) after the defeat of all the evil forces in the world (chs. 38–39; cf. 43:7–8). The temple he saw sat on "a very high mountain" in the midst of a city (40:2), signifying, again, Yahweh's supremacy over all creation.

Thus, the body of this volume is "bookended" at its front and back to highlight Yahweh's sovereign rule over everything. And yet, even though God is certainly in control of all creation, his throne resides in Israel. So while the universality of Yahweh's reign is endorsed (as it is in other Old Testament books, especially Isaiah), for Ezekiel there is a special focus on Yahweh's rule over Israel.

Figure 12.1. Ezekiel at a Glance
Ezekiel's Vision and Call (1–3)
God's Judgment on Israel (4–24)
God's Judgment on the Nations (25–32)
Israel's Future Salvation (33–48)

God's Acts for the Sake of His Own Name

As a book that emphasizes Yahweh's sovereignty, Ezekiel is certainly *theocentric*, or centered on God. More than seventy times, Ezekiel described Yahweh's motivation for acting in history (whether it be salvation or judgment) with the phrase: "that they (or you) may know that I am the Lord" (e.g. 16:62; 20:38, 44; 24:27; 38:23; 39:7, 22). In other words, God frequently intervenes in human affairs ultimately to bring glory and honor to his own holy name. More than fifteen times Ezekiel depicted Yahweh as doing something "for the sake of my name." For example, in Ezekiel 36:22, Yahweh declared, "It is *not for your sake*, O house of Israel, that I am about to act [i.e., save the remnant of Israel], but *for the sake of my holy name*, which you have profaned among the nations to which you came" (cf. 36:32). Of course Israel would benefit from God's act of salvation, and certainly God grieved over the suffering of Israel and the horrible effects of their sinful behavior (cf. Exod. 3:7–9). But Ezekiel emphasized most of all that Yahweh ultimately acts on behalf of his own name, and he has the freedom to do whatever he feels will accomplish this, as the psalmist says, "Our God is in the heavens; he does all that he pleases" (Ps. 115:3).

God's Judgment and Defeat of All Foreign Powers

Yahweh's sovereignty over the foreign nations is shown in his punishment of them. After spending the first half of the book (Ezek. 4–24) proclaiming judgment on Israel for its sin, Yahweh spoke through Ezekiel to pronounce judgment on the surrounding nations (chs. 25–32). This shows that Israel's God is no tribal deity; his power and rule are not limited to the space of land between the Jordan River and the Mediterranean Sea! (Some Israelites did have this warped thinking, and God seeks to correct it in this book.) God would judge the people of Israel for their sin, but he would also hold the nations accountable, judging them accordingly. Even in the midst of a section filled with oracles about foreign nations, a focus on the redemption of Israel appears right at the center in Ezekiel 28:25–26. This shows again that Yahweh's universal sovereignty has a special focus on the nation of Israel.

God's sovereign rule is dramatically portrayed in the oracle of Ezekiel 38–39, where we find a colorful, prophetic description of Yahweh's total destruction of Israel's enemies, who are led by a certain "Gog, of the land of Magog" (38:2). This passage has spawned all sorts of wild speculations about the identity of Gog (Augustine thought it was the Goths; Martin Luther thought it was the Turks; at the end of the twentieth century some thought it was the Russians; and so on). However, there are signals in the text that suggest we should not interpret the vision quite so literally. First, the frequent use of the number seven appears symbolic of completeness (*seven nations* in 38:1–6; burning weapons for *seven years* in 39:9; cleansing the land for *seven months* in 39:12, 14). Second, the cataclysmic events said to accompany Yahweh's intervention appear regularly in the Latter Prophets as poetic depictions of this world's reaction to the intrusion of God's presence into space and time (38:20; cf. e.g., Isa. 5:25; 64:1; Jer. 4:23–26; Mic. 1:4). Third, the

> John appears to have viewed the "Gog and Magog" prophecy of Ezekiel 38–39 as a figurative depiction of God's final defeat of evil, for in Revelation 20:7–10 "Gog and Magog" are a general reference to the nations led by Satan in an effort to thwart God's move to restore creation.

personification of animals sitting at God's dining table and feasting on human flesh seems most likely a figurative depiction of the utter destruction of evil Yahweh will bring. Regardless of how one interprets the details, the overarching point of the passage seems clear: in the end, the God of Israel will defeat all his foes in a climactic move to reestablish peace in creation. Moreover, the end goal of Yahweh's passionate intervention is his own glory: "So I will show my greatness and my holiness and make myself known in the eyes of many nations. Then they will know that I am the LORD" (Ezek. 38:23; cf. 39:21–24). The theocentric focus of this passage is astounding! The God of Ezekiel, who is supreme over all, acts ultimately for the sake of his reputation in the world.

"Gather from all around to the sacrificial feast that I am preparing for you, a great sacrificial feast on the mountains of Israel, and you shall eat flesh and drink blood" (Ezek. 39:17). *From the seventh century B.C., an Assyrian victory procession with the dead floating in a river (from the British Museum).*

The Author of Ezekiel Accentuated the Temple as Mediating *God's Glorious Presence* on Earth

The Old Testament temple was the place where God's presence dwelt on earth among his people. His presence has always been *life-giving* (Ezek. 37:1–14; 47:1–12), and this is why Ezekiel's announcement of the imminent departure of God's glory (9:3; 11:23) and subsequent destruction of the temple (24:15–27) would have been devastating to both the prophet and his audience.

The Departure and Return of God's Presence

The importance of Yahweh's presence is highlighted throughout Ezekiel. It begins in chapter 1, where God's glory appears to Ezekiel in Babylon, beside the Chebar canal (1:1–3). What is striking is that the glory is not in the temple! The Israelites conceived of Yahweh's presence as dwelling in a physical structure, the temple, but Ezekiel 1 declares that God's presence is not limited to a building (cf. 1 Kings 8:27). In fact, Yahweh himself was a "sanctuary to them for a while in the countries" where Israel lived in exile (Ezek. 11:16), even though there was no *physical* temple structure. This reality served to counter the notion that the destruction of the temple in 586 B.C. brought about the destruction of the One who dwells in the temple. Ezekiel thus showed that the glory of Yahweh departed from the temple *before* the temple is destroyed by the Babylonians (9:3; 10:4, 18; 11:23). Yahweh's house may be destroyed, but *Yahweh himself*, who rules from heaven above, will *never* be destroyed. And in the end, he will return to his people (43:1–7).

God's Presence in the Messiah's Rule and the Spirit's Indwelling

The return of Yahweh's presence becomes a main motif in the latter part of the book (chs. 34–48). In Ezekiel 34, the prophet looks forward to a time

"I will set up over them one shepherd, my servant David, and he shall feed them" (Ezek. 34:23). *Well and feeding troughs at Tantur.*

when God will gather together the lost sheep of Israel under "one shepherd, my servant David," who will be "prince among them" (34:23–24; cf. 37:24–28). Although the book does not have a pervasive messianic expectation (not nearly as much as Isaiah), these statements clearly anticipate a messianic figure who will rule over God's people. When this happens, "they shall know that I am the LORD their God *with them*"

> Ezekiel 34:20–31 and 37:24–28 look forward to a time when Yahweh's Messiah, the Son of David, will mediate God's presence to his people. This time is fulfilled in the ministry of Christ, when "the Word became flesh and dwelt (lit., *tabernacled*) among us" (John 1:14).

(34:30). God's presence, then, will be mediated to his people through the Son of David.

God's presence is also embodied in his Spirit. The divine Spirit appears often in Ezekiel's book (more so than most other Old Testament books), and no other passage is as powerful and clear as Ezekiel 36–37. Here, Yahweh's presence through his Spirit dwells in the renewed nation of Israel (36:26–27; 37:14, 26–27), giving them life (37:1–14), enabling obedience to Yahweh and their new Davidic king (36:27; 37:24–28), and vindicating Yahweh's holiness in the sight of the nations (36:23; 37:28). God's people would enjoy life with God only through his Spirit and in relation to the Davidic king.

God's Presence in the Temple

While Ezekiel saw the Messiah mediating God's presence and the Spirit embodying this presence, the prophet never abandoned his priestly temple theology. Although he anticipated and saw the fulfillment of the Babylonian destruction of Solomon's temple (24:21; 33:21), he also believed that a new temple would be rebuilt sometime in the future (chs. 40–43). Not only this, he also saw that this temple would again be filled with the divine glory

"This water flows toward the eastern region and goes down into the Arabah, and enters the [Dead] sea; when the water flows into the sea, the water will become fresh.... And on the banks ... there will grow all kinds of trees for food ... because the water from them flows from the sanctuary" (Ezek. 47:8, 12). *Nahal David flowing eastward through the Judean wilderness to En Gedi at the Dead Sea.*

(43:1–5)—an act that would result in the restoring of life to all creation. This renewal was creatively portrayed in a vision of a supernatural river flowing from Yahweh's presence in the temple down to the Dead Sea, giving life to all its inhabitants (47:1–12). Intriguingly, this "river of the water of life" is picked up by John in Revelation 22:1–2 and correlated with the river of Genesis 2:10. This life-giving flow thus signifies that God's return to his new temple in the "new Jerusalem" is in some way a return to Eden, where the Creator resided in perfect harmony with his creation. In Ezekiel's words at the end of the book, the renewed paradise of God will be called, "The LORD Is There" (Ezek. 48:35).

What are we to make of this future temple? Should we anticipate the future rebuilding of a literal temple, fully equipped with a Levitical priesthood (44:15–31) performing sacrifices of atonement for sin (45:15–17, 20)? This literal interpretation is possible and is suggested by the fact that Ezekiel is shown such detailed measurements of this temple (40:5–42:20) and given such detailed guidelines about how worship should be conducted within it (chs. 44–46). This literal interpretation runs into problems, however, when we look at the book of Hebrews, where the Old Testament sacrificial system is clearly a mere shadow pointing to the ultimate sacrifice of Christ (see esp. Heb. 10). Furthermore, the New Testament appears to treat the prophecy of this temple much like it does Isaiah's prophecy of the new creation—namely, as finding at least initial fulfillment in Christ and the church (cf. Isa. 43:18–19; 65:17 with 2 Cor. 5:17; see also 2 Peter 3:14; Rev. 21:1). Jesus clearly referred to his body as the temple (John 2:19–21), and Paul referred to the church as "the temple of God" (1 Cor. 3:16; cf. 2 Cor. 6:16; Eph. 2:20–21). Moreover, in Revelation 21:1–22:5, John envisioned a future holy city called the "new Jerusalem," which is remarkably similar to Ezekiel's temple. John, like Ezekiel, was taken by an angelic guide with a measuring rod to a high mountain (Rev. 21:10, 15; Ezek. 40:2–3). There he saw a structure: a holy city in the shape of a cube in Revelation 21:16; a perfectly square temple in Ezekiel 42:15–20. With this, both John and Ezekiel saw a "river of life" flowing from the throne of God (Rev. 22:1–2; Ezek. 47:1–12). The key difference in John's vision was that there was no temple in the city because "its temple is the Lord God the Almighty and the Lamb" (Rev. 21:22). In John's portrayal, the new heavens and new earth will include no physical

> In 1 Corinthians 6:18–20, Paul asserted: "Flee from sexual immorality.... Or do you not know that your body is a temple of the Holy Spirit within you, whom you have from God? You are not your own, for you were bought with a price. So glorify God in your body." Consider what you are and how much Jesus paid for your holiness next time you are tempted to sin!

temple to mediate God's presence, because through the Lamb, Jesus Christ, believers gain full and abundant access to God. There is no *need* for a temple!

The Author of Ezekiel Believed That *God Abhors Sin and Will Judge It Accordingly*

The book of Ezekiel makes absolutely clear that God is not soft on sin. Yahweh is, to be sure, a God of grace and love—but he is also a God of judgment. None of the prophets, Ezekiel included, ever grew weary of graciously warning Israel about God's righteous wrath against sinful behavior. Reminding Israel of the covenant curses, the prophets called Yahweh's people to repent and return to their covenant Lord and Father.

Israel's Depravity and Social Injustice

From chapters 4–24, Ezekiel predominately preached messages of judgment on Israel; in chapters 25–32 he preached messages of judgment on the surrounding nations. Like the other Hebrew prophets, Ezekiel described Israel's sin in terms of idolatry, fornication, robbery, and murder (see, e.g., Ezek. 8:5–18; 22:1–31). But this prophet went beyond all others in depicting Israel's sinful behavior with edgy—sometimes sexually graphic—rhetoric (esp. chs. 16 and 23). For instance, in Ezekiel 16, the prophet portrayed the nation as an unfaithful bride, selling herself to various lovers out of uncontrollable and excessive desire for sex (16:28–34). In Ezekiel 23, she is again pictured as longing to sleep around with her Babylonian and Egyptian playmates (23:11–21). In both contexts, Ezekiel was not trying to use racy rhetoric for rhetoric sake; rather, he was trying to shock his audience in order for them to wake up and see how horrendously disloyal and disgusting their behavior was to Yahweh. Ezekiel did not shrink back from telling Israel that she was, in theological terms, *totally depraved*.

One of the most significant ways Israel sinned against Yahweh was through their partiality and social injustice against those less fortunate. These sins included charging excessive interest on loans to the poor (18:8, 13; 22:12, 29), failing to provide housing for the needy (11:1–5), neglecting the orphans and widows in their midst (22:7), exploiting the immigrant who came to the land (22:7), and oppressing the powerless in their community (18:12). Those receiving the greatest condemnation were, of course, the leaders. They were entrusted to care for the people, but they only cared for themselves (34:2–6). Yahweh considered their failure to meet the material and economic needs in their midst to be the equivalent of *murder*. That is, when God indicted Israel for having filled "the land with violence" (8:17)

and "multiplied [their] slain in this city" (11:6), he was referring to the leaders' economic exploitation of the poor in the land (cf. 22:2–6 with 22:7 and 34:2–6). To strip the poor of all their resources seals their death—and God calls this *murder*. Much later, James would warn the rich with similar statements (James 5:4–6): "Behold, the wages of the laborers who mowed your fields, which you kept back by fraud, are crying out against you, and the cries of the harvesters have reached the ears of the Lord of hosts. You have lived on the earth in luxury and in self-indulgence. You have fattened your hearts in a day of slaughter. You have condemned and murdered the righteous person." We would do well today to learn from Ezekiel's message, always keeping in mind Jesus' words, "As you did it to one of the least of these my brothers, you did it to me" (Matt. 25:40).

"The sojourner suffers extortion in your midst; the fatherless and widow are wronged" (Ezek. 22:7). *A woman with a bag of harvest near Lebonah.*

The most powerful statement in all of Ezekiel regarding such social sin occurs in 16:49. Here, Ezekiel described the sins of Israel as going beyond the sins of Sodom. This is an outrageous claim, evoking images of the infamous attempt at homosexual gang rape at the door of Lot's house (Gen. 19:4–11). Amazingly, however, Ezekiel has something different, perhaps even *more* perverse in mind: "Behold, this was the guilt of your sister Sodom: she and her daughters had pride, excess of food, and prosperous ease, but did not aid the poor and needy" (Ezek. 16:49). The point is shocking—even disturbing, especially for those of us today who have the world's goods and yet close our heart to the disadvantaged in our midst (1 John 3:17).

> Yahweh condemned Israel not only for their mistreatment of the poor, but also for their simple apathy toward those who were needy. What would God say today to the affluent church of the West, who, like Israel, is also largely overfed and unconcerned (Ezek. 16:49)?

God's Covenant Judgment upon Israel

Because of such sins, God's fierce anger is unleashed in judgment. In the context of Ezekiel, that judgment was the destruction of Jerusalem with its temple and the massacre that followed. The prophet graphically portrayed Yahweh's wrath in that event through various "sign acts," wherein he acted out the Babylonian siege and the ensuing massacre and exile (Ezek. 4:9–11; 5:1–4). The destruction of Jerusalem was not just political, however. It was not just one nation (Babylon) conquering another nation (Israel). The massacre was *theological*. It was the inevitable outcome of Yahweh's covenant relationship with the nation, a covenant that promised not only blessings for obedience but also curses for disobedience (see Lev. 26; Deut. 28). Thus, the sword of Babylon was at the same time the sword of Yahweh (Ezek. 5:1–4; 9:1–11; 21:1–27).

The Author of Ezekiel Affirmed That *Salvation* Is Possible Only by God's Relentless, Unmerited Grace

Even though Israel would be punished for their sin, judgment is never God's final word. Grace is! Grace, for Ezekiel, is Yahweh's unmerited commitment to the nation of Israel to bring it back to its land and to give it new life. Grace is Yahweh's faithfulness to his covenant promise, the promise that stretches back to Abraham and extends through David to the exilic community. Grace is Yahweh's ability to keep his promise and to bless Israel *despite* its sinful ways.

The first two-thirds of Ezekiel is primarily about sin and judgment (Ezek. 4–32), but there are glimpses into Yahweh's future salvation of the nation (11:14–21; 16:60–63; 20:33–44; 28:25–26), a salvation that is elaborated on further in the last third of the book (chs. 33–48). For example, in Ezekiel 11:14–21, the repetition of the divine "I will" (11:17, 19) highlights God's unwavering commitment to his covenant as he grounded Israel's future salvation in the divine promise. Accordingly, Ezekiel 20:33–44 portrays Israel's salvation in terms of a "second exodus," where imagery from the original exodus account (Exod. 6–15) is used to describe the return of the exiles from Babylon (Ezek. 20:33–34; cf. Jer. 16:14–16; 23:7–8; Isa. 40–55). Similarly, in the midst of Ezekiel's prophecies against the foreign nations, there is a brief testament to Israel's future redemption in Ezekiel 28:25–26. So even before Ezekiel begins his "oracles of salvation" in chapter 34, he opens small windows early on to allow the light of God's grace to penetrate the somewhat dark "oracles of judgment." From beginning to end, then, Ezekiel's God is a God of grace.

Figure 12.2. Mosaic Covenant Blessings, Curses, and Restoration Blessings

Blessings

1. Yahweh's presence, favor, loyalty (Lev. 26:11–12)
2. Confirmation of the covenant (Lev. 26:9)
3. Be a holy people to Yahweh (Deut. 28:9)
4. Rains in season (Lev. 26:4; Deut. 28:12)
5. Abounding prosperity and productivity:
   a. General (Deut. 28:12)
   b. Fruit of the womb (Lev. 26:9; Deut. 28:4, 11)
   c. Fruit of the livestock (Deut. 28:4, 11)
   d. Fruit of the ground (Lev. 26:4–5, 10; Deut. 28:4, 8, 11)
6. General and unspecified (Deut. 28:2, 6, 8, 12–13)
7. Peace and security in the land with no fear:
   a. General (Lev. 26:5–6)
   b. From harmful animals (Lev. 26:6)
   c. From enemies (Lev. 26:6)
8. Victory over enemies (Lev. 26:7–8; Deut. 28:7)
9. Freedom from slavery (Lev. 26:13)
10. Global influence and witness (Deut. 28:1, 10, 12)

Curses

1. Anger and rejection from Yahweh (Lev. 26:17, 24, 28, 41; Deut. 4:24–25; 29:20, 24, 27–28; 31:17–18, 29; 32:16, 19–22, 30)
2. Rejection and destruction of the cult (Lev. 26:31)
3. War and its ravages:
   a. General (Lev. 26:17, 25, 33, 37; 28:25, 49, 52; 32:23–24, 30, 41–42)
   b. Siege (Lev. 26:25–26, 29; Deut. 28:52–53, 55, 57)
4. Fear, terror, and horror (Lev. 26:16–17, 36–37; Deut. 28:66–67; 32:25)
5. Occupation and oppression by enemies and aliens (Lev. 26:16–17, 32; Deut. 28:31,33, 43–44, 48, 68; 32:21)
6. Agricultural disaster and non-productivity:
   a. General (Lev. 26:20; Deut. 28:17–18, 22, 40; 29:23)
   b. Drought (Lev. 26:19; Deut. 28:22–24)
   c. Crop pests (Deut. 28:38–42)
7. Starvation, famine (Lev. 26:26, 29, 45; Deut. 28:53–56; 32:24)
8. Illness, pestilence, and contamination (Lev. 26:16; Deut. 28:21–22, 27–28, 35, 59–61; 29:22; 32:24, 39)
9. Desolation:
   a. Of holy places (Lev. 26:31)
   b. Of cities and towns (Lev. 26:31, 33)
   c. Of the land (Lev. 26:32–35, 43; Deut. 28:51; 29:23)
10. Destruction by fire (Deut. 28:24; 32:22)
11. Harm from wild animals (Lev. 26:22; Deut. 32:24)
12. Decimation and infertility:
   a. Of family (Lev. 26:22; Deut. 28:18, 59)
   b. Of cattle (Lev. 26:22; Deut. 28:18, 51)
   c. Of population generally (Lev. 26:22, 36; Deut. 4:27; 28:62; 32:36)
13. Exile and captivity:
   a. Of the people (Lev. 26:33–34, 36, 38–39, 41, 44; Deut. 4:27; 28:36–37, 41, 63–64, 68; 29:28; 30:4; 32:26)
   b. Of the king (Deut. 28:36)
14. Forced idolatry in exile (Deut. 4:28; 28:36, 64)
15. Futility (Lev. 26:16, 20; Deut. 28:20, 29–31, 33, 38–41)
16. Dishonor and degradation (Lev. 26:19; Deut. 28:20, 25, 37, 43–44, 68)
17. Loss of possessions and impoverishment (Deut. 28:31)
18. Loss of family (Deut. 28:30, 32, 41; 32:25)
19. Helplessness and stumbling (Lev. 26:36–37; Deut. 28:29, 32; 32:35–36; 38–39)
20. Psychological afflictions (Deut. 28:20, 28, 34, 65–67)
21. Lack of peace and rest (Deut. 28:65)
22. Denial of burial (Deut. 28:26)
23. Becoming like the cities of the plain (Deut. 29:23)
24. Death and destruction (Lev. 26:36, 39; Deut. 4:26; 28:20–22, 44, 48, 51, 61; 29:20; 30:15,18–19; 31:17; 32:25–26, 35, 39, 42)
25. General and unspecified (Deut. 4:30; 28:20, 24, 45, 59, 61, 63; 29:19, 21–22; 31:17, 21, 29; 32:23, 35)
26. General punishment, curse, and vengeance (Lev. 26:41, 43; Deut. 28:16, 20–21, 27; 30:19; 32:35, 41, 43)
27. Multiple punishments (Lev. 26:18, 21, 24, 28)

Restoration Blessings

1. Renewal of Yahweh's presence, favor, and loyalty (Lev. 26:42, 45; Deut. 4:29, 31; 30:3, 9)
2. Renewal of the covenant (Lev. 26:42, 44–45; Deut. 4:31)
3. Restoration of true worship and ability to be faithful (Deut. 4:30; 30:6, 8)
4. Population increase (Deut. 30:5, 9)
5. Agricultural bounty (Lev. 26:42; Deut. 30:9)
6. Restoration of general prosperity, well-being, and wealth (Deut. 30:3, 5, 9; 32:39)
7. Return from exile and repossession of the land (Deut. 30:3–5)
8. Reunification (Deut. 30:3–4)
9. Power over enemies and aliens (Deut. 30:7)
10. Freedom and restoration from death and destruction (Lev. 26:44; Deut. 30:6; 32:39)

All references are from Leviticus 26, Deuteronomy 4; 28–32. No single prophetical book, except perhaps Isaiah, mentions all categories. Prepared by Jason S. DeRouchie. The Blessings and Curses sections are adapted from pp. 1259–60 in "Malachi" by Douglas Stuart in *The Minor Prophets: An Exegetical and Expository Commentary* edited by Thomas Edward McComiskey; copyright © 1998 by Thomas Edward McComiskey. Used by permission of Baker. www.bakerpublishinggroup.com.

God's Grace Toward His Wayward Harlot: Ezekiel 16

This fact is no more clearly and creatively portrayed than in Ezekiel 16. This long chapter narrates a colorful story of Yahweh's relationship with Israel, metaphorically portrayed first as Yahweh's adoption of an abandoned child (Ezek. 16:1–7) and then as Yahweh's unmerited love for his wife (16:8–14). The Cinderella-like story ensued with God adorning his beloved bride with luxurious gifts fit only for a queen (16:9–14). But the wife "trusted in [her] beauty and played the whore because of [her] renown" (16:15). All the gifts that Yahweh gave Israel were turned into objects of idolatry and exploited by her foreign lovers (16:15–22). Thus Israel forgot about the days of her youth, when Yahweh rescued her (16:22), and her perverse behavior continued. She not only prostituted herself with every willing person but also even gave gifts for her services while receiving nothing in return (16:32–35; probably referring to Israel's political alliances with foreign nations). Thus, Ezekiel compared Israel's sin with that of Sodom, the archetypal symbol of a sinful community, and with that of Samaria, Judah's despised sister to the north. Although chosen to be a light

"I made my vow to you and entered into a covenant with you, declares the Lord GoD, and you became mine.... But you trusted in your beauty and played the whore because of your renown and lavished your whorings on any passerby" (Ezek. 16:8, 15). *An orthodox Jewish wedding.*

Spirit of life has set you free in Christ Jesus from the law of sin and death," and God "will also give life to your mortal bodies through his Spirit who dwells in you" (Rom. 8:2, 11; cf. 2 Cor. 3:3, 6).

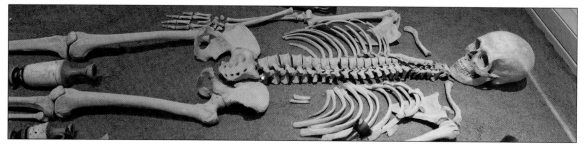

"O dry bones, hear the word of the LORD. Thus says the Lord GOD to these bones: Behold, I will cause breath to enter you, and you shall live" (Ezek. 37:4–5). *A skeleton from Kerameikos, an area in Athens, Greece (from the Athens Archaeological Museum).*

Conclusion

Through and through, Ezekiel is a book about grace. From an abandoned, bloody newborn tossed out into an open field (Ezek. 16:4–7) to a dry, dusty skeleton lying in a valley (37:1–2), Israel's life was marked with misery and despair. Left to themselves, these people would know only death. *But God*, who is rich in mercy, would not cast off his people forever. They were unworthy, *but God*, who stands supreme and sovereign over all things, would intervene. Ezekiel is a book about the unmerited intrusion of God's favor into the world of sinners. And while his primary focus is the spiritual transformation of Israel, he also gives hope to outsiders from the world's nations who might align themselves with Yahweh (16:53–63; 17:23–24; 29:13–16; 47:22–23). No one, whether Jew or Gentile, deserves the saving work of Yahweh. But because his love bubbles over toward his creation, he intervenes to save, to forgive, and to restore. We were running headlong into a pit of sin and destruction, *but God* acted on our behalf. And according to Ezekiel, that move is grace.

KEY WORDS AND CONCEPTS FOR REVIEW

Vision of God's glory	Blessings, curses, restoration blessings
Theocentric	Wayward harlot
Gog and Magog	Grace
Yahweh's presence	Spiritual rebirth
Messiah	Heart transplant
Spirit	Vision of the dry bones
Temple	But God!
Social injustice	

KEY RESOURCES FOR FURTHER STUDY

Block, Daniel I. *The Book of Ezekiel*, 2 vols. NICOT. Grand Rapids: Eerdmans, 1997, 1998.

Duguid, Iain M. *Ezekiel*. NIVAC. Grand Rapids: Zondervan, 1999.

Stuart, Douglas. *Ezekiel*. TPC. Nashville: Thomas Nelson, 2002.

Wright, Christopher J. H. *The Message of Ezekiel*. BST. Downers Grove, IL: InterVarsity, 2001.

ISAIAH

Who?

This book claims to contain the visions (Isa. 1:1), the words (2:1; 37:6–7, 21–29), the burdensome oracles (13:1), the experiences (6:1–8; 7:3–12; 8:1–4; 38:1–8, 21–22; 39:3–8), and the sign acts (20:2–6) of the prophet Isaiah. Although the introductions that mention Isaiah's name are found only here and there, most interpreters would assume that these superscriptions refer to the authorship of all the following chapters. Thus Isaiah's authorship of the burdensome oracle in 13:1 would apply to all the burdensome oracles in 15:1; 17:1; 19:1; 21:1; 22:1; and 23:1. We are told in 2 Chronicles 26:22 that Isaiah wrote about the reign of Uzziah, while 2 Chronicles 32:32 indicates that the prophet detailed material on Hezekiah in "the vision of Isaiah the prophet" (cf. Isa. 1:1).

When?

Based on information within these prophecies, Isaiah began prophesying during the reign of Uzziah (1:1; 6:1), continued in the era of Ahaz (1:1; 7:1), and finished in the time of Hezekiah (1:1; 37:1; 38:1; 39:1). This time period stretched from about 755 B.C. to a little after 700 B.C. The latest unforetold event recorded is the death of Sennacherib in 681 B.C., so the final edition of all of Isaiah's prophesies had to appear some time after that date.

Where?

The prophet Isaiah warned people in Jerusalem about the future. In 3:1 he predicted dire judgment for those living in Judah, and in 3:16 he spoke of God's coming judgment on the proud women of Jerusalem. Isaiah prophesied in Jerusalem when he gave the parable of the vineyard (5:3), had conversations with Ahaz (7:3), condemned the Assyrians (10:24), warned the inhabitants of the city (22:1–14; 29:1–4), and condemned political alliances with Egypt (30:1–5; 31:1–9). We know his location was Jerusalem in chapters 36–39, but numerous other chapters refer to the prophet speaking to the people of Jerusalem or Judah without identifying a location.

Why?

Isaiah provided both kings and the common people with Yahweh's instruction on their need to trust him:

1. When the times were good and the nation was powerful;
2. When the nation was being attacked and no alliance could help them;
2. Because the idols can do nothing, but God's Servant will bear their sins;
4. Because on the Day of Yahweh, God will judge the wicked and create a glorious new Jerusalem for the righteous people in Israel and from all nations.

CHAPTER 13

ISAIAH

Gary V. Smith

Carefully Crafted Verses from Isaiah

And the haughtiness of man shall be humbled, and the lofty pride of men shall be brought low, and the LORD alone will be exalted in that day (Isa. 2:17).

But they who wait for the LORD shall renew their strength; they shall mount up with wings like eagles; they shall run and not be weary; they shall walk and not faint (Isa. 40:31).

THE AUTHOR OF ISAIAH ...

- Warned of *the dangers of pride and unbelief*.

- Called people to *trust God*.

- Believed *the suffering Servant paid for the sins of many*.

- Longed for *God's glorious kingdom*.

" I am the LORD, and there is no other, besides me there is no God.... I form light and create darkness, I make well-being and create calamity, I am the LORD, who does all these things" (Isa. 45:5, 7).

He bore the sin of many, and makes intercession for the transgressors (Isa. 53:12).

Isaiah is an amazing book. Its expansive historical and theological scope, including its developed treatment of universal restoration under the oversight of the messianic Servant, made it a favorite of the New Testament authors and early church.

Figure 13.1. Isaiah at a Glance
Will People Trust God or Exalt Themselves? (Isa. 1–12)
Do Not Put Your Trust in the Nations (chs. 13–27)
Woes of Judgment Mixed with Threads of Hope (chs. 28–35)
God Miraculously Delivers Those Who Trust Him (chs. 36–39)
Trust God, for He Will Restore His People (chs. 40–55)
The Destiny of God's Servants and the Wicked (chs. 56–66)

The Author of Isaiah Warned of *the Dangers of Pride and Unbelief*

Warnings Against Pride and Unbelief in Judah

Ministering in Judah in the second half of the eighth century, Isaiah prophesied over four decades and through four reigns of Judean kings. During this whole time, he denounced pride and maintained a call to humility and faith in God. Judah became arrogant during the days of King Uzziah, when the nation was loaded with riches and had a very strong army of elite troops and weaponry (Isa. 2:7; 2 Chron. 26:11–15). Trusting in their own strength, Judah felt secure about their future but lost sight of Yahweh. The false security was further evidenced when the wealthy women of Jerusalem proudly strutted around the city in the finest of clothes, while failing to care for the poor in their midst (Isa. 3:15–16). In response, God would take away all their jewelry and give them the clothes of mourning (3:18–26). Indeed, on the Day of Yahweh, when God would come as warrior to definitively put an end to all his enemies, all the proud would be humbled and Yahweh alone would be exalted (2:11, 17; 5:15–16).

Amidst the reign of Ahaz, Isaiah proclaimed a similar message. After announcing that Judah would withstand the Syro-Ephraimite onslaught (734–732

> Isaiah charged, "Stop regarding man in whose nostrils is breath, for of what account is he?" (Isa. 2:22). Similarly, the psalmist urged (Ps. 146:3–5): "Put not your trust in princes, in a son of man, in whom there is no salvation. When his breath departs, he returns to the earth; on that very day his plans perish. Blessed is he whose help is the God of Jacob."

B.C.), Isaiah warned the king that if he did not believe God's promises and act upon them, he would not last (7:9). Ahaz refused to trust Yahweh and in unbelief even refused to ask for a miraculous sign in the heavens above or in the earth beneath (7:10–12). As a result, Isaiah prophesied that the Assyrians would destroy his land (7:17).

Warnings Against Pride in the Foreign Nations

The book of Isaiah makes clear that Yahweh is King not only of Israel but also of the world! In a series of oracles, Yahweh warned the kings of Judah not to make alliances with foreign peoples for he was planning to destroy all these nations due to their pride. The enemy kings of Assyria boasted that they had defeated and controlled most of the kingdoms of the world (10:13–14; 37:23–25) and that they were far more powerful than the small country of Judah and its God (36:18–20; 37:10–13). As the Assyrian lord proclaimed to the people of Judah (36:18): "Beware lest Hezekiah mislead you by saying, 'The LORD will deliver us.' Has any of the gods of the nations delivered his land out of the hand of the king of Assyria?" However, Isaiah declared that Yahweh would remove Assyria's power and destroy them (10:12; 37:29), even crushing them in the land of Judah (14:24–27). Similarly, because of its pride, the great and glorious nation of Babylon (13:19; 47:1–11), which was a potential ally for Judah (39:1–7), would become like Sodom and Gomorrah (13:19; 47:1–11). The Babylonians may have thought that their country was the most powerful nation on earth, but

"[The king of Assyria] says, '… Like a bull I bring down those who sit on thrones.' … Therefore the Lord GOD of hosts will send wasting sickness among his stout warriors" (Isa. 10:13, 16). *From Nimrud, south of Nineveh, the depiction of one of Assyrian King Ashurnasirapal II's bull hunts (ca. 860 B.C.).*

its haughty king would end up in the grave, and the city would go into mourning because of its defeat (14:11–15; 47:1). Both Moab, in the heights of the Transjordan, and Tyre, the great sea merchant city, would also be brought low due to their self-exaltation (16:6–7; 23:8–9). Yahweh had planned to crush the pride of the nations, and no one can prevent God's hand from accomplishing his purposes (14:27; 25:1; 37:26; 46:10). As such, the people of Judah needed to trust God and not look to the nations for help.

Figure 13.2. Main Characters in the Prophets	
Yahweh	The primary character; he stands as Creator, King, Father, Lover, Friend, Judge, and Savior.
Prophets	Messengers of the gods; Yahweh's prophets were his covenant enforcers, calling God's people back to their covenant obligations and reminding them of the blessings and curses.
Remnant	Those faithful few among Yahweh's people who remained dependent and loyal to their covenant with God, even through the disobedience and punishment of the community as a whole, and who would enjoy restoration after the curse of exile.
Rebels	The unfaithful majority among Yahweh's people who were not dependent and loyal to their covenant with Yahweh and who would experience God's lasting wrath.
Nations	The Gentile pagans outside Israel who practiced idolatry, who served as Yahweh's agents of judgment, and who would ultimately experience God's wrath; some among the nations would be drawn to Yahweh and be established among his restored people.

Prepared by Jason S. DeRouchie.

Warnings to Unbelievers about God's Wrath

Isaiah envisioned that, at the end of the ages, Yahweh will bring great judgment on all parts of the world and on all the unbelievers that live on the earth (24:1–23). Everyone and everything that is proud and lifted up will be brought low (2:12–17), and all who run after idols will perish before the splendor of God's glory (2:9–10, 17–21). On the Day of Yahweh, the sun and moon will be darkened, the earth will be split asunder (24:19–20), and only few people will survive (13:9–13; 24:1–13). At that time, Yahweh's anger against sin will result in the trampling of all sinners (63:1–6) and the dissolving of the heavens and the earth (34:1–4), as God destroys everything that has to do with sin (34:5–8). Sometimes Isaiah compares this day of destruction with

> What chance of survival do sinners have when they fall into the hands of an angry God (see Heb. 10:31)?

treading out the grapes (63:1–6), and at other times one hears of God's fire, whirlwind, and sword bringing just judgment on the ungodly (66:15–17). These descriptions of Yahweh's wrath are terrifying reminders that God takes sin seriously and that we should too!

The LORD declares: "I have trodden the winepress alone.... Their lifeblood spattered on my garments, and stained my apparel.... I trampled down the peoples in my anger" (Isa. 63:3, 6). *Stepping on grapes in a winepress at Avdat.*

The Author of Isaiah Called People to *Trust God*

In the midst of various trials and temptations the people of Judah were faced with the choice of trusting in Yahweh or relying on something or someone else instead of Yahweh. Because God is invisible and no one really knows when or if he will display his great power on behalf of his people, it is often tempting to trust in things that one can see and in the things that people can do to help themselves.[1]

---

1. See "The Attractions of Idolatry" at Fig. 8.3.

Trusting God in Times of War

Jesus said (Matt. 10:28): "Do not fear those who kill the body but cannot kill the soul. Rather fear him who can destroy both soul and body in hell." Isaiah's audience far too often failed at just this point. For example, the nations of Israel and Syria (i.e., Aram) attacked Judah (the Syro-Ephraimite War, 734–732 B.C.) in order to force King Ahaz to join their coalition against the powerful Assyrian King Tiglath-pileser III (Isa. 7:1; 2 Kings 16:5–7; 2 Chron. 28:5–6). Isaiah exhorted Ahaz not to fear these violent enemies, but to trust in Yahweh for deliverance. The prophet also warned the king that unless he stood firm in his faith in God, he would not last (Isa. 7:4–9). In spite of the great advantage of trusting God for deliverance from his enemies, Ahaz sent a costly bribe to Assyria's king and asked him to come and rescue Judah from its enemies (2 Kings 16:7–9). Because of this failure of faith, Isaiah predicted that the Assyrians would overpower Judah like a mighty flood (Isa. 7:17, 20; 8:7–8), and this is exactly what happened. Assyria came and did rescue Judah from Syria (i.e., Aram) and Israel, but then Assyria turned against Judah and heavily taxed the nation.

Some years later, King Hezekiah of Judah refused to pay his tribute to the Assyrian King Sennacherib (2 Kings 18:7), so Sennacherib and his army came to subdue Judah and to force them to pay their taxes (18:13). Being vastly overpowered, Hezekiah initially turned to trust in the Egyptian army (Isa. 30:1–5; 31:1–9) and later wanted to make a treaty with Babylon (39:1–6). Isaiah condemned both of these options, calling the king instead to look for help from the Holy One of Israel (31:1). Isaiah challenged Hezekiah to trust in Yahweh alone and not to depend on the horses and chariots of Egypt, for no other nations could help them. Judah needed to repent and to turn back to God, for he alone was able to defeat the Assyrians (31:6–9). "I, I am the LORD, and besides me there is no savior" (43:11). Isaiah declared that all the powerful nations on earth amounted to

"The Lord is bringing up against them the waters of the River, mighty and many, the king of Assyria and all his glory. And it will rise over all its channels and go over all its banks, and it will sweep on into Judah, it will overflow and pass on" (Isa. 8:7–8). *A relief of Assyrian King Tiglath-pileser III (ca. 728 B.C.), with whom Ahaz attempted to make a treaty (2 Kings 16:7) (from the British Museum; photo by Mark Borisuk).*

nothing in God's eyes; indeed, they were but a drop in a bucket or a speck of dust (40:15, 17). When all of Judah but the city of Jerusalem was defeated, in desperation Hezekiah finally humbled himself and went into the temple to pray for God's deliverance: "So now, O LORD our God, save us from his hand, that all the kingdoms of the earth may know that you alone are the LORD" (37:20). Soon after that Yahweh miraculously delivered Hezekiah and the city of Jerusalem from the Assyrian army by sending an angel who killed 185,000 Assyrian troops in one night (37:36).

> Because God defeated the large Assyrian army without any human assistance (Isa. 37:36), what theological principle can we draw about trusting God when we face challenges that seem insurmountable? We declare, "If God is for us, who can be against us?" (Rom. 8:31).

Trusting God Instead of Idols

An idol is anything other than Yahweh that masters one's soul or that one treasures above God. In Isaiah's day, as in our own, people far too often put their trust in things man made rather than in the One who made man. The presence of carved images and pagan temples was a smaller problem in the days of King Uzziah (2:8), but it became a major issue in the time of King Ahaz, who was a devoted worshipper of Baal (2 Kings 16:1–4; 2

"They were no gods, but the work of men's hands, wood and stone. Therefore they were destroyed. So now, O LORD our God, save us … that all the kingdoms of the earth may know that you alone are the LORD" (Isa. 37:19–20). *Left, the lion-faced Sekhmet, the Egyptian goddess of warfare (fourteenth century B.C.) (from the Vatican Museum);* **center,** *a golden head from the Oxus Treasure in Persia (fourth–fifth century B.C.) (from the British Museum);* **right,** *an idol of Phoenician god Baal-Hammon (fourth century B.C.) (from Larnaca Museum, Cyprus).*

But instead of punishing all who foolishly wander away from him, God would lay the punishment for our sins on this righteous Servant (53:4–5). This was not a big mistake; instead it was exactly what God had planned: "It was the will of the LORD to crush him" (53:10; cf. Acts 4:27–28). God intended that this Servant would be a covenant to the peoples and a light that would bring salvation to the Hebrews as well as those from all the nations of the world (Isa. 42:6; 49:6, 8). This work of the Servant would have the effect of bringing God's justice to the nations (42:1–4), of opening the eyes of those who were blind to spiritual truth, and freeing people who were held captive to false theological ideas (42:7; 49:9; 61:1–2). In the end this Servant would be vindicated by God (50:8) and consequently he would be satisfied with his work, see many who would follow him, and intercede for others (53:11–12). Having accomplished his mission, the Servant would be highly exalted (52:13, 15) because he would suffer the punishment that other people deserved.

Who Is This Servant in the Old Testament?

The suffering Servant in these poems is left largely unidentified by Isaiah, although the task of bringing justice to the nations is surely the responsibility of a king (42:1–4). Elsewhere in the book, the role of bringing justice and righteousness to this world is consciously connected to the role of the great kingly Messiah (9:7). Going along with this hint about the identity of the Servant is the fact that this Servant will grow up as a tender shoot and as a root out of dry ground (53:2), terminology that seems to connect this Servant with the Messiah who is also a shoot from the stump of Jesse, a Branch from his roots (11:1). In addition, both the messianic figure in 11:2 and the Servant in 42:1 have the blessing of God's Spirit on them and both function as a great light (9:2; 42:6; 49:6) that will bring joy to all mankind throughout the world (9:3; 42:10–13; 49:13). But Isaiah never really explains exactly how it is possible that a victorious ruling messianic king could ever become a suffering Servant who dies for the sins of others. This is the good news that is more fully explained by the writers of the New Testament.

"There shall come forth a shoot from the stump of Jesse, and a branch from his roots shall bear fruit" (Isa. 11:1). *An olive tree stump at Neot Kedumim.*

Who Is This Servant in the New Testament?

The New Testament writers and Jesus himself unequivocally identify Jesus of Nazareth as the fulfillment of these prophesies about the suffering Servant. He was the one who received a special anointing of the Holy Spirit at his baptism as well as the approval of God in the statement that Jesus was the one God loved and was the one who pleased God (Isa. 42:1; Matt. 3:17; Mark 1:11; Luke 3:22). Because Jesus went around healing the weak, Matthew 12:15–21 connects the work of Jesus with the ministry of the Servant in Isaiah 42:1–4. Jesus himself said that he came to serve others (Matt. 20:28; Phil. 2:7) and to take on himself the infirmities of others (Isa. 53:4; Matt. 8:16–17). At the Last Supper Jesus connected the blood he would spill with the establishment of the new covenant (Isa. 42:6; 49:6; Luke 22:20), and as he taught in the synagogue he connected his ministry with of the Anointed One in Isaiah 61:1–4 (Isa. 42:7; Luke 4:16–21). Certain Jewish rulers abhorred him (Isa. 53:3; John 11:53; 15:19; Acts 3:13), but others understood who he was (Isa. 52:15; Rom.15:21) and believed in him (John 12:42). He was seen as a light to the nations (Isa. 42:6; 49:6; Matt. 4:16; Luke 2:32) and the light of the world (John 1:9; 8:12; 12:35–36). The death of Christ is connected to the prophecies of Isaiah (Isa. 53:3; Luke 18:31), specifically the mocking and spitting on him (Isa. 50:6; 53:3; Matt. 28:29–30) and his bearing the sins of others (Isa. 53:5; Rom 4:25). Phillip explained to the Ethiopian eunuch that Isaiah 53:7–8 relates to Jesus, and Peter testified that Jesus was the innocent one in Isaiah 53:9 who suffered and died for our sins (1 Peter 2:21–25). Both Paul and the writer of Hebrews also connected the Servant's intercession in Isaiah 53:12 to Jesus' present ministry of interceding for others (Rom. 8:34; Heb. 7:25). Thus Jesus fulfilled the work of the suffering Servant in his first coming when he died for the sins of others, but he will also fulfill the role of the reigning Messiah when he returns a second time to rule the world in justice (Dan. 7:13–14).

> With Isaiah 53 in mind, Peter declared of Christ: "He committed no sin, neither was deceit found in his mouth…. He himself bore our sins in his body on the tree, that we might die to sin and live to righteousness. By his wounds you have been healed" (1 Peter 2:22, 24; cf. Isa. 53:4, 9, 11).

The Author of Isaiah Longed for *God's Glorious Kingdom*

Because of the sinfulness of mankind and the unbelief even within Israel, the prophet Isaiah knew that, left to themselves, there was no hope for the sinful people in this world. All their righteous deeds looked like filthy rags (Isa. 64:6). Their only hope was to know and believe Yahweh (43:10), to trust in the one who was able to blot out all their sins (43:25), and to turn to God and be saved (45:22). They needed to come and partake of the spiritual food that God offers (55:1), to seek the Lord while he may be found, and to turn to Yahweh so that he can freely pardon their sins (55:6–7). Only the redeemed, the holy people of God can ever hope to enjoy the everlasting covenant promised to David and his followers (55:3). Isaiah's messages attempted to persuade his audience to repent of their sins (59:20) and to transform their lives so that they could enjoy the glories of Yahweh's wonderful kingdom. To strengthen his appeal, Isaiah pictured the amazing glories of this new kingdom and contrasted the wonderful joy of being there with the ghastly horror of suffering under God's wrath.

The People of the New Kingdom

Yahweh's future kingdom will be glorious because he himself will be present there with his people (60:1–2). The full appearance of his glory will be that great light that will attract the nations to come with many gifts to offer to Yahweh and his people (60:3–11). He will call for the nations at the far extremities of the earth to turn to him and be saved (45:22). Then all mankind will know that Yahweh is the Savior, Redeemer, the Holy and Mighty One who is able to save them (49:26). As these nations stream into Jerusalem from all the four corners of the world, some will help Hebrew people as they travel to Jerusalem (14:1–2; 60:3), while others will go to distant nations to proclaim God's glory to people who have never heard of Yahweh's love or seen his greatness (66:19–20). People will come from afar on whatever means of transportation that is available (66:20), but their common purpose will be to honor and glorify the Lord (60:9).

"The coastlands shall hope for me, the ships of Tarshish first, to bring your children from afar…for the name of the LORD your God, and for the Holy One of Israel, because he has made you beautiful" (Isa. 60:9). *A harbor and city panorama of Samos Pythagorio, a Greek Island in the eastern Aegean Sea off the coast of Asia Minor, where Paul stopped on his third missionary journey (see Acts 20:15).*

These will all be holy people who have had their sins forgiven (4:3–4). God will teach his ways to all the people who come to Zion and eliminate all the past conflicts that existed among the nations (2:2–4). God will reign over Zion, his people, and over all the earth (24:23; 52:7). People will exalt and praise the Lord (25:1–5; 26:7) when they attend the great banquet Yahweh will provide for the righteous (25:6). At that time there will be no sorrow or death (25:8; 65:19), and the dead will come to life to enjoy God's new creation and to receive their rewards (26:19). Yahweh will pour out his Spirit, and people will live in peace and be righteous (32:15–18; 44:3; 59:21; 66:12). Those who

> What a glorious future is waiting for all who persevere in faith, trusting and treasuring God even amidst life's tragedies. Because the great salvation is only for those who call upon the name of the Lord in faith, and because people can believe only if they hear, may we share boldly and joyfully the good news of salvation (see Rom. 10:13–15)!

were previously blind will see, and the lame will walk (35:5–6). God will establish his covenant with his people (55:3; 61:8), and he will bless his servants with abundance, meeting all their needs (65:13). They will live long and enjoy the fruits of their labor (65:20–23). Such glorious images should fill all in Christ with hope and motivate us to persevere even through the toughest times in this age.

The World of the New Kingdom

Yahweh will create a new heavens and a new earth for his redeemed people (65:17; 66:22). His glory will be a protection over them (4:5–6), and God will provide abundant rain and great fertility (30:23–26; 41:17–20). The dry desert wastelands will be transformed into fertile places with beautiful flowers and trees (35:1–2, 7), and man's adversarial relationship with the fierce ani-

"The wilderness and the dry land shall be glad; the desert shall rejoice and blossom like the crocus; it shall blossom abundantly and rejoice with joy and singing…. They shall see the glory of the LORD, the majesty of our God" (Isa. 35:1–2). *A winter crocus in Odem Forest.*

mals will be a thing of the past (11:6–8; 65:25). The ransomed of the Lord will come and sing with joy and gladness (35:10), and because Yahweh's glory will be so bright, the sun and moon will almost disappear from sight (60:19). God will create a new city of Jerusalem (65:18) and give it the new names of "Praise" for its gates, "Salvation" for its walls (60:18), plus "Hephzibah" (my delight) and "Beulah" (married) to the city itself (62:4). These wonders will be enjoyed by all whom the Lord ransoms (51:11)!

The King of the New Kingdom

Significantly, all the glory for this new kingdom will go to God (43:7, 21; 60:1–2, 9), for he will rule as King forever (43:15; 44:6–8). His reign will coincide with some of the functions of the messianic Servant, for the Servant, the Messiah, and God all claim that they will be responsible for bringing about a world of justice, righteousness, and peace (9:6–7; 11:4–5; 42:1–4; 59:16–17). The Messiah will rule on the throne of David forever (9:7), the Servant will be highly exalted (52:13), and kings and princes will bow before him (49:7). In this new world, where all people gladly worship the Holy One of Israel, reflecting his worth and finding satisfaction in him, God's original plans for creating this world will be fulfilled. May we long for this day and live in the light of it, even now!

Summary

The prophet Isaiah addressed a "sinful nation, a people laden with iniquity" who had "forsaken the LORD" (Isa. 1:4). To those persisting in arrogance, he promised sure judgment. However, to all who would turn from pride and unbelief to trust in the Holy One of Israel, he trumpeted the good news that "God reigns" and that salvation is possible. In glorious hues, the book paints a hope-filled picture of global restoration under the headship of the messianic Servant, who would pay for the sins of many at the cost of his own life, establish justice and peace in the world, and make a way for ethnic Jew and Gentile alike to enjoy lasting relationship with God in the new creation. This glorious vision has begun to be fulfilled in Christ Jesus, and it will reach its consummation after he returns to earth as conquering King.

KEY WORDS AND CONCEPTS FOR REVIEW

Pride	Yahweh's incomparability
The Day of Yahweh	Servant
Wrath	Messiah
Characters in the Prophets	Suffering Servant
Trust in God	God's kingdom
Idols	New heavens and new earth

KEY RESOURCES FOR FURTHER STUDY

Motyer, J. Alec. *The Prophecy of Isaiah*. Downers Grove, IL: InterVarsity, 1998.

Oswalt, John N. *Isaiah*. NIVAC. Grand Rapids: Zondervan, 2003.

Smith, Gary V. *Isaiah*, 2 vols. NAC. Nashville: B&H, 2007, 2009.

Young, Edward J. *The Book of Isaiah*, 3 vols. Grand Rapids: Eerdmans, 1992.

PRE-EXILIC PROPHETS TO ISRAEL

Who?

Jonah, Hosea, and Amos were prophets who spoke to the kingdom of Israel before it was destroyed in 723 B.C. Jonah, the son of Ammitai, came from Gath-Hepher, a town on the tribal border of Zebulun (2 Kings 14:25). His name meant "dove"—a symbol of love and an ironic contrast with Jonah's unloving attitude toward the Assyrians to whom he was called to speak. Before he was called to be a prophet, Amos worked with sheep and fruit in the area of Tekoa, about five miles south of Jerusalem (Amos 1:1; 7:14). His name meant "burden," an appropriate name for someone with his "heavy" message. Hosea, son of Beeri, was called as a prophet to marry a "loose" woman named Gomer (Hos. 1:2–3). With her, he had three children who were given ominous names, all pointing to God's judgment on Israel. Hosea's own name meant "save," which was fitting in light of his radical message of salvation. He was probably a contemporary of Amos.

When?

Jonah was known for preaching oracles announcing the restoration of Israel during the early part of the reign of Jeroboam II (ca. 770 B.C., cf. 2 Kings 14:25–26). Amos prophesied during the reign of Jeroboam II "two years before the earthquake" (Amos 1:1), which can be dated approximately to 760 B.C. Hosea's activity was around the same time but would have lasted longer (Hos. 1:1) (ca. 760–730).

Where?

The story of Jonah began in Israel but soon moved to the capital city of Assyria, known as Nineveh. In this "City of the Fish," a prophet who had been delivered by a fish preached the need for repentance. Amos spoke to the northern kingdom in places like Samaria and Bethel (Amos 3:12, 14). As a southerner speaking in the north, he was viewed as an intruder and was told to "go home" (7:12). Because references to the northern kingdom abound in his message, Hosea served as a prophet to Israel (Hos. 4:15; 5:1; 6:8).

Why?

The book of Jonah is unique, for rather than providing a collection of oracles, it narrates a short story with a theological point. It was a meditation on the universal implications of the Israelite theological confession: God's mercy encompassed all who were truly penitent (Exod. 34:6–7, cf. Jonah 4:2). Amos proclaimed a message of judgment against the Israelites for their lack of concern for social justice. Hosea's marriage to an unfaithful wife symbolized God's union with an unfaithful Israel, and his verbal message confronted the nation.

PRE-EXILIC PROPHETS TO JUDAH

Who?

Micah, Nahum, Zephaniah, Habakkuk, Joel, and Obadiah were all prophets whose target audience was Judah before the exile. Not many specific details are known about these prophets. Micah's hometown, Moreshat-Gath, was in the western lowlands of Judah, and indicated that he probably had a rustic background (Mic. 1:1). His name meant "Who is like Yahweh?"—a rhetorical question, emphasizing God's transcendence (cf. 7:18). Nahum, from Elkosh (perhaps in Galilee), comforted the people of Judah with a prophecy of the coming destruction of Assyria's capital, Nineveh (Nah. 1:1). Appropriately, his name meant "comfort." Habakkuk ("embrace") was regarded as the prophet of "faith" (Hab. 2:4; cf. 3:17–19), who ironically wanted answers for God's apparent disregard of the righteous. Zephaniah's ("hidden by Yahweh") lengthy genealogy was a sign of his prominent status (Zeph. 1:1). Little about Joel ("Yahweh is God") is known except that he was the "son of Pethuel" (Joel 1:1), and Obadiah ("servant of Yahweh") had a message of judgment against Edom.

When?

Micah prophesied approximately between 737 and 690 B.C., with his proclamation averting an Assyrian destruction of Jerusalem in 701 B.C. Nahum's prophecy occurred after the fall of Thebes in 664 B.C. (Nah. 3:8) and before the fall of Nineveh in 612 B.C.; a likely date is around 650 B.C., while Assyria was still a major world power.

Habakkuk prophesied during the Babylonian rise to power (ca. 630 B.C.) and was likely a contemporary with Zephaniah, who prophesied around 627 B.C. during the reign of Josiah. Due to a lack of explicit internal evidence, both Joel and Obadiah are difficult to date. However, the great destruction Joel anticipates and Obadiah reflects on may be the Babylonian overpowering of Judah in 586 B.C.

Where?

All of these prophets spoke in the southern kingdom of Judah. Joel's location is more difficult to determine, but many of his oracles assume the presence of the temple (Joel 1:13; 2:1).

Why?

Micah called for a radical social and spiritual reformation, which eventually spared the city of Jerusalem (see Jer. 26:18). Nahum inspired hope with his message that the Assyrian terror of the world would finally cease. Habakkuk addressed God, not people, wanting answers for how he could judge Judah with the more evil Babylonians. Zephaniah spoke against idolatry and foretold of a great looming time of judgment known as the Day of Yahweh (Zeph. 1:14–17). In order to elicit repentance, Joel used a recent locust plague to remind Judah of a coming day of judgment, while Obadiah confronted an arrogant Edom enriching itself at Judah's expense.

POST-EXILIC PROPHETS

Who?

Haggai and Zechariah ministered at the same time and, with Malachi, were the last of the Twelve prophets. Haggai's name meant "festal," a word associated with celebration. He could have been a very aged prophet, for there is an inference that he had seen Solomon's temple (Hag. 2:3). Zechariah ("Yahweh has remembered") was the son of Berekiah, the son of Iddo (Zech. 1:1). Iddo may have been a priest who returned to Judah after the exile (Neh. 12:4), which would have made Zechariah a priest as well as a prophet, and a younger contemporary of Haggai. Malachi's name meant "my messenger," which was appropriate, because his message predicted a messenger who would suddenly come to the temple before the awesome day of Yahweh (Mal. 3:1). Since Malachi 1:1 begins with the same introductory formula as is found in Zechariah 9:1 and 12:1, many scholars assume that the book simply continued Zechariah and that the name "Malachi" did not represent a particular person but an office—one discharged with a message. This would be anomalous in the Twelve if it were so.

When?

The times of Haggai and Zechariah were precisely dated. Haggai's ministry was dated to the second year of Darius I of Persia (ca. 520 B.C.) (Hag. 1:1, 2:10), while the same date is the earliest given for Zechariah. The latest date for the latter was the fourth year of Darius (Zech. 1:1, 7; 7:1). The date for the message of Malachi is somewhat difficult to place, but linguistic peculiarities and social/spiritual conditions suggest the period of Ezra and Nehemiah's reforms or just thereafter (ca. 450 B.C.).

Where?

Each of the prophets prophesied in the Persian province of Judah, urging reform in the light of God's future plan for the nation and world.

Why?

Both Haggai and Zechariah were commissioned to encourage the rebuilding of the temple. Work on the temple had ceased shortly after the first return by the exiles. Discouraged with hard economic times and the failure to see the fulfillment of all restoration prophecies, the people began to place their own interests ahead of the kingdom of God. But both prophets emphasized the importance of seeing beyond the humble beginnings of the present moment to recognize its stupendous implications (Hag. 2:1–9, Zech. 4:6–14). A few generations later, Malachi sought to revive a people who had forgotten their identity as a result of mixed marriages, a neglect of worship, and a cynical outlook. A messenger would come and suddenly appear in the temple, signaling the final Day of Yahweh.

CHAPTER 14

THE TWELVE

Stephen G. Dempster

Carefully Crafted Verses from the Twelve

How can I give you up, O Ephraim? ... My heart recoils within me; my compassion grows warm and tender. I will not execute my burning anger; I will not again destroy Ephraim; for I am God and not a man, the Holy One in your midst, and I will not come in wrath (Hos. 11:8–9).

"Rend your hearts and not your garments." Return to the LORD your God, for he is gracious and merciful, slow to anger, and abounding in steadfast love; and he relents over disaster. Who knows whether he will not turn and relent, and leave a blessing behind him? (Joel 2:13–14).

THE AUTHOR OF THE TWELVE ...

- Compiled twelve prophetic writings into *a single, unified book*.

- Affirmed *God's amazing love* for Israel and *sin's horrific nature*.

- Clarified the implications of *Yahweh's covenantal commitment* to Israel

- Stressed the need for God's people *to reflect God's character*.

- Emphasized the future *day of judgment* for the wicked and *of salvation* for the righteous.

- Announced *the coming of a new David*, who would bring God's kingdom.

"I hate, I despise your feasts.... Even though you offer me your burnt offerings and grain offerings, I will not accept them.... Take away from me the noise of your songs.... But let justice roll down like waters, and righteousness like an ever-flowing stream" (Amos 5:21–24).

The Author of the Twelve Compiled Twelve Prophetic Writings into *a Single, Unified Book*

The Twelve are often called the Minor Prophets for their length and not their message. These covenant representatives functioned in the Old Testament much like the twelve apostles in the New—as emissaries and ambassadors of God's truth and as a foundation for God's house. It is not a coincidence that the number of writing prophets in the Hebrew Bible (fifteen: Jeremiah, Ezekiel, Isaiah, and the Twelve) matched the number of patriarchs and tribes (fifteen: Abraham, Isaac, Jacob, and the twelve tribes). The prophets were a mini-Israel calling back the larger nation to its covenant Lord.

In the Christian English Bible, the Minor Prophets consist of twelve separate books and are positioned at the end of the Old Testament. Thus Malachi's prophecy about Elijah coming to prepare the way before the great and terrible day of Yahweh is a powerful segue into the New Testament, which begins with John the Baptist and his ministry of preparation and repentance, heralding the arrival of the new age (Mal. 4:5–6; cf. Matt. 11:13–14). In Jesus' Hebrew Bible, however, these prophets comprised one scroll and were placed near the middle, closer to the Law and just before the Writings. With Jeremiah, Ezekiel, and Isaiah, the book of the Twelve provides theological commentary on Israel's checkered history (Genesis–Kings), while also pointing ahead to a brighter day. Through emphasis on Israel's sin, Yahweh's just judgment, and hope after curse, this prophetic collection describes Israel's history in the light of the covenant and so serves as a close ally of the Law, urging Israel to return to their roots as the people of God. The inclusion of twelve prophets in one scroll ensured that they sang together, not only in physical unison but also in theological harmony. Although each of the Twelve had different parts to sing in the prophetic choir, they all followed the same Conductor, conveying his message. Furthermore, when we listen to their voices together, we hear far more than if we listen only to the individual parts.

"Remember the law of my servant Moses, the statutes and rules that I commanded him at Horeb for all Israel" (Mal. 4:4). *A painting of Moses and the Ten Commandments in the chapel interior at Jebel Musa, traditional site of Mount Sinai.*

The literary sequence of the Twelve differs from the prophets' probable chronological sequence in history—a fact that suggests the biblical ordering is thematically and theologically significant. The following chart compares the difference between the biblical and chronological sequences.

It is instructive to consider why the compiler of the Twelve arranged the books the way he did. The audience of the prophets alternates between the northern and southern kingdoms for the first six prophets. God spoke to one and then to the other until the northern kingdom was decimated. Thus there was an interest in communicating to the whole nation, the entire people of God. Then three prophets spoke to the southern kingdom until it was destroyed. Finally, three post-exilic prophets spoke to a restored Judah.

Figure 14.1. The Biblical and Chronological Sequences of the Twelve

BIBLICAL SEQUENCE		CHRONOLOGICAL SEQUENCE				
Order	Message Target*	Order	Origin*	Message Target*		
Hosea	NK Israel	Jonah (ca. 770)	NK Israel	NK Israel/Assyria	Assyria	PRE-EXILE
Joel	SK Judah	Amos (ca. 760)	SK Judah	NK Israel		
Amos	NK Israel	Hosea (ca. 760–730)	NK Israel	NK Israel		
Obadiah	SK Judah/Edom	Micah (ca. 737–690)	SK Judah	SK Judah		
Jonah	NK Israel/Assyria	Nahum (ca. 650)	SK Judah	SK Judah/Assyria		
Micah	SK Judah	Habakkuk (ca. 630)	SK Judah	SK Judah	Babylon	
Nahum	SK Judah/Assyria	Zephaniah (ca. 627)	SK Judah	SK Judah		
Habakkuk	SK Judah/Babylon	Joel (ca. 600?)	SK Judah	SK Judah		
Zephaniah	SK Judah	Obadiah (ca. 586?)	SK Judah	SK Judah/Edom		
Haggai	Judah	Haggai (ca. 520)	Judah	Judah	Persia	POST-EXILE
Zechariah	Judah	Zechariah (ca. 520–518)	Judah	Judah		
Malachi	Judah	Malachi (ca. 450)	Judah	Judah		

*NK = northern kingdom; SK = southern kingdom
Prepared by Jason S. DeRouchie and Stephen G. Dempster. Most dates are taken from John H. Walton, *Chronological and Background Charts of the Old Testament* (Grand Rapids: Zondervan, 1994), 52. While probably secondary, the Septuagint has an alternative order for the first six prophets: Hosea, Amos, Micah, Joel, Obadiah, Jonah.

Figure 14.2. Yahweh's Prophets in the Flow of Israel's History

ASSYRIAN THREAT (870–626 B.C.) AND THE DEATH OF ISRAEL

Date	Prophets	SOUTHERN KINGDOM (JUDAH)		NORTHERN KINGDOM (ISRAEL)	
		Prominent Kings	Key Events	Prominent Kings	Key Events
900		**Rehoboam** (930–913)	**930–Kingdom divided; first southern king**	**Jeroboam I** (930–909)	**First northern king; worship centers at Dan and Bethel**
		Asa (910–869)	Good king		
				Omri (885–874)	Samaria made capital
850	Elijah	Jehoshaphat (872–848)*		Ahab (874–853)	No Yahweh worship; international influence
	Elisha				853–Made Assyrian vassal
				Jehu (841–814)	Omride dynasty ends
800				Jeroboam II (793–753)	Israel's political zenith
	Jonah				
750	Amos/Hosea				
	Isaiah/Micah	Ahaz (735–715)*	Foolish alliance with Assyria	Hoshea (732–723)	Last king of Israel
		Hezekiah (729–686)*	**Faithful king; reformation in Judah**		**723–Fall of Samaria to Assyria; Israel exiled**
700			701–Jerusalem delivered		
		Manasseh (696–642)*	**Most wicked Judean king;** Judah's judgment sure		
650	Nahum				

BABYLONIAN THREAT (626–539 B.C.) AND THE DEATH OF JUDAH

SOUTHERN KINGDOM (JUDAH) CONTINUED

Date	Prophets	Prominent Kings	Key Events
	Habakkuk	**Josiah (640–609)**	**Faithful king; reformation in Judah**
	Zephaniah/ Jeremiah		
			612–Assyria fell to Babylon; 605–Babylon sacked Jerusalem; Daniel and nobles exiled
600	Joel?	Jehoiachin (598–597)	597–Babylon sacked Jerusalem; King Jehoiachin, Ezekiel and nobles exiled
	Ezekiel (in Babylon)	Zedekiah (597–586)	Last king of Judah
	Obadiah?		**586–Fall of Jerusalem to Babylon; first temple destroyed; Judah exiled**

INITIAL RESTORATION UNDER PERSIA (539–323 B.C.) AND ANTICIPATIONS OF THE RESURRECTION OF GOD'S PEOPLE

Date	Prophets	Key Events in Judah	Key Events in Babylon and Persia
			Daniel as court official in Babylon and Persia
550			**539–Babylon fell to Persia; 538–King Cyrus decreed exiles could return to homelands**
	Haggai/Zechariah	**538–First return of Jewish exiles under Jeshua and Zerubbabel**	
		516–Second temple completed	
500			486–464–Esther story
		458–Second return of Jewish exiles under Ezra	
450		444–Third return of Jewish exiles under Nehemiah	
	Malachi		

*Date includes a coregency or overlapping reign.
Prepared by Jason S. DeRouchie.

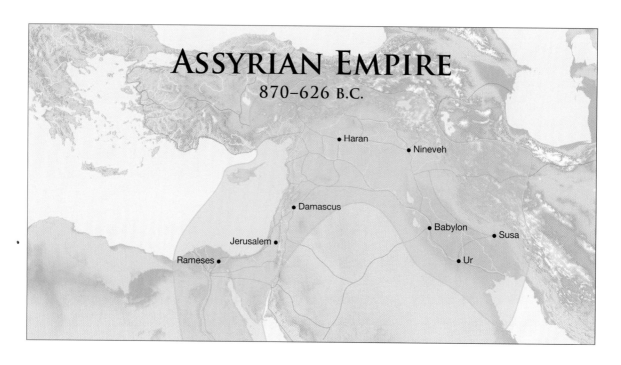

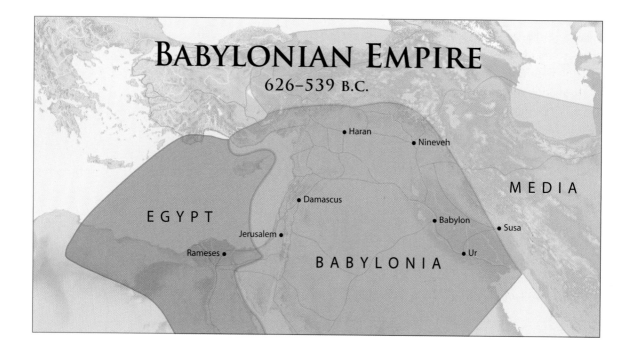

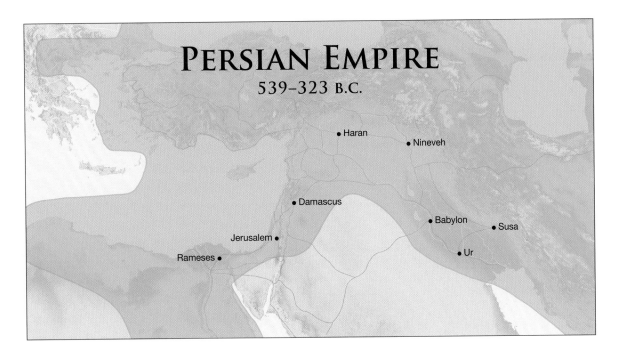

The Author of the Twelve Affirmed *God's Amazing Love* for Israel and *Sin's Horrific Nature*

Standing as the conclusion to the Latter Prophets, the book of the Twelve synthesizes the whole collection's message. One way it accomplishes this is to focus repeatedly on God's amazing love on the one hand and the tragedy of an unreciprocated love from Israel on the other.

The book of the Twelve is framed with this focus. Hosea uses the daring metaphor of marriage to symbolize this love and adultery to indicate its rejection. Malachi opens his book with the following sad and revealing words (Mal. 1:2): "'I have loved you,' says the LORD. But you say, 'How have you loved us?'" Sin is not just the violation of a norm but the desecration of a relationship—the ultimate relationship.

By using the metaphor of marriage, Yahweh enabled his people to understand more profoundly the passionate character of his love—what the Jewish philosopher Abraham Heschel has called *the pathos of God*.[1] Yahweh is not a metaphysical abstraction nor the Wholly Other; instead he is a passionate lover, near and dear, whose heart can be wounded and broken by covenant infidelity. Through Hosea's marriage to a promiscuous woman,

---

1. Abraham Heschel, *The Prophets* (New York: Harper and Row, 1969), 285–98.

"I will punish her for the feast days of the Baals when she burned offerings to them and adorned herself with her ring and jewelry, and went after her lovers and forgot me, declares the LORD" (Hos. 2:13). *A fertility pillar figurine from the time of the Twelve (from Rockefeller Museum).*

the prophet awakened Israel to the fact that she had been an unfaithful spouse to Yahweh (Hos. 1:2). Thus Hosea's life and his wife provided a lens through which Israel was to view her relationship to God. Israel's sin of adding other gods to its religion (such as the Canaanite fertility deities) was not just idolatry; it was adultery! Israel was not just being apostate by acting disloyal to Yahweh; she was a whore! Israel's disobedience to the law was not just a failure to keep a list of rules; it was a rejection of and an offence against a person—in the same category as the breaking of a marriage vow. As such, Yahweh declared: "I will punish her for the feast days of the Baals when she burned offerings to them and adorned herself with her ring and jewelry and went after her lovers and forgot me" (2:13).

Hosea's marriage to Gomer should have illustrated the profound truth of covenantal marriage, which was a symbol of the union between God and his people (cf. Eph. 5:22–33). Children would have been the result and would have provided a sign of God's blessing—of "God sowing" (Jezreel) his people in the land. The profound love Hosea had for Gomer was signified by the Hebrew word for "mercy" or "love," and the fact that Gomer now belonged to Hosea intimated a deep personal union through which God could call his people "mine"—"my people." However, the resulting unfaithfulness of Gomer led to tragedy, and the children of the marriage bore ominous names: Jezreel (Hos. 1:4–5), No Mercy/Love (1:6), and Not My People (1:9–10). Although the first name simply meant "God sows," the literal meaning had been recently overshadowed by a notorious massacre in the city of Jezreel (2 Kings 10:1–10). Thus the young child had an ominous name that symbolized an equally menacing future for the nation. The next two children bore names that indicated that the covenant with Yahweh was now broken: "Not Loved" and "Not My People." The covenant had been severed, and this was symbolized by a public divorce between Hosea and Gomer (Hos. 2:2–13; cf. Jer. 3:8; Isa. 50:1).

Yahweh was not through with Israel, however, and the book of Hosea reveals the amazing reality that God was willing to begin again. Hosea was commanded to remarry his unfaithful lover, a sign of the inextinguishable nature of the divine love. A divine soliloquy gives an insight into the inner divine struggle between justice and mercy, wrath and forgiveness, and final resolution of the tension (Hos. 11:8–9): "How can I give you up, O Ephraim? How can I hand you over, O Israel? How can I make you like Admah? How can I treat you like Zeboiim? My heart recoils within me; my compassion grows warm and tender. I will not execute my burning anger; I will not again destroy

Ephraim; for I am God and not a man, the Holy One in your midst, and I will not come in wrath." The covenant was to be renewed, as God would take his new bride into the desert for a new eschatological "honeymoon" (2:14). All nature would be transformed, and the children's names would be changed to Mercy/Loved, My People, and Jezreel (retaining now its original meaning because of the numerous descendants from this new union) (1:10–2:1).

The message to the people of Hosea's time was that judgment was coming (divorce) but that God's love was not at an end. Their responsibility after the judgment was to repent and to pursue faithfulness, steadfast love, and knowledge (4:1), all the while anticipating the full renewal of the covenant. By placing this message at the beginning of the Twelve, the incredible depth and passion of Yahweh for his people was demonstrated powerfully for all to see. The judgment of the exile did not mean the end, but it was a time for reflection and repentance, waiting in hope for God's unbounded love

> The Bible is the ultimate love story. Not only does it begin and end with a wedding, every marriage since Adam and Eve's (Gen. 2:21–25) points to the ultimate, eschatological wedding at the end of history between the last Adam and his bride, the church (Rev. 19:6–9). "Blessed are those who are invited to the marriage supper of the Lamb" (19:9)!

to begin the task of restoration. It is, therefore, telling that during the time of Malachi, right in the midst of initial restoration, most of the province of Judah did not recognize Yahweh's love. May we today not be so blind!

The Author of the Twelve Clarified the Implications of *Yahweh's Covenantal Commitment* to Israel

One objective of the book of the Twelve was to expound the implications of Israel's basic theological confession revealed to Moses at Mount Sinai: "The LORD, the LORD, a God merciful and gracious, slow to anger, and abounding in steadfast love and faithfulness, keeping steadfast love for thousands, forgiving iniquity and transgression and sin, but who will by no means clear the guilty, visiting the iniquity of the fathers on the children and the children's children, to the third and the fourth generation" (Exod. 34:6–7). From the beginning of the Twelve, where the focus is on the extravagant nature of God's love, the word *ruḥāmâ* ("mercy, love") was used to describe the renamed Israel (Hos. 1:7; 2:1). In context, this name appears to be an intentional echo of the first divine trait in the character creed—"merciful" (*raḥûm*), derived from the same linguistic root. At the end of the Hosea, a similar verbal echo appears, describing Yahweh's *compassion* to the repentant (14:3). Other notable reverberations of the confession throughout the Twelve are as follows:

- "Rend your hearts and not your garments." Return to the LORD your God, for he is gracious and merciful, slow to anger, and abounding in steadfast love; and he relents over disaster. Who knows whether he will not turn and relent, and leave a blessing behind him (Joel 2:13–14).

- "I will avenge their blood, blood I have not avenged, for the LORD dwells in Zion" (Joel 3:21).

- "O LORD, is not this what I said when I was yet in my country? That is why I made haste to flee to Tarshish; for I knew that you are a gracious God and merciful, slow to anger and abounding in steadfast love, and relenting from disaster" (Jonah 4:2).

- Who is a God like you, pardoning iniquity and passing over transgression for the remnant of his inheritance? He does not retain his anger forever, because he delights in steadfast love. He will again have compassion on us (Mic. 7:18–19).

- "The LORD is slow to anger and great in power, and the LORD will by no means clear the guilty" (Nah. 1:3).

This ancient confession of faith is the basis for both the mercy and the justice of God and bore witness to both of these qualities throughout the Twelve. As a result, the confession testified to a basic tension within God's

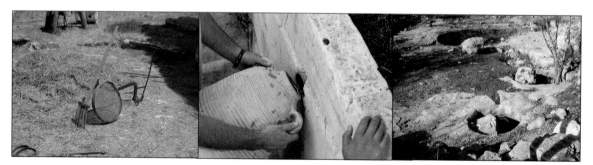

"The threshing floors shall be full of grain; the vats shall overflow with wine and oil. I will restore the years that the swarming locust has eaten, the hopper, the destroyer, and the cutter, my great army which I sent among you" (Joel 2:24–25). *Left: a threshing floor and threshing implements at Neot Kedumim; Center: collecting wine to fill the vats at Yad HaShmonah Biblical Gardens; Right: ancient wine or olive oil vats at Gibeon.*

character. Yahweh is a God of perfect holiness and justice; Yahweh is a God of immeasurable mercy and compassion. This tension was reflected repeatedly in the experience of Israel in the Twelve, and the tension was somewhat resolved by repentance in humanity.

Both Joel and Jonah showed the relevance of this creed for their situations. In both contexts, the audiences of the prophets (Judah in Joel and Nineveh in Jonah) were guilty of great sin and were going to experience the judgment of God. Joel encouraged the people to repent because they might expect to find mercy from the God of the confession. He is a God, "gracious and merciful, slow to anger, and abounding in steadfast love; and he relents over disaster" (Joel 2:13). In contrast, Jonah was discouraged when the people of Nineveh repented at his preaching; he knew that they were spared precisely because Yahweh is "a gracious God and merciful, slow to anger and abounding in steadfast love, and relenting from disaster" (Jonah 4:2).

Both prophets did not cite the entire confession but used the descriptor "relenting from disaster" to provide a commentary on the last half of the creedal statement. This short phrase was theological shorthand for "keeping steadfast love for thousands, forgiving iniquity and transgression and sin, but who will by no means clear the guilty, visiting the iniquity of the fathers on the children and the children's children, to the third and the fourth generation" (Exod 34:7). As far as Joel was concerned, the people of Judah had a chance to repent and be saved because of the confession. Consequently, he held out for them this hope. As for Jonah, this was the reason he did not wish to preach to the hated Assyrians. He knew that the God of the Mosaic Covenant and the God of the world were one and the same and that Yahweh would somehow find a reason to show mercy if he saw repentance. So in both cases God resolved the tension between justice and mercy in favor of mercy because he saw repentance. The guilty were acquitted.

Without such repentance, the book of Nahum showed the consequences to the same Assyrians generations later: "The LORD is slow to anger and great in power, and the LORD will by no means clear the guilty" (Nah. 1:3). The guilty were not acquitted. Similarly throughout the Twelve there were statements by complacent Israelites who presumed on the mercy of God and *who did not repent*:

- "All the sinners of my people shall die by the sword, who say, 'Disaster shall not overtake or meet us'" (Amos 9:10).

- [Jerusalem's] heads give judgment for a bribe; its priests teach for a price; its prophets practice divination for money; yet they lean on the LORD and say, "Is not the LORD in the midst of us? No disaster shall come upon us" (Mic. 3:11).

- "At that time I will search Jerusalem with lamps, and I will punish the men who are complacent, those who say in their hearts, 'The LORD will not do good, nor will he do ill'" (Zeph. 1:12).

- You have wearied the LORD with your words. But you say, 'How have we wearied him?' By saying, "Everyone who does evil is good in the sight of the LORD, and he delights in them." Or by asking, "Where is the God of justice?" (Mal. 2:17).

> Other biblical voices help clarify how a God of real justice and real compassion could acquit the guilty: God's righteous servant (Isa. 53), also called his high priest (Zech. 3) and good shepherd (chs. 11–13), would become a curse for us (Gal. 3:13), allowing God to extend mercy to the guilty while maintaining his justice. As Paul stated in 2 Corinthians 5:19–21: "In Christ God was reconciling the world to himself, not counting their trespasses against them.... For our sake [God] made [Christ] to be sin who knew no sin, so that in him we might become the righteousness of God."

The twelve prophets were clear. To make such statements was to live in a dream world—a dream world that would be shattered eventually by the storm of God's judgment. Yahweh may be immeasurably patient, but eventually that patience reaches a limit, a point of no return (Amos 1–2). Or as Longfellow put it, "Though the mills of God grind slowly, yet they grind exceeding small; though with patience he stands waiting, with exactness grinds he all."

The Author of the Twelve Stressed the Need for God's People *to Reflect God's Character*

The twelve prophets were convinced that living in covenant with Yahweh meant that the people of God should resemble the God of the people. Thus the theological confession, which described Yahweh's character, was to be imitated in Israel's daily routine. The chief priority was to love and honor Yahweh above all else. In Hosea, the priests had forgotten their duty to honor God and his law, and the people had misdirected their love for God to the fertility idols: "Israel has forgotten his Maker and built palaces" (Hos. 8:14). Much later in the people's history, during the initial restoration, Haggai pointed out that the returnees dire economic challenges were specifically

"I will search Jerusalem with lamps, and I will punish the men who are complacent, those who say in their hearts, "The LORD will not do good, nor will he do ill'" (Zeph. 1:12). *An oil lamp from the days of the minor prophets (from the Rockefeller Museum).*

due to their failure to make Yahweh a priority (Hag. 1:4, 6): "Is it a time for you yourselves to dwell in your paneled houses, while this house [of God] lies in ruins? … You have sown much, and harvested little. You eat, but you never have enough." Similarly, Malachi condemned the priests and people's lack of respect for Yahweh that was clearly evident in their not giving him their best (Mal. 1:6–14). Yahweh lamented (1:6): "A son honors his father, and a servant his master. If then I am a father, where is my honor? And if I am a master, where is my fear?"

Periodically in the Twelve, "mini-doxologies" occur that call for deep respect and even silence in the presence of the divine King. In Zephaniah 1:7 we read: "Be silent before the Lord God! For the day of the Lord is near." Similarly, Habakkuk 2:20 declares, "But the Lord is in his holy temple; let all the earth keep silence before him" (cf. Amos 4:13, 5:8–9, 8:3, 9:5–6; Zeph. 2:17). Because Yahweh is God, he deserves the highest praise and honor. One way the prophets highlight the calls to

> Zephaniah 2:3 and 3:2 provide lasting, basic principles to guide anyone's relationship with the Lord: Seek Yahweh, do his just commands, seek righteousness and humility, listen to the voice of correction, trust Yahweh, and draw near to your God.

reverent awe in the present is by depicting the universal scope of God's reign as it will be manifest in the end. For example, Zechariah 14:9 anticipates the day when the absolute uniqueness of Yahweh as King will be revealed for the entire world to see, as the fundamental truth of the *Shema* is manifest: "And the Lord will be king over all the earth. On that day the Lord will be one and his name one." As Yahweh takes up residence in Jerusalem, all the nations will recognize his splendor (Mal. 1:14), and his holiness will overflow so much that even the bells on horses and common cooking pots will become sanctified (Zech. 14:20). It is in the light of this grand future vision that the twelve prophets called Israel and Judah to love and honor Yahweh.

From the beginning, the Twelve focus not only on worshipping Yahweh but also on his people being transformed by a basic knowledge of his person and will. In Hosea, the priests were reprimanded for not disseminating the words of the law; as a result, there was "no faithfulness or steadfast love, and no knowledge of God in the land" (Hos. 4:1). Rather there was "swearing, lying, murder, stealing, and committing adultery"; they [broke] all bounds, and bloodshed

"On that day there shall be inscribed on the bells of the horses, 'Holy to the Lord.' And the pots in the house of the Lord shall be as the bowls before the altar" (Zech. 14:20). *Bronze bells from Assyrian horse harnesses (eighth century B.C.) (from the British Museum).*

follow[ed upon] bloodshed" (4:2). The implication was that knowing God rightly would have produced in the people both faithfulness and love. Similarly empty ritual was not acceptable to God, since it did not involve a character transformation. God desired "steadfast love and not sacrifice, the knowledge of God rather than burnt offerings" (6:6), devotion rather than devotions. Other prophets repeated the same refrain in louder tones. For Amos, worship services and religious meetings were actually repulsive to God without a life committed to a transformation of character (Amos 5:21–24): "I hate, I despise your feasts, and I take no delight in your solemn assemblies. Even though you offer me your burnt offerings and grain offerings, I will not accept them; and the peace offerings of your fattened animals, I will not look upon them. Take away from me the noise of your songs; to the melody of your harps I will not listen. But let justice roll down like waters, and righteousness like an ever-flowing stream."

This text represented the tip of a theological iceberg. The call for righteousness and justice was basic to Israelite identity (see Isa. 5:1–7). When God summoned Abraham, he called him and his offspring to a particular way of life marked by the characteristics of "righteousness and justice" (Gen. 18:19). These two words were extremely important, because they marked what God was accomplishing in the world: his way. Their frequent pairing in the Old Testament indicates they are an example of the figure of speech termed *hendiadys*—two words expressing one concept, which in this instance was a type of "social justice" that was both God-honoring and neighbor-loving. However, it is helpful to try to understand their distinctive meanings. On the one hand, righteousness is an objective word connoting "order, structure, or rightness" in God's world. It indicates conformity to Yahweh's standards or definition of right order. On the other hand, justice has to do with the maintenance of this order. So one can literally "do justice." When a judge makes a ruling that upholds law and order, he or she is doing justice, or doing right. Whenever the standard is violated, one has to do justice—a particular act—to restore the order. Both words are concerned with the upholding and maintenance of the law for all people, without discrimination. And in the context of Amos, God's point is this: Any "worship" that does not take seriously the command to

> Injustice often happens to the powerless and the defenseless—those without economic, political, and social resources. With Habakkuk, we should pray, "O Lord, how long?" (Hab. 1:2), and with Amos, we should act to alleviate all human suffering: "Let justice roll down like waters, and righteousness like an ever-flowing stream" (Amos 5:24). Many social reformers, from William Wilberforce to Martin Luther King Jr., have been inspired by God's call to aid the oppressed, poor, and broken. Care for the needy is not just an option for believers; it is a divine imperative!

"care for the least of these" without prejudice is a worship that makes God sick! James put it this way in 1:27–2:1: "Religion that is pure and undefiled before God, the Father, is this: to visit orphans and widows in their affliction, and to keep oneself unstained from the world. My brothers, show no partiality as you hold the faith in our Lord Jesus Christ." Similarly, John declared in 1 John 3:17–18: "If anyone has the world's goods and sees his brother in need, yet closes his heart against him, how does God's love abide in him? Little children, let us not love in word or talk but in deed and in truth."

The Author of the Twelve Emphasized the Future *Day of Judgment* for the Wicked and *of Salvation* for the Righteous

Abraham Heschel wrote: "To the prophets, God was overwhelmingly real and shatteringly present. They never spoke of Him as from a distance. They lived as witnesses, struck by the works of God, rather than as explorers engaged in an effort to ascertain the nature of God; their utterances were the unloading of a burden rather than glimpses obtained in the fog of groping."[2] This was particularly true when the prophets spoke of the future day when God would enter history for a final reckoning. There was an urgency and anxiety in their speech that was impossible to miss. It was important for the people not to delay repentance. Near the beginning and at the end of the Twelve an ominous note was struck:

- The LORD utters his voice before his army, for his camp is exceedingly great; he who executes his word is powerful. For the day of the LORD is great and very awesome; who can endure it? "Yet even now," declares the LORD, "return to me with all your heart, with fasting, with weeping, and with mourning" (Joel 2:11–12).

- "Behold, I will send you Elijah the prophet before the great and awesome day of the LORD comes. And he will turn the hearts of fathers to their children and the hearts of children to their fathers, lest I come and strike the land with a decree of utter destruction" (Mal. 4:5–6).

---

2. Heschel, *The Prophets*, 285–286.

This "Day" occurs repeatedly throughout the Twelve, so that one scholar regards it as *the* theme of these prophets: "No other prophetic book contains as many passages about this day, which are at the same time central for the overall structure."[3] Amos said that it would pounce like a roaring lion on a presumptuous people of God who had forgotten their mission (Amos 5:18–20); Obadiah, that it would make Edom and all the nations reel like drunkards (Obad. 15–16); Zephaniah, that it would descend like a gathering storm over the landscape of not only Judah but the world (Zeph. 1:7–18); Zechariah, that it would include a great battle, a great earthquake, and a great plague and that it would be a unique day in which Yahweh would triumph over all his enemies and bring righteousness and justice to the world (Zech. 14). In fact, Yahweh's holiness was to emanate so much from the divine center in Jerusalem that everything would become holy (14:20). By the time the end of the Twelve is reached, the Day has turned into a great conflagration (Mal. 4:1): "For behold, the day is coming, burning like an oven, when all the arrogant and all evildoers will be stubble. The day that is coming shall set them ablaze, says the LORD of hosts, so that it will leave them neither root nor branch." What judgment this Day would bring!

> The Old Testament portrays the Day of Yahweh as a time of "darkness" that will catch off guard those "asleep" from spiritual drunkenness (e.g., Joel 1:5; Amos 5:20). In this context, after asserting that "the day of the Lord will come like a thief in the night" for those in darkness, Paul asserted, "But you are not in darkness, brothers, for that day to surprise you like a thief" (1 Thess. 5:2, 4). He then urged, "Let us not sleep, as others do, but let us keep awake and be sober" (5:6).

For the prophets, nothing else mattered but to be aligned with God's vision of life in the world. This was so because everything not in keeping with the divine will would be swept aside like chaff and burned up in a fire of overwhelming judgment. So much of life then and now is preoccupied with trivialities. The twelve prophets were God's shock troops, commissioned to shake people up to realize the divine view of life and to see the transformation of their character and ultimately of their society in order to be beacons of the coming age. For the ultimate reality is to be betrothed to Yahweh in righteousness and justice, to hear his words of favor—Jezreel, Loved, and My People—and to make the incredible response, "You are my God" (Hos. 2:19–23)!

---

3. Aaron Schart, "Reconstructing the Redaction History of the Twelve Prophets: Problems and Models," in *Reading and Hearing the Book of the Twelve* (ed. J. D. Nogalski and M. A. Sweeney, SBL Symposium Series 15; Atlanta: Society of Biblical Literature, 2000), 40.

"Woe to you who desire the day of the Lᴏʀᴅ! Why would you have the day of the Lᴏʀᴅ? It is darkness, and not light, as if a man…went into the house and leaned his hand against the wall and a serpent bit him" (Amos 5:18–19). *A Palestinian Viper.*

The Lord is not slow to fulfill his promise as some count slowness, but is patient toward you, not wishing that any should perish, but that all should reach repentance. But the day of the Lord will come like a thief, and then the heavens will pass away with a roar, and the heavenly bodies will be burned up and dissolved, and the earth and the works that are done on it will be exposed.

Since all these things are thus to be dissolved, what sort of people ought you to be in lives of holiness and godliness, waiting for and hastening the coming of the day of God, because of which the heavens will be set on fire and dissolved, and the heavenly bodies will melt as they burn! But according to the promise we are waiting for new heavens and a new earth in which righteousness dwells (2 Peter 3:9–13).

Figure 14.3. The Day of Yahweh and the Coming of Christ

The New Testament makes clear that John the Baptist's ministry of repentance and reconciliation was the ministry of Elijah reconciling Israelite families before the Day of Yahweh was to come (Mal. 4:5–6; Matt. 11:9–15). John's words display that he envisioned the Day of Yahweh as one of awesome judgment: "I baptize you with water for repentance, but he who is coming after me is mightier than I, whose sandals I am not worthy to carry. He will baptize you with the Holy Spirit and fire. His winnowing fork is in his hand, and he will clear his threshing floor and gather his wheat into the barn, but the chaff he will burn with unquenchable fire" (Matt. 3:11–12). When John languished in prison, he questioned whether Jesus was the one who had brought the Day of Yahweh, for the wicked were not burning up like chaff and the righteous were not being vindicated (Matt.11:2–3). Jesus responded by alluding to Isaiah 61:1–2, suggesting that his mission now was to "proclaim the year of the LORD's favor" in anticipation of "the day of vengeance of our God" (Matt. 11:3–6). Now is the day of salvation and afterwards the time of judgment (2 Cor. 6:2; cf. Matt. 24–25). At the cross, Jesus experienced the awesome judgment of God in his identification with sinners, so that they would be spared final judgment (Isa. 53:5; 2 Cor. 5:21; 2 Peter 2:24; cf. Matt. 27:45–54). Today we still await the ultimate Day (2 Thess. 2:1–3) and are called to proclaim the good news of reconciliation to the nations in anticipation of it (2 Cor. 5:18–20). For those in Christ, the culmination of the Day of Yahweh will bring eternal salvation, not harm (Rom. 5:9; 1 Thess. 5:9). However, for those who fail to believe, Yahweh's wrath remains on them, and the ominous judgment portended by the Day will take place (John 3:36; 1 Thess. 5:1–3; 2 Thess. 1:9–10).

Prepared by Stephen G. Dempster and Jason S. DeRouchie.

The Author of the Twelve Announced *the Coming of a New David*, Who Would Bring God's Kingdom

A major emphasis in the Twelve is the person of David and the city associated with his name—Jerusalem. One of the technical terms for the end times associated with the Day of Yahweh is the expression "the latter days." Hosea said that in "the latter days" Israel would seek "the LORD their God, and David their king" (Hos. 3:5). Micah spoke of the exaltation of David's city, Zion, in the latter days, where it would become the center for world peace and world order (Mic. 4:1; cf. 5:2). This theme of David and his city is a pervasive theological theme in the Twelve. Joel prophesied of the exaltation of Zion and a spring issuing from its temple (Joel 3:18–21); Amos, of a restored Davidic kingdom (Amos 9:11–15); Obadiah, of an elevated Zion proclaiming divine rule (Obad. 21); Micah, of a leader from Bethlehem whose rule would someday extend to the ends of the earth (Mic. 5:1–5); Zephaniah, of a renewed Jerusalem over which Yahweh would exult (Zeph. 3:14–18); Haggai, of a Davidic descendant who would be God's "signet ring" or promise of the full restoration of David's house (Hag. 2:20–23); and Zechariah, of a "branch" who would sprout up to bring forgiveness, worship, and just rule (Zech. 3:8–10; 6:12); of a king who would make war forever obsolete from the world (9:9–10); and of a restored Jerusalem whose life giving streams would flow to the east and west (14:8). This prominence of David and his city represents the fulfillment of the covenant that was made with him in 2 Samuel 7, which would ultimately fulfill the promise to Abraham that in his seed all nations of the world would be blessed (Gen. 12:3, cf. 2 Sam. 7:9–10; Ps. 72:17).

Significantly, this Davidic theme becomes prominent in the next canonical division, the Writings. The mention of "Bethlehem" at the beginning of Ruth (Ruth 1:2) and of "David" at the end (4:17, 22) becomes a lightning rod for this messianic hope. This is continued in the Psalms and the Davidic wisdom literature, is highlighted in the narrative books devoted to kingdom-hope (Daniel–Ezra–Nehemiah), and is reinforced at the end of the canon in Chronicles, which opens with lengthy genealogies (1 Chron. 1–9), which begin with Adam, focus on the royal line of Judah, and set the stage for the account of David. It is as if all history was a prelude to the coming king![4]

The Old Testament's stress on David heightens anticipation for the new David, the ultimate David, David's greater Son. As King, Jesus chose twelve disciples who became a mini-Israel; he focused attention on Jerusalem by dying and rising there; and his global rule is stressed by the commissioning of his disciples to be like a city set on a hill, bringing news of reconciliation and forgiveness

"For you who fear my name, the sun of righteousness shall rise with healing in its wings. You shall go out leaping like calves from the stall. And you shall tread down the wicked … on the day when I act, says the LORD of hosts" (Mal. 4:2–3). *A young calf near the Jordan River north of the Sea of Galilee.*

It is no accident that the New Testament begins with the genealogy of Jesus, which is divided into three sequences of fourteen descendants: Abraham to David, David to the exile, and the exile to Jesus (Matt. 1:1–17). In ancient Hebrew, letters were frequently used to indicate numerical values, and the numerical value of the name David is 14. Matthew is making it absolutely clear at the beginning of his Gospel that Jesus is the ultimate David anticipated in the Old Testament!

---

4. Walter Brueggemann, *David's Truth in Israel's Imagination and Memory* (Minneapolis: Fortress, 1987), 101.

to the worlds (Matt. 5:14; 28:18–20). All these New Testament themes are initial fulfillments of the Old Testament hope—a messianic hope that has been inaugurated, yet still awaits consummation. An early church Aramaic prayer expresses this expectation: *Marana tha*, "Our Lord, come" (1 Cor. 16:22; cf. Rev. 22:20)!

Figure 14.4. Flow of Thought in the Twelve

SIN	Hosea	Israel, Yahweh has a case against you: You have played the harlot and been like an unfaithful wife, departing from faithfulness, steadfast love, and knowledge. Please return to Yahweh, your husband!
	Joel	For the Day of Yahweh is at hand, and repentance is your only hope! I will be a refuge to my people, but a roaring, devouring lion against all who fail to heed my voice!
	Amos	How secure you feel, yet how insecure you actually are! I have disciplined you, yet you have not learned from the discipline. You anticipate my coming, but for you this Day will be darkness, not light. Prepare to meet your God, for the fulfillment of my kingdom promises is only for those who truly repent!
	Obadiah	Know this: Pride and hatred have no place in my coming kingdom; this is why your brother Edom will be destroyed.
	Jonah	Yet be warned, for your own pride and hatred of others resembles that of Edom and stands in direct contrast to the mercy Yahweh gives to whomever he wills. Don't be like Jonah; be like Yahweh and extend compassion rather than gloating in others' destruction, lest God's judgment fall on you!
	Micah	Yahweh, from his courtroom, has found you and the nations guilty! Yet your final judgment day has not come, and in his mercy, he will still forgive your sins, if you but return. Soon God, through his Word and Messiah, will be exalted over all things. Will you be a part of the judgment or the redemption?
PUNISHMENT	Nahum	Know this for certain: Yahweh is a stronghold only for those who accept his terms of peace, but he will justly judge all his unrepentant enemies.
	Habakkuk	Yahweh is just, and in his time he will indeed punish all wrongdoers and preserve all who walk by faith, looking to him for help, guidance, and satisfaction.
	Zephaniah	Please be part of the remnant that draws near to God, so that the coming Day may be one of rejoicing! Yet for all who fail to heed God's voice, the Day of Yahweh the warrior will be sure destruction!
RESTORATION	Haggai	Drawing near to God necessitates that you take seriously the need for his presence in your midst, that he might bring forth the fulfillment of all he has promised, blessing for you and for the nations who surrender to him.
	Zechariah	You need God's presence among you, for his kingdom restoration will be brought not by human effort but by the power of his Spirit working through his slain and yet victorious priest-king.
	Malachi	This restoration is for you, if you will but fear and honor God in all areas of your life, awaiting the day when curse will give rise to full restoration blessing!

Prepared by Jason S. DeRouchie.

KEY WORDS AND CONCEPTS FOR REVIEW

Minor Prophets	Righteousness and justice
Interpretive framework	Social justice
Divine pathos	Imitation of God
Marriage made in heaven	Day of Yahweh
Not My People	Elijah
Divine soliloquy	New David
Theological confession	Jerusalem
Divine tension	

KEY RESOURCES FOR FURTHER STUDY

McComiskey, Thomas Edward, ed. *The Minor Prophets*. Grand Rapids: Baker, 2009.

Longman, Tremper, III, and David E. Garland, eds. "Daniel–Malachi." In *The Expositor's Bible Commentary*, vol. 8, rev. ed. Grand Rapids: Zondervan, 2008.

Alexander, T. Desmond, David W. Baker, and Bruce K. Waltke. *Obadiah, Jonah, Micah*. TOTC. Downers Grove, IL: InterVarsity, 2009.

Baldwin, Joyce G. *Haggai, Zechariah, and Malachi*. TOTC. Downers Grove, IL: InterVarsity, 2009.

Barker, Kenneth L., and Waylor Bailey. *Micah, Nahum, Habakkuk, Zephaniah*. NAC. Nashville: B&H, 1998.

Boda, Mark J. *Haggai, Zechariah*. NIVAC. Grand Rapids: Zondervan, 2004.

Garrett, Duane A. *Hosea, Joel*. NAC. Nashville: B&H, 1997.

Patterson, Richard D. *Nahum, Habakkuk, Zephaniah : An Exegetical Commentary*. Richardson, TX: Biblical Studies, 2003.

Smith, Gary V. *Hosea, Amos, Micah*. NIVAC. Grand Rapids: Zondervan, 2001.

Stuart, Douglas. *Hosea–Jonah*. WBC. Nashville: Thomas Nelson, 1987.

Taylor, Richard A., and E. Ray Clendenon. *Haggai, Malachi*. NAC. Nashville: B&H, 2004.

THE OLD COVENANT ENJOYED: WHAT THE WRITINGS ARE REALLY ABOUT

Jason S. DeRouchie

Very little was good at the end of the Prophets. The historical narrative had ended in 2 Kings with Jerusalem destroyed and God's people in exile, cursed by Yahweh because they had broken the covenant (2 Kings 18:11–12; 23:27; cf. Deut. 31:16–17). The prophetic commentary of the Latter Prophets had then added stress to Israel's covenant rebellion, highlighting the nature of the people's sins, calling attention to God's faithfulness both to bless and to curse, and declaring that kingdom hope would exist only for the repentant who would return to Yahweh.

Strikingly, even though the final three prophets of the Twelve were part of the initial restoration (Haggai, Zechariah, Malachi), none of the books announced the arrival of the new creational kingdom for which Israel longed. Instead, these volumes testified to the nation's continued failure to honor and fear God above all else (Hag. 1:9; Zech. 1:2–6; Mal. 1:6). The community's inward transformation had not been experienced, global peace and witness had not been realized, the renewed Eden had not arrived, the redeemer-king had not arisen, and the divine presence had yet to manifest itself, even in the rebuilt temple (see Ezek. 36:22–36; 37:21–28). In many respects, then, the exile still continued, and God's promises still awaited fulfillment. As such, the final word in Malachi declared judgment on the wicked, charged God-fearers to heed the law of Moses, and called readers to keep looking ahead, anticipating a new "prophet like Elijah," who would (with the "prophet like Moses") help restore the community of God (Mal. 4:1–6).

In such a context of sustained darkness, the loyal remnant needed clarity on how to maintain their faith, even amidst life's sufferings and enigmas. This is the purpose of the final section of Jesus' Bible. The Writings provided guidance to this faithful few, still in "slavery" (Ezra 9:8–9), who remained resolute in their confidence that Yahweh was on the throne and would one day right all wrongs through a royal redeemer.

In the Bible, only at the head of the Prophets (Josh. 1:8) and at the beginning of the Writings (Ps. 1:2) are believers explicitly called to "meditate day and night" on God's *law*. This catch-phrase at the "canonical seams" calls the reader to interpret both canonical divisions through the lens of the covenant. However, unlike the Prophets, which major on Israel's sin and the covenant curses and give only minor (though always evident) attention to the promise of restoration blessing, each book of the Writings is dominated by a message of kingdom hope in an all-wise, all-sovereign God, who is faithful to his own, even in the midst of pain. A minority of saints did exist who treasured God, and both the commentary of the Former Writings (Ruth/Psalms–Lamentations) and the narrative of the Latter Writings (Daniel–Chronicles) clarify how this group *enjoyed the old (Mosaic) covenant.*

The Writings open with the book of Ruth, one of only two narrative books in the Old Testament not arranged in chronological succession.[1] Because the rest of the Former Writings are all poetic and organized from longest to shortest,[2] Ruth stands out as a preface to the whole, calling the reader to interpret the remaining part of the Old Testament through a messianic lens of kingdom hope. Just as God preserved King David's ancestors through "exile" in Moab and secured their redemption by the hand of one from Bethlehem, so too God would deliver David's descendants from exile, raising up a new redeemer from this Judean town (see Mic. 5:2). For those who will trust in God, justified optimism exists even in darkness.

The rest of the Former Writings clarify *how those hoping in God's kingdom were to live.* In short, they were to embody in every setting the life of wisdom, waiting, and worship, grounded in God's Word, that was to characterize the messianic King.

---

1. The other is 1–2 Chronicles, though one could also count Jonah, which is part of the Twelve.
2. Lamentations is a little longer than the Song of Songs (2011 words vs. 1662 words). For a suggestion as to why Lamentations was put last, see note 8 in Chapter 1.

- In Psalms, those hoping for kingdom consummation express through lament, thanksgiving, or praise their faith and joy in Yahweh who reigns over all, ultimately through his Messiah.

- Job, Proverbs, and Ecclesiastes then consider the nature and pursuit of wisdom, the beginning of which for humans is the fear of the Lord. Perseverance through suffering will be experienced only by those who revere God for who he is, not for what he gives or takes away (Job). Life's purest and most lasting joy will be known only by those who act wisely, walking daily in light of the future by considering the brokenness that comes to the wicked and the blessing that awaits the righteous (Proverbs). The Creator is the Shepherd of all, who providentially guides all things and will call all actions into account; therefore, even when life in this cursed world is hard and makes little sense, wise followers of God fear him and keep his commands, both in pleasure and in pain (Ecclesiastes).

- These two contexts—pleasure and pain—then color the last two commentary books. In Song of Songs, marital love is celebrated and portrayed as a gift of God that gives hope for the ultimate kingdom blessings. And in Lamentations, even the darkest shadows of divine discipline as seen in the destruction of Jerusalem do not cancel the hope of divine mercies at dawn. God forever reigns (Lam. 5:19), and his promised Son will soon rise over the nations of the earth (see Ps. 2:7–12).

With Lamentations, the Old Testament's commentary section—begun with Jeremiah's other book—comes to a conclusion. The exilic despair highlighted in Lamentations serves as a natural bridge back into the narrative of Israel's exile departed from in 2 Kings. Through Daniel, Esther, Ezra-Nehemiah, and 1–2 Chronicles, the Old Testament narrative comes to a conclusion, all the while heightening anticipation for a further kingdom work of God.

The Latter Writings narrate the fifth of the seven stages in God's redemptive program, declaring his protection of the faithful remnant and his absolute supremacy over all things (Daniel), his providential preservation of his people in exile (Esther), and his initial restoration of his own to Jerusalem (Ezra-Nehemiah). Significantly, the narrative in 1–2 Chronicles stands out

Figure W.1. God's Kingdom-Building Program Narrated in the Latter Writings

	Preface introducing the biblical worldview: God and his purposes for people on this planet		Genesis 1:1–2:3
K	**KICKOFF AND REBELLION**	1. Creation, fall, and flood (ca. ? B.C.)	Genesis 2:4–11:9
I	**INSTRUMENT OF BLESSING**	2. Patriarchs (ca. 2100–1850 B.C.)	Genesis 11:10–50:26
N	**NATION REDEEMED AND COMMISSIONED**	3. Exodus, Sinai, and wilderness (ca. 1450–1400 B.C.)	Exodus–Deuteronomy
G	**GOVERNMENT IN THE PROMISED LAND**	4. Conquest and kingdoms (united and divided) (ca. 1400–600 B.C.)	Joshua–Kings
D	**DISPERSION AND RETURN**	5. Exile and initial restoration (ca. 600–400 B.C.)	Daniel–Chronicles
O	**OVERLAP OF THE AGES**	6. Christ's work and the church age (ca. 4 B.C.–A.D. ?)	Matthew–Acts
M	**MISSION ACCOMPLISHED**	7. Christ's return and kingdom consummation (ca. A.D. ?–eternity)	Revelation

of chronological succession, thus allowing its story to complement and in some ways contrast with the narrative that runs from Genesis 2:4 through the end of Ezra-Nehemiah. Chronicles opens with a genealogy of the line of promise beginning with Adam and therefore places the remnant of God, living in exile, within God's global kingdom purposes. The mission of Israel in relation to the nations will be fulfilled, and God's universal kingdom will be realized. The call at the end of the book for the remnant of Yahweh to enjoy God's presence and to return to Jerusalem (2 Chron. 36:23), leads naturally into the New Testament where the ultimate return to Jerusalem by One enjoying God's presence definitively secures complete kingdom restoration. This is the hope to which all the Old Testament points.

Figure W.2 overviews the flow of thought in the Writings. Figure W.3 synthesizes through images the last stage in the foundational (Old Testament) portion of God's kingdom-building program, all in anticipation of the fulfillment found in Christ and the New Testament.

Figure W.2. The Writings at a Glance

The WRITINGS: The Old Covenant ENJOYED (Yahweh as Satisfier)	
FORMER (Commentary)	
Ruth	Prelude Affirming the Kingdom Hope of Yahweh's Redeeming Grace Through the Line of David
Psalms	Hope for Those Delighting in and Submitting to God's Kingship Through His Word and Messiah
Job	Hope for Those Fearing God for Who He Is, Not for What He Gives or Takes Away
Proverbs	Hope for Those Acting Wisely—Who Fear God, Turn from Evil, and Live in Light of the Future
Ecclesiastes	Hope for Those Fearing and Following God in Pleasure and Pain Despite Life's Enigmas
Song of Songs	Hope for Those Celebrating Human Sexuality in the Context of Marriage
Lamentations	Hope for Those Remaining Confident in God's Reign and Faithfulness to His Own
LATTER (Narrative)	
Daniel	The Promise of God's Universal Kingdom Reiterated
Esther	The Preservation of God's Kingdom People Realized
Ezra-Nehemiah	The Restoration of God's Kingdom People and Land Foreshadowed
1–2 Chronicles	Yahweh's Universal Kingship and Kingdom Promises Affirmed

Figure W.3. God's K-I-N-G-D-O-M Story Through Images

KEY RESOURCES FOR FURTHER STUDY

Former Writings

Bullock, Hassell. *Encountering the Book of Psalms*. Grand Rapids: Baker, 2001.

Curtis, Edward M., and John J. Brugaletta. *Discovering the Way of Wisdom: Spirituality in the Wisdom Literature*. Grand Rapids: Kregel, 2004.

Estes, Daniel. *Handbook on the Wisdom Books and Psalms*. Grand Rapids: Baker, 2005.

Lucas, Ernest C. *Exploring the Old Testament*, vol. 3: *A Guide to the Psalms and Wisdom Literature*. Downers Grove, IL: InterVarsity, 2008.

Latter Writings

Hamilton, Victor P. *Handbook on the Historical Books*. Grand Rapids: Baker, 2001.

Howard, David M., Jr. *An Introduction to the Old Testament Historical Books*. Chicago: Moody, 1993.

Satterthwaite, Philip E., and J. Gordon McConville. *Exploring the Old Testament*, vol. 2: *A Guide to the Historical Books*. Downers Grove, IL: InterVarsity, 2005.

RUTH

Who?

The book of Ruth is an anonymous work and gives no specific clues to its author. Jewish tradition suggests Samuel, although references to David (Ruth 4:17, 22) make it unlikely that he is the author. The Hebrew idioms and syntax suggest an author during the monarchy.

When?

The author began his book with the chronological marker, "In the days when the judges ruled" (1:1); this places the events somewhere between 1380 and 1050 B.C. Although the story no doubt existed in oral form prior to the monarchy, it was written in its final form after David began to reign. The Hebrew literary style points toward a composition sometime during the monarchy, though some degree of linguistic updating probably occurred later and its placement in the Writings is a post-exilic phenomenon.

Where?

Elements of the story took place in both Israel and Moab. Ironically, Naomi and her family left the Judean city of Bethlehem (lit., "house of bread") because of a famine and dwelt in Moab (east of the Dead Sea), which was one of the nations that oppressed Israel during the period of the judges. While there, Naomi's son married Ruth, a Moabitess, who, after the death of her husband, decided to return to Bethlehem with Naomi. This move was not only a geographical journey, but also a spiritual one to the land and to Yahweh, the God of Israel.

Why?

The book of Ruth provided Israel with a telling contrast to the book of Judges. Not only had Yahweh preserved a remnant of people who did what was right in his eyes, but he would also use them to provide a "kinsman redeemer" in later generations for the nation as a whole. Throughout the book they progressively enjoyed the blessings of Yahweh for covenant faithfulness and gave promise of more to come.

In its present location, directly following the Prophets and standing as a prelude to the Writings, Ruth also:

1. Supplied an early analogy of how David's royal line experienced exile and then redemption;
2. Focused attention on the Davidic promises;
3. Built hope for full kingdom restoration.

RUTH

Chris A. Miller and
Jason S. DeRouchie

Carefully Crafted Verses from Ruth

In the days when the judges ruled … (Ruth 1:1).

"Where you go I will go, and where you lodge I will lodge. Your people shall be my people, and your God my God" (Ruth 1:16).

"The LORD repay you for what you have done, and a full reward be given you by the LORD, the God of Israel, under whose wings you have come to take refuge!" (Ruth 2:12).

"May he be blessed by the LORD, whose kindness has not forsaken the living or the dead! … The man is a close relative of ours, one of our redeemers" (Ruth 2:20).

"A son has been born to Naomi." They named him Obed. He was the father of Jesse, the father of David (Ruth 4:17).

> ## THE AUTHOR OF RUTH …
>
> - Highlighted *covenant faithfulness and Yahweh's gift of a redeemer.*
> - Emphasized *Yahweh's faithfulness* to bless the faithful and to fulfill his promises.

The Author of Ruth Highlighted *Covenant Faithfulness and Yahweh's Gift of a Redeemer*

The book of Ruth is deceptively powerful. When set within its historical and biblical context, what appears to be a simple love story between two people becomes a revolutionary tale that sounds the promise of national redemption. The book is positioned in the Hebrew canon in the Writings, likely due to its hope-filled focus on the life of the remnant and the faithfulness of God. Nevertheless, the author placed the book chronologically "in the days when the judges ruled" (Ruth 1:1), and when naturally compared with the characters in the book of Judges, Ruth and Boaz stand out like counter-revolutionaries.

> In a day when "everyone did what was right in his own eyes" (Judg. 21:25), there were at least two people who did what was right in God's eyes.

The narrative is about two women, Naomi and Ruth, and their experience of redemption through their kinsman, Boaz. The message of the book, however, is much more profound.

Figure 15.1. Ruth at a Glance			
Introduction	**Body**	**Conclusion**	
Ruth 1:1–22	2:1–4:12	4:13–17	4:18–22
Naomi emptied	Ruth and Boaz marry	Naomi filled	Genealogy of David

Dwelling in Bethlehem of Judah but caught in the midst of famine, Naomi followed her husband away from the "house of bread" and the place of redemptive hope (Mic. 5:2; cf. 1 Sam. 16:1, 12–13) into "exile" within Moab, one of Israel's oppressors. There her son married a foreigner named Ruth, who, upon the death of her father-in-law and husband, chose to follow Naomi back to Bethlehem: "Your people shall be my people, and your God my God" (Ruth 1:16). Ruth recognized that her decision likely meant she would remain a single woman without the benefit of male protection or provision. In light of the horrors of Israelite society during the period of the judges, such an act was a fearful thing (2:9, 22) and a testament of supreme faith in Yahweh, in whom she sought refuge (2:12).

Naomi said to Ruth, "Where did you glean today? ... Blessed be the man who took notice of you" (Ruth 2:19). *Women working in a field near Lebonah.*

God rewarded Ruth by bringing her into the field of a man who ruled his "kingdom" from a position of virtue and servant leadership. Boaz was the antithesis of the typical man of Judges. He did not selfishly abuse his workers (2:4) but gently provided for their needs (2:8–9, 14–16). Every time Ruth encountered Boaz she came to him *empty* but left *full* (2:14, 17; 3:17; 4:13). He unselfishly gave, cared, protected, and redeemed, all under the umbrella of faithfulness to the covenant of Yahweh.

"Then [Naomi] arose with her daughters-in-law to return from the country of Moab, for she had heard in the fields of Moab that the Lᴏʀᴅ had visited his people and given them food" (Ruth 1:6). *The fields of Moab south of the Arnon.*

In response, Ruth did not play the part of the foreign temptress who seduced the Israelite Boaz from his calling. Rather, Ruth was a "worthy woman" who inspired this Bethlehemite to follow the covenant and who, in the end, brought him honor at the city gate (3:11; 4:11; cf. Prov. 12:4; 31:10, 23).

Although Boaz would not have been forced to marry Ruth, he willingly did so in obedience to the spirit of the law of levirate marriage, wherein a man assumed the wife of a deceased relative in order to protect this relative's property and family and to continue his line at great cost to himself (Ruth 4:1–14; cf. Deut. 25:5–10). Naomi pointed to this principle when she told Ruth, "The man is a close relative of ours, *one our redeemers*" (Ruth 2:20; cf. 3:9, 12; Lev. 25:25).

This image of the "redeemer" provides part of the background for the work of Jesus, through whom God saved his own from destruction. Directly after his oracle about the Suffering Servant, who "has borne our griefs and carried our sorrows" (Isa. 53:4), the prophet Isaiah declared (54:4–5): "Fear not, for you will not be ashamed; be not confounded, for you will not be disgraced; for you will forget the shame of your youth, and the reproach of your widowhood you will remember no more. For your Maker is your husband, the LORD of hosts is his name; and the Holy One of Israel is your *Redeemer*, the God of the whole earth he is called." Ruth went to Bethlehem, seeking refuge under Yahweh's "wings" (Ruth 2:12), and Yahweh provided her with a tangible expression of his care under the "wings" of Boaz, a kinsman "redeemer" (3:9). God's protection of Ruth through Boaz was designed to give great hope of God's faithfulness to the reader.

> James coined the perfect caption for this story when he wrote, "Religion that is pure and undefiled before God, the Father, is this: to visit orphans and widows in their affliction, and to keep oneself unstained from the world" (James 1:27).

Naomi said to Ruth: "Is not Boaz our relative? ... See, he is winnowing barley tonight at the threshing floor" (Ruth 3:2). *A threshing floor with sledges and winnowing instruments.*

The Author of Ruth Emphasized *Yahweh's Faithfulness* to Bless the Faithful and to Fulfill His Promises

The Blessing of the Faithful

The entire book of Ruth draws attention to Yahweh's amazing faithfulness both to bless those who remain loyal to him and to fulfill all his promises. One way this is accomplished is by building an intentional correlation between calls for God's blessing in response to covenant faithfulness and details of a positive divine response. For example, following the death of her husband and son, Naomi blessed Ruth by declaring, "May the Lord deal kindly with you, as you have dealt with the dead and with me" (Ruth 1:8). Similarly, in reaction to Ruth's self-sacrificing care of her mother-in-law, Boaz proclaimed, "the Lord repay you for what you have done, and a full reward be given you by the Lord" (2:12). In turn, Ruth found favor in the eyes of Boaz (2:13) enjoyed provision from his hand (3:17), received his protective care as a husband, and enjoyed the blessing of a child (4:13).

A similar pattern is seen in the life of Boaz, who unrelentingly served everyone around him. Following his initial care for Ruth, Naomi prayed, "May he be blessed by the Lord, whose kindness has not forsaken the living or the dead!" (2:20). Little did she know how greatly God would answer this prayer, for through his and Ruth's offspring would come David (4:17) and ultimately Jesus, the promised son of David (Matt. 1:1, 5–6, 16).

The Fulfilling of Promises

Significantly, upon Boaz' servant-hearted declaration of intent to marry Ruth, the residents of Bethlehem asserted, "May the Lord make the woman, who is coming into your house, like Rachel and Leah, who together built up the house of Israel" (Ruth 4:11). While historically proclaimed before the nation's destruction in exile, the placement of the book of Ruth *after* the Prophets allows these words to cast hope for the full restoration of God's people. This ray of light is further highlighted when we learn that Boaz's and Ruth's son Obed was the grandfather of David, the Old Testament's royal image of hope (4:17, 22; cf. 2 Sam. 7:12–13; Jer. 23:5–6; 30:9; Ezek. 34:23–24; 37:24–25; Isa. 9:6–7; Hos. 3:5; Amos 9:11–12). God's blessing of Ruth and Boaz for their faithfulness would ultimately result in blessing to the world!

In contrast to Judges, where death was overwhelmingly prevalent, the book of Ruth finished with the promise of new life and had "David" as its final word (Ruth 4:22). With this stroke of genius, the writer sparked the reader's imagination. David would do on a *national* level what Boaz had done on a *personal* one. No difference existed in character, only in the size of the stage. The same godliness that drove Boaz would drive David to bless his nation and redeem their lives from the moral chaos of the judges. God continued to be faithful, and the characters of Boaz and David supplied hope in the son of David whose godly character and sacrificial leadership would ultimately redeem all believers from the chaos of sin and death.

This fact is also highlighted by the ten-person genealogy that ends the book. Its very presence recalls the ten-person genealogy in Genesis 5 and and the nine-person genealogy in Genesis 11 that focus on the line of promise (from Adam to Noah and from Shem to Terah, father of Abra[ha]m). Furthermore, its makeup, starting with Perez and ending with David, emphasizes the hope of redemption. Perez was the grandson of Jacob and son of Judah and Tamar, whose own story involved the institution of levirate marriage and the role of the kinsman redeemer (Gen. 38). Moreover, the link with the patriarchal narratives in general and Judah in particular brought focus to God's promise of a royal deliver who would ultimately set all evil right and provide satisfying relief to those in an oppressed and oppressive world. As Yahweh promised Abraham, "Your offspring shall possess the gate of his enemies, and in your offspring shall all the nations of the earth be blessed" (22:17–18). Or in Jacob's blessing of Judah (49:8, 10): "Judah, your brothers shall praise you; your hand shall be on the neck of your enemies; your father's sons shall bow down before you.... The scepter shall not depart from Judah, nor the ruler's staff from between his feet, until tribute comes to him; and to him shall be the obedience of the peoples."

> The New Testament opens, "The book of the genealogy of Jesus Christ, the son of David, the son of Abraham" (Matt. 1:1). This abbreviated genealogy captures the trajectory of redemptive history that the story of Ruth embraces and through which we find hope. "Boaz the father of Obed by Ruth, and Obed the father of Jesse, and Jesse the father of David the king.... Jacob the father of Joseph the husband of Mary, of whom Jesus was born, who is called Christ" (1:5–6, 16).

Yahweh had redeemed the ancestors of David from their temporary "exile" in Moab, and he would do so again for those under Persian rule. He would raise up the promised Son of David and would, through him, redeem and restore. The story of Ruth, therefore, provides a hope-filled analogy for those living apart from the complete fulfillment of the restoration promises.

"Then the women said to Naomi, 'Blessed be the LORD, who has not left you this day without a redeemer.... He shall be to you a restorer of life and a nourisher of your old age, for your daughter-in-law who loves you ... has given birth to him'" (Ruth 4:14–15). *Barley in the field near Kiriath Gat.*

Conclusion

Placed within its biblical context, the book of Ruth is clearly more than a story of the salvation of Naomi's family line. God was working in ways larger than any in Ruth's day probably ever anticipated. In nearly every way, the story of Ruth contrasts and answers the message of Judges and therefore provides a helpful prelude to the hope of the Writings. After the extended testimony in the Prophets to the ominous chaos in Israel and the nations, the book of Ruth provides great encouragement by disclosing that a remnant, faithful to Yahweh, did exist and that God was in the process of fulfilling the Davidic promises.

KEY WORDS AND CONCEPTS FOR REVIEW

Counter-revolutionaries	Covenant blessings
Worthy woman	Royal image of hope
Levirate marriage	Davidic promises
Kinsman redeemer	Genealogy
Pure religion	Exile
Covenant faithfulness	Prelude to the Writings

KEY RESOURCES FOR FURTHER STUDY

Atkinson, David. *The Message of Ruth*. BST. Downers Grove, IL: InterVarsity, 1985.

Block, Daniel I. *Judges, Ruth*. NAC. Nashville: B&H, 1998.

Duguid, Ian M. *Esther and Ruth*. REC. Phillipsburg, NJ: P&R, 2005.

Hubbard, Robert L., Jr. *The Book of Ruth*. NICOT. Grand Rapids: Eerdmans, 1989.

PSALMS

Who?

Many authors wrote the 150 psalms in the Psalter. The psalm titles appear, at the very least, to be an early, reliable tradition concerning authorship and setting. Forty-seven psalms are anonymous, but the rest are attributed to individuals:

- Moses, 1x (Ps. 90)
- Ethan the Ezrahite, 1x (89)
- Solomon, 2x (72, 127)
- The sons of Korah, 12x (42–49, 84–85, 87–88; Heman the Ezrahite is also accredited with Ps. 88)
- Asaph, 12x (50, 73–83)
- David, 73x (3–9, 11–32, 34–41, 51–65, 68–70, 86, 101, 103, 108–110, 122, 124, 131, 133, 138–145)

The high concentration of Davidic psalms at the front and back of the Psalter places a Davidic (or messianic) stamp on the whole. While many individuals played a part in writing the psalms, some person or group late in Old Testament history collected them into the book known as Psalms.

When?

The various psalms date from the time of Moses (Ps. 90) to after the return from exile (e.g. Ps. 107). The final form of the Psalter was likely shaped during the time of Ezra (ca. 458) or even later.

Some psalm titles speak of events from which the psalms arose, but the psalms themselves are almost always devoid of direct reference to specific historical situations. This fact lets the voice of the psalmist be the words of every worshipper throughout time and in ever-changing contexts. It also suggests that attempts to place the psalms too specifically into historical settings cut against the intention of the authors.

Although the historical background of individual psalms is usually unknown, certain psalms suggest the context of worship wherein they were to be used. For example, the question "Who shall ascend the hill of the LORD?" in Psalm 24:3 indicates that this psalm was intended for those anticipating corporate worship in the presence of God. Similarly, the prayer in Psalm 70:1, "Make haste, O God, to deliver me!" would be sung by one overcome with adversity.

Where?

Not much is known about the physical location in which psalms were written. A psalm's literary context is more important than its original historical context(s) in the life of the nation of Israel.

Why?

Psalms is a collection of prayers and songs designed to instruct and encourage God's people and to guide both the individual and community in the worship of Yahweh in every setting. The psalms provide tangible expressions of praise and lament, invitation and exhortation, in ways that honor Yahweh as the ultimate sovereign and supreme treasure and helper of all. Together the psalms exalt the greatness and faithfulness of Yahweh, the centrality of his Word, the hope of his messianic kingdom, and the need for persevering trust and loyalty.

CHAPTER 16

PSALMS

John C. Crutchfield

Carefully Crafted Verses from Psalms

Blessed is the man who walks not in the counsel of the wicked ... but his delight is in the law of the LORD, and on his law he meditates day and night (Ps. 1:1–2).

"You are my Son.... Ask of me, and I will make the nations your heritage, and the ends of the earth your possession" (Ps. 2:7–8).

One thing have I asked of the LORD, that will I seek after: that I may dwell in the house of the LORD all the days of my life, to gaze upon the beauty of the LORD and to inquire in his temple (Ps. 27:4).

Whom have I in heaven but you? And there is nothing on earth that I desire besides you. My flesh and my heart may fail, but God is the strength of my heart and my portion forever (Ps. 73:25–26).

Let everything that has breath praise the LORD! (Ps. 150:6).

> ## THE AUTHOR OF PSALMS ...
>
> - Used *literary forms as templates* for communicating with God.
>
> - Expressed *human emotions* in healthy and authentic ways.
>
> - Taught how to *live and think wisely*.
>
> - Encouraged *waiting for God's kingdom and Messiah*.
>
> - Called people to *worship Yahweh* in light of his person and works.

Psalms is a beautiful book, containing some of the most God-exalting and well-known poetry in the world. For thousands of years, people of faith have been singing, chanting, memorizing, and meditating on its worship poems. Psalms is the most quoted book in the New Testament, and this compilation has more chapters than any other book in the Bible (150) and also includes the longest (Ps. 119) and the shortest chapter (Ps. 117). This stated, it is more accurate to speak of "psalms" rather than "chapters" in the Psalter, though the editor(s) who collected the whole did show intentionality in the placement of the parts. Early on, the various psalms were grouped into five "books," perhaps paralleling the five books of the Law; each concludes with a brief doxology: Book I = Psalms 1–41; Book II = Psalms 42–72; Book III = Psalms 73–89; Book IV = Psalms 90–106; and Book V = Psalms 107–150. The main themes of the whole collection are captured in Psalms 1–2 (the introduction) and Psalm 150 (the conclusion). The book of Psalms teaches people how to communicate with God, to express their emotions, to live well, to understand God's kingdom, and to worship him rightly, all in a world where evil still lingers and where Yahweh's universal reign is not yet fully manifest on earth as it is in heaven.

Figure 16.1. Psalms at a Glance

		BOOK I	BOOK II	BOOK III	BOOK IV	BOOK V	
Psalm 1: Wisdom	Psalm 2: Eschatology	Psalms 3–41	Psalms 42–72	Psalms 73–89	Psalms 90–106	Psalms 107–149	Psalm 150: Worship
		Concluding Doxology: Psalm 41:13	Concluding Doxology: Psalm 72:18–19	Concluding Doxology: Psalm 89:52	Concluding Doxology: Psalm 106:48	Concluding Doxology: Psalms 146–149	
Intro.		Body					Conc.

The Author of Psalms Used *Literary Forms as Templates* for Communicating with God

A Shakespearian sonnet has certain rules that make it a sonnet, and both the writer and the reader must be aware of those rules in order for the poem to be appreciated for its beauty and creativity. The writers of the Psalms also wrote their poems with certain literary guidelines in mind. We can better understand the parts of a psalm and its message if we understand the structure of the psalm as a whole and its literary genre. In this brief survey, we will look closely at three kinds of psalms: praise, lament, and thanksgiving.

Psalms of Praise

Psalms of Praise focus the reader on who God is and what he has done. The structure is as follows:

1. Call to praise
2. Basis for praise
3. Repeated call to praise

Figure 16.2. Praise Psalm	
Psalm 117	**Praise Element**
¹ Praise the LORD, all nations! Extol him, all peoples!	Call to Praise
² For great is his steadfast love toward us, and the faithfulness of the LORD endures forever.	Basis for Praise
Praise the LORD!	Repeated Call to Praise

Psalm 117, the shortest of the psalms, is an excellent illustration of this structure (for a longer example, see Ps. 103). The final line of the poem,

"As for man, his days are like grass; he flourishes like a flower of the field; for the wind passes over it, and it is gone, and its place knows it no more. But the steadfast love of the LORD is from everlasting to everlasting on those who fear him" (Ps. 103:15–17). **Left:** *grass in the Judean Wilderness;* **Right:** *a field of yellow chamomile flowers at Kedesh.*

"Praise the LORD," is the Hebrew word that we often render "Hallelujah." Grammatically, this word consists of two elements: *halĕlû*, which is the plural imperative "praise!" and *yāh* (or "jah"), which is a shortened form of the divine name. "Hallelujah" means "You (plural) praise Yahweh!"

Psalms of Lament

One of the most important genres in Psalms is the Lament. In a Lament Psalm, the writer calls out to God and asks for help. Again we find several elements, though each one is not always present and not always in this exact order.

1. First-person address to God, often using the divine name
2. Petitions, usually for being heard
3. Description of the trouble
4. Rationale for why God should answer
5. Statement of confidence or trust
6. Promise of sacrifice or praise

Psalm 6 is a good example of this structure (cf. Ps. 13).

Figure 16.3. Lament Psalm	
Psalm 6	**Element of Lament**
¹ O LORD, rebuke me not in your anger....	First person address to God
² Be gracious to me...; heal me....	Petitions
⁴ Turn, O LORD, deliver my life; save me for the sake of your steadfast love.	Rationale
⁶ I am weary with my moaning; every night I flood my bed with tears....	Description of the trouble
⁹ The LORD has heard my plea; the LORD accepts my prayer.	Statement of confidence

Psalms of Thanksgiving

Another common literary form in the Psalter that follows the Lament is the Thanksgiving Psalm. In the Thanksgiving Psalm, the writer calls his readers to give thanks/praise to God, usually for some specific instance of God's deliverance or help.

There are several typical elements of a Thanksgiving Psalm, though they are not present in every case.

1. Praise addressed to God
2. A report of the trouble or crisis
3. Summons to praise the Lord
4. Vows, offerings, or praise

Psalm 30 is a good example of this structure (cf. Ps. 116). In each of these psalms, the writer follows a consistent literary form.

Figure 16.4. Thanksgiving Psalm	
Psalm 30	**Element of Thanksgiving**
[1] I will extol you, O Lord,	Praise addressed to God
for you have drawn me up and have not let my foes rejoice over me.	Report of the trouble
[4] Sing praises to the Lord, O you his saints, and give thanks to his holy name.	Summons to praise the Lord
[11] You have turned for me my mourning into dancing; you have loosed my sackcloth and clothed me with gladness, [12] that my glory may sing your praise and not be silent. O Lord my God, I will give thanks to you forever!	Vows, offerings, or praise

Further Comments on Genre

We cannot here review all the genres in Psalms. There are differences, for example, between individual or communal psalms. There are also Wisdom Psalms, Psalms of Trust, Torah Psalms, Imprecatory Psalms, "Kingship of Yahweh" Psalms, Zion Psalms, and others.[1]

The writers of the psalms clearly cared about the structure of their poems and used these genres as a means of giving expression to their communication with God. An awareness of these genres and their various literary structures will help the reader understand and appreciate the authors' message.

There is a danger, however, in overemphasizing the genres. Sometimes a writer will compose a psalm that includes formal features from various genres so that the psalm is not easily categorized. Heartfelt words to God are so often a combination of praise and petition, thanksgiving and plea, that we must be careful not to force a given psalm into a preconceived mold.

"We have escaped like a bird from the snare of the fowlers; the snare is broken, and we have escaped! Our help is in the name of the Lord, who made heaven and earth" (Ps. 124:7–8). *A black kite at Yotvata Hai-Bar Nature Reserve.*

---

1. For a more thorough discussion, see C. Hassell Bullock, *Encountering the Book of Psalms* (Grand Rapids: Zondervan, 2001).

We must also remember that the most important task is to understand the author's message, regardless of whether the psalm contains all elements of a genre category.

Figure 16.5. Psalms by Genre Category

GENRE	PSALM
Lament	3, 4, 5, 6, 7, 12, 13, 14 (= 53), 17, 22, 26, 27, 28, 35, 38, 39, 41, 42/43, 44, 51, 54, 55, 56, 57, 58, 59, 60, 61, 63, 64, 69, 70, 71, 74, 77, 79, 80, 82, 83, 85, 86, 88, 90, 94, 102, 106, 108, 109, 120, 123, 126, 130, 137, 140, 141, 142, 143 (Penitential Psalms = 6, 32, 38, 51, 102, 130, 143; Imprecatory Psalms = 35, 55, 59, 69, 79, 109, 137)
Praise	8, 29, 33, 46, 47, 48, 76, 84, 87, 93, 95, 96, 97, 98, 99, 100, 103, 104, 105, 111, 113, 114, 117, 122, 134, 135, 136, 145, 146, 147, 148, 149, 150 (Songs of Zion = 46, 48, 76, 84, 87; Enthronement of Yahweh Psalms = 47, 93, 96, 97, 98, 99)
Royal	2, 18, 20, 21, 45, 72, 101, 110, 132, 144
Thanksgiving	30, 66, 92, 107, 116, 118, 124, 138
Trust	11, 16, 23, 91, 121, 125, 129, 131
Wisdom	1, 37, 49, 73, 112, 127, 128
Liturgy	15, 24 (see also 136)
Historical	78 (see also 105, 106, 107, 114)
Mixed	9/10, 19, 25, 31. 32, 34, 36, 40, 65, 89, 119
Unclear	50, 52, 62, 67, 68, 75, 81, 115, 133, 139

Prepared by John C. Crutchfield; for an expanded version of this chart in canonical order with comments, see Appendix 1, Fig. A.1

Psalm 40 is a good example of a "mixed" psalm. The psalm opens like a typical Psalm of Thanksgiving (vv. 1–10), but suddenly, in verse 11, the writer shifted to the form of a Lament (vv. 11–17). We cannot treat Psalm 40 strictly as a Thanksgiving Psalm or a Lament Psalm. We must treat it as … Psalm 40! The writer was combining the two kinds of psalms into one poem. Our job is to ask why he did this.

> The most important goal of interpretation is to grasp the author's message. God spoke directly through the human authors, so to understand their words is to understand God!

The Author of Psalms Expressed *Human Emotions* in Healthy and Authentic Ways

The psalmists express a wide array of emotions in their poems, ranging from strongly negative emotions, like rage and anger, to positive emotions, like praise. The very presence of these emotions authenticates human experience. We all feel emotions; that's part of being human. The poems in the Psalter demonstrate how to channel these emotions in ways that are authentic and honest as well as healthy and positive.

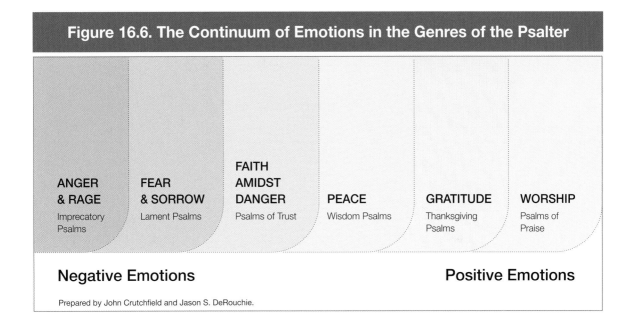

Figure 16.6. The Continuum of Emotions in the Genres of the Psalter

ANGER & RAGE
Imprecatory Psalms

FEAR & SORROW
Lament Psalms

FAITH AMIDST DANGER
Psalms of Trust

PEACE
Wisdom Psalms

GRATITUDE
Thanksgiving Psalms

WORSHIP
Psalms of Praise

Negative Emotions   **Positive Emotions**

Prepared by John Crutchfield and Jason S. DeRouchie.

Rage in the Psalms of Imprecation

The most negative of the emotions in Psalms is rage. In the Psalms of Imprecation, writers express strong anger, usually along with some kind of curse or judgment on someone. Here are some examples of these imprecations:

- Let them be put to shame and dishonor who seek after my life! (Ps. 35:4).

- "Let death steal over them" (55:15).

- "Let their eyes be darkened, so that they cannot see, and make their loins tremble continually" (69:23).

- "Add to them punishment upon punishment; may they have no acquittal from you" (69:27).

- "O daughter of Babylon, doomed to be destroyed, blessed shall he be who repays you with what you have done to us! Blessed shall he be who takes your little ones and dashes them against the rock!" (137:8–9).

Paul was convinced the Imprecatory Psalms were for Christians, for directly after quoting the Imprecatory Psalm 69, he declared, "For whatever was written in former days was written for our instruction, that through endurance and through the encouragement of the Scriptures we might have hope" (Rom. 15:4). His following words also show that he saw love of neighbor as the ultimate end (15:5–6). Trusting God to bring justice tomorrow enables us to love even our enemies today (12:18–19).

These are difficult verses to read, and some scholars have condemned these sentiments as immoral. However, we should remember that these emotions are in response to real wrong and injustice and arise often after sustained acts of love have been rejected (35:12–13; 109:4–5). Also, the writers are often concerned about God and his name, not just personal vindication. We even see where the psalmist prays for Yahweh to punish the enemies *so that* their hearts may ultimately turn toward him (83:16–18). Finally, we should remember that these emotions are expressed *in prayer*, not in a call to arms or to an angry mob. The Psalms of Imprecation authenticate the human emotions of anger and rage but submit them to God and his sovereign will. Admitting to God that we have enemies, and that we hate them, is the first step in a long process of emotional healing that ends in our ability to love our enemies.[2] Far from being immoral, the expressions of anger and rage in the Psalms teach us to submit our most violent urges and emotions to God.

"Contend, O LORD, with those who contend with me; fight against those who fight against me! ... Draw the spear and javelin against my pursuers! Say to my soul, 'I am your salvation!'" (Ps. 35:1, 3). *Spearheads from ancient Israel (from Istanbul Archaeological Museum).*

Fear in the Psalms of Lament

We live in a world of enemies and evil, of death and disappointment. The Psalms of Lament express deep emotions of fear and anxiety.

---

2. Michael Card, *A Sacred Sorrow* (Colorado Springs, CO: NavPress, 2005), 73–80.

- My soul also is greatly troubled.... I am weary with my moaning; every night I flood my bed with tears (Ps. 6:3, 6).

- "Be gracious to me, O LORD! See my affliction from those who hate me" (9:13).

- "How long must I take counsel in my soul, and have sorrow in my heart all the day?" (13:2).

- "O my God, I cry by day, but you do not answer, and by night, but I find no rest" (22:2).

- "Hear the voice of my pleas for mercy, when I cry to you for help" (28:2).

- "O LORD, rebuke me not in your anger, nor discipline me in your wrath!" (38:1).

Although the Lament Psalms express emotional pain, for several reasons they also lead to emotional and psychological health. First, the Lament protects from denial and repression. Psychologists insist that trauma victims must verbally process their experiences, and the subsequent emotions, or the ensuing mental damage can become permanent. Lament facilitates this processing. Lament is healthy because it is real and protects us from denial and hypocrisy. Second, the Lament provides verbal containers into which a person can pour his own sometimes inexpressible pain. When a person cannot verbalize his negative emotions, the biblical Laments lend him their language. Third, the very structure of the Lament brings healing. Every biblical lament but one ends with an expression of trust; that is, after the expression of negative emotion, the psalmist turns the eyes of his heart to God in faith. "But I have trusted in your steadfast love," says David in Psalm 13:5. The Lament's final expression of trust gently transforms a fit of sorrow, grief, and fear into an exercise of faith. The importance of this upward glance can hardly be exaggerated. The genius of the biblical Lament is that, although it allows for the expression of agonizing pain, it does not leave the lamenter to sit on the ash heap of his own pity. By forcing him to express his trust, the Lament leads the lamenter to the ultimate answer to his own trouble: God himself. In other words, the literary form of the biblical Lament comes equipped with its own answer.

Confidence in the Psalms of Trust

The Psalm of Trust was not a genre covered above, but it falls between the Psalm of Lament and the Psalm of Thanksgiving. In the Lament, the psalmist is very much in the midst of the crisis; in the Psalm of Thanksgiving, the crisis is clearly over. In the Psalm of Trust, the writer expresses confidence in God's imminent deliverance. Two examples will suffice: Psalms 23 and 62.

Perhaps the most loved of all the psalms, Psalm 23 expresses great certainty and rest in God's provision (vv. 1–3) and protection (vv. 4–5). "Even though I walk through the valley of the shadow of death, I will fear no evil, for you are with me.... You prepare a table before me in the presence of my enemies" (vv. 4–5). In both cases, death and danger were near, but David proclaimed trust in God's ever-present help. Psalm 62 is another Psalm of Trust. David faced opposition from outside (vv. 3–4), but he exclaimed: "For

"The LORD is my shepherd; I shall not want. He makes me lie down in green pastures. He leads me beside still waters. He restores my soul" (Ps. 23:1–3). *Baby goats in Nahal Yitla.*

God alone my soul waits in silence; from him comes my salvation…. For God alone, O my soul, wait in silence, for my hope is from him" (vv. 1, 5). In both of these psalms, the writer gave voice to confidence in God's ultimate goodness, provision, and protection.

Gratitude in the Psalms of Thanksgiving

Those who have experienced the love of God look for ways to express it. In the Psalms of Thanksgiving, the reader finds exuberant cries of gratitude. In Psalm 30, the psalmist listed at least three responses: dancing, joy, and singing (vv. 11–12). The author of Psalm 116 emphasized fulfilling vows to God, vows that may be not only sacrifice and worship but also deeds of service (vv. 12–14, 17–19). In Psalm 40 (a mixed psalm), David proclaimed God's righteousness, faithfulness, and salvation in the great assembly (vv. 9–10). Psalm 95 bids the believing community to come before God with thanksgiving, music, and song (v. 2). The title for Psalm 100 describes it as "a psalm for giving thanks." These and many others are examples of expressions of gratitude to God for salvation, works, deliverance, goodness, guidance, provision, and even for who he is. The psalmists cared about helping people express their gratitude to God in words of thanksgiving and praise.

> Thanksgiving is central to the Christian life. Paul called believers to sing "psalms and hymns and spiritual songs, *with thankfulness in your hearts to God,*" and then added, "Whatever you do, in word or deed, do everything in the name of the Lord Jesus, *giving thanks to God the Father through him*" (Col. 3:16–17).

Worship in the Psalms of Praise

The movement of the entire book of Psalms is toward praise. Lament Psalms dominate early in the book (esp. Books I–III), but as one moves into Book V, Praise Psalms appear more and more.

Worship will be discussed more fully below, but here we notice that adoration and worship of a deity moves one's focus outward away from oneself to another. Even some secular psychologists admit that believing in a supreme being is mentally and emotionally healthy. An outward focus or reference point allows one to order one's priorities around something bigger than oneself. Psalms endorses this perspective by consistently calling the believer to adoration and worship. "Tremble, O earth, at the presence of the Lord" (Ps. 114:7). "Serve (or worship) the Lord with fear, and rejoice with trembling" (2:11). One way or another, humans will worship. Those who do not worship something that is worthy will worship something that is not, and the results can be tragic (115:2–8; 135:15–18). The Psalter proclaims worship of the God of creation and redemption whose character is beautiful (27:4) and whose presence is all satisfying (16:11).

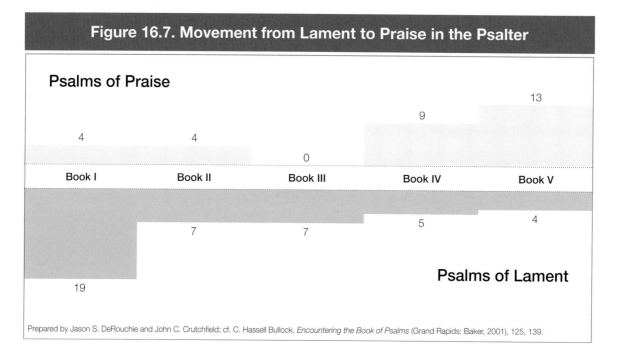

Figure 16.7. Movement from Lament to Praise in the Psalter

Psalms of Praise

Book I	Book II	Book III	Book IV	Book V
4	4	0	9	13

Book I	Book II	Book III	Book IV	Book V
19	7	7	5	4

Psalms of Lament

Prepared by Jason S. DeRouchie and John C. Crutchfield; cf. C. Hassell Bullock, *Encountering the Book of Psalms* (Grand Rapids: Baker, 2001), 125, 139.

Internal dialogue or self-talk

When the psalmist wrote, "How long must I take counsel in my soul?" (13:2), he alluded to a psychological reality: We talk to ourselves. Internal dialogue, or self-talk, is the content and tone of what a person thinks about and says to oneself. At several points throughout Psalms, the psalmists model an authentic and healthy internal wrestling.

Psalms 42–43 together form a single Lament. The writer expressed deep desire for spiritual communion with God (42:1–3) and wistfully remembered days of open fellowship (42:4). Then in 42:5–6 he began to preach to himself: "Why are you cast down, O my soul, and why are you in turmoil within me? Hope in God; for I shall again praise him, my salvation and my God." At this point he began to recall Yahweh's work in his past (42:6b–8), to express his fears and concerns to God (42:9–10), then repeated his self-talk, using the same words he had before (42:11). He then requested vindication and help, while promising to worship and praise

(43:1–4). He concluded at the end with the same charge to himself to find hope in God (43:5). The repetition of the rhetorical question followed by the personal exhortation to hope and the statement of confidence in God holds Psalms 42–43 together. This is an example of self-talk in the context of lament.

"Why are you cast down, O my soul, and why are you in turmoil within me? Hope in God" (Ps. 42:5). *A couple of young Nubian Ibex wild goats drinking in Nahal David.*

In Psalm 116, the psalmist thanked God for deliverance from death. In verse 7, the writer used his personal experience in the past, and God's character and attributes, as the ground for a call to his own soul to be at rest in the present. "Return, O my soul, to your rest; for the LORD has dealt bountifully with you." This is self-talk in the context of thanksgiving.

Psalms 103, 104 and 146 are all Psalms of Praise. In 103, the psalmist called on his soul to praise the Lord for "all his benefits" (v. 2). In 104, the psalmist called on his soul to praise the Lord for his work in creation. In 146, the psalmist contrasted the faithfulness of Yahweh with the transience of princes and mortal men. In all these psalms, the psalmists exhorted their own souls to move from an acknowledgement of God's character and works to heartfelt worship. This is self-talk in the context of praise and worship.

In commenting on Psalm 42, the preacher D. Martyn Lloyd-Jones asserted: "Have you realized that most of your unhappiness in life is due to the fact that you are listening to yourself instead of talking to yourself…. Now this man's treatment [in Ps. 42:5, 11] was this; instead of allowing this self to talk to him, he starts talking to himself. 'Why art thou cast down, O my soul?' he asks. His soul had been depressing him, crushing him. So he stands up and says: 'Self, listen for a moment, I will speak to you'." When spiritually depressed, we would do well to open a text like Romans 8:31–35 and preach the gospel to ourselves!

In conclusion, by means of expressing a wide range of human emotions and by repeated self-exhortations, the psalmists demonstrated authentic human experience as well as healthy and godly internal dialogue. Their personal charges were based *not* on the disappointments and dangers of this world but on the truth of God's person and works.

The Author of Psalms Taught How to *Live and Think Wisely*

Psalms 1–2 introduce the whole Psalter. Psalm 1, a Wisdom Psalm, presents the themes of how to live and think wisely. The first of these themes, called by some "*tôrâ* piety," calls the reader to value the instruction in the Law (Genesis–Deuteronomy) as God's revelation and to live in conscious conformity to it. Psalm 1 contrasts torah piety with the wicked, the sinful, and those who mock (Ps. 1:1–2). It is only one whose "delight is in the law of the Lord" who will flourish and enjoy lasting life (1:2). Similarly, Psalm 19 compares God's law with the sun, both of which *reveal* something; the sun *reveals* physical reality, while the law *reveals* God's will and guides and convicts the believer of sin. Psalm 119 also focuses on torah piety, with the entire psalm being structured to provide an exhaustive description of a life circumscribed by the Word of God.

The Psalter also addresses the issue of theodicy—the presence of evil in a world that an all-good and all-powerful God has created and controls. Psalm 73 begins with the premise, "Truly God is good to Israel" (v. 1). This stated, the psalmist immediately related what appeared on the surface to stand in contrast to this truth: the prosperity of the wicked (vv. 2–12). While this observation was initially troubling to his faith, in the context of worship, he came to a deeper understanding of God and his world (vv. 13–17). The psalmist explained (vv. 18–28) that the premise of verse 1 is still true but that the "goodness" God shows to Israel is not necessarily material or physical prosperity; rather, the goodness God gives to the "pure in heart" is God himself, which cannot be taken away and which is infinitely more valuable and lasting than health and wealth. Psalm 73 demonstrates how a believer can make sense of the world.

The book of Psalms contrasts the way of the righteous with the way of the wicked. Psalm 1 compares the righteous with a healthy, fruit-bearing tree but the wicked with worthless chaff, separated by the winnowing process from the kernel of wheat (vv. 3–4). The psalm concludes by contrasting

"[The man whose] delight is in the law of the LORD … is like a tree planted by streams of water that yields its fruit in its season, and its leaf does not wither. In all that he does, he prospers" (Ps. 1:2–3). *Ein Perat with tree and running water.*

the final end of the wicked with that of the righteous. The wicked cannot stand in the righteous assembly but will perish, whereas the righteous are protected by God (vv. 5–6). This contrast between the righteous and the wicked surfaces throughout the whole collection (e.g., Pss. 5; 9–10; 34; 37; 140).

Like the Old Testament books that are devoted wholly to wisdom (Prov. 1:7, 9:10; Eccl. 12:13; Job 1:1, 28:28), the Psalter calls people to "fear the Lord." Fearing God is *an intellectual and emotional recognition of who God is that results in right behavior.* The fear of the Lord is the beginning of wisdom (Ps. 111:10) and is closely linked with God's law (19:9). The one who fears Yahweh serves him (2:11) and is blessed by him (112:1; 115:13; 128:1, 4). God teaches and confides in those who fear him (25:12, 14); he is good to them (31:19), provides for them (34:9; 111:5; 145:19), and protects them (33:18; 34:7; 60:4). Yahweh loves and has compassion on those who fear him (103:11, 13, 17; 118:4). Indeed, he delights in them (147:11)!

> Psalm 1 teaches that there are only two ways in this world: the way of the righteous and the wise and the way of wicked and the fool. Jesus said that while the first way is hard it leads to life; the second way is easy but leads to destruction (Matt. 7:13–14). John put it this way (1 John 3:7–8): "Whoever practices righteousness is righteous…. Whoever makes a practice of sinning is of the devil."

Torah piety, theodicy, the righteous versus the wicked, and the fear of Yahweh. Psalms uses all these themes to instruct people how to live and think wisely. May God "teach us to number our days that we may get a heart of wisdom" (90:12).

The Author of Psalms Encouraged *Waiting for God's Kingdom and Messiah*

Psalm 2, the second half of Psalter's introduction, describes the kings and princes of the earth opposing Yahweh's kingdom and reign through his "Anointed" (v. 2). The writers of the Psalms cared deeply about God's rule in the world.

Yahweh's Reign and Kingdom

Yahweh is sovereign over the world (Pss. 9:7; 10:16; 47:2, 7–8; 103:19; 145:13; 146:10), and his people call on him as "King" (5:2; 145:1). In terms of extent, he rules over his people (28:9; 68:7; 77:15, 20; 80:1; 114:2), over the nations of the globe (47:2, 7–9; 96:10; 99:1), and even over the whole creation (97:2–6; 103:19; 104; 135:6–7; 147:15–18). In terms of time, his kingdom is eternal (9:7; 10:16; 29:10; 45:6; 55:19; 66:7;

102:12; 145:13; 146:10). God's kingdom reflects his character (9:4; 11:4; 47:8; 89:14; 97:1–2) and is an extension of his role as creator (95:3–5; 96:5, 10).

Yahweh's Anointed One

But Yahweh not only *is* a king, he also *has* a king (2:6; 18:50). The earthly Israelite king was a manifestation of God's heavenly rule. In Psalm 2, Yahweh responds to the rebellion of the kings of the earth by proclaiming

"Give the king your justice, O God.... May he judge your people with righteousness, and your poor with justice! Let the mountains bear prosperity for the people, and the hills, in righteousness!" (Ps. 72:1–3). *A pear orchard in Dan with a view of Mount Hermon to the northeast (photo by David Bivin).*

the installation of his earthly king. Sometimes it is hard to tell whether the writer is talking about the heavenly divine king, Yahweh, or about the earthly human king (e.g., Ps. 45); their attributes and reign are very similar. The earthly human king is described as Yahweh's "anointed one," meaning anointed with oil as a symbol of God's special equipping with abilities to accomplish a task (2:7–12; 89:19–24). Specifically, the king was set apart by God to rule his people with justice and righteousness (72:1). Due to the failures of these human Israelite kings, the expectation of a righteous king was gradually transferred to an ideal "anointed one" of the future, an eschatological king who would one day fulfill the expectations both of God and his people. In Hebrew the word for "anointed one" is *māšîaḥ*, from which we get the word "Messiah" (*christos* in Greek).

> "Christ" is not Jesus' second name; it is the title "Messiah" and embodies all the Old Testament hopes of God's kingdom. When we read in the first verse of the New Testament, "The book of the genealogy of Jesus Christ, the son of David, the son of Abraham" (Matt. 1:1), we should be filled with as much anticipation for God's kingdom as the wise men from the east, who sought "the king of the Jews" (2:2).

The book of Psalms encourages people to believe in and submit to Yahweh's absolute rule, which oversees his people, the nations, and the whole earth. Psalms also calls people to wait patiently for the perfect manifestation of that kingdom through a coming "anointed one," or Messiah, whom God will one day send to deliver, purify, protect, defend, and rule over his people with justice, righteousness, and might (Ps. 72). Because Yahweh will punish, subdue (2:9; 144:3; 149:7–9), and ultimately destroy (1:6; 2:9; 92:9; 94:20–23; 110:5–6; 141:6–7; 145:20) those who reject his rule, the psalmists encourage their readers to embrace God's kingdom by submitting to God's authority, especially as expressed through his Messiah (2:8–12; 110).

The Author of Psalms Called People to *Worship Yahweh* in Light of His Person and His Works

"Praise the Lord.... Praise him for his mighty deeds; praise him according to his excellent greatness! Praise him with trumpet sound; praise him with lute and harp!" (Ps. 150:1–3). *An image of a harpist (from the Oriental Institute, USA).*

Psalm 150 concludes the Psalter and gives expression to its ultimate goal: *worship*. Psalms turns the reader's heart to God in adoration, thanks, and praise. In Psalm 150:1, the psalmist first issues a command to praise ("Hallelujah!") and then addresses two main spheres of worship: "his sanctuary" (physical, earthly) and "his mighty heavens" (spiritual, heavenly). In verse 2, the psalmist calls the reader to worship Yahweh for two reasons: "his mighty deeds" (works) and "his excellent greatness" (person). The same dual focus is in the doxology of Book II, Psalm 72:18–19: "Blessed be the Lord, the God of Israel, who alone does wondrous things. Blessed be his glorious name forever; may the whole earth be filled with his glory!" Similarly, Psalm

86:10 declares, "You are great and do wondrous things; you alone are God." In Psalms, the scope of why God deserves praise is difficult to summarize, but these two general rubrics—works and person—help to focus our thoughts.

God's Works

The psalmists regularly cite God's creative power as a reason for praise and worship. For example, upon considering "your heavens, the work of your fingers," and their relationship to "man," the psalmist proclaims, "O Lord, our Lord, how majestic is your name in all the earth!" (Ps. 8:3–4, 9; cf. 19:1). Yahweh protects and delivers those who love him (3:3, 5; 34:4, 17, 19; 35:9; 37:39–40; 54:7; 56:12–13; 68:19–20; 97:10–12), and his works call for meditation (77:12; 111; 143:5; 145:5), joy (92:4; 104:31), and fear (33:5–9; 64:9; 96:4–5). God is sovereign over the nations (2:8; 22:28; 33:10; 46:8–10; 47:2–3, 8; 60:6–8 [=108:7–9]; 66:5–7; 67:4; 99:1–2; 102:15; 111; 113:4), especially over the history of the nation of Israel (22:3; 44; 53:6; 78; 80:1; 81; 105–106; 111:6; 135:10–12; 136). And this is but a short list of God's "glorious deeds" (78:4).

God's Person

The person of God occupies so much of Psalms that attempting a summary is challenging. Within the collection, Yahweh is praised because he is:

- *Righteous* (7:10, 12, 17; 11:7; 33:5; 35:28; 36:6; 71:15–16, 19; 89:14; 98:2; 111:3; 116:15; 119:137; 145:17);
- *Good* (13:6; 25:7–8; 34:8; 54:6; 73:1, 28; 86:5; 100:5; 106:1; 107:1; 116:7; 118:1, 29; 119:68; 135:3; 136:1; 145:9);
- *Faithful* (33:4; 36:5; 57:10 [=108:4]; 71:22; 86:15; 91:4; 100:5; 115:1; 117:2; 119:90; 145:13; 146:6);
- *Strong* (24:8; 62:11; 65:6; 66:3; 68:34–35; 89:9; 93:4; 99:4; 147:5);
- *Great* (48:1; 77:13; 86:10; 95:3; 96:4; 99:2–3; 104:1; 135:5; 145:3; 147:5);
- *Holy* (22:3; 71:22; 77:13; 99);
- *Forgiving* (86:5; 99:8; 103:3; 130:4);
- *Forever loving with unfailing love* (13:5; 32:10; 33:5; 36:7; 48:9; 52:8; 130:7).

This is our amazing God, who deserves our trust and our praise.

Conclusion

Psalms begins with walking (Ps. 1) and waiting (Ps. 2); it ends with worship (Ps. 150). Though the reader faces death and disappointment, enemies and evil, the collection of psalms continues to call people to find their ultimate safety, security, joy, and purpose in God and his royal Son (2:12). In Yahweh's presence alone "are pleasures forever more" (16:11). "Let everything that has breath praise the LORD! Praise the LORD!" (150:6).

KEY WORDS AND CONCEPTS FOR REVIEW

Psalm titles	"Self-talk"
Historical context	Torah piety
Five books	Theodicy
Psalms of Praise, Lament, Thanksgiving, Imprecation, and Trust	Righteous versus wicked
	Fear of Yahweh
Hallelujah	Messiah
Mixed genre	Worship
Most important goal of interpretation	
Expression of trust	

KEY RESOURCES FOR FURTHER STUDY

Longman, Tremper, III. *How to Read the Psalms*. Downers Grove, IL: Inter-Varsity, 1988.

VanGemeren, Willem A. "Psalms." In *The Expositor's Bible Commentary*, vol. 5, rev. ed. Grand Rapids: Zondervan, 2008.

Wilcock, Michael. *The Message of Psalms*, 2 vols. BST. Downers Grove, IL: InterVarsity, 2001.

Wilson, Gerald H. *Psalms, Volume 1*. NIVAC. Grand Rapids: Zondervan, 2002.

JOB

Who?

The author of Job is unknown, but the book's theological perspective and the regular use of Yahweh, Israel's covenant name for God (Job 1:6, 21; 12:9; 42:10), suggest that the author was an Israelite who took a true story involving non-Israelite characters and, under the inspiration of God, crafted it into one of the world's great literary masterpieces.

When?

The dates for both the events described in Job and the composition of the book are uncertain. The prologue (1:1–5) and epilogue (42:10–17) suggest that the story took place in a patriarchal setting, though one outside Israel. Unfortunately, this provides little help in dating the events because a patriarchal culture could have continued in the Transjordan long after it had ended in Israel. Scholars have suggested dates for the book ranging from the patriarchal period (ca. 2100–1800 B.C.) to the postexilic period (after ca. 538 B.C.), and many posit a date during Solomon's reign (ca. 970–930 B.C.) because social and economic conditions then created an environment where such literature could flourish. The Hebrew used in Job is quite different from that found elsewhere in the Hebrew Bible and so provides little help in dating the book.

Where?

The story of Job took place in the land of Uz, east of the Jordan River (1:1). Other biblical passages associate Uz to the north in Aram (Gen. 10:23), in Edom to the southeast of Israel (Lam. 4:21), and in an area farther to the south (Jer. 25:20). Ambiguities regarding the book's authorship and date of composition and the events' date and location are perhaps related to the fact that the problem dealt with in the book is a universal one rather than an issue that involved uniquely Israelite concerns.

Why?

Job teaches basic lessons about who Yahweh is and how he works in the world; it also deals with the question of how a godly person should appropriately respond in circumstances that seem to call into question God's love and justice. Job highlights the sovereignty of Yahweh even in a world that includes suffering and evil. Job emphasized human limits in understanding the work of God and the folly of presuming that our understanding of how God works is comprehensive or that God's working in the world must correspond to our theological categories. The book shows that Yahweh accepts the honest cries and complaints of his hurting people, and it affirms that the godly person's proper response in difficult and perplexing circumstances is to fear God and to turn from evil (Job 28:28).

CHAPTER 17

JOB

Edward M. Curtis

Carefully Crafted Verses from Job

And the LORD said to Satan, "Have you considered my servant Job, that there is none like him on the earth, a blameless and upright man, who fears God and turns away from evil? Then Satan answered the LORD and said, "Does Job fear God for no reason?" (Job 1:8–9).

"Shall we receive good from God, and shall we not receive evil?" In all this Job did not sin with his lips (Job 2:10).

"Behold, the fear of the LORD, that is wisdom, and to turn away from evil is understanding" (Job 28:28).

"I know that you can do all things, and that no purpose of yours can be thwarted.... I have uttered what I did not understand, things too wonderful for me, which I did not know" (Job 42:2–3).

THE AUTHOR OF JOB ...

- Affirmed *Yahweh's sovereignty* over all things.

- Showed that *personal sin is not the only reason humans suffer*.

- Acknowledged *humanity's inability* to fully grasp God's work and purposes.

- Recognized that *God accepts the honest cries of his hurting people*.

- Clarified *how to respond* when God's justice and goodness appear questionable.

- Believed that *people should fear God* for who he is rather than for what he gives.

The Author of Job Affirmed *Yahweh's Sovereignty over All Things*

People have long struggled with the theological problems created by the suffering of righteous people. Usually, the answers given either raise questions about whether God wants to prevent such situations (that is, whether God is good and just) or whether God is able to prevent such things (that is, whether he is all-powerful and sovereign). The author of Job clearly affirmed God's sovereignty over all things including suffering (cf. Deut. 32:39; Isa. 45:7; 1 Peter 4:19). For example, after Job lost his livestock, servants, and children, he declared, "The LORD gave, and the LORD has taken away; blessed be the name of the LORD" (Job 1:21). And lest we think Job's perspective was wrong, the inspired narrator added, "In all this Job did not sin or charge God with wrong" (1:22). Similarly, after Job's own health deteriorated and his wife called him to curse God, Job said, "Shall we receive good from God, and shall we not receive evil?" (2:10; cf. 42:11; Exod. 4:11). Again, the narrator immediately affirmed, "In all this Job did not sin with his lips" (Job 2:10). God is the Creator of all things; he is sovereign over the cosmic realm including Satan and the forces at his disposal (cf. Gen. 3:1; Col. 1:16–17 with 2:15). The book of Job makes it clear that what happened to Job did not catch God by surprise nor did it in any way threaten God or his purposes. In Job's words at the end of the book: "I know that you [the LORD] can do all things, and that no purpose of yours can be thwarted" (Job 42:2). Rather, the sovereign Lord used Job's experience to accomplish his good ends.

Figure 17.1. Job at a Glance

Act 1	Prologue (1–2)
Act 2	Dialog with Three Friends (chs. 3–31)
	3–26: Interchange with Three Friends 27–28: Job's Extended Response with Meditation on the Nature of Wisdom 29–31: Job's Final Defense
Act 3	Elihu's Speeches (32–37)
Act 4	Yahweh's Speeches (38:1–42:6)
Act 5	Epilogue (42:7–17)

Prepared by Jason S. DeRouchie.

"Do you know when the mountain goats give birth?" (Job 39:1). *A Nubian Ibex wild goat on a cliff in Machtesh Ramon of the Negeb.*

The Author of Job Showed That *Personal Sin Is Not the Only Reason Humans Suffer*

Both Job and his friends assumed that the doctrine of retribution (that is, that people reap what they sow) constituted a comprehensive explanation of how God works in the world. They applied this idea to Job's situation, and the debate between Job and his friends revolved around this concept. As Eliphaz asserted, "As I have seen, those who plow iniquity and sow trouble, reap the same" (Job 4:8). Job was unaware of anything he had done that would account for his suffering (9:20; 10:7; 31:1–40), and so this experience raised questions about how Job's suffering was consistent with God's justice and goodness. The friends could not see how it was possible for Job to be innocent without casting aspersions on God's justice—"Does God pervert justice? Or does the Almighty pervert the right?" (8:3). As such, Job's suffering prompted them to insist that he must have sinned. Job is described as "blameless and upright" and as one "who fears God and turns away from evil" (1:1, 8), and this makes clear that *Job's suffering was not the result of his sin.* The author's description of events that took place in heaven between God and Satan (1:6–12; 2:1–7) shows that what happened to Job was related to purposes of God having little to do with justice and retribution. In fact Job's piety was essential for God's purposes to be accomplished in this situation. The book recognizes that people do suffer for their own sins, but they also suffer because of the sins of others. Job pointed out that sometimes wicked people prosper and do very well and then finally die at a good old age without reaping the consequences of their evil (21:7–34). Job did not present anything like a comprehensive list of reasons why people suffer, but he made it clear that many things besides a person's personal sin explain the suffering that occurs in human experience. The book makes it clear that retribution, while generally true, is inadequate as a comprehensive explanation for suffering in the world.

> Many in Jesus' day were equally confused regarding the relationship of suffering, sin, and God's purposes. In John 9:2, the disciples asked of a man born blind, "Who sinned, this man or his parents…?" Jesus responded, "It was not that this man sinned, or his parents, but that the works of God might be displayed in him" (9:3). For a similar interchange with a grave warning attached, see Luke 13:1–5!

The Author of Job Acknowledged *Humanity's Inability* to Fully Grasp God's Work and Purposes

As Job and his friends struggled to understand the reason for and meaning of Job's suffering, they identified a number of reasons why people suffer. At the same time no one came close to discovering the real reason for Job's pain. As chapters 1 and 2 make clear, there are sometimes aspects of reality, especially happenings in the spiritual realm, that are unknown to us but are essential for fully understanding suffering in a particular instance. The same point is made in Job 28:20–21, 23, where we read: "From where, then, does wisdom come? And where is the place of understanding? It is hidden from the eyes of all the living and concealed from the birds of the air…. God understands the way to it, and he knows its place" (cf. Job 42:2–6; Eccl. 6:10–12).

Job also demonstrates the damage that can be done to others, especially to those who are suffering, when "comforters" or "counselors" presume to analyze a situation and then deliver dogmatic pronouncements about what

God is doing and what his purposes involve. Job 28 shows that there are situations in life where human finitude makes it impossible to understand the works and ways of God and that the proper course in such situations is to fear God and turn from evil (Job 28:28; cf. Eccl. 12:13). After Eliphaz counseled Job to turn from his sin and to ask God for forgiveness, Job observed how unhelpful such directives were because he did not

> Tragedies that seem inexplicable to us may be used by the sovereign, all-wise God to accomplish his good purposes which sometimes remain unknown to us. God "works all things according to the counsel of his will" (Eph. 1:11) and will work all things for good for those who love him (Rom. 8:28).

know anything to confess. In chapter 6, he observed that what a suffering person needs in such circumstances is kindness from his friend rather than theological advice and analysis which, in Job's case, only intensified his pain. Job himself asserted those who lack such care have forsaken "the fear of the Almighty" (Job 6:14), and Yahweh later affirmed how his anger burned against the three whose words were filled with foolishness (42:7). The book

"From where, then, does wisdom come? And where is the place of understanding? It is hidden from the eyes of all living and concealed from the birds of the air" (Job 28:20–21). *White storks above Caesarea on the coast of the Mediterranean Sea making their annual migration from Europe to Africa.*

of Job, therefore, clearly warns against the arrogance of assuming that our theological categories constitute a comprehensive statement about how God works.

"He who withholds kindness from a friend forsakes the fear of the Almighty. My brothers are treacherous as a torrent-bed, as torrential streams that pass away.... When it is hot, they vanish from their place" (Job 6:14–15, 17). *Nahal Arugot riverbed.*

The Author of Job Recognized That *God Accepts the Honest Cries of His Hurting People*

After sitting in silence for a week, Job began the conversation with his friends by stating that he wished he had never been born, since that would have kept him from enduring such great tragedy (Job 3:1–23). His friends were caught off guard by his response, because they apparently felt that a man as godly as they supposed Job to be should not speak with such rash and impious words. Job conceded that his words had been rash (6:3; cf. 42:3), but he also argued that they had misunderstood the significance of his cries. Eliphaz concluded from Job's words that he was foolish and lacked appropriate piety, but Job insisted that his friend should have recognized from his rash words how much pain he felt. Job's laments—or those of Jeremiah or the authors of many psalms—make clear that God accepts such cries of pain and that even blameless and upright people sometimes respond to profound tragedy in such ways. At the end of the book, Yahweh told Job's friends in 42:7, "You have not spoken of me what is right, as my servant Job has." The Lord's statements suggest that God's people can be honest with him—telling him exactly how they feel in their pain and distress—and still speak right words about God. The Lord knows the difference between words of pain and confusion coming from his hurting people and words of blasphemy and disdain. When the former are involved, he responds to his children as a loving father would to a hurting child.

The Author of Job Clarified *How to Respond* When God's Justice and Goodness Appear Questionable

Given all that happened to Job, neither he nor his friends could see how Job could be innocent and Yahweh could be just and good. The friends saw

God's justice as the given and so declared that Job must be guilty of great sin. Job grew in confidence that he was innocent and at points seemed willing to give up God's justice rather than deny his integrity (Job 27:1–6; cf. ch. 31). Indeed, Job spent more energy justifying his own claims of innocence than asserting God's right to rule his world as he will. In Elihu's words (36:22–23): "Behold, God is exalted in power; who is a teacher like him? Who has prescribed for him his way, or who can say, 'You have done wrong'?" Elihu's anger burned against Job "because he justified himself rather than God" (32:2) and did not "ascribe righteousness to my Maker" (36:3), and the Yahweh speeches make clear that in this he was correct. How little we understand of God's ways!

> With echoes of these texts, Paul spoke in similar tones (Rom. 9:20; 11:33): "Who are you, O man, to answer back to God? Will what is molded say to its molder, 'Why have you made me like this?' … Oh, the depth of the riches and wisdom and knowledge of God! How unsearchable are his judgments and how inscrutable his ways!"

"He loads the thick cloud with moisture; the clouds scatter his lightning. They turn around and around by his guidance, to accomplish all that he commands them on the face of the habitable world. Whether for correction or for his land or for love, he causes it to happen" (Job 37:11–13). *Sunset over the Mediterranean Sea, as the storm clouds dissipate.*

continued to trust God—this even as Job remained unclear of how God was working out his purposes.

The book illustrates the point made many other places in Scripture that the answer to suffering does not lie in understanding why it happened but rather is found in a knowledge of God. Only such knowledge allows one to continue trusting the Lord even when no explanation for the suffering is forthcoming. When the test began, Job was a man who knew God and lived his life by faith. As the test continued, Job struggled to understand how these experiences could be consistent with the God he knew and trusted. Through the test, Job persevered in trusting the Lord, even as he questioned him and cried out in distress. Significantly, God never abandoned Job, and through the ordeal, Job experienced God's grace in ways that brought him into an even deeper and more intimate knowledge of the sovereign Lord: "I had heard of you by the hearing of the ear, but now my eye sees you" (42:5). May we, with Job, fear God for who he is, not for what he gives.

Summary

Job is a book that addresses human pain, but it never deals with questions like, "Why is the suffering this hard?" or "Why is it this long?" Instead, the book calls those experiencing unexplained hardship to affirm the absolute sovereignty of God over all things, to recognize that personal sin is not the only reason humans suffer, and to cry out to God from the midst of one's pain, confident that he cares. The book also stresses that God is free to rule his world as he will and that we as humans must acknowledge our inability to fully grasp God's work and purposes. In the end, even amidst life's trials, we must continue to revere God for who he is, not because of what we receive from him. He is worth trusting in simply because he is good, gracious, just, and the Creator of all.

KEY WORDS AND CONCEPTS FOR REVIEW

Suffering	Creator versus creature
God's sovereignty	Mystery
Satan	Fear of the Lord
Doctrine of retribution	Disinterested piety
God's justice and goodness	Answer to suffering
Job's piety	Test
Laments	Knowledge of God
Loving Father	

KEY RESOURCES FOR FURTHER STUDY

Andersen, Francis I. *Job*. TOTC. Downers Grove, IL: InterVarsity, 2008.

Hartley, John E. *The Book of Job*. NICOT. Grand Rapids: Eerdmans, 1994.

Konkel, August, and Tremper Longman. *Job, Ecclesiastes, and Songs*. CBC. Carol Stream, IL: Tyndale, 2006.

Wilson, Gerald H. *Job*. NIBCOT. Grand Rapids: Baker, 2007.

PROVERBS

Who?

Proverbs 1:1 suggests that Solomon's words fill the book, and this agrees well with the description of Solomon as a wise man in 1 Kings 3–4. Included in the book is a collection of Solomonic sayings edited during the reign of Hezekiah (729–686 B.C.) (Prov. 25:1), and the final two chapters are attributed to Agur and Lemuel (30:1; 31:1). Apparently, Solomon was a major figure in the development of the wisdom sayings that are included in Proverbs, and successive generations continued the study and teaching of wisdom that he championed.

The primary intended audience of Proverbs is reflected in the frequent address to "my son" (1:8; 2:1; 3:1; 27:11; 31:2). This could refer to the biological child of the teacher, but it could also be intended more generally for young men as the students of wisdom. The examples that the teacher uses imply that the students were in the transitional period as they emerged from adolescents into adulthood. They would be comparable to high school and college students today.

When?

Apart from the references to the various authors, there is little evidence in the book of Proverbs to indicate when it was written. Nothing is known about Agur and Lemuel aside from the brief mention of them in Proverbs 30:1 and 31:1. If Solomon and Hezekiah were involved in the composition and editing of the sayings found in Proverbs, then the book developed throughout much of the history of Israel and Judah, from tenth century to the seventh century B.C.

Where?

The sayings in Proverbs are drawn from a variety of settings in ancient Israel. Some of the proverbs reflect a rural setting, but others assume village or city life. References to the king suggest that scribal schools at the royal court may have transmitted and taught these sayings (14:28; 20:28). However, references to teaching by the father and the mother (1:8; 6:20) suggest that the home was also a vital setting for instruction in ancient Israel.

Why?

Proverbs endeavored to persuade its readers to choose God's narrow path of wisdom rather than to follow the broad path of folly. By examining a wide selection of life experiences, Proverbs made clear how wisdom and folly are demonstrated in practical life. Its overall purpose is to transform immature people into adults who are wise, mature, and God-honoring. For this reason, the book continues to have great relevance for life today.

CHAPTER 18

PROVERBS

Daniel J. Estes

Carefully Crafted Verses from Proverbs

Blessed is the one who finds wisdom, and the one who gets understanding, for the gain from her is better than gain from silver and her profit better than gold (Prov. 3:13–14).

The wise will inherit honor, but fools get disgrace (Prov. 3:35).

The fear of the LORD is the beginning of wisdom, and the knowledge of the Holy One is insight (Prov. 9:10).

THE AUTHOR OF PROVERBS ...

- Pictured *life as a journey*.

- Contrasted the path of *wisdom* with the path of *folly*.

- Portrayed *the nature of wisdom* in memorable ways.

- Asserted that true wisdom is grounded in *the fear of Yahweh*.

- Gave practical *guidance for wise living*.

The Author of Proverbs Pictured *Life as a Journey*

Throughout the book of Proverbs the author repeatedly used language that speaks of life as a journey. The Hebrew word *dérek* occurs about seventy-five times in Proverbs with the sense of "a way, a road, a journey" or of "a manner of life." In addition, other synonyms such as "a path or track of life" reflect similar ideas. All of these terms are related to the familiar biblical metaphor of life as a walk. For example, Genesis 6:9 recorded: "Noah was a righteous man, blameless in his generation. Noah walked with God." The following verses are just a sampling of how Proverbs uses this imagery:

- My son, if sinners entice you, do not consent.... Do not walk in *the way* with them; hold back your foot from *their paths*, for their feet run to evil (1:10, 15–16).

- "So you will walk in *the way* of the good and keep to *the paths* of the righteous" (2:20).

- "*The way* of the LORD is a stronghold to the blameless, but destruction to evildoers" (10:29).

- "*The way* of the wicked is an abomination to the LORD, but he loves him who pursues righteousness" (15:9).

Using similar language, Jesus asserted that he was *the way* to the Father (John 14:6). He also declared that "*the way* is easy that leads to destruction" but that "*the way* is hard that leads to life" (Matt. 7:13–14).

By speaking of life as a journey, Proverbs considers a person's behavior as expressing the general character of one's life. The call, therefore, is to "keep your heart with all vigilance, for from it flow the springs of life" (Prov. 4:23).

"You will walk in the way of the good and keep to the paths of the righteous" (Prov. 2:20). *Bedouin on camels near Serabit el-Khadim.*

Or, in Jesus' WORDS, "Out of the abundance of the heart the mouth speaks" (Matt. 12:34; cf. Luke 6:35). A person's actions and attitudes propel him either in the direction of virtue and maturity, or toward vice and immaturity. As the wise teacher addressed his students, he challenged them to become committed to a lifetime journey that honors God. "Those of crooked heart are an abomination to the LORD, but those of blameless ways are his delight" (Prov. 11:20).

The book of Proverbs describes the overall direction that one's journey should take. As stated in 21:16, 21: "One who wanders from the way of good sense will rest in the assembly of the dead.... Whoever pursues righteousness and kindness will find life, righteousness, and honor." As a journey, life has a final destination that governs each step on the way. Every particular action, then, will either advance the person toward the proper goal of life or away from life and toward destruction.

> The emphasis on life as a journey echoes the biblical theme of walking with God. Christians are to walk in "good works" (Eph. 2:10), to "walk in love," to "walk as children of light," and to "walk, not as unwise but as wise" (5:2, 8, 15). When we "walk by the Spirit," we "will not gratify the desires of the flesh" (Gal. 5:16).

The Author of Proverbs Contrasted the Path of *Wisdom* with the Path of *Folly*

As Proverbs presents life as a journey, it pictures two antithetical ways that humans can take. In doing this, Proverbs echoes a theme that resonates throughout the Bible. For example, in Deuteronomy 30:15–20, Moses set before the Israelites two alternatives: a way of life and blessing or a way of death and curse. In Psalm 1, the way of the righteous is contrasted to the way of the wicked. Similarly, in Matthew 7:13–14, Jesus spoke of the narrow way that leads to life and the wide way that leads to destruction. All of these passages contrast a course of life that pleases God with a course of life that results in divine judgment.

In Proverbs, wisdom and folly are moral rather than intellectual concepts. Wisdom refers to skill in living within the moral order of Yahweh's world, but folly is rooted in an inability or unwillingness to conform to Yahweh's order. This folly may be caused by careless neglect, or it may be the result of a conscious choice to reject the way of the Lord. Folly may

Figure 18.1. Proverbs at a Glance

Extended Instructions of Wisdom (Prov. 1–9)
Individual Sayings of Wisdom (chs. 10–31)

confuse what is good and bad, it may be too smug to learn what is right and wrong, or it may treat God with contempt by scoffing at his way. As Proverbs 12:15 indicates, the fool presumes that he knows the right way, but the wise person listens to godly counsel.

The book of Proverbs often links wisdom with righteousness and folly with wickedness (Prov. 3:33–35; 10:1–3, 7–8; 14:32–33). The Hebrew term for righteousness describes something that measures up to a standard. Wisdom, then, is evidenced by actions, attitudes, and values that correspond to the will and character of Yahweh. By contrast, folly is evidenced by behaviors that deviate from Yahweh's will and character.

"The Lord does not let the righteous go hungry, but he thwarts the craving of the wicked. A slack hand causes poverty, but the hand of the diligent makes rich. He who gathers in summer is a prudent son, but he who sleeps in harvest is a son who brings shame" (Prov. 10:3–5). *Arabs gathering grapes.*

These two contrasting paths lead to very different destinations. In Proverbs 8:35–36, personified wisdom declared, "For whoever finds me finds life and obtains favor from the Lord, but he who fails to find me injures himself; all who hate me love death." The path of wisdom and righteousness, then, leads toward life in all its positive dimensions. By contrast, folly in its wickedness leads toward death in all its negative dimensions.

> Throughout the Bible we are challenged by commands, warnings, and examples that set before us the path that leads to God's blessing in contrast to the path that leads to destruction. If we are wise, we will obey God's instructions, heed his cautions, and make good use of the patterns that have been given us in the Bible.

The Author of Proverbs Portrayed *the Nature of Wisdom* in Memorable Ways

The book of Proverbs contains two general kinds of literature. For the most part, chapters 1–9 are extended instructions addressed to "my son." In contrast, chapters 10–31 are predominantly individual sayings (or *proverbs*, as traditionally understood) that often resist structural organization. A proverb is a brief maxim—like "a stitch in time saves nine"—that condenses a lot of experience into a highly memorable saying. It is not intended to be understood as a promise, a law, or a guarantee, but rather as a general principle of life that has been carefully crafted to stick in the mind of the hearer. Proverbs contain guidelines to direct lives, rather than fixed formulas about how life always works. Because the proverbs function in this way, we even find sets of sayings like Proverbs 26:4–5 that must be read together, or else they would form a contradiction: "Answer not a fool according to his folly, lest you be like him yourself. Answer a fool according to his folly, lest he be wise in his own eyes."

> The book of Proverbs is designed to help us to remember to follow God's way. As we grasp its memorable sayings, they become hidden in our hearts, guiding us to make wise choices that are pleasing to the Lord.

The Author of Proverbs Asserted That True Wisdom Is Grounded in *the Fear of Yahweh*

The Concept of Fearing God

The message of the book of Proverbs can be summarized well in the words of Proverbs 9:10, "The fear of the Lord is the beginning of wisdom." This idea of fearing the Lord occurs in the opening (Prov. 1:7) and closing (31:30) of Proverbs and a total of eighteen times scattered throughout the book. The concept is rooted in the law that Yahweh gave to Moses (Deut. 10:12), and it is reaffirmed by the prophets.

Just as Proverbs 1:7 and 9:10 present the fear of Yahweh as the first precept of wisdom, so Proverbs 2:5 teaches that this same fear is the final goal of wisdom. The fear of Yahweh guides the wise person from start

"The unjust heir who does not support a wife, who does not support a son, is not raised to prosperity" (A Sumerian proverb; cf. Prov. 11:29). *One of nearly forty clay cuneiform tablets from Nippur (ca. 1900–1800 B.C.) containing Sumerian proverbs (from the Istanbul Archaeological Museum). Like biblical proverbs, most Sumerian proverbs focus on daily activities of life rather than communal worship. Unlike biblical proverbs, however, those in the Sumerian collection do not express any clear concept of "wisdom" and do not display any compositional strategy or theological agenda. Only few of the Sumerian proverbs find any parallel with the teaching of Scripture. The example above is translated from COS 1:563.9b.*

to finish on the path toward life. Every wise motivation and choice, action and attitude, must reflect this fundamental value.

The English term "fear" usually evokes a negative fright that prompts one to hide or run. In contrast, the Hebrew term used in this expression is *yir'â*, which refers to an overwhelming awe that causes humans to tremble before God in dread or to turn to him in reverence. This is the appropriate stance that humans should take before the awesome Creator of the universe, in contrast to arrogant rebellion or disdain toward him. When we fear the Lord, we embrace what he desires and avoid what he disapproves. The person who fears or reveres Yahweh humbly submits to his Word and faithfully follows his way.

"If you seek [wisdom] like silver and search for it as for hidden treasures, then you will understand the fear of the Lᴏʀᴅ and find the knowledge of God" (Prov. 2:4–5). *Beth Shean excavation of a wall from the time of the patriarchs.*

The Fruit of Fearing God

Although Proverbs gives many instructions about practical matters of life, its agenda is much broader than just that. The wisdom in Proverbs is not to make its readers successful in their careers and relationships. Rather, at its heart, the book teaches its readers how to respect Yahweh by obeying what he has said and imitating his own holy character (Prov. 9:10). "My son, do not forget my teaching, but let your heart keep my commandments, for length of days and years of life and peace they will add to you" (3:1–2). Biblical wisdom is grounded ultimately in a positive relationship with Yahweh that causes one to adopt his values as the pattern for life.

Just as Yahweh's order permeates his physical creation (3:19–20; 8:22–31), so his moral character is the foundational authority for ethics in his universe (8:32–36). The values that are embodied in his holy character, then, are the objective standard by which all human behavior must be measured. Yahweh's character and his commands, which are verbal expressions of that character, are the fixed standard for measuring what is right and wrong. Thus the instructions in Proverbs are the outworking of Yahweh's command in Leviticus 19:2, "You shall be holy, for I the LORD your God am holy." Furthermore, wisdom is a path of behavior that is righteous as measured against the intrinsic character of the holy Yahweh, and folly is behavior that diverges from his holy character.

In contrast to wisdom, folly at its heart is the arrogant pursuit of freedom or autonomy, when humans declare their independence from Yahweh's authority. "Pride goes before destruction, and a haughty spirit before a fall" (Prov. 16:18). As in the chaotic days of the judges, moral collapse occurs when people do what is right in their own eyes rather than obeying the law of Yahweh (Judg. 21:25). At the heart of folly is moral relativism that exalts personal freedom above living according to the objective moral standard of Yahweh embodied in his character and expressed in his Word. Because of this, Proverbs 3:5 urges, "Trust in the LORD with all your heart, and do not lean on your own understanding."

> The author of Proverbs would be struck by how little difference there is between the values of many contemporary Christians and those of our culture as a whole. The paths of wisdom and folly should look very different, because wisdom deeply reveres the Lord by imitating and obeying him, but folly chooses to take its own way regardless of what the Lord desires.

The Author of Proverbs Gave Practical *Guidance for Wise Living*

The wise teacher in Proverbs acts as a guide to his students: "Let the wise hear and increase in learning, and the one who understands obtain guidance" (Prov. 1:5). The term that is used for guidance in this verse refers elsewhere in the book to expertise in navigation (11:14). Thus, the teacher functions as the navigator or coach who assists the learner to find and follow the way of wisdom. This image of the teacher as a guide is also expressed in Proverbs 4:11: "I have taught you the way of wisdom; I have led you in the paths of uprightness." Similarly, referring to parental instructions and echoing Deuteronomy 6:7, Proverbs 6:22 states, "When you walk, they will lead you; when you lie down, they will watch over you; and when you awake, they will talk with you."

"It is better to be of a lowly spirit with the poor than to divide the spoil with the proud" (Prov. 16:19). *A Bedouin woman starting a fire.*

The main objective of the wise teacher is to guide the learner to live wisely in Yahweh's world. When the learner is young and inexperienced, the teacher provides a high degree of direction, but as the learner grows in his ability to make good decisions, the teacher steps back to allow the learner to develop his independent competence. By his wise counsel, the teacher provides a framework within which the learner can have the freedom to learn to choose wisely for himself. The teacher's role is to guide the learner into personal maturity that sets him on a lifelong course on the path of wisdom.

The wise teacher endeavors to instruct the learner in understanding or insight. The Hebrew term for insight refers to the ability to make discerning choices among competing alternatives. Without insight, the learner would likely default to what looks most attractive or most convenient to him, rather than choosing the alternative that respects Yahweh. Because of this, personified wisdom called out in Proverbs 9:6, "Leave your simple ways, and live, and walk in the way of insight."

Proverbs is particularly addressed to young people who are emerging from childhood and adolescence into adulthood. This period of life, roughly equivalent to high school and undergraduate college years today, is a crucial time when most of the key commitments of a lifetime are forged. The appeal in Proverbs 4:7 can be paraphrased in the following terms: "The primary thing is wisdom; so purchase wisdom, and at the price of all that you own, purchase insight." In these words, the youth is challenged to adopt a radical reorientation of life in which the pursuit of wisdom becomes the prime driving value. Wisdom, then, seeks to guide people into a wise commitment to God and his way. Instead of passively adopting the religious practices in which they grow up or assimilating to the patterns of the culture around them, those who are wise choose to make a robust genuine adult commitment to the Lord. It is this personal commitment that propels them on to the path of wisdom that leads to life.

"Those who forsake the law praise the wicked, but those who keep the law strive against them.... If one turns away his ear from hearing the law, even his prayer is an abomination" (Prov. 28:4, 9). *An open Torah scroll with the pointer on the story of the making of the bronze serpent in Numbers 21:4–9 (cf. John 3:14–15).*

Ultimately, Proverbs focuses on the development of wise character. Although it speaks of many overt behaviors, such as speech, business dealings, and relationships, it is most concerned with the heart, because "from it flow the springs of life" (Prov. 4:23). Wisdom is not just a set of pious activities. It is neither a checklist of things to do and things to avoid, nor a cosmetic makeover that alters the external appearance. Rather, wisdom works from the inside out to transform the entire person, including the thoughts, the feelings, and the choices. The ultimate goal of wisdom is the formation of responsible moral character that corresponds to the righteous standards of Yahweh. Although Proverbs is a very practical book, it endeavors to do nothing less than to transform a life that is predisposed by its sin nature toward folly into a life directed by and toward godly wisdom.

Summary

In a dark and broken age filled with deceit and evil, every person needs sound guidance to enjoy life in a way that honors the Lord. The book of Proverbs provides a manual for wise living in God's world. It pictures life as a journey and contrasts in memorable ways the path of wisdom to the path of folly. The book calls the old to instruct well and calls the young to passionately pursue wisdom at all cost—true wisdom that is understood only in relation to God. Any successful navigation through life's temptations and pains begins with a proper fear of the Lord.

KEY WORDS AND CONCEPTS FOR REVIEW

My son	Fear of Yahweh
Journey	Imitation of Yahweh
Two ways	Autonomy
Wisdom	Guidance
Folly	Maturity
Righteousness	Insight
Wickedness	Character
Life	

KEY RESOURCES FOR FURTHER STUDY

Garrett, Duane A. *Proverbs, Ecclesiastes, Song of Songs.* NAC. Nashville: B&H, 1993.

Longman, Tremper, III. *How to Read Proverbs.* Downers Grove, IL: InterVarsity, 2002.

Koptak, Paul E. *Proverbs.* NIVAC. Grand Rapids: Zondervan, 2003.

Steinmann, Andrew E. *Proverbs.* CC. St. Louis, MO: Concordia, 2009.

ECCLESIASTES

Who?

The body of Ecclesiastes is attributed to Qoheleth (often translated "the Preacher"), which appears to be a sort of official title for one who gathered others together for teaching or worship (Eccl. 1:1–2; 12:8–10). Apart from this ambiguous term, the author of the book is not clearly identified. Certain statements imply that King Solomon was the author (1:1, 12, 16; 2:4–10), and early Jewish and Christian tradition attributed the book to him. At the same time, this figure's apparent inability to change government incompetence and corruption suggests someone other than Solomon (3:16; 4:1; 5:8; 8:11, 14; 10:5–7), and the Hebrew in the book may point to a much later time. We are left, then, with some uncertainty about the identity of this author.

When?

If Solomon wrote this book, it would be dated between about 970 and 930 B.C. Some Jewish tradition places the date toward the end of this period, believing the book to be his final-days' reflections on a life that failed to live up to its potential (1:16; 4:13; cf. 1 Kings 3:10–14; 9:1–5 with 11:1–13). If Solomon was not the author, the most likely date, based on some views of the Hebrew in the book, would be several centuries later.

Where?

The author was perhaps from Jerusalem and its environs (Eccl. 1:1, 2; 2:9).

Why?

In Israel, a sage's main objective seems to have been to develop skill in living according to Yahweh's order, and this was Qoheleth's goal. He was committed to the idea that this skill must be rooted in an accurate understanding of reality, both about life "under the sun" and about the work of God. He also wanted to show that the meaning of life is not found in the pursuit of things or in human accomplishments, but in a life characterized by the fear of the Lord. His observations often create significant tensions and raise questions about the character and providence of God and about whether life has meaning. Given the realities that Qoheleth pointed out, he asked whether there is a way to live life so as to gain some profit or advantage, perhaps even a profit that death cannot erase. The author rarely answered such questions, and many seem impossible to answer, at least on the basis of the data provided "under the sun." An important part of Qoheleth's teaching method was to show us that the only way such questions can be answered is by accepting God's special revelation to us (that is, living by faith).

ECCLESIASTES

Edward M. Curtis

Carefully Crafted Verses from Ecclesiastes

Vanity of vanities, says the Preacher, vanity of vanities! All is vanity. What does man gain by all the toil at which he toils under the sun? (Eccl. 1:2–3)

He has made everything beautiful in its time. Also, he has put eternity into man's heart, yet so that he cannot find out what God has done from the beginning to the end (Eccl. 3:11).

Behold, what I have seen to be good and fitting is to eat and drink and find enjoyment in all the toil with which one toils under the sun the few days of his life that God has given him, for this is his lot (Eccl. 5:18).

The end of the matter; all has been heard. Fear God and keep his commandments, for this is the whole duty of man (Eccl. 12:13).

THE AUTHOR OF ECCLESIASTES ...

- Raised more *questions* than he answered.

- Acknowledged *numerous challenges* to living "under the sun."

- Affirmed *God's mysterious providence* in all of life.

- Provided important *instruction about living well* "under the sun."

- Highlighted the key to a *meaningful and significant life*.

The Author of Ecclesiastes Raised More *Questions* Than He Answered

Ecclesiastes is a book of queries and conclusions. It reflects the kind of teaching described in 12:11 where the words of the wise are compared with pointed sticks ("goads") used to guide animals to a desired destination. Israel's sages sought to help students to develop skills in living according to Yahweh's order, and such skills had to be based on an accurate understanding of the way things are, including realities that believers are sometimes reluctant to acknowledge. Qoheleth knew that simply giving students "right answers" would not produce this outcome, so he challenged students and saw spiritual and educative benefits in struggling with difficult issues. Qoheleth's examples force one to ask whether life has meaning or whether a person can live life so as to gain some benefit, perhaps even one that death cannot erase. His wrestlings raise questions about God's goodness and justice—questions that remain unanswered in this book. His

> Some of Qoheleth's questions find answers elsewhere in the Old Testament; others only find clear resolve in the New Testament, and still others will likely await eternity to gain clarity.

"The words of the wise are like goads ... they are given by one Shepherd" (Eccl. 12:11). *Sheep and a shepherd with a goad in eastern Samaria.*

queries about life's meaning and about the way God works in his world make clear that the evidence available to us from experience is often too ambiguous to provide full answers. Resolve to such tensions can only be enjoyed by faith—that is, in the fear of God. No other means can provide a solution.

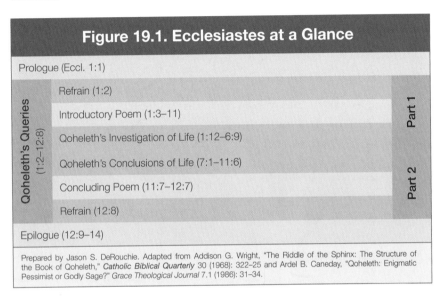

Figure 19.1. Ecclesiastes at a Glance

Prologue (Eccl. 1:1)		
Qoheleth's Queries (1:2–12:8)	Refrain (1:2)	**Part 1**
	Introductory Poem (1:3–11)	
	Qoheleth's Investigation of Life (1:12–6:9)	
	Qoheleth's Conclusions of Life (7:1–11:6)	**Part 2**
	Concluding Poem (11:7–12:7)	
	Refrain (12:8)	
Epilogue (12:9–14)		

Prepared by Jason S. DeRouchie. Adapted from Addison G. Wright, "The Riddle of the Sphinx: The Structure of the Book of Qoheleth," *Catholic Biblical Quarterly* 30 (1968): 322–25 and Ardel B. Caneday, "Qoheleth: Enigmatic Pessimist or Godly Sage?" *Grace Theological Journal* 7.1 (1986): 31–34.

The Author of Ecclesiastes Acknowledged *Numerous Challenges* to Living "under the Sun"

Life "under the sun" is life as we experience it in a world that is fallen and cursed by God (Eccl. 1:15; 7:13) and that is filled with significant challenges, which are often hard to understand (3:11; 6:12; 8:17). The author's experience demonstrated the difficulty in discovering the key to a meaningful and significant life (1:12–2:26). Qoheleth emphasized that there are many things that we can neither figure out nor control. For example, timing is critical in achieving desired outcomes, but people are often unable to determine the right timing (3:1–14), and even when they can, circumstances beyond their control sometimes prevent them from taking advantage of it. Similarly, Qoheleth recognized the reality of injustice and the difficulties in eliminating such inequities (3:16; 5:8). Life is filled with anomalies and tensions that make it difficult to see order and meaning, and what happens often depends less on skill or ability than on factors outside our knowledge or power (9:11–12). Finally Qoheleth made it clear that human beings can neither understand nor direct the work of God, which ultimately determines outcomes (3:11; 9:1–2).

The Author of Ecclesiastes Affirmed *God's Mysterious Providence* in All of Life

Qoheleth believed in the bigness of God and the smallness of mankind (Eccl. 3:18; 5:2). He affirmed that God is the Creator of all things (12:1), the one who makes everything (11:5) and whose purposes are unchangeable (3:14; 7:13). Both righteous and wicked are in God's hands (9:1), for he alone creates and sustains life (8:15; 12:7), gives mankind his work (1:13; 3:10), brings both prosperity and adversity (7:14), and grants or withholds wisdom and satisfaction (2:24, 26; 5:19; 6:2). He is to be feared in the

"Remember also your Creator in the days of your youth, before the evil days come and the years draw near of which you will say, 'I have no pleasure in them'" (Eccl. 12:1). *An almond blossom near Aijalon.*

present (3:14; 5:7; 8:12–13; 12:13), for he will bring all deeds under judgment in the future (11:9; 12:14).

While Qoheleth affirmed that the sovereign providence of God lies behind everything that happens, he also acknowledged the importance of human choice, while clearly recognizing that people have a limited understanding of the work of God (3:11; 6:12; 8:17; 11:5). For example, he observed, "[God] has put eternity into man's heart, yet so that he cannot find out what God has done from the beginning to the end" (3:11). Similarly, he asserted (8:17): "Then I saw all the work of God, that man cannot find out the work that is done under the sun. However much man may toil in seeking, he will not find it out."

Qoheleth recognized that God causes things to work out the way they do, but the sage does not indicate whether this is good or disconcerting. Sometimes hindsight allows us to see God's goodness in experiences that initially showed few signs of his beneficence. However, as one honestly and broadly observes life, it is apparent that for

> Qoheleth described the providence of God exactly the manner we experience it—in ways that seldom come with interpretations.

"In the morning sow your seed, and at evening withhold not your hand, for you do not know which will prosper, this or that, or whether both alike will be good" (Eccl. 11:6). *An Arab farmer plowing with a donkey near Mount Gerizim.*

every experience demonstrating God's goodness, there are others that seem random, with few hints of goodness. Much of life is beyond our understanding and ability to control. Life can be exasperating and complex, and many things seem arbitrary and defy explanation. Sometimes things work to our advantage; sometimes they seem to work to our disadvantage. It is hard to deny the truth that Qoheleth affirmed in this book; his description of life is frustratingly exact.

The Author of Ecclesiastes Provided Important *Instruction about Living Well* "under the Sun"

Qoheleth also provided important instruction about living well. Despite wisdom's limits, he affirmed the importance of living wisely (Eccl. 7:19; 9:13–16) and of avoiding folly (9:18–10:1). Wisdom is essential for living according to Yahweh's order, and it will deliver us from the disasters of foolishness. Specifically, the sage commended the importance of diligence and emphasized that one cannot wait for absolute guarantees before doing things (10:8–9, 11; 11:1–6). Instead, one must wisely assess risks, weigh them against benefits, and then proceed with wisdom. Furthermore, he affirmed the value of cultivating beneficial and enjoyable relationships and the tragedy of being so obsessed with money or power that one fails to do so (4:7–12). He warned against putting trust in the wrong things (e.g., money, power, pleasure, accomplishments), and he affirmed the importance of wisdom in relating with the rich and powerful (8:2–7; 10:4, 20). Qoheleth emphasized the importance of balance, even in one's religious life (4:4–6; 5:1–7; 7:16–18), and he affirmed the value of enjoying life (3:12–13; 5:18–20; 9:7–9). Delight in the present, however, must be had only in light of the future judgment, which God will bring to all (11:9; 12:13–14).

> Qoheleth calls all of us to seek out opportunities for pleasure that come from God's hand—whether in prosperity or in need, finding delight in food and drink, family and friends (Eccl. 3:12–13; 5:18–20; 9:7–9). Look for examples of God's steadfast love, and take delight in the good things he provides. "For everything created by God is good, and nothing is to be rejected if it is received with thanksgiving" (1 Tim. 4:4).

The Author of Ecclesiastes Highlighted the Key to *a Meaningful and Significant Life*

Qoheleth began and ended his book by declaring that everything is vanity/*hébel* (Eccl. 1:2; 12:8), and he identified many examples of *hébel* throughout the book. *Hébel* literally denotes a puff of air. In Ecclesiastes, the metaphor describes the temporal nature of human life and those aspects of life that refuse to yield to human understanding and control. Given all that characterizes life, his advice was, "Fear God and keep his commandments, for this is the whole duty of mankind" (12:13; cf. 3:14; 5:7; 8:12–13). In calling his audience to fear God, he is calling them to a life of faith and trust in God. He recognized that even in a world characterized by *hébel*, many good gifts come from God and attest to his goodness. He exhorted his students to enjoy those

> Qoheleth (Eccl. 8:12), the author of Job (Job 28:28), and many other biblical figures (including Jesus, Matt. 10:28) taught that hope exists for all who fear God, even when life makes little sense.

"I perceived that there is nothing better for them than to be joyful and to do good as long as they live; also that everyone should eat and drink and take pleasure in all his toil—this is God's gift to man" (Eccl. 3:12–13). *A Bedouin market in Beer-sheba (photo by David Bivin).*

things to the full while acknowledging their source. Qoheleth also saw that the frustrating realities of life and the inability of humans to fully comprehend God's work have the power to draw people to faith and trust in the sovereign Lord who always accomplishes his purposes (3:11–14; 7:13), and this, for Qoheleth, was the only way to experience life with meaning and significance.

Summary

Some interpreters view Qoheleth's queries as overwhelmingly filled with bad theology, more like Job's three friends than the wisdom of Solomon. Although the sage of Ecclesiastes raised many unanswered (and even unanswerable) questions and rightly recognized numerous challenges to living "under the sun," he maintained a right view of God and man, properly called readers to enjoy life in light of the future judgment, and stressed the need to fear and obey God always. The wisdom of Ecclesiastes is not unorthodox but is rather needed in this cursed and broken world, which often makes little sense. And for the believing remnant who still struggles through life's enigmas while maintaining hope in the coming kingdom, Ecclesiastes provides a good reminder of how to live.

KEY WORDS AND CONCEPTS FOR REVIEW

Qoheleth	Profit/advantage
Solomon	Wisdom
Sage	Folly
Questions and answers	Joy
Fear of God	Future judgment
Under the sun	Vanity/*hébel*
Life's meaning and significance	Commandment keeping
Mysterious providence	

KEY RESOURCES FOR FURTHER STUDY

Fredericks, Daniel C., and Daniel J. Estes. *Ecclesiastes and Song of Songs.* AOTC. Downers Grove, IL: InterVarsity, 2010.

Garrett, Duane A. *Proverbs, Ecclesiastes, Song of Songs.* NAC. Nashville: B&H, 1993.

Provan, Iain W. *Ecclesiastes, Song of Songs.* NIVAC. Grand Rapids: Zondervan, 2001.

Wilson, Douglas. *Joy at the End of the Tether: The Inscrutable Wisdom of Ecclesiastes.* Moscow, ID: Canon, 1999.

Song of Songs

Who?

The initial verse of the Song of Songs links the book with Solomon, the son of David and third monarch of the united kingdom of Israel. The Hebrew clause translated "which is Solomon's" could indicate that Solomon was the author of the book, but it could also mean that the book is about Solomon, for Solomon, dedicated to Solomon, or in a style resembling that of Solomon. Because it is unclear whether Solomon actually composed the Song, many scholars refer to book as the Song of Songs rather than the Song of Solomon.

The Song is lyrical poetry that celebrates love and intimacy God's way. Although it portrays a royal courtship and marriage, the audience is unspecified and general, so that every husband is called to treat his wife as a queen and every wife her husband as a king.

The connection to Solomon may indicate that the Song belonged to Israel's ancient wisdom tradition (see 1 Kings 3:12), much like Job, Proverbs, and Ecclesiastes. This literature was addressed in particular to young people, primarily men, as they prepared to enter into the challenges and joys of adult life.

When?

The date of the writing of the Song of Songs is tied directly to the identity of its author. If Solomon wrote the book, then it must have been composed in the tenth century B.C., which would make the book roughly contemporaneous with similar love lyrics from Egypt in the twelfth century B.C. Perhaps because of the poetic character of the text, the Hebrew used in the Song is quite unusual, with some of its features pointing toward an early date in the time of Solomon, but other features suggesting a later period in the history of the language. Scholars, therefore, have not reached a consensus on when the Song was originally written.

Where?

The Song contains references to many geographical places that are spread throughout the land of Israel, from the mountains in the extreme north to Engedi in the Dead Sea region in the south. The focus of the book is on the capital city of Jerusalem, but it appears that the Shulammite, the book's main female character, grew up in a rural area, likely in the northern part of the country.

Why?

The Song of Songs extols the richness of human love and intimacy as God's good gift (Song 8:6). By describing in realistic and positive terms how intimacy grows and develops, the Song endeavored to encourage its primarily young readers to follow God's wise path that leads to the delights of marital intimacy. At the same time, it warned them against trying to find sexual pleasure outside the boundaries of marriage, as so many people attempt to do (2:7; 3:5; 8:4).

SONG OF SONGS

Daniel J. Estes

Carefully Crafted Verses from the Song of Songs

My beloved speaks and says to me: "Arise, my love, my beautiful one, and come away" (Song 2:10).

I adjure you, O daughters of Jerusalem, that you not stir up or awaken love until it pleases" (Song 8:4).

Set me as a seal upon your heart, as a seal upon your arm, for love is strong as death, jealousy is fierce as the grave. Its flashes are flashes of fire, the very flame of the LORD. Many waters cannot quench love, neither can floods drown it. If a man offered for love all the wealth of his house, he would be utterly despised (Song 8:6–7).

THE AUTHOR OF SONG OF SONGS ...

- Traced *the progress of intimacy* from initial attraction to maturity.

- Extolled *erotic love within marriage* as God's good gift.

- Described *the transforming power of love.*

The Author of the Song of Songs Traced *the Progress of Intimacy* from Initial Attraction to Maturity

Traditionally, the Song of Songs most often has been read as an allegory of the love of God for his people, either the nation of Israel or the church. However, in recent years, most interpreters have come to understand it to speak of human love. Some see the book as a collection of unrelated love songs; however, the refrains (Song 2:7; 3:5; 8:4), consistent characters, repeated images, and overall flow suggest that the Song is more likely a unified, intentionally structured document.

Rather than telling a complete story, the lyrics in the duet are like a collection of pictures that trace the growth of a relationship. The baritone is Solomon (1:1; 3:6; 8:11–12), whom his girl called "my beloved." His "lover" is the soprano, known as the Shulammite (6:13), and the two are introduced in the first scenes in chapter 1. Throughout this impressionistic song cycle, their love grows and develops from that initial attraction into a deep, mature intimacy. In the first three chapters, ten short scenes lead up to their wedding procession. In chapter 4, the couple celebrates their wedding night together. In the final half of the Song, their love continues to grow throughout their married life. In the final scene in 8:5–14, the Shulammite is leaning on her husband, perhaps suggesting that they are

> In our contemporary culture, in which love is too often replaced by lust and in which nearly half of all marriages end in divorce, the message of the Song of Songs is especially relevant. We cannot afford to ignore what God teaches about genuine intimacy.

"Behold, you are beautiful, my love, behold, you are beautiful! Your eyes are doves behind your veil" (Song 4:1–2). *An orthodox Jewish wedding ceremony.*

elderly, and the two lovers reminisce about what they have learned regarding love and intimacy through their years together.

Figure 20.1. Song of Songs at a Glance
Progressing Toward Marriage (Song 1–3)
Wedding Celebration (ch. 4)
Growing in Intimacy (chs. 5–8)

The Author of the Song of Songs Extolled *Erotic Love Within Marriage* as God's Good Gift

In the ancient world, marriage was regularly a financial contract between families or nations, and its purpose was often limited to the procreation of children. Only rarely does the ancient literature or the Bible speak of erotic or sexual love within the marital bond. In fact, when the Bible does speak of sexual activity, it typically condemns sex outside of marriage as sin, in contrast to the debased standards of the civilizations outside of Israel (Deut. 22:13–29).

> Our contemporary culture too often diminishes sex by removing it from the marital relationship and turning it into mere recreation. In God's design, sex is a celebration and expression of the intimate closeness of a husband and a wife who are pledged to one another in committed love.

Echoing the exhortation of Proverbs 5:15–19 and using images drawn from dress, warfare, nature (gardens, mountains, forests, animals, plants, and spices), and architecture (towers, walls, and cities), Song of Songs extols the richness of sexual delight within marriage as God's good gift. Indeed, it is "the very flame of the Lord" (Song 8:6)! This precious provision needs to be enjoyed, nurtured, and protected so that it can produce the intimacy that God designed for married couples. Using symbolic language, God says to Solomon and the Shulammite on their wedding night, "Eat, friends, drink, and be drunk with love!" (5:1). Twice in this song cycle, we see the couple delighting in one another as they make love together (4:10–5:1; 7:1–9).

Significantly, three times in the Song the Shulammite sings a refrain that cautions singles away from lust and away from entering into sexual intimacy with another before marriage: "I adjure you, O daughters of Jerusalem, that you not stir up or awaken love until it pleases" (8:4; cf. 2:7; 3:5). The flame of unrestrained, guiltless, and pure love is kindled only in the context of marriage, where it unites a husband and wife in an "unquenchable" way. Such a treasure is a gift that no person can purchase (8:6–7).

"How beautiful is your love, my sister, my bride! How much better is your love than wine, and the fragrance of your oils than any spice! … Your shoots are an orchard of pomegranates with all choicest fruits" (Song 4:10, 13). *Pomegranates on a tree near Lachish (photo by Daniel Frese).*

The Author of the Song of Songs Described *the Transforming Power of Love*

Although the Song speaks directly about the nature of love only in 8:6–7, it has much to say indirectly about the life-changing effect of love. The mutual and exclusive intimacy that Solomon and the Shulammite come to enjoy together contrasts with the damaging effects that sin brought into the human family in Genesis 3. After Adam and Eve disobeyed the Lord's commandment, he pronounced a curse upon them. The Lord said to Eve that though her desire would be for her husband, he would rule over her (Gen. 3:16). In other words, sin turned their relationship into a struggle for power.

In the Song of Songs 7:10, the same word "desire" is used, but in a very different sense. There, the Shulammite says, "I am my beloved's, and his desire is for me." As God designed it, love can diminish the damaging effects of sin, and regain God's original intention that the man and wife should become one flesh in marriage (Gen. 2:24), ultimately displaying the unrelenting and unrestrained covenant love of Christ and his church (Eph. 5:31–32).

> Within God-honoring marriage, we can discover the delights that satisfy the deepest hunger of our hearts, and we can be transformed from the self-centeredness that too often drives our lives.

"How beautiful and pleasant you are, O loved one, with all your delights! Your stature is like a palm tree, and your breasts are like its clusters" (Song 7:6–7). *Date palm trees near the Dead Sea.*

Summary

Even in this cursed world, intimacy in marriage can still be celebrated. The Song of Songs traces the progress of intimacy from initial attraction through the wedding and on into maturity. In the Song, erotic love within marriage is extolled as God's good gift, the "flame of the Lord" that is to continue blazing through the storms of life into old age. Where such love is maintained, the damaging effects of sin are diminished, and a display of God's goodness is manifest to a world too familiar with the brokenness of relationships.

KEY WORDS AND CONCEPTS FOR REVIEW

Solomon	Impressionistic song cycle
King and queen	Erotic love
Wisdom	Imagery and symbolism
Love lyrics	The cautioned refrain
Intimacy	Desire
Allegory	One flesh
Shulammite	

KEY RESOURCES FOR FURTHER STUDY

Fredericks, Daniel C., and Daniel J. Estes. *Ecclesiastes and Song of Songs*. AOTC. Downers Grove, IL: InterVarsity, 2010.

Garrett, Duane A., and Paul R. House. *Song of Songs / Lamentations*. WBC. Nashville: Thomas Nelson, 2004.

Gledhill, Tom D. *The Message of the Song of Songs*. BST. Downers Grove, IL: InterVarsity, 1994.

Provan, Iain W. *Ecclesiastes, Song of Songs*. NIVAC. Grand Rapids: Zondervan, 2001.

LAMENTATIONS

Who?

The book of Lamentations is anonymous, but ancient Jewish tradition posits that Jeremiah was the author. We know this "weeping prophet" uttered laments (2 Chron. 35:25) and called for deep mourning (Jer. 4:8; 6:26; 7:29; 9:20; 49:3). The heading of Lamentations in the Septuagint connects the book with Jeremiah, as do English versions that locate it after the prophetic book bearing his name. Even if not Jeremiah, the author was someone like him, who experienced and mourned the exile of Judah, who was convinced Jerusalem's destruction was divine judgment for the people's sins, and who retained a deep confidence in Yahweh's faithfulness.

The initial recipients of the five laments would have been Jews who just experienced the defeat and exile of Judah. They were the survivors who had neither died nor been taken into captivity in Babylon.

When?

This book seems to have been written shortly after Judah's downfall in 586 B.C., when Babylon destroyed Jerusalem and its temple. The expressions here seem to reflect a very recent tragedy and raw emotions that are still very fresh and painful.

Where?

The author of Lamentations seems to be still living in Jerusalem and experiencing the ongoing effects of God's devastating judgment.

Why?

As the title indicates, this book contains five laments, which express grief and mourning over Judah's sins and over the recent judgment of God that resulted from them. The book has much the same function as a funeral dirge, disclosing outbursts of anguish from three voices: the author (Laments 1–5, alone in 3), the city of Jerusalem/Zion (personified in Laments 1–2), and the people of God (Laments 4–5). Thus, the book is in the form of both individual and communal laments. Significantly, every lament expresses or presupposes deep conviction in Yahweh's faithfulness to his promises and his compassionate character (esp. Lam. 3:21–25, 31–33). As such, Lamentations aptly serves as a bridge back into the Old Testament's narrative history, which halted at the end of 2 Kings. In Daniel through Chronicles, which follow, suffering saints are encouraged to hope in the complete restoration of God's kingdom.

Today, ethnic Jews read Lamentations annually on the ninth of Ab (mid-July) to commemorate and mourn the Babylonian (586 B.C.) and Roman (A.D. 70) destructions of Jerusalem. Jews also regularly read it at Jerusalem's Western (or Wailing) Wall, which contains remains from the temple complex destroyed by the Romans. However, in Messiah Jesus, God is rebuilding a spiritual temple in which he dwells (Eph. 2:19–22), and for all who are reconciled to God through Jesus (2:4–5, 16), the honest cries of Lamentations can be echoed in confidence that the God whose wrath has been appeased (Rom. 3:24–25; 5:8–9; 8:1) and who is completely for us (8:31) will indeed graciously meet us in our hour of need (8:32).

LAMENTATIONS

Daryl Aaron

Carefully Crafted Verses from Lamentations

The roads to Zion mourn, for none come to the festival; all her gates are desolate; her priests groan; her virgins have been afflicted, and she herself suffers bitterly. Her foes have become the head; her enemies prosper, because the LORD has afflicted her for the multitude of her transgressions; her children have gone away, captives before the foe (Lam. 1:4–5).

THE AUTHOR OF LAMENTATIONS …

- Acknowledged *Israel's sin and God's uprightness* in judging it.

- Was *brutally honest with God* about emotional and spiritual pain.

- Stressed *God's faithfulness* as the basis for hope in suffering.

The steadfast love of the LORD never ceases; his mercies never come to an end; they are new every morning; great is your faithfulness. "The LORD is my portion," says my soul, "therefore I will hope in him" (Lam. 3:22–24).

You, O LORD, reign forever; your throne endures to all generations. Why do you forget us forever, why do you forsake us for so many days? Restore us to yourself, O LORD, that we may be restored! (Lam. 5:19–21).

The Author of Lamentations Acknowledged *Israel's Sin and God's Uprightness* in Judging It

A terrible tragedy had recently occurred in Judah. The Babylonians had sacked Jerusalem; destroyed the temple of Yahweh; slaughtered or ravaged hundreds of men, women, and children; and took many Jewish captives into exile. In the mind of the author of Lamentations, such disaster was expected, for God had been warning Israel for hundreds of years that its sin would incur punishment. Specifically, if God's people did not follow God's law, heeding his covenant, he would curse them climaxing in his expelling them from the Land of Promise (Lev. 26:14–39; Deut. 28:15–68). The prophets had continued to remind God's people of this, even after the northern kingdom was destroyed, but Judah remained deaf (e.g., Jer. 3:6–11).

> God hates sin, and so should we. Indeed, we should grieve over it! Humble confession and repentance should be the common practice of those who confess Jesus as Savior and Lord (1 John 1:8–10).

Now, as the author recognized, the Lord had executed what he had said he would do. "The LORD has done what he purposed; he has carried out his word, which he commanded long ago; he has thrown down without pity; he has made the enemy rejoice over you and exalted the might of your foes" (Lam. 2:17; cf. 3:37–38). Even though the Babylonians were the immediate cause of the devastation of Judah, the sovereign God of Israel was the ultimate cause (1:12, 17; 2:21; 3:37, 38; 4:16). The reason for God's judgment of Israel was "the multitude of her transgressions" (1:5, cf. 1:8, 14, 22), which the author readily confessed (1:18–20; 3:40–42; 5:7, 16). Therefore, the author accepted that the suffering the nation was experiencing was flowing from the righteous wrath of God (1:18; 2:1–8, 21–22; 3:37–39; 4:11).

The Author of Lamentations *Was Brutally Honest with God* about Emotional and Spiritual Pain

Like Job, Jeremiah, Habakkuk, the lamenters in Psalms, and Jesus himself, the author of Lamentations honestly and vigorously vented his feelings to and about God. One way the author highlighted this was by building each of the five laments around the number 22, reflecting the letters of the Hebrew alphabet. In Laments 1–2, each of the 22 three-line stanzas begins with a consecutive Hebrew letter. In Lament 3, all three lines in each stanza begin with a consecutive letter,

> God wants us to honor him with our trust by being honest and open with him about our feelings.

and English Bibles have highlighted this by numbering each line (thus 66). Lament 4 begins each of its 22 two-line stanzas with a consecutive letter, and Lament 5 has only 22 single-line stanzas with no alphabetic acrostic. Through this structure, the lamenter seems to have been focusing on the completeness of his grief, for he drew on every letter that could be used to express the depth of his pain.

This is seen most clearly in Lament 3, which includes the most developed form of the acrostic and is the only lament dominated solely by the author's voice. He deeply felt the effects of Yahweh's judgment (Lam. 3:1), and he expressed how God seemed to have turned against him (vv. 2–9), was deaf to his prayers (vv. 8, 44), stalked and attacked him like a wild beast or an enemy soldier (vv. 10–13), humiliated him (v. 14), and robbed him of his peace and hope only to leave him in despair (vv. 17–20). Such honesty acknowledges the emotional tension that often accompanies serious trial. For a brief moment, the author had lost hope in Yahweh (v. 18), but immediately he affirmed that hope was still alive (v. 21). He felt as though God did not hear his prayers (vv. 3, 44), yet he expressed confidence that God had heard (vv. 55–57). The author stated five times that there was no one to bring comfort (1:2, 9, 16, 17, 21), yet the entire book is an appeal to God for comfort (e.g., 2:19–22; 5:1). Even as the author pleaded with

"The old men have left the city gate, the young men their music. The joy of our hearts has ceased; our dancing has been turned to mourning. The crown has fallen from our head; woe to us, for we have sinned!" (Lam. 5:14–16). *A wooden harp from Egypt's Second Intermediate Period during the days of the patriarchs (from the Oriental Institute, USA).*

"Why do you forget us forever, why do you forsake us for so many days? Restore us to yourself, O Lᴏʀᴅ, that we may be restored! Renew our days as of old—unless you have utterly rejected us, and you remain exceedingly angry with us" (Lam. 5:20–22). *A man praying at Jerusalem's Western ("Wailing") Wall, the nearest point of access for Jews to the destroyed temple.*

God for restoration (5:21), he admitted his fear that God would never do that (5:20, 22). Such are the mixed emotions that are so characteristic of suffering people.

Figure 21.1. Lamentations at a Glance				
Lament 1	Lament 2	Lament 3	Lament 4	Lament 5
Jerusalem's Sorrow	God's Punishment	Jeremiah's Pain	Jerusalem's Siege	Jeremiah's Plea

The Author of Lamentations Stressed *God's Faithfulness* as the Basis for Hope in Suffering

Even though Yahweh's people were experiencing the depths of his wrath, their story had not come to an end. God is righteous and will punish sin, just as he said he would. But he is also faithful to his covenant promises and people, and he will forgive sin, just as he said he would (cf. Lev. 26:40–45; Deut. 30:1–10; Hos. 2:19–23). Therefore, those who look to God have real hope—the confident assurance that he will meet the repentant with real mercy in accordance with his character and promise.

> God's ability to justly forgive sin is fully bound up in the good news that on the cross Jesus bore the wrath that we deserved—our sins imputed to him and his righteousness imputed to us (Rom. 3:24–26; 5:8–9, 19; 2 Cor. 5:21; Phil. 3:9; 1 Peter 2:24).

After the author despaired that hope was lost (Lam. 3:18), further reflection helped him recognize that hope still existed, due to the character of God (as Job discovered). "But this I call to mind, and therefore I have hope: The steadfast love of the LORD never ceases; his mercies never come to an end; they are new every morning; great is your faithfulness" (3:21–23; cf. vv. 31–33; Exod. 34:6–7). Therefore, the appropriate response from the people of God to discipline and suffering is trust and patience (Lam. 3:24–26): "'The LORD is my portion,' says my soul, 'therefore I

> Even in the midst of deep suffering, we should have hope that God will eventually deliver us and give us all that he has promised in Jesus Christ (Rom. 8:32, 38–39).

will hope in him.' The LORD is good to those who wait for him, to the soul who seeks him. It is good that one should wait quietly for the salvation of the LORD."

Conclusion

This hope in Yahweh's salvation of his people is what was hinted at when the narrative of Kings came to an end—God's kingdom promises still stand, and he will preserve a royal remnant (2 Kings 25:25–30). The same hope echoed through the messages of the Latter Prophets (Jeremiah–the Twelve) and has resonated through the commentary portion of the Writings (Ruth/Psalms–Lamentations). It is this confidence in God's mercy and faithfulness that provides the context for reading Daniel through Chronicles. Lamentations, therefore, provides an apt bridge back into the final narrative portion of Jesus' Bible. Here Israel's narrative history picks up again, but the focus is future-oriented, filled with anticipation of complete restoration, the destruction of all God's enemies, and the global establishment of the divine kingdom through the Messiah.

"The steadfast love of the LORD never ceases; his mercies never come to an end; they are new every morning; great is your faithfulness" (Lam. 3:22–23). *Sunrise over the Mount of Olives in Jerusalem.*

KEY WORDS AND CONCEPTS FOR REVIEW

Weeping prophet	Divine wrath
586 B.C.	Alphabetic acrostic
Jerusalem	Mixed emotions
Lament	Yahweh's faithfulness and compassion
Funeral dirge	Forgiveness
Sin	Hope
Covenant curses	Bridge to the Latter Writings
Babylonians	

KEY RESOURCES FOR FURTHER STUDY

Provan, Iain. *Lamentations*. NCBC. Grand Rapids: Eerdmans, 1991.

Dearman, J. Andrew. *Jeremiah, Lamentations*. NIVAC. Grand Rapids: Zondervan, 2002.

Garrett, Duane A., and Paul R. House. *Song of Songs/Lamentations*. WBC. Nashville: Thomas Nelson, 2004.

Longman, Tremper, III. *Jeremiah, Lamentations*. NIBCOT. Grand Rapids: Baker, 2008.

DANIEL

Who?

The frequent use of "I" or "I, Daniel" in chapters 7–12 suggests that Daniel had a significant part in writing at least the second half of the book that bears his name (Dan. 7:2; 8:1; 9:2; 10:2). Jesus' reference to "the abomination of desolation spoken of by the prophet Daniel" (Matt. 24:15; cf. Dan. 11:31; 12:11) strongly supports this idea. However, the third-person introductions to some of the visions (e.g., Dan. 7:1, "Daniel saw a dream.... He wrote"; cf. 10:1), and the third-person narrative throughout chapters 1–6 suggest that someone else, perhaps later, could have edited the visions and brought the book into the form we now have. Clearly the visions and narrative were written for conquered Israelites living under the control of Babylon and subsequent foreign powers.

When?

The book begins in 605 B.C. as the Babylonians sacked Jerusalem and took Daniel and friends captive. Much of the rest of the book records events during the rule of the Babylonian empire, which fell to the Persians in 539 B.C. The last dated event took place in the third year of Cyrus of Persia in the mid-530s B.C. Thus the book spans approximately seventy years, making Daniel an old man by the time he was thrown to the lions and received the final visions in the book.

Where?

The conquest described in the first few verses occurred in Jerusalem, Daniel's apparent home, but the location quickly shifted as Daniel and his friends were exiled to Mesopotamia. Their Babylonian captors would have marched them more than seven hundred miles northward to the Euphrates, then southeast along the river to the city of Babylon, where most of the rest of the events took place.

Why?

King Nebuchadnezzar was quickly establishing Babylon as the dominant power in the ancient Near East, raising the question of absolute control. Who was really in charge: Nebuchadnezzar and the subsequent kings of Babylon and Persia, or Yahweh, the God of the conquered Israelites? Despite the conquest and continued domination by current and future pagan powers, the author of Daniel showed that Israel's God was still sovereign, reigning supremely over both the present and the future. As such, the oppressed Israelites needed to remain faithful to Yahweh, confident that his kingdom would ultimately triumph.

DANIEL

Boyd Seevers

Carefully Crafted Verses from Daniel

"There is a God in heaven who reveals mysteries, and he has made known ... what will be in the latter days" (Dan. 2:28).

"The God of heaven will set up a kingdom that shall never be destroyed "(Dan. 2:44).

"Our God whom we serve is able to deliver us from the burning fiery furnace, and he will deliver us out of your hand, O king. But if not, be it known to you, O king, that we will not serve your gods or worship the golden image that you have set up" (Dan. 3:17–18).

THE AUTHOR OF DANIEL ...

- Emphasized Israel's *God's complete control* of human history and powers.

- Stressed the need to *remain faithful to God* even under oppression.

- Illustrated how the wise can successfully *navigate life's challenges*.

- Showed that *human pride is evil and results in God's judgment*.

- Taught *the ultimate triumph of God's kingdom* over evil influence.

"The Most High rules the kingdom of men and gives it to whom he will" (Dan. 4:17, 25).

"There came one like a son of man, and he came to the Ancient of Days and was presented before him. And to him was given dominion and glory and a kingdom, that all peoples, nations, and languages should serve him" (Dan. 7:13–14).

The Author of Daniel Emphasized Israel's *God's Complete Control* of Human History and Powers

In a time when people thought that military conquest demonstrated the superiority of the victor's god(s), the author of Daniel emphasized that the Babylonian subjection of Judah did not negate the sovereignty of Israel's God. Babylon's king and gods did not conquer Yahweh; instead, "the Lord gave" Babylon both the Israelite king and sacred articles from the temple (Dan. 1:2). He then protected and blessed Daniel and others in

> Just as Yahweh ruled despite present and future hard times for the Israelites, so God still controls the destinies of his people, regardless of any difficult circumstances in the present or future.

"In the days of those kings the God of heaven will set up a kingdom that shall never be destroyed, nor shall the kingdom be left to another people. It shall break in pieces all these kingdoms and bring them to an end, and it shall stand forever" (Dan. 2:44). *The Colossi by the eighth pylon at Karnak Temple in Luxor, Egypt, remnants of another earthly kingdom that has passed away.*

captivity. Only the sovereign Yahweh could reveal hidden things (2:22; cf. 2:28, 47) like the king's dream (2:11, 19), which saved the lives of Daniel and his friends. Though his chosen nation had been vanquished, Yahweh retained control over all nations, including Babylon. He ruled kingdoms as he wished (4:17, 32), and even foreign kings paid him homage (2:46–47; 3:28–29; 4:34–37; 6:25–27). "The Most High rules the kingdom of men and gives it to whom he will" (4:32; cf. 5:21).

Figure 22.1. Daniel at a Glance	
Historical Narratives from Daniel's Time (Dan. 1–6)	**Apocalyptic Prophecies of the Future (Dan. 7–12)**
Training in Babylon (ch. 1)	Vision of Four Beasts/Kingdoms (ch. 7)
Nebuchadnezzar's Dream (ch. 2)	Vision of a Ram and Goat (ch. 8)
Fiery Furnace (ch. 3)	Prayer, 70 Weeks (ch. 9)
Nebuchadnezzar's Insanity (ch. 4)	Vision of Kings, End (chs. 10–12)
Belshazzar's Feast (ch. 5)	
The Lion's Den (ch. 6)	

Yahweh's sovereignty continued despite Babylon's current dominance, and it would extend into the future even as subsequent ancient Near Eastern powers continued to dominate Israel. Chapters 7–12 are written as apocalyptic prophecy, describing future events through visions that use fantastic images to describe later realities. The visions of the four beasts (ch. 7), the ram and goat (ch. 8), and the kings of the south and north (ch. 11) all described future empires that would control God's people during a time framed as "seventy weeks" (lit., "seventy sevens," 9:24). Sadly for Israel, its earlier dominance would not return during these later times, but God showed that he determined who would rule and when. "Blessed be the name of God forever and ever, to whom belong wisdom and might. He changes times and seasons; he removes kings and sets up kings; he gives wisdom to the wise and knowledge to those who have understanding" (2:20–21).

The Author of Daniel Stressed the Need to *Remain Faithful to God Even under Oppression*

Since the Israelites had been conquered and would continue to be ruled by pagan overlords for many years, how were they to respond to the pressure to submit to their conquerors' gods? Should they give in or resist, knowing that their decision could lead to persecution or even death? The author of Daniel showed that Israelites had to remain true to their God, who was worth serving, whether through life or by death (cf. Phil. 1:20–21).

Daniel and his three friends were immersed in Babylonian culture as they trained for service in the royal court (Dan. 1), but when they drew the line about what foods they would eat, God granted them favor and success in their training (1:3–20). Shadrach, Meshach, and Abednego refused to worship the king's statue and to break God's commands against idolatry (ch. 3). They were confident that God would rescue them, but were determined to remain faithful even if he did not (3:17–18): "Our God whom we serve is able to deliver us from the burning fiery furnace, and he will deliver us out of your hand, O king. But if not, be it known to you, O king, that we will not serve your gods or worship the golden image that you have set up." Likewise, Daniel stayed faithful in his devotion, even in the face of death (6:10), and Yahweh both rescued him from the lions and provided a testimony of the greatness of Israel's God. We read of Daniel that "no kind of harm was found on him, because he had trusted in his God" (6:23). The result was King Darius's decree (6:26–27): "In all my royal dominion people are to tremble and fear before the God of Daniel, for he is the living God, enduring forever; his kingdom shall never be destroyed, and his dominion shall be to the end. He delivers and rescues; he works signs and wonders in heaven and on earth, he who has saved Daniel from the power of the lions." History tells us that God did not rescue every faithful Jew during this era, but the charge to stay true remained nonetheless.

"[Daniel said to the steward,] 'Test your servants for ten days; let us be given vegetables to eat and water to drink….' At the end of ten days it was seen that they were better in appearance and fatter in flesh than all the youths who ate the king's food" (Dan. 1:12, 15). *A woman buying vegetables at Jerusalem's Mahane Yehuda market.*

Different cultures apply various kinds of pressure on believers at different times; regardless, believers must not compromise God's clear standards.

"Daniel was taken up out of the [lion's] den, and no kind of harm was found on him, because he had trusted in his God" (Dan. 6:23). *Created under the leadership of King Nebuchadnezzar, who exiled Daniel in 605 B.C, this image of a lion on glazed brick was found along ancient Babylon's Processional Way en route to the Ishtar Gate on the north side of the city (from the Istanbul Archaeological Museum); Ishtar was the Assyrian and Babylonian goddess of fertily and war and is parallel to the Canaanite deity Asherah.*

The Author of Daniel Illustrated How the Wise Can Successfully *Navigate Life's Challenges*

In addition to remaining faithful, Daniel provided an excellent illustration of a believer who received wisdom from God (Dan. 1:17; 2:21, 23), which set him apart from others and gave him the skill to handle difficult situations (1:20; 5:11, 14). Daniel always seemed to know just what to say and do. He tactfully and repeatedly requested to change his prescribed diet and suggested the test that finally won permission from his overlord to do so (1:8–16). When the inability of others threatened his life, Daniel wisely requested information, time, and then prayer, and God answered by giving him the knowledge that saved his life and the lives of his friends (2:14–47). His ability and faithfulness in carrying out his responsibilities were above reproach (6:4), and they repeatedly won him favor with the kings he served.

Significantly, what distinguished Daniel and made him so wise was his ever-present fear of Yahweh and intentionality to draw attention not to himself but to God. As Daniel declared to Nebuchadnezzar when asked to interpret the king's dream (2:27–28, 30): "No wise men … can show to the king the mystery that the king has asked, but there is a God in heaven who reveals mysteries…. This mystery has been revealed to me, not because of any wisdom that I have more than all the living, but in order that the interpretation may be made known to the king." Daniel illustrated how true wisdom, which finds its source alone in God, can guide a believer through the toughest challenges, even while serving pagan kings or when one's very survival hangs in the balance.

> Living in this cursed world, our lives regularly present us with challenging circumstances, and God can also give us the wisdom to handle them skillfully.

Daniel said, "Blessed be the name of God forever and ever…. To you, O God of my fathers, I give thanks and praise, for you have given wisdom and might, and … have made known to us the king's matter" (Dan. 2:20, 23). *The priestly blessing at the Feast of Booths.*

The Author of Daniel Showed That *Human Pride Is Evil and Results in God's Judgment*

The point just made highlights the need for humility and the danger of pride. Rather than acting wisely and submitting themselves to Yahweh's sovereignty, several kings in Daniel demonstrated arrogance and suffered judgment from Yahweh as a result. Nebuchadnezzar was certain that no god could rescue the three Hebrews from his furnace (Dan. 3:15), but he then witnessed their deliverance and praised the God who carried it out (3:24–29). Later, the same king proudly boasted about his accomplishments (4:30; cf. 5:20), but God made him like a beast until he acknowledged that God indeed ruled over him (4:31–34). The king's own reflections on his deliverance are noteworthy: "Now I, Nebuchadnezzar, praise and extol and honor the King of heaven, for all his works are right and his ways are just; and those who walk in pride he is able to humble" (4:37). His later successor Belshazzar refused to learn the same lesson (5:18–23) and lost his life and kingdom as a result (5:30–31). Because Belshazzar failed to honor God with a humble heart (5:22–23), God numbered the days of his kingdom and brought them to an end (5:26). An unnamed future ruler portrayed as a horn in Daniel's visions

> We are wise to remember that God is sovereign and that we should humbly submit to him; to forget this is to invite God's discipline or judgment.

"The tree you saw, which grew and became strong, so that its top reached to heaven ... under which beasts of the field found shade, and in whose branches the birds of the heavens lived—it is you, O king" (Dan. 4:20–22). *An oak tree in Nahal Akhbara.*

would likewise demonstrate great self-exaltation (7:8; 11:36–37) that would earn him God's judgment (7:11; 11:45). "God opposes the proud" (James 4:6), and all who exhibit pride without repentance will suffer God's subsequent punishment.

The Author of Daniel Taught the *Ultimate Triumph of God's Kingdom over* Evil Influence[1]

The proud, evil kings of Babylon and subsequent nations did and would control and often persecute God's people (Dan. 7:25; 8:9–12, 23–25). The author of Daniel encouraged his embattled current and future readers by reminding them that God's people and kingdom would eventually prevail. Injustice and hardship may be widespread in the present, but Yahweh would be true to his promise to eradicate evil, to deliver his own, and to exalt himself as King over all.

- "And in the days of those kings the God of heaven will set up a kingdom that shall never be destroyed, nor shall the kingdom be left to another people. It shall break in pieces all these kingdoms and bring them to an end, and it shall stand forever" (2:44).

- How great are his signs, how mighty his wonders! His kingdom is an everlasting kingdom, and his dominion endures from generation to generation (4:3).

- "And the kingdom and the dominion and the greatness of the kingdoms under the whole heaven shall be given to the people of the saints of the Most High; his kingdom shall be an everlasting kingdom, and all dominions shall serve and obey them" (7:27; cf. 7:18, 21–22).

The truths of these texts are highlighted through the book in dreams or visions, each of which is interpreted. For example, the vision in chapter 2 portrays a giant image made of four metals, each representing different kingdoms of the world. God's kingdom is then depicted as a divinely cut

---

1. With the author's approval, Jason S. DeRouchie significantly developed and expanded this final section.

rock that would eventually smash the other parts of the statue (i.e., kingdoms) and fill the earth (2:31–45).

In chapter 7, a comparable vision is had of four beasts. Here the kingdoms of men are shown as beastly compared with the one "the Ancient of Days" gives to "one like a son of man" (7:13). "To him was given dominion and glory and a kingdom, that all peoples, nations, and languages should serve him; his dominion is an everlasting dominion, which shall not pass away, and his kingdom one that shall not be destroyed" (7:14). Significantly, at first glance, the immediate interpretation appears to identify the Son of Man with "the saints of the Most High," who suffer tribulation (7:22, 25) and then later receive the kingdom from God (7:18, 22, 27)—some only after resurrection (12:1–3). However, it is more likely that the Son of Man represents the saints of God and delivers over and oversees their rule, for the third masculine *singular* pronouns in 7:27 appear to point to an individual whose reign is carried out through God's people (see ESV footnote): "And the kingdom … shall be given to the people of the saints of the Most High; *his* kingdom shall be an everlasting kingdom, and all dominions shall serve and obey *him*" (cf. Luke 22:22, 28–30). At the very least, the broader biblical context shows a close link between the kingdom community and its representative ruler, the Messiah.

> Daniel declared that after "one like a son of man" came "with the clouds of heaven" to "the Ancient of Days," he was given universal authority (Dan. 7:13–14). Years later, Jesus identified himself with this figure, promising, "You will see the Son of Man seated at the right hand of Power, and coming with the clouds of heaven" (Mark 14:62).

Figure 22.2. Kingdoms in Daniel

Ch. 2 Vision	Ch. 7 Vision	Ch. 8 Vision	Kingdom	Supporting Text
Head of gold	Winged lion		*Babylonia* (626–539 B.C.)	Dan. 2:37
Chest and arms of silver	Bear	Ram	*Medo-Persia* (539–330 B.C.)	Dan. 8:20; cf. 5:28
Belly and thighs of bronze	Winged leopard	Goat	*Greece* (330–63 B.C.)	Dan. 8:21
Legs of irion; feet of clay and iron mixed	Terrifying, dreadful and strong beast with iron teeth and ten horns		*Rome?* (63 B.C.–A.D. 135)	
Stone → mountain	Ancient of Days gives dominion to one like a Son of Man		*Kingdom of God in Christ*	Dan. 7:13–14; Mark 14:61–62

Prepared by Jason S. DeRouchie.

Jesus builds the most important connection in this regard by identifying himself as the Son of Man of Daniel 7. After giving "his life as a ransom for many" (Mark 10:45; cf. 9:12), he would come on the clouds of heaven and establish his kingdom in power (14:61–62)—images drawn directly from Daniel 7:13–14. As the Son of Man, Jesus was exalted or glorified through the cross event (John 3:14; 8:28; 12:23, 34; 13:31) and was given "all authority in heaven and on earth" from the Father (Matt. 28:18)—authority to save and to judge, to bestow life and to punish unto death (13:41–43; John 5:27; 6:27; 8:28). Those who identify with him will ultimately rule with him (Matt. 19:28; Rev. 3:21). To enjoy the future resurrection unto life rather than unto death (Dan. 12:1–3; John 5:27–29),

> Many centuries have passed since the times described in Daniel's prophecies, and God's people must continue to wait and trust that God in Christ will indeed destroy all evil and consummate his perfect kingdom when the time is right.

Jesus' call and promise are this: "Everyone who looks on the Son and believes in him should have eternal life, and I will raise him up on the last day" (John 6:40; cf. 6:53–54; Rev. 14:14–16). Those who heed this call in the present—even in the midst of deep suffering—can rest confidently in hope that God's kingdom will triumph, evil will be eradicated, and universal peace will be enjoyed. "He will wipe away every tear from their eyes, and death shall be no more, neither shall

"I saw in the night visions, and behold, with the clouds of heaven there came one like a son of man, and he came to the Ancient of Days and was presented before him" (Dan. 7:13). *Sunset from the Golan Heights.*

there be mourning, nor crying, nor pain anymore, for the former things have passed away…. No longer will there be anything accursed, but the throne of God and of the Lamb will be in it, and his servants will worship him" (Rev. 21:4; 22:3).

KEY WORDS AND CONCEPTS FOR REVIEW

Abomination that causes desolation	Wisdom
Babylon	Pride
Persia	Kingdom of God
Exile	Four beasts
Nebuchadnezzar	Ancient of Days
Sovereignty of God	Son of Man
Apocalyptic prophecy	Resurrection
Faithfulness to God	

KEY RESOURCES FOR FURTHER STUDY

Baldwin, Joyce G. *Daniel*. TOTC. Downers Grove, IL: InterVarsity, 2009.
Longman, Tremper, III. *Daniel*. NIVAC. Grand Rapids: Zondervan, 1999.
Steinmann, Andrew E. *Daniel*. CC. St. Louis, MO: Concordia, 2008.
Young, Edward J. *The Prophecy of Daniel*. Grand Rapids: Eerdmans, 2009.

ESTHER

Who?

There is no statement that specifically identifies who wrote the book of Esther. Because the story chronicles the thinking and personal experiences of both Mordecai and Esther, it makes sense to suggest that one of them wrote this book, although some church fathers thought Ezra was the author.

When?

All the events described in Esther fit into the reign of the Persian King Ahasuerus, also known as Xerxes I (485–464 B.C.; Esther 1:1). This places the story after the first returnees left Persia for Jerusalem in 538 B.C. but before the returns under Ezra (458 B.C.) and Nehemiah (444 B.C.). Since the book does not include linguistic influence from the Greek language, one can conclude that it was written shortly after the end of the reign of Ahasuerus (ca. 460–430 B.C.) and well before the Greek era in 331 B.C.

Where?

The Persian Empire during the time of Ahasuerus spanned "from India to Ethiopia," covering more than 120 provinces (1:1). Mordecai and Esther were the descendents of Hebrews from Judah who were taken into Babylonian captivity in 586 B.C. Around 538 B.C., Cyrus of Persia allowed the Israelites to go back to Judah and rebuild the temple (Ezra 1:1–6). About fifty-thousand Hebrews returned (2:64–65), but the families of Mordecai and Esther apparently chose to stay in Mesopotamia. They lived in the Persian city of Susa (Esther 2:5–7), where Mordecai initially worked at the gate of the king's palace (2:19, 21) and then later was raised to second in rank to the king (8:2; 10:3). King Ahasuerus and Queen Esther lived in the royal palace in Susa (1:1–2; 2:3).

Why?

The book of Esther provided the Israelites with an explanation of how God preserved the people who did not return to Judah. It illustrates why and how the Jews,

1. Were threatened with extermination by evil men (3:5–9; 5:9–14);
2. Were preserved through the prayers, fasting, and the bravery of faithful people (4:1–5:8);
3. Were raised to power to intervene on behalf of others (7:1–6; 8:1–8);
4. Established the feast of Purim (9:27–32).

ESTHER

Gary V. Smith

Carefully Crafted Verses from Esther

Now Esther was winning favor in the eyes of all who saw her (Esther 2:15).

"For if you keep silent at this time, relief and deliverance will rise for the Jews from another place, but you and your father's house will perish. And who knows whether you have not come to the kingdom for such a time as this?" (Esther 4:14).

THE AUTHOR OF ESTHER ...
• Explained the origin of *the Feast of Purim*.
• Demonstrated *God's mysterious providential* care of his people.
• Emphasized the *God-ordained purpose of everything* that happens.
• Sought to *create hope* in God's power and faithfulness.

"Go, gather all the Jews to be found in Susa, and hold a fast on my behalf, and do not eat or drink for three days, night or day. I and my young women will also fast as you do. Then I will go to the king, though it is against the law, and if I perish, I perish" (Esther 4:16).

The Author of Esther Explained the Origin of *the Feast of Purim*

The book of Esther is a story of preservation and providence, of power struggles and answered promises. It recounts how a Jewish girl named Esther became queen of Persia and with her older cousin Mordecai thwarted a plot by the villain Haman to

> In a world filled with turmoil, recalling with thanksgiving what God did yesterday gives us confidence that he is both willing and able to help us in our present time of need (Phil. 4:6–7).

annihilate the Jews. The Feast of Purim (drawn from Haman's casting of "lots" [Hebrew = *pûrîm*] in Esther 3:7; cf. 9:26) is the joyous celebration that commemorates God's wonderful deliverance of the Hebrew people

"The Jews firmly obligated themselves...that these days should be remembered and kept throughout every generation ... and that these days of Purim should never fall into disuse among the Jews, nor should the commemoration of these days cease among their descendants" (Esther 9:27–28). *Jewish children in Purim costumes ready for remembrance and celebration (photo by David Bivin).*

from Haman's evil scheme (9:18–32) and God's gracious protection of the Hebrews on the dreadful day when thousands of them were supposed to be killed (9:5–17). This celebration started on March 7, 473 B.C., and Jews today continue to observe it as a day of joy and giving of gifts to the poor (9:22).

The Author of Esther Demonstrated *God's Mysterious Providential Care* of His People

The narrative of Esther is striking both in its lack of any explicit reference to God (the only such book in the Bible) and in its clear witness to the work of God in the details of life. No one can question that some unusual things happened in the lives of Mordecai and Esther, and some readers may consider their ability to avoid death as good luck or chance. However, the book's placement within the biblical context of kingdom hope makes absolutely clear that behind the scenes God was providentially orchestrating events to bring about his will in the lives of his people.

Figure 23.1. Esther at a Glance

Ahasuerus Replaces Queen Vashti with Esther (1:1–2:18)
Plots Against Ahasuerus and the Jews (2:19–3:15)
Esther Bravely Intercedes While Haman Plots (4–5)
Ahasuerus Rewards Mordecai and Executes Haman (6–7)
The Enemies of the Jews Are Defeated (8:1–9:19)
The Origin of the Feast of Purim (9:20–32)
Mordecai Is Honored (10)

God's Providential Care for Mordecai

While serving King Ahasuerus at the palace gate, Mordecai "just happened" to overhear a plot to assassinate the monarch (Esther 2:21–23). After an investigation the criminals were punished, but it "just happened" that Mordecai was never rewarded. Nevertheless, years later the king "just happened" to remember this fact when a servant read to the king this story from the royal chronicles (6:1–3). So the king decided to honor Mordecai by letting him ride through the streets of Susa on the king's horse while wearing one of the king's robes. Incidentally, it was Haman, the scoundrel who hated Mordecai, who was commanded to honor the Jew as they walked through Susa (6:10–11).

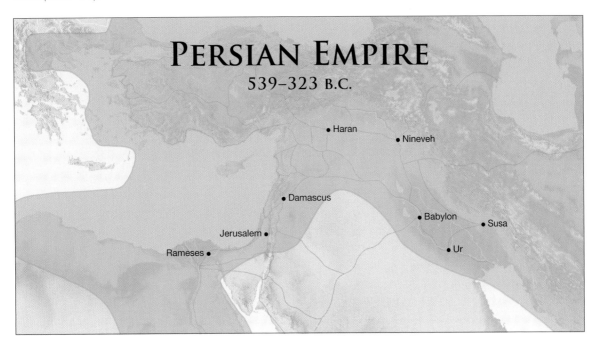

God's Providential Care for Esther

Esther appeared to be an unlucky poor orphan who was raised by Mordecai (2:7). However, as "chance" would have it, she was named the new queen of Persia (2:17–18). Later, when the powerful Haman plotted to kill all the Hebrews (3:5–9), Esther put her life on the line by going to see the king without an invitation (5:1–2). She was "lucky," though, for the king welcomed her into his presence

> If the author of Esther published a diary of your life, what examples might it include of God's providential protection, guidance, and leading through life's so-called "coincidences"?

and volunteered to do anything she asked (5:3; cf. 5:6; 7:2). Driven by apparent God-given conviction, she boldly accused Haman of plotting to kill her and all the Hebrews in the land (7:3–6). At this point the king was angry, so Haman pleaded with Esther to have mercy on him. But in the process of begging, Haman "accidentally" slipped and landed on the queen's lap just as the king was entering the room (7:8). Thus Haman's plot backfired, and he was executed on the very gallows he had prepared for Mordecai (7:10). Ironically, the king decided to give Esther all of Haman's property (8:1) and Haman's job to Mordecai (8:2; 10:3).

"[King Ahasuerus] showed the riches of his royal glory and the splendor and pomp of his greatness for many days" (Esther 1:4). *Left:* a column capital with the depiction of a man-bull, from the reign of Ahasuerus (Xerxes I), the Persian king of the Esther story; *Right:* a colossal bull head from the Persian Empire from dating the days of Ahasuerus (Xerxes I) and Artaxerxes I, the Persian king during Ezra and Nehemiah (from the Oriental Institute, USA).

The Author of Esther Emphasized the *God-ordained Purpose of Everything* That Happens

When life went badly or when unusual things happened in the lives of Esther and Mordecai, the author did not boldly or explicitly clarify God's reason for allowing the events to play out the way they did. Instead, the coincidental nature of these events was emphasized in order to clarify that God's mysterious purposes were being fulfilled. By telling the story this way, the author implied that God's intentions were accomplished even when the king got rid of Queen Vashti, because then it was possible for Esther to become queen (Esther 1:10–2:18). God's purposes were fulfilled when Esther became queen, for then she was able to intervene with the king and save the Hebrews whom Haman had condemned to death (4:1–5:8; 7:1–10). God's plan was that Mordecai should not be rewarded at the time he

> Can you see how some of your successes and challenges of the past few years were not mere "accidents" but were part of God's great plan for your life?

"And the king said to Queen Esther, 'In Susa the citadel the Jews have killed and destroyed 500 men and also the ten sons of Haman. What then have they done in the rest of the king's provinces? Now what is your wish? It shall be granted you'" (Esther 9:12). *The Citadel of David minaret in Jerusalem with a full moon.*

revealed the conspiracy against the king (2:21–23) so that Haman could be humiliated by honoring Mordecai at a later time (6:10–13). God raised up Mordecai as prime minister (8:1–2) so that he and Esther could encourage the king to grant another decree that would allow the Hebrews to defend themselves if people tried to kill them (8:3–14). The story of Esther is a case study for the truth that "for those who love God *all things* work together for good, for those who are called according to his purpose" (Rom. 8:28).

The Author of Esther Sought to *Create Hope* in God's Power and Faithfulness

Intentionally interwoven into the book's plot is a stress on Yahweh's faithfulness to his past promises to preserve his own and to curse those who curse his people (Gen. 12:3; Num. 24:9). Mordecai's conviction in God's trustworthiness was expressed in his own call for Esther to represent her people before the king (Esther 4:14): "If you keep silent at this time, *relief and deliverance will rise for the Jews from another place*, but you and your father's house will perish. And who knows whether you have not come to the kingdom for such a time as this?"

The narrative makes clear a number of times that the rogue Haman was an "Agagite" (3:1, 10; 8:3, 5; 9:24). This ethnic title appears to be an intentional echo of Agag, king of the Amalekites, whom King Saul had long ago failed to execute, thus disobeying God's word (1 Sam. 15:8–9, 19–22). As with Sodom and Gomorrah (Gen. 18:20–21; 19:29) and the pagan inhabitants of the Promised Land (15:16; Deut. 9:5), Yahweh had declared a war of judgment on Amalek for its attempt to destroy the Israelites when they first left Egypt (Exod. 17:8–16; cf. Deut. 25:17–19; 1 Sam. 15:2). Now in Esther's day, another "Agagite" had declared genocide on the Jews (Esther 3:6; 7:4). However, whereas Saul—a Benjaminite and son of Kish (1 Sam. 9:1–2)—had failed in his judicial obligations, Mordecai—also a Benjaminite and descendant of Kish (Esther 2:5)—would succeed in seeing the death of Haman and all his sons (7:10; 9:14). In 1 Samuel 15:28, Saul's authority was taken away and given to his "neighbor" who was "better than" him—namely, to David, the Old Testament image of messianic hope. In Esther, this hope is again echoed when the power was shifted out of Persian hands to a new "neighbor" (ESV =

"Mordecai the Jew was second in rank to King Ahasuerus, and he was great among the Jews and popular with the multitude of his brothers, for he sought the welfare of his people and spoke peace to all his people" (Esther 10:3). *A sixth century B.C. glazed brick relief panel of a wealthy Persian from Susa (from the British Museum).*

"another") who was "better" (Esther 1:19)—namely, Queen Esther and her God-honoring guardian Mordecai!

The Lord is both powerful and faithful. None of his purposes can be thwarted, and the careful crafting of this book testifies to this fact. For those on God's side, the story of Yahweh's deliverance in the days of Mordecai and Esther gives great confidence that God is still working for them. Just as he thwarted the conspiracy of Haman, he will also one day put an end to all evil, delivering his people and fulfilling all his kingdom promises.

> "May the God of hope fill you with all joy and peace in believing, so that by the power of the Holy Spirit you may abound in hope" (Rom. 15:13).

KEY WORDS AND CONCEPTS FOR REVIEW

Mordecai	Coincidences
Esther	Purposes
Ahasuerus/Xerxes I	Hope
Persia	Curse
Exile	Agagite
Haman	Amalekites
Purim	God's power and faithfulness
Providence	

KEY RESOURCES FOR FURTHER STUDY

Allen, Leslie C., and Timothy S. Laniak. *Ezra, Nehemiah, Esther*. NIBCOT. Peabody, MA: Hendrickson, 2003.

Baldwin, Joyce. *Esther*. TOTC. Downers Grove, IL: InterVarsity,

Duguid, Ian M. *Esther and Ruth*. REC. Phillipsburg, NJ: P&R, 2005.

Jobes, Karen H. *Esther*. NIVAC. Grand Rapids: Zondervan, 1999.

EZRA-NEHEMIAH

Who?

Ancient Jewish tradition considered Ezra-Nehemiah a single book and posited that the priest-scribe Ezra was the author of both this volume and Chronicles. These two documents may indeed be connected because the closing verses of Chronicles are roughly the same as the opening verses of Ezra-Nehemiah, and the books contain similar themes and emphases. That Ezra had his hand in composing the book is clear from the first-person perspective found throughout his "memoirs" (Ezra 7:27–9:15; cf. Neh. 8–10). However, the fact that Nehemiah the governor also has first-person narrative (Neh. 1:1–7:73; 12:27–13:31) renders the issue of final authorship unclear. More recent scholars have argued that the author-editor of Ezra-Nehemiah is anonymous and not the same as that of Chronicles. They have also asserted that, in addition to his own original narrative, this unnamed author included the memoirs of Ezra and Nehemiah and other primary source material, such as letters and official documents.

When?

The events recorded in this book span almost a century, running from around 538 B.C. when Cyrus decreed that the Jewish exiles could return to the Promised Land, through the return under Ezra just after Esther (458 B.C.), and into the governorship of Nehemiah, which began in 444 B.C. The latter two figures, whose lives most likely overlapped with that of the prophet Malachi, both ministered during the reign of the Persian King Artexerxes I (also known as Longimanus, 464–424 B.C.). The final form of this literary work could be dated to around 400 B.C.

Where?

Both the author and audience of Ezra-Nehemiah were located in Judah. Most of the events recorded took place in Jerusalem and its surroundings, along with a few that are set in Persia.

Why?

Some of the Jews who returned to the Promised Land after the Babylonian exile had experienced trauma, having witnessed the defeat and destruction of their homeland, capital, and temple and having been taken forcibly into exile. Others had been born in exile, under the burden of God's judgment due to the nation's persistent sin. The people of Israel had now been permitted to return to Judah, but they remained slaves (Ezra 9:8–9; Neh. 9:36–37), and they faced opposition, challenges, and questions. Had God forsaken them forever? Were they still the chosen people of God? Were God's promises to them still good?

The author of Ezra-Nehemiah wrote both to encourage and to challenge his readers. To encourage, he assured them that God was still their God and on their side, that his covenant relationship with them was still in effect, and that his promises would still be fulfilled. To challenge, he stressed their need to repent of their ongoing sinfulness, to recommit themselves to their covenant resposibilities, and to faithfully obey and worship God according to his standards.

24

EZRA-NEHEMIAH

Daryl Aaron and
Jason S. DeRouchie

Carefully Crafted Verses from Ezra-Nehemiah

The good hand of his God was on him. For Ezra had set his heart to study the Law of the LORD, and to do it and to teach his statutes and rules in Israel (Ezra 7:9–10).

"The hand of our God is for good on all who seek him, and the power of his wrath is against all who forsake him" (Ezra 8:22).

"Do not be grieved, for the joy of the LORD is your strength" (Neh. 8:10).

THE AUTHOR OF EZRA-NEHEMIAH ...

- Stressed *God's sovereignty and faithfulness* in restoring his people to the land.

- Acknowledged *the threat of opposition* to God's people and purposes.

- Emphasized *the need for spiritual, social, and physical boundaries*.

- Called for *covenant loyalty* through conformity to the law of Moses.

- Demonstrated how *God favors those who dependently seek him*.

They read from the book, from the Law of God, clearly, and they gave the sense, so that the people understood the reading.... And all the people went their way ... to make great rejoicing, because they had understood the words that were declared to them (Neh. 8:8, 12).

The Author of Ezra-Nehemiah Stressed God's *Sovereignty and Faithfulness* in Restoring His People to the Land

The Babylonians exiled the Judeans in three increasingly devastating deportations, climaxing in the destruction of the Jerusalem temple (605, 597, 586 B.C.). Historically, Ezra-Nehemiah is about the three Babylonian exiles put in reverse, for the book tells of three returns to Jerusalem, all focused on the reconstitution of worship and the restoration of life in the Promised Land (538, 458, 444 B.C.).

Figure 24.1. Ezra-Nehemiah at a Glance

The First Return to Jerusalem: The Temple Rebuilt (Ezra 1–6)
The Second Return to Jerusalem: The People Revived (Ezra 7–10)
Nehemiah Rebuilds the Walls of Jerusalem (Neh. 1–7)
Nehemiah and Ezra Revive the People (Neh. 8–13)

Theologically, Ezra-Nehemiah addressed the concern of these returnees: Would God fulfill his promises to them and restore them wholly as his people? The unified testimony of the book is that the "Lord God of heaven" is indeed "the great and awesome God who keeps covenant and steadfast love with those who love him and keep his commandments" (Neh. 1:5; cf. 9:32; Deut. 7:9, 21). In context, this reference provides the basis for Nehemiah's request for divine help. Two elements in the statement are clear: (1) Yahweh is sovereign as the "God of heaven," and (2) Yahweh is faithful to his covenant promises and people.

Yahweh's Sovereignty in the Restoration

From start to finish, the book testifies to Yahweh's sovereign control over the Jews' reestablishment in Judah. The book opens: "In the first year of Cyrus king of Persia, that the word of the Lord by the mouth of Jeremiah might be fulfilled, *the Lord stirred up the spirit of Cyrus*" (Ezra 1:1). The text is further explicit that God directed not only Cyrus but also two other Persian kings to encourage the Jewish return to Jerusalem and to support the building projects and worship there (6:14, 22; 7:27–28), and God was also the one who blessed his people, moving, enabling, and protecting them through the entire process of initial restoration to the land (1:5; 5:5; Neh. 2:12; 6:16; 7:5). Yahweh's governing oversight was stressed in the recurring statement "the hand of the

Figure 24.2. The Three Returns from Exile

	Return 1	Return 2	Return 3
Bible Reference	Ezra 1–6	Ezra 7–10	Nehemiah 1–13
Date Initiated	538 B.C.	458 B.C.	444 B.C.
Persian King	Cyrus II	Artaxerxes I	Artaxerxes I
Jewish Leaders	Sheshbazzar and then Zerubbabel as governors; Jeshua as priest	Ezra as priest	Nehemiah as governor
Prophets	Haggai and Zechariah	Malachi?	
Elements of the Decree	All who wished could return to Judah; the Jerusalem temple was to be rebuilt, partially financed from the royal treasury; all sacred vessels taken from Jerusalem were restored (Ezra 1:1–11; 6:1–5).	All who wished could return; worship at the Jerusalem temple was to be performed and any repairs or restorations completed, partially financed from the royal treasury; allowed to have civil magistrates (Ezra 7:6–26).	Allowed to rebuild the Jerusalem temple and city wall and gates, partially financed from the royal treasury; protection by the royal army (Neh. 2:1–9).
Number Returning	42,360 (returnees) + 7,337 (servants) 49,697 (Ezra 3:64–65)	1,496 (men) 38 (Levites) + 220 (helpers) 1,754 (Ezra 8:1–20)	Unknown
Events Accomplished	Temple begun; sacrifices instituted and Feast of Booths celebrated; Samaritans cause trouble, and work ceases until 520 B.C.; temple completed in 516 B.C.	Problems with interfaith marriage; communal confession of sins.	Jerusalem temple and city wall and gates rebuilt in fifty-two days, despite enemy opposition; problems with oppression of the poor and interfaith marriage; the Book of the Law read with communal rejoicing and the celebration of the Feast of Booths; communal confession of sins, covenant renewal, dedication of the wall, and further reforms.

Prepared by Jason S. DeRouchie. Adapted from p. 35 in *Chronological and Background Charts of the Old Testament* by John H. Walton; copyright © 1994 by John H. Walton. Used by permission of Zondervan. www.zondervan.com.

LORD was on him/me/us" (Ezra 7:6, 9, 28; 8:18, 22, 31; Neh. 2:8, 18), and this same sovereign rule was testified to in the title "the God of heaven" that both Persian kings and Jewish leaders employed (Ezra 1:2; 6:9–10; 7:12, 21, 23; Neh. 1:5).

"By [Marduk's] exalted [word], … I returned the (images of) the gods to the sacred centers [on the other side of] the Tigris whose sanctuaries had been abandoned for a long time, and I let them dwell in eternal abodes. I gathered all their inhabitants and returned (to them) their dwellings" (The *Cyrus Cylinder*). *The Cyrus Cylinder provides King Cyrus of Persia's own account of his rise to power and of his restoration policy for all exiles (from the British Museum; photo by William L. Krewson; translation from COS 315.28–36; cf. ANET 316). Significantly, what Cyrus attributes to "Marduk, the great lord of the gods" on the cylinder, the Bible rightly attributes to "the LORD, the God of heaven" (Ezra 1:2; cf. 2 Chron. 36:23).*

Yahweh's Faithfulness in Restoring to the Land

This God, who governs all, would be faithful to his covenant promises. Nehemiah's confidence in this is stressed in his echo of God's words through Moses: "If you are unfaithful, I will scatter you among the peoples, but if you return to me and keep my commandments and do them, though your outcasts are in the uttermost parts of heaven, from there I will gather them and bring them to the place that I have chosen, to make my name dwell there" (Neh. 1:8–9; cf. Lev. 26:33, 39–42; Deut. 4:25–31; 28:64; 30:2, 3).

Israel's prophets confirmed this promise repeatedly, proclaiming in advance even specific details like the name of Cyrus as the instrument of initial restoration and the specific timeframe of "seventy years" (see Ezra 1:1):

- "When seventy years are completed for Babylon, I will visit you, and I will fulfill to you my promise and bring you back to this place" (Jer. 29:10; cf. 25:12–13).

- "Thus says the LORD, your Redeemer, … who says of Cyrus, 'He is my shepherd, and he shall fulfill all my purpose'; saying of Jerusalem, 'She shall be built,' and of the temple, 'Your foundation shall be laid.'… He shall build my city and set my exiles free" (Isa. 44:24, 28; 45:13).

Clearly, part of the purpose of Ezra-Nehemiah was to show how Yahweh was accomplishing what he promised to do.

Yahweh's Faithfulness in Restoring His People

Another way Ezra-Nehemiah calls attention to God's covenant faithfulness is by establishing the returnees' continuity with pre-exilic Israel and thus the promises given them. What God had started in the past, he was continuing with the post-exilic community. Their link with the earlier generations is highlighted through the numerous genealogies and lists of people found in the book (Ezra 2:3–70; 8:1–14; Neh. 7:6–73; 11:3–19; 12:1–26). It is also indicated by the *re*-building of the temple and walls of Jerusalem; the Jewish *re*-population of Jerusalem; the *re*-establishment of the priesthood and temple worship; and the *re*-focusing on the Law, holy days, and covenant responsibilities of the people of God.

> God continues to be faithful to his covenant promises to ethnic Jews and Gentiles who are in a (new) covenant relationship with him through faith in Jesus Christ (Heb. 8:7–13; cf. Gal. 3:27–29).

The Author of Ezra-Nehemiah Acknowledged *the Threat of Opposition* to God's People and Purposes

Yahweh sovereignly works to accomplish his purposes, but opposition is always to be expected in this life due to the presence of those who hate God and his people. As Jesus asserted, "If they persecuted me, they will also persecute you" (John 15:20). And

> We as Christians should still expect opposition, and we should deal with it as Nehemiah did: trusting God for protection and deliverance and faithfully continuing to do the work that God has called us to do.

as Paul noted, "Through many tribulations we must enter the kingdom of God" (Acts 14:22; cf. 2 Tim. 3:12). This reality is certainly apparent in Ezra-Nehemiah, where we are told that many peoples of the land arose to keep the Jewish remnant from being reestablished in Jerusalem and its surroundings. There was hostility against rebuilding the temple (Ezra 4:1–24) and enmity against reconstructing Jerusalem's walls (Neh. 2:10, 19; 4:1–23; 6:1–14). The opposition included insincere requests at cooperation (Ezra 4:1–3), intimidation (4:4; Neh. 6:9), attempts to dissuade the Persian kings (Ezra 4:6–16), ridicule (Neh. 2:19; 4:1–3), and threats of physical violence against workers and leaders (4:8–15; 6:1–4). In response, the Jewish leaders depended upon and appealed to God to protect them (2:20; 4:4–5; 6:9, 14), and they took action, whether through restarting the temple rebuilding in defiance of the king's unjust order (Ezra 5:1–2) or in calling the workers to defend themselves in battle if they were attacked (Neh. 4:13–23). These two aspects come together in Nehemiah 4:14, 20 where Nehemiah said to his people: "Do not be afraid of them. Remember the LORD, who is great and awesome, and fight for your brothers, your sons, your daughters, your wives, and your homes…. Our God will fight for us."

"And they offered great sacrifices that day [Jerusalem's walls were completed] and rejoiced, for God had made them rejoice with great joy; the women and children also rejoiced. And the joy of Jerusalem was heard far away" (Neh. 12:43). *An image of an Egyptian priest slaughtering a calf (from the Oriental Institute, USA).*

The Author of Ezra-Nehemiah Emphasized the Need for Spiritual, Social, and Physical Boundaries

Israel's ability to serve as a channel of blessing to the world (Gen. 12:3) was always contingent on their remaining true to God and uninfluenced by the evil of the world. "You shall be holy to me, for I the LORD am holy and have separated you from the peoples, that you should be mine" (Lev. 20:26). As Israel stood distinct from the pagans, heeding God's voice and keeping his covenant, they would in turn operate as a kingdom of priests and a holy nation, directing the nations to the unique worth of Yahweh (Exod. 19:5–6; cf. Deut. 4:5–8; 1 Peter 2:9). This expectation remained for Israel even after the exile. As the "remnant" (Ezra 9:8–15; Neh. 1:3), the "holy race" (Ezra 9:2), they needed to maintain spiritual, social, and even physical boundaries from the pagan influences borne by the other inhabitants of the land (4:3; Neh. 2:20; 9:2; 10:28; 13:1–3).

In Ezra-Nehemiah, this stress shows up most directly in the recurring problem of inter-faith marriage—an issue confronted by both Ezra (Ezra 9–10) and Nehemiah (Neh. 13:1–3, 23–27). Earlier through Moses, God had warned parents not to allow their children to marry nonbelievers. The

"I went out by night by the Valley Gate to the Dragon Spring and to the Dung Gate, and I inspected the walls of Jerusalem that were broken down and its gates that had been destroyed by fire" (Neh. 2:13). *City of David excavations northward up the Kidron Valley to the temple mount (left) and Mount of Olives (right).*

What the Old Testament Authors Really Cared About

reason was clear (Deut. 7:4): "They would turn away your sons from following me, to serve other gods. Then the anger of the LORD would be kindled against you, and he would destroy you quickly." Israel's history was dotted with failure related to this issue, and the results were always destructive (Judg. 3:5–8; 1 Kings 11:1–13; 16:30–33; cf. 2 Kings 17:8; 21:9). How then could the returnees, the "holy race," be found to have "mixed itself with the peoples of the lands" (Ezra 9:2)? Was pleasing God not important to them? Did they not care about seeing him exalted in the sight of others? Were they so uninterested in restoration and life that they would choose a path toward eternal death? On this basis, Ezra charged them: "Separate yourselves from the peoples of the land and from the foreign wives" (10:11).

> If Ezra were here today, he would charge all Christians who are single to be vigilant in their pursuit of God with respect to their relationships.

The importance of rebuilding the walls of Jerusalem symbolized in a physical way the necessity for these boundaries (Neh. 1:3; 2:3). The walls not only were protection from outside threats but also signified the

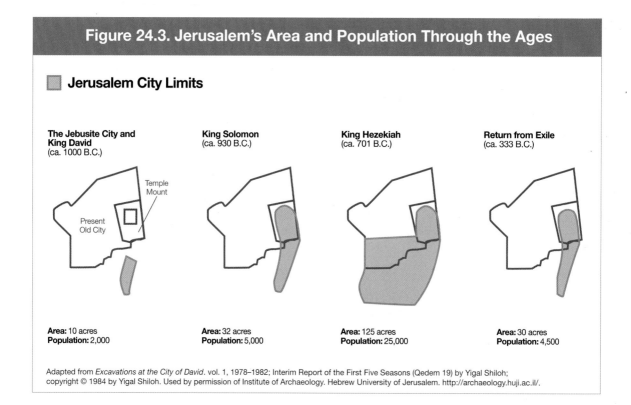

Figure 24.3. Jerusalem's Area and Population Through the Ages

Jerusalem City Limits

The Jebusite City and King David
(ca. 1000 B.C.)

Temple Mount

Present Old City

Area: 10 acres
Population: 2,000

King Solomon
(ca. 930 B.C.)

Area: 32 acres
Population: 5,000

King Hezekiah
(ca. 701 B.C.)

Area: 125 acres
Population: 25,000

Return from Exile
(ca. 333 B.C.)

Area: 30 acres
Population: 4,500

Adapted from *Excavations at the City of David*. vol. 1, 1978–1982; Interim Report of the First Five Seasons (Qedem 19) by Yigal Shiloh; copyright © 1984 by Yigal Shiloh. Used by permission of Institute of Archaeology. Hebrew University of Jerusalem. http://archaeology.huji.ac.il/.

uniqueness and separateness of those within (7:3–4). The city of Jerusalem had become an important symbol of Israel's identity as the people of God. Even in exile, their identity had been tied to the Holy City (Ps. 126:1–2; cf. Dan. 6:10), for it was the location God chose to make his presence dwell (Ezra 1:4; 6:12; Neh. 9:1).

Social and physical boundaries were important in that they also provided a spiritual boundary. Unhealthy intermingling with pagans inevitably leads to spiritual defection or idolatry. This is why God clearly and repeatedly commanded Israel not to do it (Exod. 34:12–16; Deut. 7:1–6; cf. Ezra 9:10–12).

> As he did with Old Testament Israel, God calls for Christians to be set apart, to live in a way that is distinctively God-like (1 Peter 1:14–16; cf. 1 Thess. 4:3–8).

The Author of Ezra-Nehemiah Called for *Covenant Loyalty* Through Conformity to the Law of Moses

God was faithful to his covenant promises, but he continued to expect his people to be faithful to their covenant responsibilities, specifically in keeping the instructions given through Moses. Many of the exiles who returned clearly understood that their captivity was due to their covenant violation: "We have acted very corruptly against you and have not kept the commandments, the statutes, and the rules that you commanded your servant Moses" (Neh. 1:7; cf. 9:13–17, 26–30; Ezra 9:6–15). They saw the return as a "brief moment" of divine favor—"a little reviving in our slavery" (Ezra 9:8), and what they needed was to dependently follow God in the present rather than to spurn his grace by rebelling like their ancestors had.

Such a revived covenant loyalty necessitated reprioritizing their lives around God's Word—a feature that came to characterize post-exilic Judaism. In short, from Ezra onward, the Jews came to be regarded as a "people of the Book." Ezra himself played an important role in this because he was "a scribe skilled in the Law of Moses" who "had set his heart to study the Law of the LORD, and to do it and to teach his statutes and rules in Israel" (7:6, 10). This devotion can be seen in Nehemiah 8 as he and his fellow-Levites publicly "read from the book, from the Law of God, clearly, and they gave the sense, so that the people understood the reading" (Neh. 8:8). The result was that "all the people went their way … to make great rejoicing, because they understood the words that were declared to them" (8:12).

> Ezra's own life is a portrait of Paul's call, "Do you your best to present yourself to God as one approved, a worker who has no need to be ashamed, rightly handling the word of truth" (2 Tim. 2:15).

One way Ezra-Nehemiah emphasized the revitalized focus on the centrality of Scripture was through highlighting the rebuilding of the temple and the reinstituting of the Levitical priesthood, the sacrifices, and the holy days (Ezra 3:2–10; 6:13–22; Neh. 8:13–18; 12:44–47; 13:4–9, 15–22, 28–31). These ceremonial or cultic laws helped distinguish Israel from the nations and provided parables of more fundamental truths about God and relating to him (see Col. 2:16–17; Heb. 9:11–14). Along with these more symbolic laws, God also called Israel to keep the various criminal, case, family, and compassion laws—all of which displayed love for God and neighbor in the community (see Fig. 3.4). The issues highlighted most directly in this book were the care of the poor and Levites (Neh. 5:1–13;

"Ezra had set his heart to study the Law of the LORD, and to do it and to teach his statutes and rules in Israel" (Ezra 7:10). *A Jewish scribe writing (photo by Kim Guess).*

What the Old Testament Authors Really Cared About

13:10–14); the keeping of the Sabbath (13:15–22); and the purity of marriage, the community, the priesthood, and the temple (Ezra 9–10; Neh. 13:1–9, 23–31).

The Author of Ezra-Nehemiah Demonstrated How *God Favors Those Who Dependently Seek Him*

Prayer expressed through confession and covenant renewal plays a central role in the events recorded in Ezra-Nehemiah. Whether the prayers are short (Neh. 2:4; 4:4–5; 5:19; 13:14, 22, 29, 31) or long (Ezra 9:6–15; Neh. 1:5–11; 9:5–38), their content demonstrates great humility and dependent longing for God.

For example, Ezra pleaded with God on behalf of the returnees, who had engaged in sinful behavior (Ezra 9:13–15), and his cries were accompanied with corporate weeping and brokenness (10:1) and the recognition that the assembly had "broken faith with our God" (10:2). The people were convinced, however, that "even now there is hope for Israel in spite of this" (10:2), and they committed to Yahweh through covenant to separate themselves from those peoples that stood as obstacles in their pursuit of living for God (10:3).

"In your great mercies you did not make an end of them or forsake them, for you are a gracious and merciful God…. You have been righteous in all that has come upon us, for you have dealt faithfully and we have acted wickedly" (Neh. 9:31, 33). *Men praying at the Western Wall, Jerusalem.*

Why were they convinced that there was still hope? The reason is made clear in the record of a similar commitment that was formalized years later under the leadership of Nehemiah (Neh. 9:38). Caught up in the midst of an extended revival centered on the reading and exposition of God's Word, the people gathered together for a solemn assembly, to hear from the Book of the Law and to confess their sins and worship Yahweh God (9:1–3). Nehemiah 9:5–37 is an amazing prayer of covenant renewal. In it the returnees recognized Yahweh as the only true God and as the one who entered into a covenant relationship with them; they affirmed their own covenant failures throughout history and praised God's faithfulness to them despite their sin. With a frequency paralleled only in Hosea 1–2, Nehemiah 9 glories in the "mercy-filled" nature of God's character (9:17, 19, 27–28, 31; cf. Exod. 24:6), and it is on this basis that the repentant returnees pleaded to "the great, the mighty, and the awesome God, who keeps covenant and steadfast love" (Neh. 9:32), to help them in their present need. There was hope, because God was merciful! As such, before God and with one another they entered "into a curse and an oath to walk in God's Law that was given by Moses the servant of God, and to observe and do all the commandments of the LORD our God and his rules and his statutes" (10:29).

> Our inward propensity to sin is *always* challenging our desire to obey God. Therefore renewal is *always* necessary.

As one overviews the prayers in the book, a number of features are common. The people's humility and dependence flowed from their confession of sin (Ezra 9:6–7, 10–11, 15; Neh. 1:6–7; 9:16–31) and from their recognition of (1) God's faithfulness to his covenant promises (Ezra 9:9; Neh. 1:5; 9:8); (2) his grace and mercy (Ezra 9:8–9, 13; Neh. 9:17, 31), which had flowed out in compassion, patience, forgiveness, and deliverance (Neh. 9:17, 19, 27–28, 30); and (3) his ever-present provision and protection (9:9–15; 20–21, 25). While God's justness in dealing with their sinfulness was freely acknowledged (Ezra 9:7, 13; Neh. 9:27–28, 30, 33), his people appealed to him on the basis of his faithful and merciful character (Neh. 1:8–9; 9:32) to graciously grant success (1:11; 5:19; 6:9; 13:14, 22, 31) and protection (4:4–5, 9; 6:14). The foundational truth that governs such pleas is this: "The hand of our God is for good on all who seek him, and the power of his wrath is against all who forsake him" (Ezra 8:22; cf. 7:6, 9–10, 28; Neh. 2:8, 18).

> The prayers in Ezra-Nehemiah show us what prayers ought to be—human expressions of humility and insufficiency that are both dependent on and confident in God's grace and all-sufficiency.

Conclusion

The book of Ezra-Nehemiah ends with a brief plea: "Remember me, O my God, for good" (Neh. 13:31). This small sentence captures the heart of Israel's hopes for restoration. Only where God remembers for good will the kingdom be established.

Unfortunately, the Jews' desire to be obedient to God's laws was continually challenged by their inward propensity to sin. Even after the formal covenant renewal highlighted in Nehemiah 8–10, the problems of interfaith marriage continued to arise, as did numerous other challenges regarding purity and holiness (ch. 13). While restoration was initialized, Israel's enslavement continued—not only to Persia (Ezra 9:8–9; Neh. 9:36–37) but also to sin. Yet in light of God's sustained mercies (Neh. 9:31), hope remained (Ezra 10:2), as Israel longed for the more complete, ultimate restoration of God's kingdom.

KEY WORDS AND CONCEPTS FOR REVIEW

Ezra and Nehemiah's memoirs	Boundaries
Persia	Remnant
Exile	Interfaith marriage
Post-exile	People of the Book
Three returns from exile	Prayer
Sovereignty	Covenant renewal
Faithfulness	Mercy
Opposition	

KEY RESOURCES FOR FURTHER STUDY

Fensham, F. Charles. *The Books of Ezra and Nehemiah*. NICOT. Grand Rapids: Eerdmans, 1982.

Kidner, Derek. *Ezra and Nehemiah*. TOTC. Downers Grove, IL: InterVarsity, 2009.

Steinmann, Andrew E. *Ezra and Nehemiah*. CC. St. Louis, MO: Concordia, 2010.

Yamauchi, Edwin M. "Ezra and Nehemiah." In *The Expositor's Bible Commentary*, vol. 4, rev. ed. Grand Rapids: Zondervan, 2010.

1–2 CHRONICLES

Who?

The author of 1–2 Chronicles is never named, so any attempt to identify him is speculative. Ancient Jewish tradition held that Ezra wrote this work together with Ezra-Nehemiah, and the similarity of the ending of 2 Chronicles with the beginning of Ezra may support this view. The emphasis on the temple and the Levitical priesthood also points to Ezra, or perhaps another priest, as the book's author. But the Chronicler could have been a historian with a priestly perspective. Because the book was recognized as the Word of God, it is safe to conclude that it was written by a divine spokesman—that is, a prophet, but beyond that we do not know. As with the books of Samuel and Kings, 1–2 Chronicles began as a single work in the Hebrew and was later expanded to two parts when the consonant-only Hebrew text was translated into Greek, which includes vowels and thus required more space.

When?

If Ezra wrote 1–2 Chronicles, then the book must be dated around 450 B.C., during the time he lived in Jerusalem. Another possibility is that the book was written shortly after the return from exile in 538 B.C. This would explain the last historical reference in the book dating to the time of Cyrus' decree (2 Chron. 36:22–23), and it may account for the largely optimistic view of the future generally absent in Ezra-Nehemiah. Furthermore, the two major themes of 1–2 Chronicles, the temple and the Davidic dynasty, were central to the returnees' aspirations, as can be seen in the construction of the temple by 516 B.C. and the similar emphases of the contemporary prophets Haggai and Zechariah. All interpreters agree that Chronicles was written after Samuel–Kings and that the writer expected his readers to be familiar with that history.

Where?

Nothing explicitly locates the origin of this book, but its focus upon the temple and its audience of post-exilic Judeans indicate a Jerusalem origin. As 1–2 Chronicles so eloquently describes, Jerusalem was chosen as Yahweh's dwelling place on earth.

Why?

The writer of 1–2 Chronicles desired to show Israel's place in Yahweh's plan in order to help those in the nation believe that Yahweh was still committed to them. Those who had returned from exile likely questioned their relationship to God and sought direction for the future. The Chronicler wanted them to know that God's promises to the house of David remained true but required patient trust. He pointed them to pure worship at God's dwelling place in the temple and repeatedly emphasized the consequences of obedience and disobedience to the Mosaic (old) covenant.

1–2 CHRONICLES

Todd Bolen

Carefully Crafted Verses from 1–2 Chronicles

"When your days are fulfilled to walk with your fathers, I will raise up your offspring after you, one of your own sons, and I will establish his kingdom. He shall build a house for me, and I will establish his throne forever" (1 Chron. 17:11–12).

"O LORD, God of Israel, there is no God like you, in heaven or on earth, keeping covenant and showing steadfast love to your servants who walk before you with all their heart" (2 Chron. 6:14).

And all Judah rejoiced over the oath, for they had sworn with all their heart and had sought him with their whole desire, and he was found by them, and the LORD gave them rest all around (2 Chron. 15:15).

THE AUTHOR OF 1–2 CHRONICLES ...

- Stressed God's commitment to the *Davidic dynasty*.

- Emphasized *the centrality of God's temple-presence* in his people's worship.

- Demonstrated how covenant loyalty brought *blessings or curses*.

- Called for *seeking Yahweh in humility and faith*.

- Exalted Yahweh as *the sovereign Lord* over Judah, Israel, and the nations.

The Author of 1–2 Chronicles Stressed God's Commitment to the *Davidic Dynasty*

The book of Chronicles is often compared with the history recorded in the books of Samuel and Kings. Some have felt that 1–2 Chronicles is redundant, and the Septuagint even called the book "the things omitted." The ordering of most Christian English Bibles encourages this misrepresentation, but both the book's content and its placement at the end of the Hebrew Bible highlight its distinctiveness. The author of Chronicles was well-acquainted with Samuel and Kings, but he wrote a different history, designed to explain and stress truths critical for God's people returning from the exile. In particular, Chronicles elaborates on the wonderful word play that Yahweh made with David when he established his covenant with him. David had asked to build God a "house" (temple; 1 Chron. 17:1, 4; 22:7), but Yahweh responded that he would build David a "house" (dynasty; 17:10). This book is really about these two houses—how God raised up the Davidic *dynasty* as a beacon of hope and how David's royal house constructed and maintained Yahweh's *temple*.

From the start, the Chronicler focused on David, as he traced the genealogy from Adam to Abraham and from Abraham to the twelve tribes (ch. 1). The first tribal genealogy he gave was not that of the oldest, Reuben, or even of Joseph, who had the rights of the firstborn, but of Judah, from whom the royal redeemer was to rise (2:1–5:2; cf. Gen. 49:10).

"[Solomon] shall build a house for my name. He shall be my son, and I will be his father, and I will establish his royal throne in Israel forever" (1 Chron. 22:10). *Left: a westward look at the temple mount from the Mount of Olives; the Islamic Dome of the Rock stands roughly where the temple stood, but Israel's temple would have been approximately one-third higher (photo by David Bivin).* **Right:** *the Damascus Gate and Dome of the Rock from the north (photo by Tom Powers).*

David's children and his royal descendants occupy the central portion of Judah's family list (1 Chron. 3:1–24). After the other tribes are listed, the author almost entirely passed over Saul's reign, explaining that "the LORD put [Saul] to death and turned the kingdom over to David" (10:14).

	Figure 25.1. Kings vs. Chronicles	
	1–2 KINGS	**1–2 CHRONICLES**
Theme	Covenant Failure	Covenant Continuity, Transformation, and Theological Stability
Focus	Doom	Hope
Emphases	Apostasy, Idolatry, and the Role of the Kings and Prophets	Retribution Theology (Blessings or Curses) and the Role of the Priests and Levites
Ending	Judgment and Captivity with Hint of Hope	Shift from Monarchy to Theocracy with Dominant Hope of Full Kingdom Restoration
Audience and Their Question	Exilic Community Questioning, "Why Did the Exile Happen?"	Post-exilic Community Questioning, "Will the Kingdom Be Restored?"
Recurrent Motifs	Sins of Jeroboam and Promises to David	The Davidic Dynasty and Yahweh's Kingship over All; Repentance and Reform as the Means to God's Favor

Prepared by Jason S. DeRouchie. Adapted from p. 194 in *Chronological and Background Charts of the Old Testament* by John H. Walton; copyright © 1994 by John H. Walton. Used by permission of Zondervan. www.zondervan.com.

Yahweh's Placement of David on the Throne

David's rise to the throne was not the mere product of human ingenuity but was ordained by God. David honored the Lord in his life, even leading Israel to victory while Saul was still king. Therefore Yahweh told David, "You shall be shepherd of my people Israel, and you shall be prince" (1 Chron. 11:2). The Chronicler recorded that "all Israel" recognized David as their king, and he even listed each tribe and the number of military men "who came to David in Hebron to turn the kingdom of Saul over to him" (12:23–40). David obeyed God's commands, and the Lord gave him victory and caused all nations to fear him (14:16–17). His patient reliance on Yahweh was rewarded: "David knew that the LORD had established him as king over Israel, and that his kingdom was highly exalted for the sake of his people Israel" (14:2).

What the Old Testament Authors Really Cared About

Yahweh's Promise to David of an Everlasting Dynasty

Readers looking for a complete biography of David's life and reign will not find it in Chronicles, for the writer is almost silent regarding the king's faults, choosing instead to focus on God's promises to David and the king's faithful obedience. Because David's sins with Bathsheba and Uriah do not contribute to these emphases, the Chronicler did not repeat the sad stories of 2 Samuel. Instead, twelve of the Chronicler's nineteen chapters about David's years as king describe his preparation for the construction of the temple. Even this, however, is secondary to the covenant that God made with David. Yahweh was pleased with David's desire to build him a temple, but God denied his request (1 Chron. 17:4; 28:3). In its place, he made a covenant with David—a perpetual and unswerving grant that would never fail or be changed. The words that Yahweh spoke to David should be read slowly (17:11–13a): "When your days are fulfilled to walk with your fathers, I will raise up your offspring after you, one of your own sons, and I will establish his kingdom. He shall build a house for me, and I will establish his throne forever. I will be to him a father, and he shall be to me a son." This was a promise of substance, for the first king, Saul, lost his dynasty when he sinned, and the northern kingdom had ten different dynasties in its brief two-hundred-year history. Yet God declared that he would *never* remove his steadfast love from the Davidic dynasty (17:13). David recognized with humility the great honor God had given him, and he knew that its fulfillment would glorify God's name forever (17:24).

Yahweh's Preservation of David's Dynasty

King David lived to see the beginning of the fulfillment of God's promise to him. He crowned Solomon as his successor and declared, "Of all my sons … [the LORD] has chosen Solomon my son to sit on the throne of the kingdom of the LORD over Israel" (1 Chron. 28:5; cf. 2 Chron. 6:10). Significantly, this verse stressed a central truth that every Israelite king needed to recognize: Though he sits on the throne over Israel, the kingdom was still Yahweh's! David reminded Solomon of God's promise: "I will establish his kingdom forever if he continues strong in keeping my commandments and my rules, as he is today" (1 Chron. 28:7). However, neither Solomon nor any other Davidic king was completely faithful, and each passed away and was succeeded by his son. In other words, the Davidic covenant would stand forever, but the present experience of Davidic rule depended upon the king's

> If the writer of Chronicles were here today, he would rejoice that God fulfilled his promise to David in sending Jesus as the eternal King (Matt. 1:1; Luke 1:32–33).

loyalty to the national constitution, the Mosaic (old) covenant (22:13; 28:8; cf. Deut. 17:18–20).

The book of Chronicles describes how Yahweh maintained his promise to David while punishing the kings who were disloyal to Israel's true King. When a ruler forsook the Lord, God sent enemies to attack or disease to kill. Several of Judah's kings were assassinated, but *always* God ensured that the next son in line was placed upon the throne. One example of this was King Jehoram, who was so wicked that he was compared with Ahab! Yahweh punished him severely with multiple rebellions in his kingdom, with a personal rebuke by the prophet Elijah, and with a disease so severe that his bowels came out (2 Chron. 21:4–19). But even his sin was not enough to turn God's love from David's house, for the Chronicler wrote, "Yet the LORD was not willing to destroy the house of David, because of the covenant that he had made with David, and since he had promised to give a lamp to him and to his sons forever" (21:7). Shortly thereafter, Judah experienced a dark hour when Ahab's daughter Athaliah seized David's throne, slaughtered the royal family, and made herself queen. Yahweh, however, protected one baby and hid him in the temple, and thus the Davidic line was saved (22:10–12).

The readers of Chronicles needed to know that God had made this promise to David and that he would never fail to keep his word. Although the people had violated God's word and had thus been carried into exile (1 Chron. 9:1), Yahweh would not turn; he would remain trustworthy. No Davidic ruler sat on the throne in Jerusalem when the Chronicler wrote these words, so the people naturally questioned the status of the Davidic covenant. The book of Chronicles provided a clear answer: God has always been faithful to the Davidic dynasty, and he has not forgotten his promises. One of the rewards that comes from studying the genealogies is the recognition that, although Jerusalem was destroyed and Judah deported, Yahweh protected David's descendants and brought them back, ready to rule when God decreed (3:17–24).

"They put [Athaliah] to death there. And Jehoiada [the priest] made a covenant between himself and all the people and the king [Joash] that they should be the LORD's people. Then all the people went to the house of Baal and tore it down; his altars and his images they broke in pieces" (2 Chron 23:16–17). *From Ras Shamra in northern Syria, a stele of the Canaanite god Baal with lightning from the fifteenth to thirteenth century B.C. (from Muse'e du Louvre).*

The Author of 1–2 Chronicles Emphasized *the Centrality of God's Temple-Presence* in His People's Worship

The emphases of the book of Chronicles are apparent from a brief survey of the book. The first nine chapters provide the genealogies. The next twenty-nine chapters describe the seventy-three years when David and Solomon ruled from Jerusalem during the united monarchy. The last twenty-seven chapters survey all 345 years of the kingdom of Judah. Of the reigns of David and Solomon, eighteen chapters focus on the temple planning and construction. Of the kings that followed, the Chronicler regarded their treatment of the temple as a "weathervane" of their relationship to Yahweh.

Figure 25.2. Chronicles at a Glance

Genealogies (1 Chron. 1–9)	9 chapters	>3,500 years
David and Solomon in Jerusalem (1 Chron. 10–2 Chron. 9)	29 chapters	73 years
Kingdom of Judah (2 Chron. 10–36)	27 chapters	345 years

The Chronicler's interest was not in a building of wood and stone, but rather in Yahweh who moved into the temple to live among his people. For the writer, to seek the temple was to seek the Lord, for the temple signified God's very presence on earth. The northern tribes were guilty because they erected other worship centers (2 Chron. 11:13–16), but those who sought Yahweh at his temple in Jerusalem were filled with joy (7:10).

The Temple, Constructed by God's Design

Yahweh's concern for his temple began with selecting the location. Many people think that the story of David's census is primarily describing the king's sin of faithlessness, but in fact the emphasis in the story is on God's mercy. The Lord judged David by sending a plague on the land, but he ordered the angel to halt over a threshing floor in Jerusalem. The place where God showed mercy became the site of the temple where God would continually pour out forgiving and reconciling mercy upon his people. Yahweh confirmed that this was his will by sending fire down from heaven to consume the sacrifice on David's altar (1 Chron. 21:26; 22:1; cf. 2 Chron. 3:1).

The desire for a glorious temple motivated David to begin preparations during his reign. In his own words (1 Chron. 22:5): "Solomon my son is young and inexperienced, and the house that is to be built for the LORD must be exceedingly magnificent, of fame and glory through all lands. I will therefore make preparations for it." David prepared not only the construction materials (22:2–5), but also the Levites, priests, musicians, gatekeepers, and other officials (23:1–26:32). He gave to Solomon the blueprints for the temple, its vessels, and its staff—the written plan, which came from the hand of the LORD

"David also provided … cedar timbers without number, for the Sidonians and Tyrians brought great quantities of cedar to David. For David said, '… The house that is to be built for the LORD must be exceedingly magnificent, of fame and glory throughout all lands'" (1 Chron. 22:3–5; cf. 2 Chron. 2:8–9). *A relief of cedars of Lebanon being transported by boat for Assyrian king Sargon II (721–705 B.C.) (from Muse'e du Louvre).*

What the Old Testament Authors Really Cared About

(28:11–12, 19; cf. Exod. 25:9, 40). The Chronicler saw Solomon and the craftsman Huram-Abi as similar to the two Spirit-filled artisans who built the tabernacle, Bezalel and Oholiab (2 Chron. 2; Exod. 35).

The Temple, Inhabited by God's Presence

The narrative high point of the book of Chronicles is the temple dedication ceremony when the glory of Yahweh filled the Most Holy Place (2

In the days of King Hezekiah, "when all this [Passover celebration] was finished, all Israel who were present went out to the cities of Judah and broke in pieces the pillars and cut down the Asherim and broke down the high places and the altars throughout all Judah and Benjamin, and in Ephraim and Manasseh, until they had destroyed them all" (2 Chron. 31:1). *Located at Beersheba, the kingdom of Judah's southern border city, this large four-horned altar is a replica of one from the time of Israel's divided kingdom that was made with well-dressed stones and found in secondary use in later walls of the city. The presence of the altar suggests that the city housed a temple and was a center for syncretistic worship; it was likely torn down during King Hezekiah's reforms.*

Chron. 6–7). Though in some ways it is difficult to understand, the writer maintained that the Lord literally inhabited this man-made structure. As the Lord himself said (7:16): "I have chosen and consecrated this house that my name may be there forever. My eyes and my heart will be there for all time." On the other hand, Solomon rightly recognized that "heaven and the highest heaven cannot contain you, how much less this house that I have built!" (6:18). Yahweh is far greater than the temple, but he chose a single place on earth as his holy habitation. Again God sent fire down from heaven to consume the sacrifices and express his pleasure (7:1).

The Temple, Treasured by God's People

A holy God living among sinful people naturally required very careful attention to personal purity and holiness. Yahweh demanded that only one tribe, the Levites, serve at his altar, and for this reason the Chronicler gave lengthy genealogies and lists so that the Israelites would know who was permitted to perform the priestly duties (e.g., 1 Chron. 6). On one occasion, a Levite named Uzzah lost his life because he dared to touch God's "throne," the ark of the covenant (13:9–10). On another occasion, a Davidic king unwisely entered the Holy Place, but he was pursued by the Levitical priests who rebuked him saying, "It is not for you, Uzziah, to burn incense to the LORD" (2 Chron. 26:18). The Lord struck the king with leprosy because he had violated the laws of purity and taken the presence of God lightly.

The kings of Judah demonstrated whether and how much they treasured the Lord by the way they maintained the temple. This reality is exemplified in the life of Joash, who, with his counselors, "abandoned the house of the LORD, the God of their fathers, and served the Asherim and the idols" (24:18). Similarly, the wicked Ahaz "shut up the doors of the house of the LORD" (28:24), and his grandson Manasseh "built altars in the house of the LORD … provoking him to anger" (33:4, 6). By contrast, the godly kings were consistently commended for their devotion to the temple—opening its doors, purifying its courts, resuming its sacrifices, and repairing its features (e.g., 24:2–4; 29:2–3; 34:8).

When the people obeyed Yahweh, the temple was a place of great joy and blessing. David gathered the Israelites to the future site of the temple and commanded them to "bless the LORD your God" (1 Chron. 29:20). The people praised the Lord and

> Today, the Lord does not dwell in a building but resides within each believer. As Paul said (1 Cor. 6:19–20): "Do you not know that your body is a temple of the Holy Spirit...? You are not your own, for you were bought with a price. So glorify God in your body."

his king, offered sacrifices, and "ate and drank before the LORD on that day with great gladness" (29:21–22). After the dedication of the temple, Solomon "sent the people away to their homes, joyful and glad of heart for the prosperity that the LORD had granted" (2 Chron. 7:10). When worship at the temple was restored in the days of Hezekiah, "all the people rejoiced" in light of God's great provision (29:36). At times, the people's delight in Yahweh was accompanied by lavish giving of their personal resources to the Lord (1 Chron. 29:2–9; 2 Chron. 31:4–10). Clearly, the Chronicler would have affirmed the words of the psalmist: "In your presence there is fullness of joy; at your right hand are pleasures forevermore" (Ps. 16:11).

The Author of 1–2 Chronicles Demonstrated How Covenant Loyalty Brought *Blessings or Curses*

With God's wonderful promise to David's dynasty, the audience may have needed to be reminded that the nation continued under the Mosaic (old) covenant with its close relationship between covenant faithfulness and divine blessing or curse. An important distinction between the history of Samuel–Kings and the book of Chronicles is that the former highlights the nation's sin to explain why the exile occurred. In contrast, the Chronicler wrote after the exile to a people who were granted a new opportunity to choose whether to obey or reject God's law.

The Demands of the Mosaic (Old) Covenant

Perhaps even more than Samuel–Kings, Chronicles draws the nation's attention back to the Mosaic (old) covenant. David himself stressed the binding authority of the Law when he told Solomon: "You will prosper if you are careful to observe the statutes and the rules that the LORD commanded Moses for Israel" (1 Chron. 22:13). Kings were judged on the basis of whether they complied with the national constitution. Of Amaziah, it is written that he acted "according to what is written in the Law, in the Book of Moses" (2 Chron. 25:4). Similarly, it was "hearing all the words of the Book of the Covenant" that sparked Josiah to lead the nation in covenant renewal, committing "to walk after the LORD and to keep his commandments and his testimonies and his statutes, with all his heart and all his soul, to perform the words of the covenant that were written in this book" (34:30–31). The standard for obedience was the revelation that God had given through Moses in the Pentateuch.

The Certainty of Reward

Consequently, the history related in Chronicles is almost entirely predictable. When the king led the nation in loyalty to God's Word, the people received the promised blessings (Lev. 26:3–13; Deut. 28:1–14). And when the king and the people ignored or violated the commandments, the threatened curses came upon them (Lev. 26:14–39; Deut. 28:15–68). This is made clear in Yahweh's words through Huldah the prophetess in the days of King Josiah: "I will bring disaster upon this place and upon its inhabitants, all the curses that are written in the book … because they have forsaken me and have made offerings to other gods" (2 Chron. 34:23–25).

A superb example of this retribution principle is provided in the speech of King Abijah when he confronted the northern kingdom in battle (13:4–12). The Israelites, he declared, rejected the covenant by driving out the

"Abijah stood up on Mount Zemaraim that is in the hill country of Ephraim and said, 'Hear me, O Jeroboam and all Israel! … Do not fight against the LORD, the God of your fathers, for you cannot succeed" (2 Chron. 13:4, 12). *An aerial looking westward at the likely region of Mount Zemaraim, near Bethel and Ai.*

Levites and appointing priests from any tribe. Abijah summarized the situation (13:11–12, author's translation): "We keep the charge of the LORD our God, but you have forsaken him. Behold, God is our leader." The outcome proved that Abijah had spoken the truth, for even though he had only half as many soldiers, his army defeated the northern kingdom. Even more, the Chronicler records (13:20–21): "[The northern king] Jeroboam did not recover his power…. the LORD struck him down, and he died. But Abijah grew mighty."

When the nation was disloyal to the Lord and his covenant, they suffered war, destruction of the army, loss of wealth, looting of the temple, deportation of the people, and ultimately exile (12:14–15; 25:24; 28:6–8; 36:20). These consequences were not "coincidental" but were the direct covenantal judgments that resulted from the actions of the king and the people. Key words that underscore the cause-effect relationship are "because" and "therefore." Ahaz "walked in the ways of the kings of Israel…. *Therefore* the LORD his God gave him over into the hand of the king of Syria [i.e., Aram]" (28:2, 5). Ahaz's father, however, was blessed: "Jotham became mighty *because* he ordered his ways before the LORD his God" (27:6). The Chronicler relentlessly emphasized God's faithfulness to bless and judge according to his covenant.

Accordingly, in the mind of the Chronicler, the ultimate reason for military success was *not* careful planning, advanced strategy, or superior forces. It was God, who favored those who trusted in him! When Asa faced a huge army near Mareshah, he prayed, expressing his complete dependence on the Lord (14:11). In response, "the LORD defeated the Ethiopians" (14:12). Similarly, the faithful Jehoshaphat did not marshal a formidable force, but "when they began to sing and

"When [the Levites under King Jehoshaphat] began to sing and praise, the LORD set an ambush against the men of Ammon, Moab, and Mount Seir, who had come against Judah, so that they were routed" (2 Chron. 20:22). *A Neo-Assyrian eighth century orthostat with musicians from Sinjerli in Asia Minor (from Istanbul Archaeological Museum).*

praise, the LORD set an ambush against the men … who had come against Judah, so that they were routed" (20:22). Joash, however, lost the battle despite his strength (24:24): "Though the army of the Syrians [i.e., Arameans] had come with few men, the LORD delivered into their hand a very great army, because Judah had forsaken the LORD, the God of their fathers. Thus they executed judgment on Joash." The only real weapon of consequence in Israel's arsenal was the Lord himself.

The Necessity of Perseverance

Covenant obedience, however, was not a one-time decision. Loyalty to Yahweh required a daily submission to his will. The Chronicler recalled many kings who started faithfully but then strayed from the path. Again, King Asa serves as an excellent example of this. "Asa did what was good and right in the eyes of the LORD his God" (2 Chron. 14:2), and when confronted by the Ethiopians, God delivered him in an awesome display of power (14:9–15). But near the end of his life, Asa foolishly sought help from a foreign king rather than from the Lord. A prophet confronted Asa, but not only did Asa refuse to repent, he also put the prophet in prison and "inflicted cruelties" upon some of his people (16:10). Unfortunately, Asa never returned to Yahweh, and he died in defiance (16:1–14).

A similar story is recounted for Uzziah, who early in life was radically committed to covenant obedience. However, the Chronicler adds this ominous note (26:5, 16): "*As long as* he sought the LORD, God made him prosper…. But when he was strong, he grew proud, to his destruction. For he was unfaithful to the LORD his God." As a result, he died an isolated leper (26:21). With these and other examples, the Chronicler warned that early faithfulness does not guarantee later faithfulness. The exhortation is not simply to be loyal to the Lord, but to remain true to the end.

> In the New Testament we are told that "God opposes the proud, but gives grace to the humble" (James 4:6; 1 Peter 5:5) and that "we have come to share in Christ, if indeed we hold our original confidence firm to the end" (Heb. 3:14; cf. 1 John 2:19). Thanks be to God that Christ's obedience has secured for believers every spiritual blessing and the promise of full inheritance (Rom. 5:18–21; Eph. 1:3, 13–14) and that our God of grace is both able and willing to sanctify us and keep us blameless until Christ's return (2 Cor. 9:8; Phil. 1:6; 1 Thess. 5:23–24).

The Author of 1–2 Chronicles Called for *Seeking Yahweh in Humility and Faith*

Faithfulness to the Lord requires seeking him with all of one's life. David charged the leaders of Israel, "Now set your heart and soul to seek the LORD your God" (1 Chron. 22:19, author's translation). Similarly, the men of Asa's day committed "to seek the LORD, the God of their fathers, with all their heart and with all their soul" (2 Chron. 15:12). This is not a vain pursuit, for "if you seek him, he will be found by you" (1 Chron. 28:9; cf. Deut. 4:29).

The Plea for Genuine Humility

The most well-known verse of Chronicles emphasizes the need to seek the Lord in humility: "If my people who are called by my name humble themselves, and pray and seek my face and turn from their wicked ways,

"If my people who are called by my name humble themselves, and pray and seek my face and turn from their wicked ways, then I will hear from heaven and will forgive their sin and heal their land" (2 Chron. 7:14). *A Jewish man praying at the Western Wall in Jerusalem.*

then I will hear from heaven and will forgive their sin and heal their land" (2 Chron. 7:14). Solomon knew that the people would never be able to keep Yahweh's commands perfectly, and so he exhorted them to repent and confess, "We have sinned and have acted perversely and wickedly" (6:36–37). God heard the cries of those who sought him in humility, and he delivered repentant kings from his wrath and from foreign invasion (12:7; 32:20–26). The classic example is Manasseh, whose evil set new records, but whom God forgave and restored when the king "entreated the favor of the Lord his God and humbled himself greatly before the God of his fathers" (33:12).

Repentance is not a matter of reciting certain words, for the Chronicler repeatedly showed that repentance results in a new direction of life. For example, after Manasseh repented, he "knew that the LORD was God," and he destroyed the idols in the land and restored the altar of the Lord (33:13–16). Similarly, when the people turned from their sinful practices and made a covenant to be "the LORD's people," they tore down the temple of Baal and smashed the pagan altars (23:16–17). When Josiah heard the Book of the Law read, he ripped his royal robes as a sign of his deep sorrow over sin, and he instituted far-reaching reforms (34:19–33). Josiah's son Zedekiah, however, "did not humble himself before Jeremiah the prophet," and Jerusalem was destroyed, the temple burned, and the king deported to Babylon (36:12–20).

The Need for Complete Trust

The one who humbles himself recognizes both his own weakness and his need to rely on another. Some kings were humbled by their circumstances, but they did not seek God in faith. Other kings turned to the Lord, and the Chronicler preserved a magnificent collection of prayers that exalted God and brought blessing. Asa's prayer is an exemplary model of humility and faith (2 Chron. 14:11): "O LORD, there is none like you to help, between the mighty and the weak. Help us, O LORD our God, for we rely on you, and in your name we have come against this multitude. O LORD, you are our God; let not man prevail against you." Here both God-dependence and a passion for Yahweh's supremacy ring forth. Asa's son Jehoshaphat must have learned this lesson from his father, for he prayed, "We do not know what to do, but our eyes are on you" (20:12). It is difficult to imagine a national leader in our own day publicly humbling himself and trusting God alone!

> Jesus tells us that the Father loves for his children to seek him: "Ask, and it will be given to you; seek, and you will find; knock, and it will be opened to you" (Matt. 7:7).

Trust must be complete—there is no such thing as partially trusting the Lord. One who trusts in something *in addition to* God is, in fact, not trusting Yahweh at all. This was the sad conclusion of Asa's life, when the prophet condemned him with these familiar words: "For the eyes of the LORD run to and fro throughout the whole earth, to give strong support to those *whose heart is blameless toward him*" (16:9). Because Asa trusted in a foreign king instead of Yahweh, he was condemned to be at war the rest of his life. When Hezekiah, however, was asked by the Assyrian king Sennacherib, "On what are you trusting?" he refused to waver but "prayed … and cried to heaven," and Yahweh wiped out the army of the enemy (32:10–22).

"This same Hezekiah closed the upper outlet of the waters of Gihon and directed them down to the west side of the city of David" (2 Chron. 32:30). *Hezekiah's Tunnel under the City of David, which redirected the water of the Gihon Spring, thus securing a sustained water source for the Judeans during King Sennacherib's siege (2 Chron. 32:2–4; 2 Kings 20:20; Isa. 22:9, 11; Ben Sira 48:17; see also the Siloam Tunnel Inscription from the time of Hezekiah,* ANET *321;* COS *2:145–146).*

The Author of 1–2 Chronicles Exalted Yahweh as *the Sovereign Lord* over Judah, Israel, and the Nations

Though the focus of Chronicles largely centers on Jerusalem and the tribe of Judah, the Chronicler's message is a universal one, meant for all people of all nations. Yahweh is not just the God of Judah, but of all twelve tribes of Israel, and indeed of every nation on earth. He is the creator of all men, and he is not owned or controlled by any single group or nation.

The True King in Jerusalem

Although Chronicles tells the stories of twenty(-two) kings of Judah, all of them were more properly "vice-regents," ruling at the decision of God.

Yahweh was the true king of Israel—a fact recognized even by the Queen of Sheba who declared to Solomon: "Blessed be the LORD your God, who has delighted in you and set you *on his throne* as king" (2 Chron. 9:8). Or as David declared (1 Chron. 29:11–12): "Yours is the kingdom, O LORD, and you are exalted as head above all…. You rule over all." The Lord was not sovereign in name alone, for he chose Judah as the leader and David from among all of Judah's families (17:7; 28:4–5). God selected Jerusalem as the place for his Name, and he installed Solomon as David's successor and appointed him temple builder (2 Chron. 6:6–9). Just as many earthly monarchs made covenants with their subjects, so the heavenly king established a covenant with his people (6:14).

The Merciful Protector of Israel

One distinctive of Chronicles is the omission of information about the northern kingdom, Israel. The book of Kings described the reigns of Israel's rulers at length, but Chronicles insisted that Yahweh rejected any nation that rejected him. In not addressing the north, however, the Chronicler was not saying that the northern tribes had been "lost," since a faithful remnant was indeed preserved within Judah. The genealogies attest to this reality (1 Chron. 5, 7), since there would be no point in listing the northern tribes if they had disappeared.

Faithful men and women in the north immigrated to Judah when Jeroboam led the nation into idolatry (2 Chron. 11:13–16). Large numbers from "Ephraim, Manasseh, and Simeon deserted to [Asa] from Israel when they saw that the LORD his God was with him" (15:9). When Hezekiah held the great Passover celebration, he invited "all Israel and Judah … from Beersheba to Dan" (30:1, 5), and while some ridiculed, others "humbled themselves and came to Jerusalem" (30:10–11). Josiah carried out religious reforms in the north, and "all the remnant of Israel" contributed to the temple purification (34:6–9). The remnant that returned from exile in Babylon included northerners, and truly they could rejoice in God's faithful hand of protection (1 Chron. 9:1–3).

The Great God over the Nations

Yahweh ruled not only over not only the twelve tribes of Israel, but also all of the nations. As David sang, "For all the gods of the peoples are worthless idols, but the LORD made the heavens" (1 Chron.

> The Chronicler would tell us to declare God's supreme worth among all peoples—in our families, in our community, in our country, and around the world!

16:26). On this basis, every person owes his complete allegiance to his Maker. Yahweh chose Israel to be a light to the nations, and when godly kings ruled, "all the nations feared" Yahweh and his people (14:17; 2 Chron. 17:10–11; cf. 9:23). King Hiram of Tyre even declared Yahweh's supremacy over all: "Blessed be the Lord God of Israel, who made heaven and earth" (2 Chron. 2:12). In his dedicatory prayer at the temple, Solomon recognized the foreigner who came "from a far country for the sake of [God's] great name," and he asked Yahweh to "do according to all for which the foreigner calls to you, in order that all the peoples of the earth may know your name and fear you" (6:32–33). David captured the great commission of Chronicles in his song, "Let them say among the nations, 'The Lord reigns!'" (1 Chron. 16:31).

"For all the gods of the peoples are worthless idols, but the Lord made the heavens. Splendor and majesty are before him; strength and joy are in his place.... Let the heavens be glad, and let the earth rejoice, and let them say among the nations, 'The Lord reigns!'" (1 Chron. 16:26, 31). *Sunset over the Mediterranean Sea.*

Conclusion

Standing at the end of the Old Testament, Chronicles calls Yahweh's post-exilic community to learn the best from the past and to always see God as one who is faithful, sovereign, and gracious. It calls people to pursue God in the present, looking through punishment to renewal, through curse to restoration blessing. Such a quest is grounded in the Lord's faithfulness to his purpose begun with Adam and to his promises to his people, especially David.

Ezra-Nehemiah begins where Chronicles ends (Ezra 1:1–3; 2 Chron. 36:22–23), but the placement of Chronicles as the conclusion to Jesus' Bible and after Ezra-Nehemiah (in reverse chronological order) causes the Old Testament to end on an eschatological note.[1] That is, the canonical arrangement suggests that the initial restoration detailed in Ezra-Nehemiah and observed in Chronicles (1 Chron. 3:17–23; 9:1–44) was only the beginning and that Yahweh's people must continue to look ahead in faith, toward Jerusalem, in hope of God's full kingdom restoration. More was to come, and the fulfillment begins to be disclosed on the Bible's next page, which opens, "The book of the genealogy of Jesus Christ, the son of David" (Matt. 1:1). The charge of King Cyrus in the final verse of Chronicles becomes a rallying cry of hope that the work God had started, he would complete (2 Chron. 36:23): "The LORD, the God of heaven … has charged me to build him a house at Jerusalem, which is in Judah. Whoever is among you of all his people, may the LORD his God be with him. Let him go up."

---

1. So M. J. Selman, "Chronicles," in *New Dictionary of Biblical Theology* (Downers Grove, IL: InterVarsity, 2000), 192–193; Stephen G. Dempster, *Dominion and Dynasty: A Theology of the Hebrew Bible* (NSBT 15; Downers Grove, IL: InterVarsity, 2003), 224.

KEY WORDS AND CONCEPTS FOR REVIEW

Post-exile	Humility, faith
Jerusalem	Seek, forsake
Chronicler	Yahweh's sovereignty
1–2 Kings versus 1–2 Chronicles	Vice-regents
Davidic covenant	Remnant
Temple	Nations
Mosaic (old) covenant	Eschatological note
Retribution principle	

KEY RESOURCES FOR FURTHER STUDY

Boda, Mark J. *1–2 Chronicles*. CBC. Carol Stream, IL:Tyndale, 2010.

Hill, Andrew. *1 and 2 Chronicles*. NIVAC. Grand Rapids: Zondervan, 2003.

Selman, Martin J. *1 Chronicles* and *2 Chronicles*. TOTC. Downers Grove, IL: InterVarsity, 2008.

Thompson, J. A. *1, 2 Chronicles*. NAC. Nashville: B&H, 1994.

EXPANDED FIGURES

Figure A.1. The Genres of the Psalms in Canonical Order

Key	(i)	Individual	David (73x)	Asaph (12x)		Solomon (2x)	Ethan the Ezrahite (1x)
	(c)	Corporate	Anonymous	The Sons of Korah (12x)		Moses (1x)	

Ps.	Genre	Comment	Ps.	Genre	Comment
BOOK 1			19	Mixed	Praise, Wisdom/Torah
1	Wisdom	Introduction: Theme 1–Right living by Torah (Wisdom)	20	Royal	
			21	Royal	
2	Royal	Introduction: Theme 2–Eschatology	22	Lament (i)	
			23	Trust (i)	
3	Lament (i)		24	Liturgy	
4	Lament (i)	Strong element of trust	25	Mixed	Acrostic; Lament = vv. 1–7, 16–27; Wisdom = vv. 8–15
5	Lament (i)				
6	Lament	1st Penitential Psalm	26	Lament (i)	
7	Lament (i)		27	Lament (i)	Strong element of trust
8	Praise	Creation emphasis	28	Lament (i)	
9/10	Mixed	Acrostic; Originally one psalm	29	Praise	
11	Trust (i)		30	Thanksgiving (i)	
12	Lament (c)		31	Mixed	Lament/Thanksgiving
13	Lament (i)		32	Mixed	Thanksgiving/Wisdom; 2nd Penitential Psalm
14	Lament (c)	= Psalm 53			
15	Liturgy		33	Praise	
16	Trust (i)		34	Mixed	Thanksgiving/Wisdom; Acrostic
17	Lament (i)				
18	Royal	Thanksgiving	35	Lament (i)	Contains "imprecations"

36	Mixed	Wisdom, Praise, Lament
37	Wisdom	Acrostic
38	Lament (i)	3rd Penitential psalm
39	Lament (i)	
40	Mixed	Thanksgiving = vv. 1–10; Lament = vv. 11–17
41	Lament (i)	

BOOK 2

42/43	Lament (i)	Originally one psalm
44	Lament (c)	
45	Royal	A wedding song
46	Praise	1st "Song of Zion"
47	Praise	"Enthronement of Yahweh" Psalm
48	Praise	2nd "Song of Zion"
49	Wisdom	
50	Unclear	Prophecy? Praise?
51	Lament (i)	4th Penitential Psalm
52	Unclear	Lament? Prophecy?
53	Lament (c)	= Psalm 14
54	Lament (i)	
55	Lament (i)	Contains "imprecations"
56	Lament (i)	
57	Lament (i)	
58	Lament (c)	
59	Lament (i)	Contains "imprecations"
60	Lament (c)	
61	Lament (i)	
62	Unclear	Trust? Lament?
63	Lament (i)	
64	Lament (i)	
65	Mixed	Praise? Thanksgiving? Creation?
66	Thanksgiving	Individual? Corporate?
67	Unclear	Praise? A meditation on Numbers 6:24–26?
68	Unclear	Praise? Thanksgiving?
69	Lament (i)	Contains "imprecations"
70	Lament (i)	
71	Lament (i)	
72	Royal	

BOOK 3

73	Wisdom	
74	Lament (c)	
75	Unclear	Thanksgiving or Praise
76	Praise	3rd "Song of Zion"
77	Lament	Individual or Corporate
78	Historical	
79	Lament (c)	Contains "imprecations"
80	Lament (c)	
81	Unclear	Praise? Liturgy?
82	Lament (c)	
83	Lament (c)	
84	Praise	4th "Song of Zion"
85	Lament (c)	
86	Lament (i)	
87	Praise	5th "Song of Zion"
88	Lament (i)	By "Heman the Ezrahite," a son of Korah
89	Mixed	Praise = vv. 1–37; Lament = vv. 38–51

BOOK 4

90	Lament (c)	
91	Trust (i)	
92	Thanksgiving (i)	
93	Praise	"Enthronement of Yahweh" Psalm
94	Lament	
95	Praise	
96	Praise	"Enthronement of Yahweh" Psalm
97	Praise	"Enthronement of Yahweh" Psalm
98	Praise	"Enthronement of Yahweh" Psalm
99	Praise	"Enthronement of Yahweh" Psalm
100	Praise	

101	Royal	
102	Lament (i)	By "an afflicted man"
103	Praise	
104	Praise	Creation emphasis
105	Praise	Historical emphasis
106	Lament (c)	Historical emphasis

BOOK 5

107	Thanksgiving	
108	Lament (c)	Vv. 1–5 = Ps. 57:7–11; Vv. 6–13 = Ps. 60:5–12
109	Lament (i)	Contains "imprecations"
110	Royal	
111	Praise	Acrostic
112	Wisdom	Acrostic
113	Praise	
114	Praise	
115	Unclear	Trust, Praise, Petition
116	Thanksgiving (i)	
117	Praise	
118	Thanksgiving	
119	Mixed	Acrostic; Wisdom/Torah, Praise, Lament
120	Lament (i)	A "Psalm of Ascent"
121	Trust	A "Psalm of Ascent"
122	Praise	A "Psalm of Ascent"
123	Lament (c)	A "Psalm of Ascent"
124	Thanksgiving (c)	A "Psalm of Ascent"
125	Trust (c)	A "Psalm of Ascent"

126	Lament (c)	A "Psalm of Ascent"
127	Wisdom	A "Psalm of Ascent"
128	Wisdom	A "Psalm of Ascent"
129	Trust	A "Psalm of Ascent"
130	Lament (i)	A "Psalm of Ascent" – 6th Penitential Psalm
131	Trust (i)	A "Psalm of Ascent"
132	Royal	A "Psalm of Ascent"
133	Unclear	A "Psalm of Ascent"
134	Praise	A "Psalm of Ascent"
135	Praise	
136	Praise	
137	Lament (c)	Contains "imprecations"
138	Thanksgiving (i)	
139	Unclear	
140	Lament (i)	
141	Lament (i)	
142	Lament (i)	
143	Lament (i)	7th Penitential psalm
144	Royal	
145	Praise	Acrostic
146	Praise	
147	Praise	
148	Praise	Creation emphasis
149	Praise	
150	Praise	Conclusion: Theme 3–Worship

Prepared by John C. Crutchfield. For an abridged version of this material that only lists the psalms by genre category, see chapter 16, Fig. 16.5.

Figure A.2. General Content Distinctions of Old Testament Laws

Rom. 13:8–10. Owe no one anything, except to love each other, for the one who loves another has fulfilled the law. For the commandments ... are summed up in this word: "You shall love your neighbor as yourself." Love does no wrong to a neighbor; therefore love is the fulfilling of the law.

	Description	Example
Criminal	Laws governing crimes or offenses that put the whole community at risk; the offended party is the state or national community, and therefore the punishment is on behalf of the whole community in the name of the highest state authority, which in Israel meant Yahweh.	1. Kidnapping (Exod. 21:16; Deut. 24:7) 2. Sustained insubordination to parents (Exod. 21:15, 17; Deut. 21:18–21) 3. Homicide / Premeditated or avoidable murder (Exod. 21:14; Num. 35:16–21, 30–31; Deut. 19:11–13) 4. Religious malpractice like Sabbath breaking (Exod. 31:14–15; 35:2; cf. Num. 15:32–36); false prophecy (Deut. 13:1–5; 18:20); idolatry (Exod. 22:20; Lev. 19:4; Deut. 13:1–18; 17:2–7); child sacrifice (Lev. 20:1–5); witchcraft (Exod. 22:18; Lev. 19:26, 31; 20:27); blasphemy (see Lev. 24:14–23) 5. Sexual offenses like adultery when married or engaged (Lev. 20:10; Deut. 22:22–24; cf. Gen. 38:24); concealed premarital unchastity (Deut. 22:20–21); rape of an engaged girl (Deut. 22:25); prostitution of a priest's daughter (Lev. 21:9); incest (Lev. 20:11–12, 14); homosexuality (Lev. 20:13); bestiality (Exod. 22:19; Lev. 20:15–16) 6. False witness in a capital case (Deut. 19:16–21) *Note: Nearly all the commands and prohibitions in the Decalogue are considered criminal offenses.

Exod. 21:23–25. You shall pay life for life, eye for eye, tooth for tooth, hand for hand, foot for foot, burn for burn, wound for wound, stripe for stripe. Deut. 17:8–9. If any case arises ... within your towns that is too difficult for you, then you shall arise and go up to the place that the LORD your God will choose. And you shall come to the Levitical priests and to the judge .... and you shall consult them, they shall declare to you the decision.

	Description	Example
Civil	Laws governing private disputes between citizens in which the public authorities are appealed to for judgment or called upon to intervene; the offended party is not the state or national community.	1. Non-premeditated killing like accidental death (Exod. 21:13; Num. 35:9–15; Deut. 19:1–13) or death due to self-defense (Exod. 22:2) 2. Assault whether human against human (Exod. 21:18–19, 22), animal against human (21:28–32), animal against animal (21:33–36) 3. Breaches of trust like theft (Exod. 22:1–4, 7–9, 12; Lev. 19:11, 13) or destruction of property (Exod. 22:5, 6, 14) 4. Falsehood as a witness in non-capital case (Exod. 23:1–3) or in commerce/trade (Lev. 19:35–36) 5. Limited family issues like premarital unchastity between consenting adults, whether real (Exod. 22:16–17; Lev. 19:20–22; Deut. 22:28–29) or potential (Deut. 22:13–21); post-divorce situations (Deut. 24:1–3); the mistreatment of slaves (Exod. 21:20–21, 26–27; the handling of runaway slaves (Deut. 23:15–16); failure to accept levirate marriage duties (25:7–10)

Deut. 11:18–20. You shall therefore lay up these words of mine in your heart and in your soul, and you shall bind them as a sign on your hand, and they shall be as frontlets between your eyes. You shall teach them to your children, talking of them when you are sitting in your house, and when you are walking by the way, and when you lie down, and when you rise. You shall write them on the doorposts of your house and on your gates.

	Description	Example
Family	Non-civil, domestic laws governing the Israelite household.	1. Levirate marriage (Deut. 25:5–6) 2. Inheritance (Deut. 21:15–16) 3. Jubilee and the redemption of land and persons (Lev. 25) 4. Family discipleship (Deut. 6:6, 20–25; 11:18–21) 5. Respect of and obedience to parents (Exod. 20:20; Lev. 19:3; Deut. 5:16) 6. Turning a daughter into a prostitute (Lev. 19:29) 7. Slavery including limits of service, inheritance, and protection (Exod. 21:2–11; Deut. 15:1–23) 8. Maintaining gender distinctions (Deut. 22:5)

What the Old Testament Authors Really Cared About

Lev. 20:25–26. You shall not make yourselves detestable by beast or by bird or by anything with which the ground crawls, which I have set apart for you to hold unclean. You shall be holy to me, for I the LORD am holy and have separated you from the peoples, that you should be mine.

Cultic/Ceremonial

Laws governing the visible forms and rituals of Israel's religious life, including those sacred symbols that distinguished Israel from the nations and provided parables of more fundamental truths about God and relating to him.

Sacrifice:

1. Altar and sacrifices (Exod. 20:24–26)
2. Offering of firstfruits (Exod. 22:29–30; 23:19)
3. Sacrifices: general guidelines (Exod. 23:18; 29:38–46; Lev. 1–7; 19:5–8; Day of Atonement (Lev. 16); location (Lev. 17:1–9; Deut. 12)

Sacred Calendar:

4. Weekly Sabbaths (Exod. 20:8–11; 23:12; 31:12–17; 35:1–3; Lev. 19:3, 30; Deut. 5:12–15)
5. Sabbatical year (Exod. 23:10–11; Lev. 25:3–7; Deut. 15:1–6)
6. Feasts & sacred days (Exod. 23:14–19; 34:22–23; Lev. 23:9–22; Deut. 16:1–17)
7. Jubilee (Lev. 25:8–55)

Sacred Symbolism and Distinction:

8. Tabernacle (Exod. 25–30)
9. Priesthood: garments (Exod. 28); consecration (Exod. 29:1–37; Lev. 8); administration of sacrifices (Exod. 29:38–46; Lev. 6–7)
10. Ritual Purity (Clean/Unclean): food laws (Lev. 11:2–47; 20:24–26; Deut. 14:4–20) and the eating of blood (Lev. 17:10–16; 19:26); childbirth (Lev. 12); leprosy (Lev. 13–14); bodily discharges (Lev. 15)
11. Distinction from the pagan nations in cases like "interbreeding/mixing" of cattle, seeds, garments (Lev. 19:19; Deut. 22:9–11) and trimming of sideburns, cutting of body, tattoos (Lev. 19:27–28)

Compassion

Deut. 24:17–18. You shall not pervert the justice due to the sojourner or to the fatherless, or take a widow's garment in pledge, but you shall remember that you were a slave in Egypt and Yahweh your God redeemed you from there; therefore I command you to do this.

"Laws" dealing with charity, justice, and mercy toward others.

1. Protection and care of others like the sojourner (Exods. 22:21; 23:9; Lev. 19:9–10, 33–34; Deut. 14:28–29; 24:19–22); the widow and orphan (Exod. 22:22–24; Deut. 14:28–29; 24:19–22); the poor (Exod. 22:25–27; 23:6; Lev. 19:9–10; Deut. 15:7–11; 24:10–13, 19–22); one's neighbor (19:13, 16–18); the disabled (Lev. 19:14; Deut. 27:18); the Levite (Deut. 14:28–29); the released slave (Deut. 15:12–15); hired servant (Deut. 24:14–15)
2. Justice and impartiality (Exod. 23:7–8; Lev. 19:15; Deut. 24:17–18; 27:19, 25)
3. Honor of the elderly (Lev. 19:32)
4. Return of an enemy or brother's lost goods (Exod. 22:4; Deut. 22:1–3)
5. Help of an enemy or brother in need (Exod. 23:5; Deut. 22:4)
6. Excusal from war for a new homeowner (Deut. 20:5); a new business owner (Deut. 20:6); a newly married man (Deut. 20:7; 24:5)
7. Marriage to foreign widows of war (Deut. 20:10–14)
8. Preservation of means for food for future generations (Deut. 20:6–7; 25:4)
9. Building safe homes (Deut. 20:8)
10. Respect for other's means of sustenance (Deut. 23:24–25; 24:6)

Prepared by Jason S. DeRouchie and Kenneth J. Turner. The categories are taken from Christopher J. H. Wright, *Old Testament Ethics for the People of God* (Downers Grove, IL: InterVarsity, 2004), 288–301, which he adapted from Anthony Phillips, *Ancient Israel's Criminal Law: A New Approach to the Decalogue* (New York: Schocken Books, 1970), 2, 13. The examples are only illustrative. For an abridged version of this material, see chapter 3, Fig. 3.4.

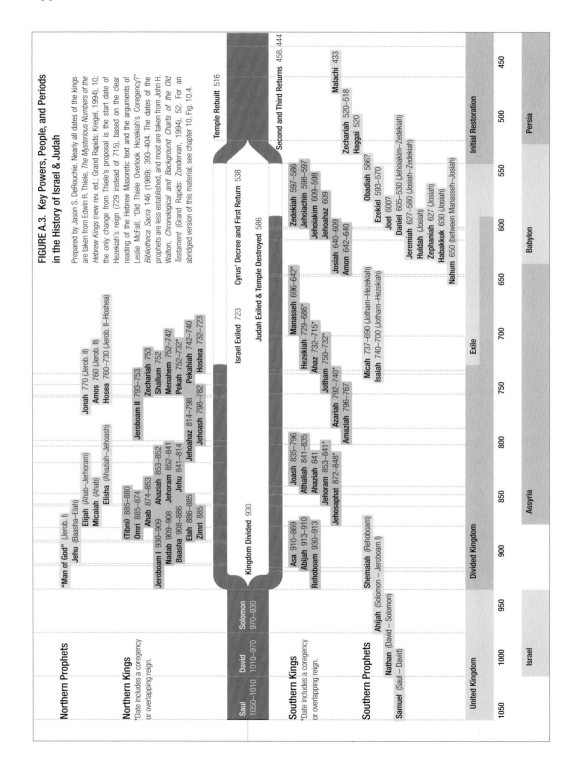

FIGURE A.3. Key Powers, People, and Periods in the History of Israel & Judah

Prepared by Jason S. DeRouchie. Nearly all dates of the kings are taken from Edwin R. Thiele, *The Mysterious Numbers of the Hebrew Kings* (new rev. ed.; Grand Rapids: Kregel, 1994), 10; the only change from Thiele's proposal is the start date of Hezekiah's reign (729 instead of 715), based on the clear reading of the Hebrew Masoretic text and the arguments of Leslie McFall, "Did Thiele Overlook Hezekiah's Coregency?" *Bibliotheca Sacra* 146 (1989): 393–404. The dates of the prophets are less established, and most are taken from John H. Walton, *Chronological and Background Charts of the Old Testament* (Grand Rapids: Zondervan, 1994), 52. For an abridged version of this material, see chapter 10, Fig. 10.4.

KEY OLD TESTAMENT CHAPTERS

To understand a biblical author's main point, it is sometimes helpful to know which chapters are most crucial to a book's message. The list below attempts to capture these "key chapters."

LAW
Gen. 1–3, 9, 12, 15, 17, 22, 49
Exod. 3–4, 7, 9, 12–15, 19–20, 24, 32–34
Lev. 9–10, 16, 19, 26
Num. 1–2, 13–14, 22, 24
Deut. 4–11, 28–30, 32

PROPHETS
Josh. 1, 6–8, 24
Judg. 2–3, 19–21
1 Sam. 1–3, 8, 12, 15–17
2 Sam. 7, 11–12, 24
1 Kings 3, 8, 11–12, 18, 22
2 Kings 17–19, 21–23, 25
Jer. 1, 7–9, 16, 23, 31–33, 36, 39
Ezek. 1, 8–11, 36–37
Isa. 6–11, 40–42, 44, 49, 52–53, 65–66
Hos. 1–3
Joel 1–2
Amos 4–5, 9
Obad. 1
Jonah 2, 4
Mic. 3–4

PROPHETS CONTINUED
Nah. 1
Hab. 1, 3
Zeph. 2–3
Hag. 1–2
Zech. 3–4, 8
Mal. 3:16–4:6

WRITINGS
Ruth 3–4
Pss. 1–2, 8, 19, 23, 42–43, 51, 72, 89, 110, 136, 145–150
Job 1–2, 19, 28, 38–42
Prov. 1–2, 8–9, 31
Eccl. 1, 6, 9, 12
Song 7–8
Lam. 3
Dan. 1, 2, 7, 9
Esther 3–4, 7–10
Ezra 7, 9–10
Neh. 1, 8–9
1 Chron. 17, 29
2 Chron. 3–7, 16–17, 34–36
Prepared by Jason S. DeRouchie

THE KINGDOM BIBLE READING PLAN

In Deuteronomy, Moses sets forth the following pattern for enjoying life with God: the *reading* of Scripture opens the door for *hearing* from God, which enables one to *learn to fear* him, which leads to *following* him (Deut. 31:12–13; cf. 6:1–3; 17:19–20; John 6:44–45). How foundational God's written revelation is to our very existence! "It is no empty word for you, but your very life" (Deut. 32:47). Only through an encounter with God's pure, perfect, true, and abiding Word (Pss. 12:6; 119:96, 160) can people be:

- Reborn in Christ (Ps. 119:93; Rom. 10:17; James 1:18); 1 Peter 1:23
- Empowered for holiness (Ps. 119:50; John 17:17; 2 Tim. 3:17; 2 Peter 1:4),
- Sustained to glory (Deut. 8:3; Rom. 1:16; 2 Tim. 3:15),
- Satisfied always (Pss. 1:2; 19:10; 1 Peter 2:3).

Man lives through "every word that comes from the mouth of God" (Matt. 4:4; cf. Deut. 8:3), so our whole being must be saturated in Scripture (Deut. 6:7; Josh. 1:7–8; Pss. 1:3; 78:5–8). We must seek its truths like silver, think deeply over its teachings, and we must passionately desire our study to generate reverence, dependence, and obedience and to overflow in proclamation—all in a way that points to the worth of the One who has revealed himself in it (Isa. 66:2; Prov. 2:4; Ezra 7:10; 2 Tim. 2:7, 15; 1 Peter 4:11).

As God's disclosure of himself and his purposes in a way we can understand, the Bible is about the good news of God's kingdom—a kingdom established through covenant for God's glory in Christ (Luke 4:43; 24:44–47;

Acts 1:3; 20:25; 26:22–23; 28:23, 31). The KINGDOM Bible Reading Plan derives its name from the Bible's kingdom framework. The plan is distinguished by the following features:

- Proportionate weight is given to the Old and New Testaments in view of their relative length, the Old receiving three readings per day and the New getting one reading per day.

- The Old Testament readings follow the arrangement of Jesus' Bible (Luke 24:44—Law, Prophets, Writings), with one reading coming from each portion per day.

- In a single year, one reads through Psalms twice and all other biblical books once; the second reading of Psalms (highlighted in blue) supplements the readings through the Law (Genesis–Deuteronomy).

- Only twenty-five readings are slated per month in order to provide flexibility in daily devotions.

- The plan can be started at any time of the year, and if four readings per day are too much, the plan can simply be stretched to two or more years (reading from one, two, or three columns per day).

May you grow in grace as you read the Scripture. I hope you enjoy the KINGDOM Bible Reading Plan.

—Jason S. DeRouchie

JANUARY

Days	OT Law (and Pss.)	OT Prophets	OT Writings	NT
	Gen.	Josh.	Ruth	Matt.
1.	❏ 1:1–2:3	❏ 1–2	❏ 1	❏ 1
2.	❏ 2:4–25	❏ 3–4	❏ 2	❏ 2
3.	❏ 3	❏ 5–6	❏ 3–4	❏ 3
			Pss.	
4.	❏ 4	❏ 7	❏ 1–2	❏ 4
5.	❏ 5:1–6:8	❏ 8	❏ 3–4	❏ 5:1–20
6.	❏ 6:9–7:24	❏ 9	❏ 5–6	❏ 5:21–48
7.	❏ 8	❏ 10	❏ 7–8	❏ 6
8.	❏ 9	❏ 11–12	❏ 9	❏ 7
9.	❏ 10:1–11:9	❏ 13–14	❏ 10	❏ 8
10.	❏ 11:10–32	❏ 15–16	❏ 11–12	❏ 9
11.	❏ 12	❏ 17–18	❏ 13–14	❏ 10
12.	❏ 13	❏ 19	❏ 15–16	❏ 11
13.	❏ 14	❏ 20–21	❏ 17	❏ 12:1–21
14.	❏ 15	❏ 22	❏ 18	❏ 12:22–50
15.	❏ 16	❏ 23–24	❏ 19	❏ 13:1–30
		Judg.		
16.	❏ 17	❏ 1	❏ 20–21	❏ 13:31–58
17.	❏ 18	❏ 2	❏ 22	❏ 14
18.	❏ 19	❏ 3	❏ 23–24	❏ 15
19.	❏ 20	❏ 4	❏ 25	❏ 16
20.	❏ 21	❏ 5	❏ 26	❏ 17
21.	❏ 22	❏ 6	❏ 27	❏ 18
22.	❏ 23	❏ 7	❏ 28–29	❏ 19
23.	❏ 24:1–28	❏ 8	❏ 30	❏ 20
24.	❏ 24:29–67	❏ 9	❏ 31	❏ 21:1–22
25.	❏ 25	❏ 10–11	❏ 32–33	❏ 21:23–46

FEBRUARY

Days	OT Law (and Pss.)	OT Prophets	OT Writings	NT
	Gen.	Judg.	Pss.	Matt.
1.	❏ 26	❏ 12–13	❏ 34	❏ 22
2.	❏ 27	❏ 14–15	❏ 35	❏ 23
3.	❏ 28	❏ 16	❏ 36	❏ 24:1–28
4.	❏ 29	❏ 17–18	❏ 37	❏ 24:29–51
5.	❏ 30	❏ 19	❏ 38	❏ 25
6.	❏ Pss. 1–2	❏ 20	❏ 39	❏ 26:1–35
7.	❏ Pss. 3–4	❏ 21	❏ 40	❏ 26:36–75
		1 Sam.		
8.	❏ 31:1–24	❏ 1:1–2:11	❏ 41	❏ 27:1–31
9.	❏ 31:25–55	❏ 2:12–36	❏ 42–43	❏ 27:32–66
10.	❏ 32	❏ 3–4	❏ 44	❏ 28
				Mark
11.	❏ 33	❏ 5–6	❏ 45	❏ 1:1–20
12.	❏ Pss. 5–6	❏ 7–8	❏ 46–47	❏ 1:21–45
13.	❏ Pss. 7–8	❏ 9	❏ 48	❏ 2
14.	❏ 34	❏ 10–11	❏ 49	❏ 3
15.	❏ 35	❏ 12	❏ 50	❏ 4
16.	❏ 36:1–37:1	❏ 13	❏ 51	❏ 5
17.	❏ Pss. 9–10	❏ 14	❏ 52–54	❏ 6:1–29
18.	❏ Pss. 11–13	❏ 15	❏ 55	❏ 6:30–56
19.	❏ 37:2–36	❏ 16	❏ 56	❏ 7
20.	❏ 38	❏ 17	❏ 57	❏ 8:1–9:1
21.	❏ 39	❏ 18	❏ 58	❏ 9:2–29
22.	❏ 40	❏ 19	❏ 59	❏ 9:30–50
23.	❏ Pss. 14–16	❏ 20	❏ 60–61	❏ 10:1–31
24.	❏ Ps. 17	❏ 21–22	❏ 62	❏ 10:32–52
25.	❏ Ps. 18	❏ 23–24	❏ 63–64	❏ 11

MARCH

Days	OT Law (and Pss.)	OT Prophets	OT Writings	NT
	Gen.	1 Sam.	Pss.	Mark
1.	❏ 41:1–36	❏ 25	❏ 65	❏ 12:1–17
2.	❏ 41:37–57	❏ 26–27	❏ 66–67	❏ 12:18–44
3.	❏ 42	❏ 28–29	❏ 68	❏ 13
4.	❏ Ps. 19	❏ 30–31	❏ 69	❏ 14:1–31
		2 Sam.		
5.	❏ Pss. 20–21	❏ 1	❏ 70–71	❏ 14:32–72
6.	❏ 43	❏ 2	❏ 72	❏ 15
7.	❏ 44	❏ 3	❏ 73	❏ 16
				Luke
8.	❏ 45	❏ 4–5	❏ 74	❏ 1:1–38
9.	❏ 46	❏ 6	❏ 75–76	❏ 1:39–80
10.	❏ 47	❏ 7	❏ 77	❏ 2:1–21
11.	❏ Ps. 22	❏ 8–9	❏ 78:1–39	❏ 2:22–52
12.	❏ Pss. 23–24	❏ 10–11	❏ 78:40–72	❏ 3
13.	❏ 48	❏ 12	❏ 79	❏ 4:1–30
14.	❏ 49	❏ 13	❏ 80	❏ 4:31–44
15.	❏ 50	❏ 14	❏ 81–82	❏ 5
16.	❏ Ps. 25	❏ 15	❏ 83	❏ 6:1–16
17.	❏ Ps. 26	❏ 16	❏ 84	❏ 6:17–49
	Exod.			
18.	❏ 1–2	❏ 17	❏ 85	❏ 7:1–35
19.	❏ 3:1–4:17	❏ 18	❏ 86–87	❏ 7:36–50
20.	❏ 4:18–5:23	❏ 19	❏ 88	❏ 8:1–25
21.	❏ 6	❏ 20	❏ 89	❏ 8:26–56
22.	❏ 7	❏ 21	❏ 90	❏ 9:1–27
23.	❏ Ps. 27	❏ 22	❏ 91	❏ 9:28–62
24.	❏ Pss. 28–29	❏ 23	❏ 92–93	❏ 10:1–20
25.	❏ Ps. 30	❏ 24	❏ 94	❏ 10:21–42

APRIL

Days	OT Law (and Pss.)	OT Prophets	OT Writings	NT
	Exod.	1 Kings	Pss.	Luke
1.	❏ 8	❏ 1	❏ 95	❏ 11:1–26
2.	❏ 9	❏ 2	❏ 96	❏ 11:27–54
3.	❏ 10–11	❏ 3	❏ 97	❏ 12:1–21
4.	❏ Ps. 31	❏ 4–5	❏ 98–99	❏ 12:22–59
5.	❏ Ps. 32	❏ 6	❏ 100–101	❏ 13
6.	❏ 12:1–28	❏ 7	❏ 102	❏ 14
7.	❏ 12:29–51	❏ 8	❏ 103	❏ 15
8.	❏ 13	❏ 9	❏ 104	❏ 16
9.	❏ 14	❏ 10	❏ 105	❏ 17
10.	❏ 15	❏ 11	❏ 106	❏ 18
11.	❏ Ps. 33	❏ 12	❏ 107	❏ 19:1–27
12.	❏ Ps. 34	❏ 13	❏ 108	❏ 19:28–48
13.	❏ Ps. 35	❏ 14	❏ 109	❏ 20:1–26
14.	❏ 16	❏ 15	❏ 110–111	❏ 20:27–47
15.	❏ 17	❏ 16	❏ 112–114	❏ 21
16.	❏ 18	❏ 17	❏ 115	❏ 22:1–38
17.	❏ Ps. 36	❏ 18	❏ 116–117	❏ 22:39–71
18.	❏ Ps. 37	❏ 19	❏ 118	❏ 23:1–25
19.	❏ 19	❏ 20	❏ 119:1–40	❏ 23:26–56
20.	❏ 20	❏ 21	❏ 119:41–72	❏ 24:1–12
21.	❏ 21	❏ 22	❏ 119:73–104	❏ 24:13–53
		2 Kings		John
22.	❏ 22	❏ 1–2	❏ 119:105–136	❏ 1:1–28
23.	❏ 23	❏ 3	❏ 119:137–176	❏ 1:29–51
24.	❏ Ps. 38	❏ 4	❏ 120–122	❏ 2
25.	❏ Ps. 39	❏ 5	❏ 123–125	❏ 3

MAY

Days	OT Law (and Pss.)	OT Prophets	OT Writings	NT
	Exod.	2 Kings	Pss.	John
1.	24	6	126–128	4
2.	25	7	129–131	5
3.	Ps. 40	8	132–133	6:1–40
4.	Ps. 41	9	134–135	6:41–71
5.	26	10	136	7:1–24
6.	27	11–12	137–138	7:25–52
7.	28	13	139	7:53–8:30
8.	Pss. 42–43	14	140	8:31–59
9.	Ps. 44	15	141–142	9
10.	Ps. 45	16	143	10
11.	29	17	144	11:1–27
12.	30	18	145	11:28–57
13.	31	19	146	12:1–19
14.	Pss. 46–47	20	147	12:20–50
15.	Ps. 48	21	148	13
16.	Ps. 49	22	149–150	14
			Job	
17.	32	23	1	15
18.	33	24	2	16
19.	34	25	3	17
		Jer.		
20.	Ps. 50	1	4	18
21.	Ps. 51	2	5	19
22.	Pss. 52–54	3	6	20
23.	35	4	7	21
				Acts
24.	36	5	8	1
25.	37	6	9	2:1–41

JUNE

Days	OT Law (and Pss.)	OT Prophets	OT Writings	NT
	Exod.	Jer.	Job	Acts
1.	38	7	10	2:42–3:26
2.	39	8	11	4
3.	40	9	12	5
4.	Ps. 55	10	13	6
5.	Ps. 56	11–12	14	7:1–29
6.	Ps. 57	13	15	7:30–60
	Lev.			
7.	1–2	14	16	8
8.	3–4	15–16	17	9:1–19
9.	5:1–6:7	17	18	9:20–43
10.	6:8–29	18	19	10
11.	7	19–20	20	11
12.	Ps. 58	21	21	12
13.	Ps. 59	22	22	13:1–12
14.	Pss. 60–61	23	23	13:13–52
15.	8	24–25	24	14
16.	9	26	25–26	15
17.	10	27	27	16
18.	Pss. 62–63	28	28	17
19.	Pss. 64–65	29	29	18
20.	Pss. 66–67	30	30	19
21.	11	31	31	20
22.	12:1–13:37	32	32	21
23.	13:38–59	33	33	22
24.	Ps. 68	34	34	23
25.	Ps. 69	35	35	24

JULY

Days	OT Law (and Pss.)	OT Prophets	OT Writings	NT
	Lev.	Jer.	Job	Acts
1.	14	36	36	25
2.	15	37	37	26
3.	16	38	38	27
4.	Pss. 70–71	39–40	39	28
				Rom.
5.	Ps. 72	41–42	40	1
6.	17	43–45	41	2
7.	18	46–47	42	3
			Prov.	
8.	19	48	1	4
9.	20	49	2	5
10.	Ps. 73	50	3	6
11.	Ps. 74	51	4	7
12.	Pss. 75–76	52	5	8
		Ezek.		
13.	21	1	6	9
14.	22	2–3	7	10
15.	23	4–5	8	11
16.	24	6–7	9	12
17.	Ps. 77	8–9	10	13
18.	Ps. 78:1–39	10–11	11	14
19.	Ps. 78:40–72	12	12	15
20.	25:1–46	13	13	16
				1 Cor.
21.	25:47–26:13	14–15	14	1
22.	26:14–46	16	15	2
23.	17	17	16	3
24.	Ps. 79	18–19	17	4
25.	Ps. 80	20	18	5

AUGUST

Days	OT Law (and Pss.)	OT Prophets	OT Writings	NT
	Num.	Ezek.	Prov.	1 Cor.
1.	1	21	19	6
2.	2	22	20	7
3.	3	23	21	8
4.	Pss. 81–82	24	22	9
5.	Ps. 83	25–26	23	10
6.	4	27	24	11
7.	5	28	25	12
8.	6	29	26	13
9.	Ps. 84	30	27	14
10.	Ps. 85	31	28	15:1–34
11.	7:1–41	32	29	15:35–58
12.	7:42–89	33	30	16
				2 Cor.
13.	8	34–35	31	1
			Eccl.	
14.	Pss. 86–87	36	1	2
15.	Ps. 88	37	2	3
16.	Ps. 89	38	3	4
17.	9	39	4	5
18.	10	40	5	6
19.	11	41–42	6	7
20.	Ps. 90	43	7	8
21.	Ps. 91	44	8	9
22.	Pss. 92–93	45	9	10
23.	12–13	46	10	11
24.	14:1–19	47	11	12
25.	14:20–45	48	12	13

What the Old Testament Authors Really Cared About

SEPTEMBER

Days	OT Law (and Pss.)	OT Prophets	OT Writings	NT
	Num.	Isa.	Song	Gal.
1.	15	1	1	1
2.	16:1–24	2	2	2
3.	16:25–50	3–4	3	3
4.	17	5	4	4
5.	Ps. 94	6–7	5	5
6.	Ps. 95	8	6	6
				Eph.
7.	Ps. 96	9	7	1
8.	18	10	8	2
			Lam.	
9.	19	11–12	1	3
10.	20	13	2	4
11.	Ps. 97	14	3	5
12.	Pss. 98–99	15–16	4	6
				Phil.
13.	Pss. 100–101	17–18	5	1
			Dan.	
14.	21	19–20	1	2
15.	22	21	2	3
16.	23	22	3	4
				Col.
17.	Ps. 102	23	4	1
18.	Ps. 103	24	5	2
19.	24	25–26	6	3
20.	25	27	7	4
				1 Thess.
21.	26	28	8	1
22.	27	29	9	2
23.	Ps. 104	30	10	3
24.	Ps. 105	31–32	11	4
25.	Ps. 106	33	12	5

OCTOBER

Days	OT Law (and Pss.)	OT Prophets	OT Writings	NT
	Num.	Isa.	Esther	2 Thess.
1.	28	34–35	1	1
2.	29	36	2	2
3.	30	37	3–4	3
				1 Tim.
4.	Ps. 107	38–39	5–6	1
5.	Ps. 108	40	7–8	2
6.	Ps. 109	41	9–0	3
			Ezra	
7.	31	42	1–2	4
8.	32	43	3–4	5
9.	33	44	5	6
				2 Tim.
10.	Pss. 110–112	45	6	1
11.	Pss. 113–114	46–47	7	2
12.	Ps. 115	48	8	3
13.	34	49	9	4
				Titus
14.	35	50	10	1
			Neh.	
15.	36	51	1–2	2
16.	Pss. 116–117	52–53	3	3
				Philem.
17.	Ps. 118	54–55	4	1
	Deut.			Heb.
18.	1:1–18	56	5–6	1
19.	1:19–46	57	7	2
20.	2	58	8	3
21.	3	59	9	4
22.	4:1–43	60–61	10	5
23.	Ps. 119:1–40	62–63	11	6
24.	Ps. 119:41–72	64–65	12	7
25.	Ps. 119:73–104	66	13	8

NOVEMBER

Days	OT Law (and Pss.)	OT Prophets	OT Writings	NT
	Deut.	Hos.	1 Chron.	Heb.
1.	4:44–6:3	1	1	9
2.	6:4–25	2–3	2	10:1–18
3.	7	4	3–4	10:19–39
4.	8	5–6	5	11:1–22
5.	Ps. 119:105–136	7	6	11:23–40
6.	Ps. 119:137–176	8	7	12
7.	Pss. 120–122	9	8	13
				James
8.	9	10	9–10	1
9.	10	11–12	11	2
10.	11	13–14	12	3
		Joel		
11.	Pss. 123–125	1	13–14	4
12.	Pss. 126–128	2	15	5
				1 Peter
13.	12	3	16	1
		Amos		
14.	13	1	17	2
15.	14	2	18–19	3
16.	15	3	20–21	4
17.	Pss. 129–131	4	22	5
				2 Peter
18.	Pss. 132–134	5	23	1
19.	16	6	24–25	2
20.	17	7	26	3
				1 John
21.	18	8	27	1
22.	Ps. 135	9	28	2
		Obad.		
23.	Ps. 136	1	29	3
		Jonah	2 Chron.	
24.	19	1–2	1–2	4
25.	20	3–4	3–4	5

DECEMBER

Days	OT Law (and Pss.)	OT Prophets	OT Writings	NT
	Deut.	Mic.	2 Chron.	2 John
1.	21	1	5:1–6:11	1
				3 John
2.	22	2	6:12–42	1
				Jude
3.	23	3	7	1
				Rev.
4.	Pss. 137–138	4	8	1
5.	Ps. 139	5	9	2
6.	24	6	10–11	3
7.	25	7	12–13	4
		Nah.		
8.	26	1–2	14–15	5
9.	Ps. 140	3	16–17	6
		Hab.		
10.	Pss. 141–142	1	18–19	7
11.	27:1–28:14	2	20	8
12.	28:15–29:1	3	21	9
		Zeph.		
13.	Ps. 143	1	22–23	10
14.	Ps. 144	2	24	11
15.	Ps. 145	3	25	12
		Hag.		
16.	29:2–29	1–2	26	13
		Zech.		
17.	30	1–2	27–28	14
18.	31:1–29	3–5	29	15
19.	Ps. 146	6–7	30	16
20.	Ps. 147	8	31	17
21.	31:30–32:52	9–10	32	18
22.	33	11–12	33	19
23.	34	13–14	34	20
		Mal.		
24.	Ps. 148	1–2	35	21
25.	Ps. 149–150	3–4	36	22

THE LAW, PROPHETS, AND WRITINGS AT A GLANCE

The LAW: The Old Covenant ESTABLISHED	
(Yahweh as Savior)	
Genesis	Prologue to God's Universal Kingdom: The Need and Provision for Universal Blessing
Exodus	King Yahweh and His Global Purpose through Israel: God's Presence and Israel's Salvation and Mission
Leviticus	Holy Yahweh and the Need for Holiness: Pursuing God through His Sanctifying Presence and Promises
Numbers	Faithful Yahweh and His Unfaithful People: Learning to Wait and Follow amidst Seasons of Discipline
Deuteronomy	Israel's Constitution: A Call to Lasting Covenant Relationship and Its Eschatological Realization
The PROPHETS: The Old Covenant ENFORCED	
(Yahweh as Sovereign)	
FORMER (Narrative)	
Joshua	Yahweh's Covenant Faithfulness and the Call for Israel's Covenant Faithfulness
Judges	Israel's Covenant Faithlessness and the Need for God's Kingship
1–2 Samuel	The Importance of Honoring Yahweh and the Davidic Kingdom Hope
1–2 Kings	Covenant Failure, Kingdom Destruction, and the Hope of Kingdom Restoration
LATTER (Commentary)	
Jeremiah	Israel's Lack of Covenant Loyalty and the Eschatological Promise of Covenant Loyalty
Ezekiel	Israel's Loss of God's Presence and the Eschatological Promise of His Spirit
Isaiah	Israel's Rejection of God's Kingship and the Eschatological Promise of His Universal Kingdom
The Twelve	Israel's Spiritual Unfaithfulness and the Eschatological Promise of Divine Faithfulness

The WRITINGS: The Old Covenant ENJOYED
(Yahweh as Satisfier)

FORMER (Commentary)	
Ruth	Prelude Affirming the Kingdom Hope of Yahweh's Redeeming Grace through the Line of David
Psalms	Hope for Those Delighting in and Submitting to God's Kingship through His Word and Messiah
Job	Hope for Those Fearing God for Who He Is, Not for What He Gives or Takes Away
Proverbs	Hope for Those Acting Wisely—Who Fear God, Turn from Evil, and Live in Light of the Future
Ecclesiastes	Hope for Those Fearing and Following God in Pleasure and Pain Despite Life's Enigmas
Song of Songs	Hope for Those Celebrating Human Sexuality in the Context of Marriage
Lamentations	Hope for Those Remaining Confident in God's Reign and Faithfulness to His Own
LATTER (Narrative)	
Daniel	The Promise of God's Universal Kingdom Reiterated
Esther	The Preservation of God's Kingdom People Realized
Ezra-Nehemiah	The Restoration of God's Kingdom People and Land Foreshadowed
1–2 Chronicles	Yahweh's Universal Kingship and Kingdom Promises Affirmed

Prepared by Jason S. DeRouchie.

What the Old Testament Authors Really Cared About

KEY OLD TESTAMENT THEMES IN ENGLISH BIBLE ORDER

The divine author of the Old Testament ...

- Supplied *authoritative kingdom instruction* for God's people.
- Recorded *the progression and purpose of God's covenants* in redemptive history.
- Distinguished *the Law, Prophets, and Writings.*
- Highlighted *how the old (Mosaic) covenant was established, enforced, and enjoyed.*

The author of Genesis ...

- Used genealogy to highlight *the divine origin and significance of all creation.*
- Emphasized *the purpose of creation* in relation to its *one, loving, transcendent Creator.*
- Identified *human revolt against God* as the base cause of global wickedness and death.
- Stressed *God's promise to restore creation* through a specific family line and human being.

The author of Exodus ...

- Portrayed the continuing fulfillment of *Yahweh's promises and mission.*
- Stressed *Yahweh's passion to be known* by all in the world.
- Celebrated *Yahweh's power to redeem his people* from slavery.
- Disclosed *Yahweh's gracious provision of his covenant* with Israel.

- Emphasized the significance of *Yahweh's presence* among his people.
- Called *Israel to respond* to Yahweh's disclosure of himself and his will.

The author of Leviticus ...

- Proclaimed the reality and implications of *God's holiness*.
- Clarified the place of *sacrifice and atonement* in covenant worship.
- Distinguished *the holy and common, the unclean and clean* in covenant worship.
- Called Israel to *display holiness* through the practice of covenant ethics.

The author of Numbers ...

- Developed God's *covenant promises* of offspring and land.
- Explained how Israel responded to *God's gracious presence*.
- Detailed the role of *Moses' mediation* for Israel, as well as other agents.
- Emphasized the *wilderness* as a unique place of *Israel's spiritual maturity*.

The author of Deuteronomy ...

- Provided a *constitution* for guiding Israel's relationship with God.
- Stressed the importance of taking *God and his Word* seriously.
- Emphasized the *centrality of love* in one's relationship with God.
- Detailed the *perils* of sin, the *pleasures* of surrender, and the *promise* of grace.
- Defined the goal of love as *God-exalting influence* on the nations.
- Affirmed the *supremacy of Yahweh God* over all.

The author of Joshua ...

- Clarified *God's perspective on Israel's conquest* of Canaan.
- Emphasized *the character of Israel's God* in light of the conquest.
- Stressed *the need to know and heed God's expectations* for his people.
- Defined *Israel's relationship to the Promised Land*.

The author of Judges ...

- Recorded how *sin compromised Israel's national identity and mission*.

What the Old Testament Authors Really Cared About

- Traced how Israel's *covenant disloyalty forfeited blessings and brought curses.*
- Described *the moral failure of the judges and the need for a virtuous king.*
- Highlighted *the covenant faithfulness of Yahweh* in providing for Israel's need.

The author of Ruth ...
- Highlighted *covenant faithfulness and Yahweh's gift of a redeemer.*
- Emphasized *Yahweh's faithfulness* to bless the faithful and to fulfill his promises.

The author of 1–2 Samuel ...
- Explained the *transition in Israel's leadership* from judges to monarchy.
- Demonstrated the need to take seriously *Yahweh's holy, powerful, and dangerous presence.*
- Displayed *God's ideal for kingship* by contrasting Saul's failures with David's successes.
- Underscored the crucial role of *God's covenant with David* in redemptive history.
- Portrayed *David's sin and its consequences* to show the need for one greater than David.

The author of 1–2 Kings ...
- Stressed the *role of kingship* in the nation's disobedience, division, and destruction.
- Showed the *importance of Yahweh's prophets* in Israel's history.
- Measured *kingdom success* in the light of past covenants.
- Gave *hope for kingdom restoration* beyond exile.

The author of 1–2 Chronicles ...
- Stressed God's commitment to the *Davidic dynasty.*
- Emphasized *the centrality of God's temple-presence* in his people's worship.
- Demonstrated how covenant loyalty brought *blessings or curses.*
- Called for *seeking Yahweh in humility and faith.*

- Exalted Yahweh as *the sovereign Lord* over Judah, Israel, and the nations.

The author of Ezra-Nehemiah ...

- Stressed *God's sovereignty and faithfulness* in restoring his people to the land.
- Acknowledged *the threat of opposition* to God's people and purposes.
- Emphasized *the need for spiritual, social, and physical boundaries.*
- Called for *covenant loyalty* through conformity to the Law of Moses.
- Demonstrated how *God favors those who dependently seek him.*

The author of Esther ...

- Explained the origin of *the Feast of Purim.*
- Demonstrated *God's mysterious providential care* of his people.
- Emphasized the *God-ordained purpose of everything* that happens.
- Sought to *create hope* in God's power and faithfulness.

The author of Job ...

- Affirmed *Yahweh's sovereignty* over all things.
- Showed that *personal sin is not the only reason humans suffer.*
- Acknowledged *humanity's inability* to fully grasp God's work and purposes.
- Recognized that *God accepts the honest cries of his hurting people.*
- Clarified *how to respond* when God's justice and goodness appear questionable.
- Believed that *people should fear God* for who he is rather than for what he gives.

The author of Psalms ...

- Used *literary forms as templates* for communicating with God.
- Expressed *human emotions* in healthy and authentic ways.
- Taught how to *live and think wisely.*
- Encouraged *waiting for God's kingdom and Messiah.*
- Called people to *worship Yahweh* in light of his person and works.

What the Old Testament Authors Really Cared About

The author of Proverbs …

- Pictured *life as a journey*.
- Contrasted the path of *wisdom* with the path of *folly*.
- Portrayed *the nature of wisdom* in memorable ways.
- Asserted that true wisdom is grounded in *the fear of Yahweh*.
- Gave practical *guidance for wise living*.

The author of Ecclesiastes …

- Raised more *questions* than he answered.
- Acknowledged *numerous challenges* to living "under the sun."
- Affirmed *God's mysterious providence* in all of life.
- Provided important *instruction about living well* "under the sun."
- Highlighted the key to a *meaningful and significant life*.

The author of the Song of Songs …

- Traced *the progress of intimacy* from initial attraction to maturity.
- Extolled *erotic love within marriage* as God's good gift.
- Described *the transforming power of love*.

The author of Isaiah …

- Warned of *the dangers of pride and unbelief*.
- Called people to *trust God*.
- Believed *the suffering Servant paid for the sins of many*.
- Longed for *God's glorious kingdom*.

The author of Jeremiah …

- Presented *Yahweh's case against Judah* for her covenant infidelity.
- Documented *Judah's refusal to repent and to heed* Jeremiah's message.
- Voiced *the prophet's anguish* over his calling and ministry.
- Portrayed *Babylon as God's instrument and object of judgment*.
- Emphasized *the global extent of Yahweh's judgment and salvation*.
- Promised *restoration and a new covenant* between Yahweh and his people.

The author of Lamentations …

- Acknowledged *Israel's sin and God's uprightness* in judging her.
- Was *brutally honest with God* about emotional and spiritual pain.

- Stressed *God's faithfulness* as the basis for hope in suffering.

The author of Ezekiel …

- Emphasized *God's sovereignty* over creation and especially over Israel.
- Accentuated the temple as mediating *God's glorious presence* on earth.
- Believed that *God abhors sin and will judge* it accordingly.
- Affirmed that *salvation* is only possible by *God's relentless, unmerited grace.*

The author of Daniel …

- Emphasized *Israel's God's complete control* of human history and powers.
- Stressed the need to *remain faithful to God* even under oppression.
- Illustrated how the wise can successfully *navigate life's challenges.*
- Showed that *human pride is evil and results in God's judgment.*
- Taught *the ultimate triumph of God's kingdom* over evil influence.

The author of the Twelve …

- Compiled twelve prophetic writings into *a single, unified book.*
- Affirmed *God's amazing love* for Israel and *sin's horrific nature.*
- Clarified the implications of *Yahweh's covenantal commitment* to Israel.
- Stressed the need for God's people *to reflect God's character.*
- Emphasized the future *day of judgment* for the wicked and *of salvation* for the righteous.
- Announced *the coming of a new David*, who would bring God's kingdom.

APPENDIX

6

CHAPTER INDEX OF KEY WORDS AND CONCEPTS

---

1. Chapter, not page number, in parentheses.

What the Old Testament Authors Really Cared About

What the Old Testament Authors Really Cared About

Two ways (18)

U
Under the sun (19)
Unity (7)

V
Vanity/*hébel* (19)
Vice regents (25)
Vision of God's glory (12)

W
Warrior (7)
Wars of Judgment (7)
Wayward Harlot (12)

Weeping prophet (11, 21)
Wickedness (18)
Wilderness (5)
Wisdom (18, 19, 20, 22)
Worship (16)
Worthy woman (15)
Wrath (13)

Y
Yahweh's faithfulness and compassion (21)
Yahweh's incomparability (13)
Yahweh's presence (12)
Yahweh's sovereignty (25)
Yahweh/the LORD (3)

CHAPTER AND TOPICAL INDEXES OF PHOTOGRAPHS

What the Old Testament Authors Really Cared About

TOPICAL INDEX OF PHOTOGRAPHS

CULTURE AND NATURE

Dwellings and Daily Life

Farming

Fauna/Animals

Flora/Plants

Holidays and Worship Activity—True or False

What the Old Testament Authors Really Cared About

What the Old Testament Authors Really Cared About